Family spending in the UK: financial year ending 2022

Contents

Main tables

Office for
National Statistics

Data and analysis from Census 2021

Family spending in the UK: April 2021 to March 2022

Average weekly household expenditure on goods and services in the UK, by age, income, economic status, socio-economic class, household composition and region.

Contact:
Emma Barnes, Lee Colvin, Paula Croal

Release date:
31 May 2023

Next release:
To be announced

Table of contents

1. Main points

- Average weekly household expenditure was £528.80 in the financial year ending (FYE) 2022; a nominal increase of £47.30 (10%) since FYE 2021, this remains £59.10 (10%) below FYE 2020 and the start of the coronavirus (COVID-19) pandemic.

- After adjusting for inflation, this was a real terms increase in average weekly household expenditure of £28.80 (6%) in FYE 2022 consistent with easing of COVID-19 restrictions; but remained £78.80 (13%) below pre-pandemic spending in FYE 2020.

- The greatest annual increases were across restaurants and hotels, transport, and recreation and culture, which were consistent with the easing of coronavirus restrictions, however, expenditure in these categories for FYE 2022 remained below FYE 2020.

- On average, the richest fifth of households spent a total of £811.20 per week, while the poorest fifth spent less than half this amount at £329.80 per week.

2. Family spending in the UK

Household spending has increased yet remains below FYE 2020

The collection of data used for this bulletin spans April 2021 to March 2022, during which coronavirus (COVID-19) restrictions started to ease across the UK. This includes the indoor venues being reopened, and spectators could attend sporting events. Some coronavirus restrictions remained in place towards the end of 2021 and households experienced new financial pressures; domestic energy prices rose in the last six months of the financial year ending (FYE) 2022, as explained in the research briefing on the UK Parliament webpage (https://commonslibrary.parliament.uk/research-briefings/cbp-9491/#:~:text=They%20started%20to%20increase%20towards,much%20of%20the%20last%20decade.), and the energy price cap was raised in October 2021.

Changes in spending can result from both changes in the price of goods and services, and changes in consumer behaviour, such as the amount and type of good and services purchased. By adjusting for the rate at which the prices of goods and services bought by households rise or fall (consumer price inflation), we can better isolate trends in the amount of goods and services purchased. Notably, in the year leading to March 2022, UK inflation rates rose significantly, reaching a 30-year high, as reported in the Consumer Prices Index (CPI) in our consumer price inflation time series (https://www.ons.gov.uk/economy/inflationandpriceindices/timeseries/d7g7/mm23).

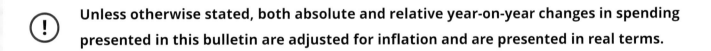 **Unless otherwise stated, both absolute and relative year-on-year changes in spending presented in this bulletin are adjusted for inflation and are presented in real terms.**

Changes in consumption throughout FYE 2022 are reflected in these annual expenditure estimates. Average weekly expenditure for all households saw a nominal increase of £47.30 (10%) to £528.80 per week. Despite this increase, average weekly expenditure remained £59.10 (10%) below FYE 2020. After adjusting for inflation, this was a real terms increase in average weekly household expenditure of £28.80 (6%) in FYE 2022; £78.80 (13%) below FYE 2020. Mean household disposable income remained comparable to FYE 2021, as shown in our Average household income, UK: financial year ending 2022 bulletin (https://www.ons.gov.uk/peoplepopulationandcommunity/personalandhouseholdfinances/incomeandwealth/bulletins/householddisposableincomeandinequality/financialyearending2022).

Figure 1: In financial year ending (FYE) 2022, average weekly expenditure increased by 6% per week while average household disposable income remained stable

Average weekly household expenditure and average weekly household disposable income in the UK, FYE 2002 to FYE 2022, at FYE 2022 prices

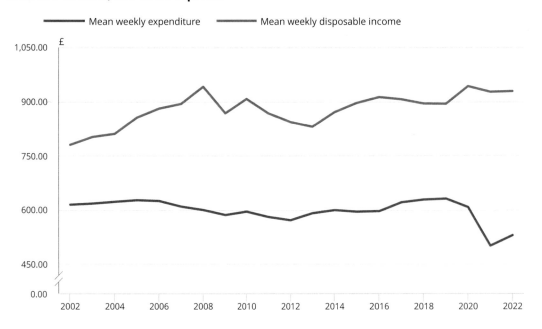

Source: Household Finances Survey, Living Costs and Food Survey from the Office for National Statistics

Notes:

1. Expenditure figures are adjusted for inflation using the Consumer Prices Index (CPI) specific to the classification of individual consumption by purpose (COICOP) category. Total real expenditure is generated as a sum of the deflated COICOP categories 1 to13.

2. Incomes are adjusted for inflation using the consumer prices index including owner-occupiers' housing costs (CPIH) excluding council tax.

3. All values are deflated to FYE 2022 prices

4. Household expenditure figures are on a financial year basis FYE 2002 to FYE 2006, calendar years 2007 to 2013, and financial years FYE 2015 to FYE 2022.

5. Weekly household disposable income figures are from the household disposable income and inequality statistics. Disposable income figures are on a financial year basis. Estimates of income from 2001 to 2002 onwards have been adjusted for the under-coverage and under-reporting of the top earners.

Households spent the highest proportion of their weekly expenditure on housing, fuel and power, and transport

The average UK household spent the largest proportion of their expenditure on housing (net), fuel and power (17%) followed by transport (14%). Within housing (net) fuel and power, £51.60 was spent on rentals for housing, while £25.70 was spent on electricity, gas and other fuels. Of the proportion of expenditure spent on transport, £30.90 of this was spent on the purchase of vehicles, most notably the purchase of second-hand cars, while £30.70 was spent on the operation of personal transport, most notably purchasing petrol, diesel, and other motor oils.

Figure 2: Housing, fuel and power, and transport were the highest expenditure categories for UK households in FYE 2022

Average household weekly expenditure in the UK, FYE 2022

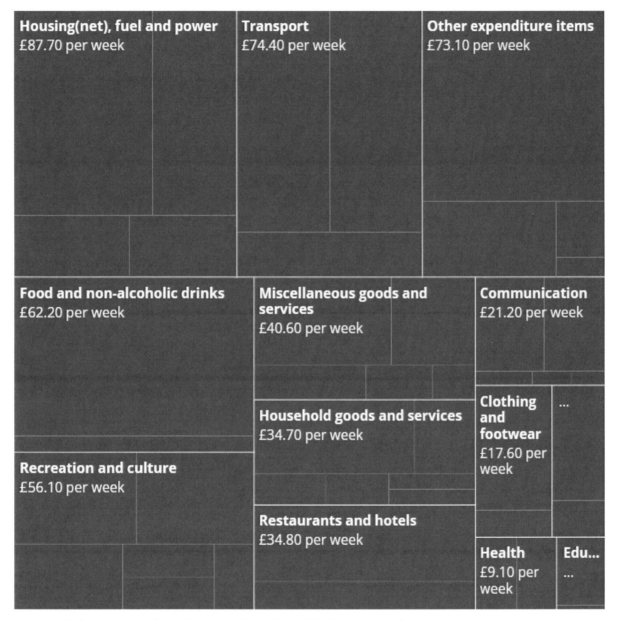

Total household spend: £528.80 per week

Housing(net), fuel and power
£87.70 per week

Transport
£74.40 per week

Other expenditure items
£73.10 per week

Food and non-alcoholic drinks
£62.20 per week

Miscellaneous goods and services
£40.60 per week

Communication
£21.20 per week

Household goods and services
£34.70 per week

Clothing and footwear
£17.60 per week

...

Recreation and culture
£56.10 per week

Restaurants and hotels
£34.80 per week

Health
£9.10 per week

Edu...
...

Source: Living Costs and Food Survey from the Office for National Statistics

Note: This is a snapshot of an interactive image, to view the full image please go to: https://www.ons.gov.uk/peoplepopulationandcommunity/personalandhouseholdfinances/expenditure/bulletins/familyspendingintheuk/april2021tomarch2022

Notes:

1. Spending is categorised using Classification of individual consumption by purpose (COICOP) categories. As such, Mortgage interest payments, Council Tax and Northern Ireland rates are categorised as Other expenditure items rather than Housing (net) fuel and power. Other expenditure items also includes Licenses, fines and transfers,

Holiday Spending and Money transfers and credit.

2. Components of spending based on fewer than 20 recording households, or where the average rounds to 0, do not appear in the tree map.

Download the data

.xlsx (https://www.ons.gov.uk/visualisations/dvc2596/datadownload.xlsx)

In FYE 2022, spending patterns continued to vary across the income distribution. Notably, changes in expenditure relating to actual rental and mortgage interest payments. This coincides with a larger proportion of lower-income households being either private or social renters, while a large proportion of higher-income households are owner occupiers, this data is available in Table A50 in Workbook 4: Expenditure by household characteristic (https://www.ons.gov.uk/peoplepopulationandcommunity/personalandhouseholdfinances/expenditure/bulletins/familyspendingintheuk/april2021tomarch2022#family-spending-data).

The poorest fifth of households continued to spend the greatest proportion of their total expenditure (25%) on housing (net), fuel and power. This is largely because of spending on actual rentals for housing (24% of their total expenditure). Meanwhile, the richest fifth of households spent the greatest proportion of their total expenditure (17%) on other expenditure items, which is largely because of spending on mortgage interest payments (6% of their total expenditure). Mortgage interest payments are included under other expenditure items according to the classification of individual consumption by purpose (COICOP (https://www.ons.gov.uk/peoplepopulationandcommunity/personalandhouseholdfinances/expenditure/bulletins/familyspendingintheuk/april2021tomarch2022#glossary)) classification. Capital repayments are not included within owner occupier expenditure as they are classified as an accrual of wealth; more information is available in our Household total wealth in Great Britain: April 2018 to March 2020 bulletin (https://www.ons.gov.uk/peoplepopulationandcommunity/personalandhouseholdfinances/incomeandwealth/bulletins/totalwealthingreatbritain/april2018tomarch2020).

Figure 3: Poorer households continue to proportionally spend more on housing, fuel and power in FYE 2022

Average weekly household expenditure as a percentage of total weekly expenditure, by quintile group, UK, financial year ending (FYE) 2022

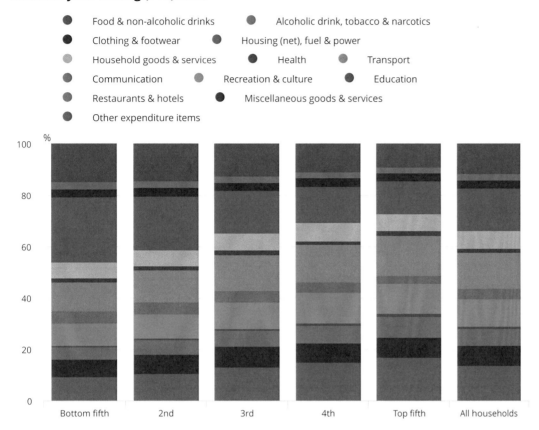

Source: Living Costs and Food Survey from the Office for National Statistics

Notes:

1. Individuals are ranked by their equivalised household disposable incomes, using the modified OECD scale.

2. Spending is categorised using classification of individual consumption by purpose (COICOP) categories. As such, mortgage interest payments, Council Tax and Northern Ireland rates are categorised as other expenditure items rather than housing (net) fuel and power. Other expenditure items also include licenses, fines and transfers, holiday spending and money transfers and credit.

Household spending in FYE 2022 varied across the income distribution, with the richest fifth of households' total weekly expenditure more than twice that of the poorest fifth of households (£811.20 and £329.80, respectively). In comparison, mean household disposable income was six times greater in the richest fifth of households than the poorest fifth, as shown in our Average household income, UK: financial year ending 2022 bulletin (https://www.ons.gov.uk/peoplepopulationandcommunity/personalandhouseholdfinances/incomeandwealth/bulletins/householddisposableincomeandinequality/financialyearending2022). This likely reflects a much greater capacity for saving in richer households than in poorer households.

Rises in spending were largely contributed to by increases in spending on transport, recreation and culture, and restaurants and hotels

In FYE 2022, increases in weekly expenditure were largely contributed to by expenditure on transport (£7.80 increase to £74.40), recreation and culture (£9.30 increase to £56.10), restaurants and hotels (£15.70 increase to £34.80). Despite these increases, spending in these categories remained below FYE 2020, prior to the coronavirus pandemic.

Spending on food and non-alcoholic drinks fell by £8.20 to £62.20 per week, £2.70 below FYE 2020. Spending on housing (net), fuel and power decreased in FYE 2022 by £0.60 to £87.70 per week yet remained £2.00 above FYE 2020.

Figure 4. Average weekly household spending remains below FYE 2020 across most expenditure categories

Average weekly household expenditure by COICOP categories, UK, financial year ending (FYE) 2020; FYE 2021 and FYE 2022 at FYE 2022 prices

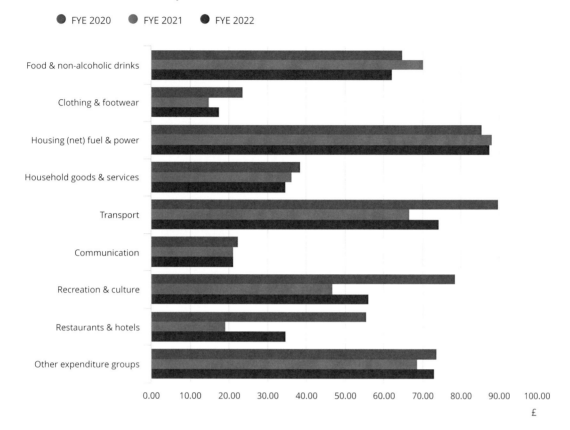

Source: Living Costs and Food Survey from the Office for National Statistics

Notes:

1. Expenditure figures are adjusted for inflation using the Consumer Prices Index (CPI) specific to the classification of individual consumption by purpose (COICOP) category. All values are deflated to FYE 2022 prices.

2. Spending is categorised using classification of individual consumption by purpose (COICOP) categories. As such, mortgage interest payments, Council Tax and Northern Ireland rates are categorised as other expenditure items rather than housing (net) fuel and power. Other expenditure items also include licenses, fines and transfers, holiday spending and money transfers and credit.

3. For clarity, not all COICOP categories are presented.

Spending increased inside and outside the home

In FYE 2022, the largest contributor to rises in spending on restaurants and hotels were increases in spending on catering services, such as restaurants and cafés, which increased by £11.20 (79%). Expenditure on recreational and cultural services such as sports admissions, subscriptions, and leisure class fees in FYE 2022 rose by £4.30 (37%) yet remained £4.90 (24%) below FYE 2020. This is consistent with the easing of coronavirus restrictions.

Housing (net), fuel and power expenditure is comparable with FYE 2021, but within this there was an increase in expenditure on electricity, gas and other fuels £1.50 (6%), which was contributed to by an increase in electricity expenditure of £0.70 (6%) compared with 2021. It is worth noting that in October 2021, the energy price cap rose by 12%. More information is available in our Consumer price inflation, UK: November 2021 bulletin (https://www.ons.gov.uk/economy/inflationandpriceindices/bulletins/consumerpriceinflation/november2021).

Figure 5: Weekly spending on restaurants and hotels increased by 82% in FYE 2022, yet remained 37% below FYE 2020

Percentage change in average weekly household expenditure by COICOP categories, UK, financial year ending (FYE) 2020; FYE 2021 and FYE 2022 at FYE 2022 prices

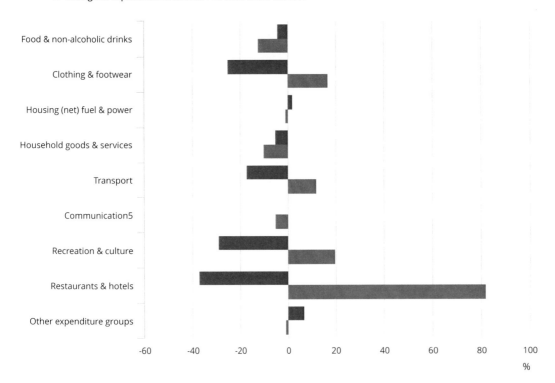

● Change in expenditure between FYE 2020 and FYE 2022
● Change in expenditure between FYE 2021 and FYE 2022

Source: Living Costs and Food Survey from the Office for National Statistics

Notes:

1. Expenditure figures are adjusted for inflation using the Consumer Prices Index (CPI) specific to the classification of individual consumption by purpose (COICOP) category. All values are deflated to FYE 2022 prices.

2. Spending is categorised using classification of individual consumption by purpose (COICOP) categories. As such, mortgage interest payments, Council Tax and Northern Ireland rates are categorised as other expenditure items rather than housing (net) fuel and power. Other expenditure items also include licenses, fines and transfers, holiday spending and money transfers and credit.

3. For clarity, not all COICOP categories are presented.

More personal transport, less public transport usage

The increase in transport expenditure was attributed to an increase in spending on the use of personal transport, such as fuel and maintenance. Weekly expenditure on petrol, diesel and other motor oils increased by £6.60 (53%) between FYE 2021 and FYE 2022. This is consistent with our Behavioural impacts of rising automotive fuel prices on consumer fuel demand, UK: July 2021 to August 2022 article (https://www.ons.gov.uk/economy/economicoutputandproductivity/output/articles/behaviouralimpactsofrisingautomotivefuelpricesonconsumerfueldemandukjuly2021toaugust2022/2022-09-02), which reported that in the week ending 17 February 2022, total automotive fuel sales growth was at 41% in comparison with the same week in the previous year.

Household spending on transport has not returned to FYE 2020 levels. Expenditure on transport services, such as bus and rail, has reduced by £11.10 (46%) between FYE 2020 and FYE 2022. Meanwhile, spending dedicated to purchasing new and second-hand vehicles was £30.90 per week, an increase of £2.00 (7%) in comparison with FYE 2020.

Decreases in international air fares are met with decreases in holidays abroad

In FYE 2022, spending on international air fare remained £5.30 (71%) below FYE 2020. Household spending on recreation and culture remained below FYE 2020, largely resulting from reductions in spending on package holidays, in particular package holidays abroad, which remained £18.20 (68%) below FYE 2020. Average weekly spending on accommodation abroad remained £4.20 (76%) below FYE 2020. Findings from our Overseas travel and tourism: April 2022 provisional results (https://www.ons.gov.uk/peoplepopulationandcommunity/leisureandtourism/bulletins/overseastravelandtourism/april2022provisionalresults) further show that in April 2022 UK residents' visits overseas estimates had not yet reached the levels seen in April 2019.

While spending on international travel and holidays abroad fell, in FYE 2022 spending on holiday accommodation in the UK increased by £1.40 (21%) above FYE 2020.

3. Family spending data

Family spending workbook 1: detailed expenditure and trends
(https://www.ons.gov.uk/peoplepopulationandcommunity/personalandhouseholdfinances/expenditure/datasets/familyspendingworkbook1detailedexpenditureandtrends)

Dataset | Released 31 May 2023

Detailed breakdown of average weekly household expenditure on goods and services in the UK. Data are shown by place of purchase, income group (deciles) and age of household reference person.

Family spending workbook 2: expenditure by income
(https://www.ons.gov.uk/peoplepopulationandcommunity/personalandhouseholdfinances/expenditure/datasets/familyspendingworkbook2expenditurebyincome)

Dataset | Released 31 May 2023

Data are shown by region, age, income (including equivalised) group (deciles and quintiles), economic status, socio-economic class, housing tenure, output area classification, urban and rural areas (Great Britain only), place of purchase and household composition.

Family spending workbook 3: expenditure by region
(https://www.ons.gov.uk/peoplepopulationandcommunity/personalandhouseholdfinances/expenditure/datasets/familyspendingworkbook3expenditurebyregion)

Dataset | Released 31 May 2023

Data are shown by region, age, income (including equivalised) group (deciles and quintiles), economic status, socio-economic class, housing tenure, output area classification, urban and rural areas (Great Britain only), place of purchase and household composition.

Family spending workbook 4: expenditure by household characteristic
(https://www.ons.gov.uk/peoplepopulationandcommunity/personalandhouseholdfinances/expenditure/datasets/familyspendingworkbook4expenditurebyhouseholdcharacteristic)

Dataset | Released 31 May 2023

Data are shown by region, age, income (including equivalised) group (deciles and quintiles), economic status, socio-economic class, housing tenure, output area classification, urban and rural areas (Great Britain only), place of purchase and household composition.

Family spending workbook 5: expenditure on housing
(https://www.ons.gov.uk/peoplepopulationandcommunity/personalandhouseholdfinances/expenditure/datasets/familyspendingworkbook5expenditureonhousing)

Dataset | Released 31 May 2023

Data are shown by region, age, income (including equivalised) group (deciles and quintiles), economic status, socio-economic class, housing tenure, output area classification, urban and rural areas (Great Britain only), place of purchase and household composition.

Definition of household expenditure
(https://www.ons.gov.uk/peoplepopulationandcommunity/personalandhouseholdfinances/expenditure/dataset s/definitionofhouseholdexpendituretable21)

Dataset | Released 19 March 2020

Provides a detailed breakdown on the definition of household expenditure.

 A number of tables within the family spending workbooks have been placed under review to be removed from future publications. Tables under review are specified within the workbooks. If you use these for your analysis, please contact us via family.spending@ons.gov.uk.

4. Glossary

COICOP categories

Spending is presented using classification of individual consumption by purpose (COICOP) categories, unless otherwise stated. COICOP is an internationally recognised classification system consistent with that used by UK National Accounts. It does not include all types of payments, for example, capital mortgage repayments are excluded as they are not a consumable item and instead add to personal wealth.

Disposable income

Disposable income is the amount of money that households have available for spending and saving after direct taxes (such as Income Tax National Insurance and Council Tax) have been accounted for. It includes earnings from employment, private pensions, and investments, as well as cash benefits provided by the state.

Equivalisation

Equivalisation is the process of accounting for the fact that households with many members are likely to need a higher income to achieve the same standard of living as households with fewer members. Equivalisation considers the number of people living in the household and their ages, acknowledging that while a household with two people in it will need more money to sustain the same living standards as one with a single person, the two-person household is unlikely to need double the income.

This analysis uses the modified Organisation for Economic Co-operation and Development (OECD) equivalence scale in taxes and benefits analysis (PDF, 166KB) (https://webarchive.nationalarchives.gov.uk/ukgwa/20160105160709/http:/www.ons.gov.uk/ons/rel/elmr/economic-and-labour-market-review/no--1--january-2010/using-the-oecd-equivalence-scale-in-taxes-and-benefits-analysis.pdf).

Our analysis ranks individuals by their equivalised household disposable incomes, using the modified OECD scale.

Mean expenditure

The mean measure of expenditure divides the total expenditure of households by the number of households. When considering changes in expenditure by classification of individual consumption by purpose (COICOP) expenditure categories, the mean allows for these changes to be analysed in an additive way.

Nominal change

Estimates of economic activity are typically available in "nominal" or "real" terms. "Nominal" estimates reflect the cash value of expenditure, such as the amount consumers would have spent in a shop at the time of purchase. These can change over time, reflecting movements in prices and quantities purchased.

Real change

Estimates of economic activity are typically available in "nominal" or "real" terms.

"Real" estimates take into account how the average price of items change over time and are adjusted to the price-levels captured in the most recent data point – for example, in this bulletin, the prices of goods and services are adjusted to the average prices in the financial year ending (FYE) 2022. Real estimates also can change over time, reflecting only the movements in the quantities purchased.

All real estimates used in this article are generated using the datasets from our Consumer price inflation time series (https://www.ons.gov.uk/economy/inflationandpriceindices/datasets/consumerpriceindices).

5. Measuring the data

Survey description

All the findings in this bulletin are taken from data collected on the Living Costs and Food Survey (LCF). The LCF is a UK household survey designed to provide information on household expenditure patterns and food consumption.

The LCF is a voluntary sample survey of private households. Each individual in a selected household is asked to complete a household interview and then an expenditure diary for two weeks. The survey is continuous, interviews being spread evenly over the year to ensure that seasonal effects are covered. Further information about changes to data collection and processing resulting from the coronavirus (COVID-19) pandemic can be found in Section 6: Strengths and limitations (https://www.ons.gov.uk/peoplepopulationandcommunity/personalandhouseholdfinances/expenditure/bulletins/familyspendingintheuk/april2021tomarch2022#strengths-and-limitations).

Care is taken to ensure complete confidentiality of information and to protect the identity of LCF households. Only anonymised data is supplied to users. The LCF is reviewed every year and changes are made to keep it up to date. Therefore, year-on-year changes should be interpreted with caution.

Values reported in this statistical bulletin

This bulletin uses the mean when referring to averages unless stated otherwise. Therefore, total average weekly household expenditure is equal to the total weekly expenditure of households divided by the number of households. All spending estimates are rounded to the nearest £0.10, therefore the sum of component items does not necessarily add to the totals shown.

This release compares household expenditure across the income distribution. Households have been ranked in ascending order of equivalised household disposable income using the modified Organisation for Economic Co-operation and Development (OECD) scale and then divided into five equal parts; quintiles or fifths. Households with the lowest income are referred to as being in the bottom fifth, and those with the largest income are referred to as being in the top fifth.

6. Strengths and limitations

Adjusting for inflation

This release provides deflated expenditure values. These are calculated by taking an average of the quarterly estimates of our Consumer Price Index (CPI) by classification of individual consumption by purpose (COICOP) category in each financial year and re-basing them to financial year ending (FYE) 2022 prices.

Comparisons between expenditure and income

It is important to note that the annual expenditure statistics published in this bulletin are not directly comparable against our annual income statistics published in our Average household income, UK: financial year ending 2022 bulletin (https://www.ons.gov.uk/peoplepopulationandcommunity/personalandhouseholdfinances/incomeandwealth/bulletins/householddisposableincomeandinequality/financialyearending2022). One reason for this is because the weights used to improve the representation of our national expenditure and national income statistics differ. Further to this, the data sources used in our average household disposable income statistics are derived from the Household Finances Survey (HFS) using both the Living Costs and Food Survey (LCF) and the Survey of Living Conditions (SLC), while our expenditure statistics are generated using LCF Survey data alone. Work is currently being carried out to investigate how and whether we can align these statistics for comparability, alongside the Office for National Statistics' (ONS) household finance transformation project.

Quality

Further quality and methodology information on strengths, limitations, appropriate uses, and how the data were created is available in our Living Costs and Food Survey technical report: financial year ending March 2022 (https://www.ons.gov.uk/peoplepopulationandcommunity/personalandhouseholdfinances/expenditure/methodologies/livingcostsandfoodsurveytechnicalreportfinancialyearendingmarch2022) and our Living Costs and Food Survey Quality and Methodology Information (QMI) (https://www.ons.gov.uk/peoplepopulationandcommunity/personalandhouseholdfinances/incomeandwealth/methodologies/livingcostsandfoodsurveyqmi). The technical report for FYE 2022 is provisionally scheduled for release in autumn 2023.

National Statistic status for family spending in the UK

Family spending in the UK has been designated as National Statistics (https://osr.statisticsauthority.gov.uk/national-statistics/), in accordance with the Statistics and Registration Service Act 2007 (https://www.gov.uk/government/statistics/how-national-and-official-statistics-are-assured/how-national-and-official-statistics-are-assured) and signifying compliance with the Code of Practice for Statistics (https://code.statisticsauthority.gov.uk/).

7. Related links

Average household income, UK: financial year ending 2022
(https://www.ons.gov.uk/peoplepopulationandcommunity/personalandhouseholdfinances/incomeandwealth/b
ulletins/householddisposableincomeandinequality/financialyearending2022)

Bulletin | Released 25 January 2023

Final estimates of median and mean household income in the UK, with analysis of how these measures have
changed over time, accounting for inflation and household composition.

Consumer trends, UK: October to December 2022
(https://www.ons.gov.uk/economy/nationalaccounts/satelliteaccounts/bulletins/consumertrends/octobertodece
mber2022)

Bulletin | Released 31 March 2023

Household final consumption expenditure (HHFCE) for the UK, as a measure of economic growth. Includes all
spending on goods and services by members of UK households.

8. Cite this statistical bulletin

Office for National Statistics (ONS), released 31 May 2023, ONS website, statistical bulletin, Family Spending in
the UK: April 2021 to March 2022
(https://www.ons.gov.uk/peoplepopulationandcommunity/personalandhouseholdfinances/expenditure/bulletin
s/familyspendingintheuk/april2021tomarch2022)

Contact details for this statistical bulletin

Emma Barnes, Lee Colvin, Paula Croal
family.spending@ons.gov.uk
Telephone: +44 1633 651927

Data and analysis from Census 2021

Average household income, UK: financial year ending 2022

Final estimates of average household income in the UK, with analysis of how these measures have changed over time, accounting for inflation and household composition.

Correction

25 January 2023 12:00

We have corrected a formatting error in Figure 4 'Changes in disposable income across the income distribution were driven by changes in original income, with a reduction in poorer households and an increase in richer households' which resulted in incorrect data to be displayed for 'All individuals'.

Contact:

Emily Andrews, Paula Croal

Release date:

25 January 2023

Next release:

To be announced

Table of contents

1. Other pages in this release

• Household income inequality, UK: financial year ending 2022 (https://www.ons.gov.uk/peoplepopulationandcommunity/personalandhouseholdfinances/incomeandwealth/bulletins/householdincomeinequalityfinancial/financialyearending2022)

2. Main points

• Median household disposable income in the UK was £32,300 in the financial year ending (FYE) 2022, a decrease of 0.6% from FYE 2021, based on estimates from the Office for National Statistics (ONS) Household Finances Survey.

• Median disposable income for the poorest fifth of the population decreased by 3.8% to £14,500 in FYE 2022; reductions were also observed in mean original income and cash benefits.

• Median disposable income increased by 1.6% to £66,000 for the richest fifth of people; increases were also observed in mean original income where the effect was not offset by the increases in direct taxes.

• Median household disposable income increased by an average 0.7% per year between FYE 2020 and FYE 2022, in comparison with a longer-term increase by an average 1.7% per year over the 10 years leading up to 2022 (FYE 2013 to FYE 2022); income estimates for FYE 2021 and FYE 2022 were affected by the coronavirus (COVID-19) pandemic and the range of financial support measures introduced to alleviate potential financial pressures.

3. Analysis of average disposable income

Unless otherwise stated, this analysis is based on a disposable income (https://www.ons.gov.uk/peoplepopulationandcommunity/personalandhouseholdfinances/incomeandwealth/bulletins/householddisposableincomeandinequality/financialyearending2022#glossary) measure, which is the amount of money households have available for spending and saving after direct taxes have been accounted for. It includes earnings from employment, private pensions and investments as well as cash benefits provided by the state.

Median income decreased by 0.6% between the financial year ending (FYE) 2021 and FYE 2022. This follows an increase of 2.0% between FYE 2020 and FYE 2021, the period covering the first year of the coronavirus (COVID-19) pandemic. Mean income increased by 0.9% between FYE 2021 and FYE 2022, following a reduction of 0.6% between FYE 2020 and FYE 2021.

Household income is reported using both means and medians (https://www.ons.gov.uk/peoplepopulationandcommunity/personalandhouseholdfinances/incomeandwealth/bulletins/householddisposableincomeandinequality/financialyearending2022#glossary). A limitation of using the mean is that it can be influenced by just a few individuals with very high incomes. Median household income shows what the middle person would be if all individuals in the UK were sorted from poorest to richest and provides a good indication of the standard of living of the "typical" individual in terms of income.

Financial support measures and policy changes were put in place during the coronavirus pandemic to alleviate financial pressures. Notably, the Coronavirus Job Support Scheme (CJRS), the Self-Employment Income Support Scheme (SEISS) and the uplift to the Universal Credit standard allowance basic element were made available between Spring 2020 and Autumn 2021. As such, income estimates for FYE 2022 remain affected by such schemes.

Figure 1: Mean income increased by 0.3% and median income increased by 1.5% between financial year ending (FYE) 2020 and FYE 2022

Mean and median equivalised household disposable income of individuals, UK, financial year ending (FYE) 2020 to 2022

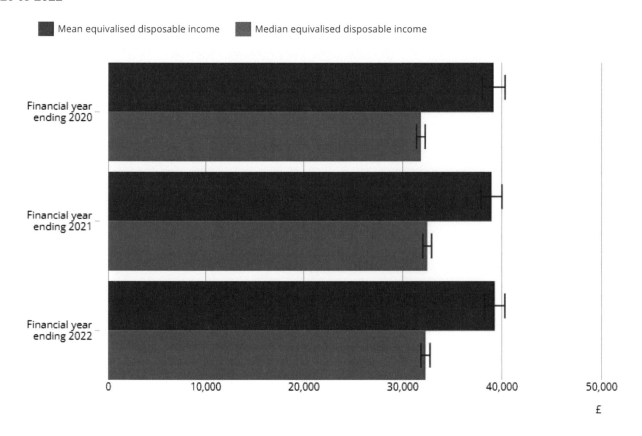

Source: Office for National Statistics – Household Finances Survey

Embed code

Notes:

1. Incomes are adjusted for inflation using the consumer prices index including owner-occupiers' housing costs (CPIH) excluding council tax.

2. FYE 2022 represents the financial year ending 2022, (April to March), and similarly for all other years expressed in this format.

Download the data

.xlsx (https://www.ons.gov.uk/visualisations/dvc2438/fig1/datadownload.xlsx)

During the 10 years leading up to FYE 2022 (FYE 2013 to FYE 2022), median income grew by 16.2%, at an average rate of 1.7% per year (Figure 2). Meanwhile, mean income grew at a slower rate of 1.4% per year, with an increase of 13.2% over the same 10-year period.

Figure 2: Median income has increased during the 10 years leading up to financial year ending 2022

Median and mean real equivalised household disposable income of individuals, UK, 1977 to financial year ending 2022

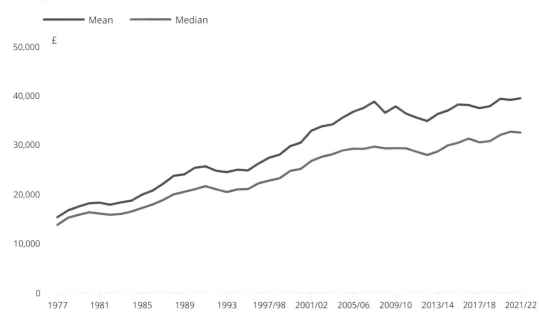

Source: Office for National Statistics – Household Finances Survey

Notes:

1. Incomes are adjusted for inflation using the consumer prices index including owner-occupiers' housing costs (CPIH) excluding council tax.

2. Estimates of income from FYE 2002 onwards have been adjusted for under-coverage of top earners.

3. 2021/22 represents the financial year ending 2022, (April to March), and similarly for all other years expressed in this format. Estimates prior to FYE 1995 are measured on a calendar year basis.

4. Estimates up to and including financial year ending (FYE) 2017 are sourced from the Living Costs and Food (LCF) survey. Estimates from FYE 2018 onwards are based on the Household Finances Survey, which the LCF is part of.

Median income for the poorest fifth of people decreased by 3.8% between FYE 2021 and FYE 2022 (Figure 3). This follows a 2.0% reduction between FYE 2020 and FYE 2021. In the 10 years leading up to 2022 (FYE 2013 to FYE 2022), income in this group increased at an average rate of 0.3% per year.

Median income for the richest fifth of people increased by 1.6% between FYE 2021 and FYE 2022 (Figure 3), following a reduction of 1.0% between FYE 2020 and FYE 2021. However, in the 10 years leading up to 2022 (FYE 2013 to FYE 2022), income in this group increased at an average rate of 1.2% per year. The impact of these changes across the income distribution can be found in our Household income inequality, UK: financial year ending 2022 bulletin (https://www.ons.gov.uk/peoplepopulationandcommunity/personalandhouseholdfinances/incomeandwealth/bulletins/householdincomeinequalityfinancial/latest).

Figure 3: Median income fell by 3.8% for the poorest fifth of people, whilst increasing by 1.6% for the richest fifth of people in financial year ending (FYE) 2022

Median equivalised household disposable income of individuals by quintile group, UK, financial year ending (FYE) 2020, FYE 2021 and FYE 2022

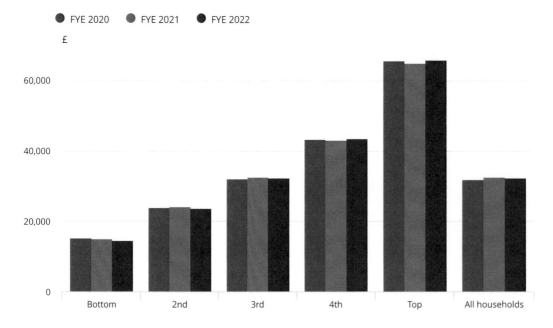

Source: Office for National Statistics – Household Finances Survey

Notes:

1. Incomes are adjusted for inflation using the Consumer Prices Index including owner-occupiers' housing costs (CPIH) excluding council tax.

2. FYE 2022 represents the financial year ending 2022, (April to March), and similarly for all other years expressed in this format.

Median income for retired households (https://www.ons.gov.uk/peoplepopulationandcommunity/personalandhouseholdfinances/incomeandwealth/bulletins/householddisposableincomeandinequality/financialyearending2022#glossary) decreased by 1.6% in FYE 2022, from £26,300 to £25,900. In the 10 years leading up to 2022 (FYE 2013 to FYE 2022), retired household income has seen an average annual growth of 1.3%. Median income for non-retired households decreased by 0.3% in FYE 2022, from £34,100 to £34,000, following a 1.0% increase in the previous year, with an average annual growth of 1.7% in the 10 years leading up to 2022 (FYE 2013 to FYE 2022).

Figure 4: Changes in disposable income across the income distribution were driven by changes in original income, with a reduction in poorer households and an increase in richer households

Contributions to changes in equivalised disposable income change between the financial year ending (FYE) 2021 and FYE 2022

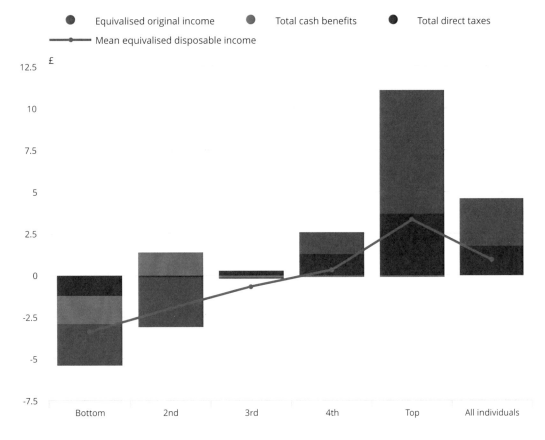

Source: Office for National Statistics – Household Finances Survey

Notes:

1. Incomes are adjusted for inflation using the Consumer Prices Index including owner-occupiers' housing costs (CPIH) excluding council tax.

2. Because of the deductive nature of taxes, a reduction in taxes will contribute to an increase in disposable income.

The largest contribution to change in disposable income across all households is attributable to original income, driven by a decrease of 4.0% in the poorest fifth of people between the financial year ending (FYE) 2021 and FYE 2022, compared with an increase of 5.4% in the richest fifth of people (Figure 4). Meanwhile, the middle of the income distribution has remained stable. More specifically, wages and salaries increased by 3.2% across all households, however, the poorest fifth of people saw a 7.5% decrease, while the richest fifth saw a 7.8% increase.

For the poorest fifth of people, income was further reduced by a real-term reduction in cash benefits of 2.6% (a nominal £80 increase) between FYE 2021 and FYE 2022, which was not fully offset by a reduction in taxes. A nominal increase in cash benefits was seen across the whole income distribution, coinciding with an increase in personal independence payments (PIP) in all but the richest fifth of people, consistent with recent reports of increased PIP claims between July 2021 and July 2022 (https://ifs.org.uk/publications/number-new-disability-benefit-claimants-has-doubled-year).

There are challenges in interpreting annual growth rates across quintiles during the coronavirus pandemic, in part because of compositional changes across the distribution. Throughout FYE 2021 and part of FYE 2022, household finances were affected by restrictions and subsequent financial support measures implemented during the coronavirus pandemic. Income estimates presented here include income from Coronavirus Job Support Scheme (CJRS), as well as policy changes such as the uplift to Universal Credit standard allowance basic element and the Income Tax and coronavirus support scheme. More information on how the pandemic affected income statistics is described in our Interpreting changes in UK estimates during the coronavirus pandemic: financial year ending 2021 article (https://www.ons.gov.uk/peoplepopulationandcommunity/personalandhouseholdfinances/expenditure/articles/interpretingchangesinukincomeestimatesduringthecoronaviruspandemic/financialyearending2021).

4. Average household income data

The effects of taxes and benefits on household income, disposable income estimate (https://www.ons.gov.uk/peoplepopulationandcommunity/personalandhouseholdfinances/incomeandwealth/datasets/householddisposableincomeandinequality)
Dataset | Released 28 March 2022
Average UK household incomes taxes and benefits by household type, tenure status, household characteristics and long-term trends in income inequality.

5. Glossary

Confidence intervals

Confidence intervals use the standard error to derive a range in which we think the true value is likely to lie, provide an indication of the degree of uncertainty of an estimate and help to decide how precise a sample estimate is. It specifies a range of values likely to contain the unknown population value. These values are defined by lower and upper limits. The width of the interval depends on the precision of the estimate and the confidence level used. A greater standard error will result in a wider interval; the wider the interval, the less precise the estimate is.

This release uses 95% confidence intervals to communicate uncertainty in UK-level estimates of mean and median income. An observed change is statistically significant at the 5% level if there is less than a 1 in 20 chance of the observed change being calculated by chance or the variable nature of the sample if there is actually no underlying change.

View more information on Uncertainty and how we measure it for our surveys (https://www.ons.gov.uk/methodology/methodologytopicsandstatisticalconcepts/uncertaintyandhowwemeasureit).

Disposable income

Disposable income is arguably the most widely used household income measure. Disposable income is the amount of money that households have available for spending and saving after direct taxes, such as Income Tax, National Insurance and Council Tax, have been accounted for. It includes earnings from employment, private pensions and investments as well as cash benefits provided by the state.

Equivalisation

We compare different types of individuals and households (such as retired and non-retired, or rich and poor) over time after income has been equivalised. Equivalisation is the process of accounting for the fact that households with many members are likely to need a higher income to achieve the same standard of living as households with fewer members. Equivalisation considers the number of people living in the household and their ages, acknowledging that while a household with two people in it will need more money to sustain the same living standards as one with a single person, the two-person household is unlikely to need double the income.

This analysis uses the modified Organisation for Economic Co-operation and Development (OECD) equivalisation scale (PDF, 165KB). (http://webarchive.nationalarchives.gov.uk/20160105160709/http://www.ons.gov.uk/ons/rel/elmr/economic-and-labour-market-review/no--1--january-2010/using-the-oecd-equivalence-scale-in-taxes-and-benefits-analysis.pdf)

Mean and median income

The mean measure of income divides the total income of individuals by the number of individuals. A limitation of using the mean is that it can be influenced by just a few individuals with very high incomes and therefore does not necessarily reflect the standard of living of the "typical" person. However, when considering changes in income and direct taxes by income decile or types of households, the mean allows for these changes to be analysed in an additive way.

Many researchers argue that growth in median household incomes provides a better measure of how people's well-being has changed over time. The median household income is the income of what would be the middle person if all individuals in the UK were sorted from poorest to richest. Median income provides a good indication of the standard of living of the "typical" individual in terms of income.

Retired and non-retired households

A retired household is one where more than 50% of its income is sourced from retired people. A retired person requires satisfying one of the following criteria:

- their self-defined employment status is "Retired", and they are aged over 50 years
- their self-defined employment status is "Sick or Injured," not seeking work, and aged at or above the State Pension age

As such, analysis of the average income of people living in retired households can include much younger people and potentially exclude older people. However, the strength of this measure is that it highlights those individuals who are most likely to be affected by policy, societal or economic changes that disproportionately affect pension income.

6. Measuring the data

This release provides headline estimates of average disposable income, calculated using the Household Finances Survey (HFS) data. Data are derived from both the Living Costs and Food (LCF) Survey (https://www.ons.gov.uk/peoplepopulationandcommunity/personalandhouseholdfinances/incomeandwealth/methodologies/livingcostsandfoodsurvey)and the Survey on Living Conditions, with harmonised income collection, covering around 17,000 private households in the UK. The Office for National Statistics (ONS) estimates of household income from 1977, up to and including the financial year ending (FYE) 2017, are based on the LCF. From FYE 2018 onwards, estimates have been revised to include data from the HFS and remain comparable with those produced using the LCF for the same period. Further detail is available in Improving the measurement of household income (https://www.ons.gov.uk/peoplepopulationandcommunity/personalandhouseholdfinances/incomeandwealth/methodologies/improvingthemeasurementofhouseholdincome).

The UK has two main, official data sources of household income statistics: the Family Resources Survey (FRS) run by the Department for Work and Pensions (DWP) and the HFS run by the ONS. The FRS estimates underpin DWP's Households Below Average Income (HBAI) series, which is the UK's official source of poverty estimates. With a larger sample size, it is also the main source on household and individual incomes. HFS data are used to produce the ONS's Household Disposable Income Inequality (HDII) (https://www.ons.gov.uk/peoplepopulationandcommunity/personalandhouseholdfinances/incomeandwealth/datasets/householddisposableincomeandinequality) and Effects of Taxes and Benefits (ETB) (https://www.ons.gov.uk/peoplepopulationandcommunity/personalandhouseholdfinances/incomeandwealth/bulletins/theeffectsoftaxesandbenefitsonhouseholdincome/financialyearending2021/relateddata) series. These outputs are the main source for considering the overall financial well-being of households.

There are some important methodological differences between the two series, which means that their income estimates are different. For example, the FRS focuses on respondents' weekly incomes at the time of interview, whereas HFS focuses more on annual income. The treatment of pension contributions also differs, with the ONS's estimate of Gross Household Income being calculated before pension contributions. Further details are available in our income and earnings statistics guide (https://www.ons.gov.uk/employmentandlabourmarket/peopleinwork/earningsandworkinghours/methodologies/aguidetosourcesofdataonearningsandincome).

To make robust comparisons over time, unless otherwise stated, data have been adjusted for effects of inflation and are equivalised to account for changes in household composition. When growth rates are quoted, they compare the average for a group of households in one period to the average for a different set of households in the next period. These statistics are assessed fully compliant with the Code of Practice for Statistics (https://code.statisticsauthority.gov.uk/) and are designated as National Statistics (https://uksa.statisticsauthority.gov.uk/list-of-national-statistics/). Detailed information on quality, methodology and how the data were created is available in the Effects of taxes and benefits on household income QMI (https://www.ons.gov.uk/peoplepopulationandcommunity/personalandhouseholdfinances/incomeandwealth/methodologies/theeffectsoftaxesandbenefitsonukhouseholdincome).

A newly released Income and Earnings interactive tool
(https://analysisfunction.civilservice.gov.uk/dashboard/tools/income-and-earnings-statistics/database.html) allows
data to be compared across a range of sources and can be filtered by topic area, data source, and geographic
coverage.

Transformation of data

The ONS is seeking to transform household financial statistics, covering income, expenditure and wealth of UK
households. Our aim is to ensure that the household financial statistics and analysis we produce continue to meet
the evolving needs of policymakers, citizens and other data users. Our ambition is that our statistics and analysis
should provide inclusive, coherent, timely and granular insights into wide aspects of the financial well-being of
households with improved coverage and accuracy. More information on our plans for household financial statistics
transformation, and an opportunity to give us your views, can be found in the Household Financial Statistics
Transformation (HFST) consultation (PDF 763KB) (https://consultations.ons.gov.uk/external-affairs/transforming-
household-financial-
statist/supporting_documents/Con%20Doc%20%20Transforming%20the%20ONSs%20household%20financial%20st
atistics.pdf), which closes 23 February 2023.

7. Strengths and limitations

Comparable estimates are available back to 1977, allowing analysis of long-term trends. This release also provides
the earliest survey-based analysis of the household income distribution available annually, allowing timely insight
into the evolution of living standards.

Data remain subject to limitations. The Household Finances Survey (HFS) is a sample of the private household
population and does not include those who live in institutionalised households, such as care homes and hostels, or
people who are homeless. Therefore, many of the poorest in society are likely not captured.

Household income surveys can suffer from under-reporting at the top and bottom of the income distribution. While
an adjustment to address survey under-coverage
(https://www.ons.gov.uk/economy/nationalaccounts/uksectoraccounts/compendium/economicreview/february2020/
topincomeadjustmentineffectsoftaxesandbenefitsdatamethodology) of the richest people has been introduced for
statistics covering the financial year ending (FYE) 2002 onwards, measurement issues at the bottom remain. The
Effects of taxes and benefits on household income (ETB) QMI
(https://www.ons.gov.uk/peoplepopulationandcommunity/personalandhouseholdfinances/incomeandwealth/metho
dologies/theeffectsoftaxesandbenefitsonukhouseholdincome) provides further details.

8. Related links

Income estimates for small areas, England and Wales: financial year ending 2018
(https://www.ons.gov.uk/peoplepopulationandcommunity/personalandhouseholdfinances/incomeandwealth/b
ulletins/smallareamodelbasedincomeestimates/financialyearending2018)

Bulletin | Released 5 March 2020

Small area model-based income estimates covering local areas called Middle layer Super Output Areas (MSOAs)
in England and Wales.

Effects of taxes and benefits on UK household income FYE 2021
(https://www.ons.gov.uk/peoplepopulationandcommunity/personalandhouseholdfinances/incomeandwealth/b
ulletins/theeffectsoftaxesandbenefitsonhouseholdincome/latest)

Bulletin | Released 29 July 2022

The redistribution effects on individuals and households of direct and indirect taxation and benefits received in
cash or kind, analysed by household type.

Employee earnings in the UK: 2022
(https://www.ons.gov.uk/employmentandlabourmarket/peopleinwork/earningsandworkinghours/bulletins/annu
alsurveyofhoursandearnings/2022)

Bulletin | Released 26 October 2022

Measures of employee earnings, using data from the Annual Survey for Hours and Earnings (ASHE).

Household below average income: for financial years ending 1995 to 2021
(https://www.gov.uk/government/statistics/households-below-average-income-for-financial-years-ending-1995-
to-2021)

Report | Published 31 March 2022

Statistics on the number and percentage of people living in low-income households for financial years between
1995 and 2021.

The effects of taxes and benefits on household income, technical report: financial year ending 2019
(https://www.ons.gov.uk/peoplepopulationandcommunity/personalandhouseholdfinances/incomeandwealth/ar
ticles/theeffectsoftaxesandbenefitsonhouseholdincome/financialyearending2019)

Article | 25 June 2020

The redistribution effects on households of direct and indirect taxation and benefits received in cash or kind
analysed by household type, and the changing levels of income inequality over time.

Income and earnings coherence workplan (https://analysisfunction.civilservice.gov.uk/government-statistical-
service-and-statistician-group/user-facing-pages/income-and-earnings-statistics/income-and-earnings-
coherence-work-plan/)

Report | Released 18 January 2023

The Government Statistical Service (GSS) income and earnings coherence workplan sets out the actions needed to achieve the GSS vision for coherence of income and earnings statistics.

9. Cite this statistical bulletin

Office for National Statistics (ONS), published 25 January 2023, ONS website, statistical bulletin, Average household income, UK: financial year ending 2022 (https://www.ons.gov.uk/peoplepopulationandcommunity/personalandhouseholdfinances/incomeandwealth/bulletins/householddisposableincomeandinequality/financialyearending2022)

Contact details for this statistical bulletin

Emily Andrews, Paula Croal
hie@ons.gov.uk
Telephone: +44 1633 651927

Office for
National Statistics

Data and analysis from Census 2021

Living Costs and Food Survey QMI

Details the strengths, limitations, uses, users and methods used for the Living Costs and Food Survey.

Contact:
Kate Pugh

Last revised:
1 August 2023

Table of contents

1. Output information

- National Statistic: yes.

- Survey name: Living Costs and Food Survey (LCF).

- Data collection: face-to-face field interviewing.

- Frequency: annual.

- How compiled: cross sectional sample survey.

- Geographic coverage: UK.

2. About this Quality and Methodology Information (QMI) report

This QMI contains information on the quality characteristics of the data (including the European Statistical System five dimensions of quality) as well as the methods used to create it.

The information in this report will help you to:

- understand the strengths and limitations of the data

- learn about existing uses and users of the data

- understand the methods used to create the data

- help you to decide suitable uses for the data

- reduce the risk of misusing data

3. Important points

- The Living Costs and Food Survey (LCF) became part of the Household Finances Survey (HFS) in financial year ending (FYE) 2020 alongside the Survey for Living Conditions (SLC); for more information on the HFS, please see our Household Finances Survey Quality and Methodology Information (QMI) (https://www.ons.gov.uk/peoplepopulationandcommunity/personalandhouseholdfinances/incomeandwealth/methodologies/householdfinancessurveyqmi).

- The Northern Ireland LCF (https://www.nisra.gov.uk/statistics/find-your-survey/northern-ireland-living-costs-and-food-survey#:~:text=The%20Living%20Costs%20and%20Food%20Survey%20%28LCF%29%20is,food%20consumption%20and%20nutrition.%20Details%20of%20the%20Survey), the companion survey to the Great Britain LCF, is conducted by the Central Survey Unit of the Northern Ireland Statistics and Research Agency (NISRA) (https://www.nisra.gov.uk/).

- Results from the LCF are published in our Family spending bulletins (https://www.ons.gov.uk/peoplepopulationandcommunity/personalandhouseholdfinances/expenditure/bulletins/familyspendingintheuk/previousReleases) and GOV.UK's Family food statistics (https://www.gov.uk/government/collections/family-food-statistics); our bulletin provides a comprehensive overview of household expenditure and income and includes background information on the survey's history and methodology, whereas the family food statistics, produced by the Department for Environment, Food and Rural Affairs (DEFRA), provides detailed statistical information on the purchase and consumption of food and drink.

- Microdata for the LCF are available from the UK Data Service (UKDS) (https://beta.ukdataservice.ac.uk/datacatalogue/studies/?Search=Living+cost+and+foods#!?Search=Living%20cost%20and%20foods&Page=1&Rows=10&Sort=1&DateFrom=440&DateTo=2023), Secure Research Service (SRS) (https://www.ons.gov.uk/aboutus/whatwedo/statistics/requestingstatistics/secureresearchservice) or the Integrated Data Service (IDS) (https://integrateddataservice.gov.uk/).

- All reasonable attempts have been made to ensure that the data are as accurate as possible; however, there are two potential sources of error that may affect the reliability of estimates and for which no adequate adjustments can be made, known as sampling and non-sampling errors (more information can be found in our Uncertainty and how we measure it for our surveys methodology (https://www.ons.gov.uk/methodology/methodologytopicsandstatisticalconcepts/uncertaintyandhowwemeasureit)).

4. Quality summary

Overview

The Living Costs and Food Survey (LCF) (https://www.ons.gov.uk/surveys/informationforhouseholdsandindividuals/householdandindividualsurveys/livingcostsandfoodsurvey) is an annual survey, designed primarily to measure household expenditure on goods and services. It also gathers information about the income of household members. Respondents, including children, keep a detailed diary of expenditure for two weeks. Respondents also record the weights and measures of food and drink items bought.

The LCF is a voluntary sample survey of private households. The basic unit of the survey is the household. The LCF (in line with other government social surveys) uses the harmonised definition of a household: a group of people (not necessarily related) living at the same address who share cooking facilities and share a living room or sitting room or dining area. The LCF omits communal establishments such as student halls of residence and armed forces, however, both students and armed forces are included if they live in private accommodation.

Information about regular expenditure, such as rent and mortgage payments, is obtained from a household interview along with retrospective information on certain large, infrequent expenditures such as those on vehicles. Each individual aged 16 years or over in the household visited is asked to keep diary records of daily expenditure for two weeks. Children aged between 7 and 15 years keep a simplified diary.

Detailed questions are asked about the income of each adult member of the household. In addition, personal information such as age, sex and marital status is recorded for each household member.

For the financial year ending (FYE) 2021, during the coronavirus (COVID-19) pandemic, respondents did not complete a face-to-face interview with questions on regular items of household expenditure and income details. Instead, respondents participated in telephone interviews. The knock to nudge intervention was also introduced, as discussed in our Impact of COVID-19 on Office for National Statistics (ONS) social survey data collection methodology (https://www.ons.gov.uk/peoplepopulationandcommunity/healthandsocialcare/conditionsanddiseases/methodologies/impactofcovid19ononssocialsurveydatacollection#:~:text). This involves interviewers visiting households to "nudge" those selected to participate in ONS surveys (following stringent health and safety protocols).

Once interviewed, LCF respondents were asked to provide copies of receipts (electronic or paper) for the two-week diary period, and interviewers recorded non-receipt-based expenditure via regular telephone calls during the two-week diary period. As a result of these changes and changes to data processing, not all the collected data could be processed, this is detailed in our Living Costs and Food Survey technical report: FYE March 2021 (https://www.ons.gov.uk/peoplepopulationandcommunity/personalandhouseholdfinances/expenditure/methodologies/livingcostsandfoodsurveytechnicalreportfinancialyearendingmarch2021). In October 2022, the LCF survey returned to face-to-face interview mode.

Uses and users

The LCF is the primary source of official information on household expenditure on goods and services and is also an important and detailed source of income data which can shed light on the impact of real-world events on expenditure patterns for different groups of people. LCF data feeds into four sets of national statistics: our Family spending (https://www.ons.gov.uk/peoplepopulationandcommunity/personalandhouseholdfinances/expenditure/bulletins/familyspendingintheuk/april2021tomarch2022), Average household income (https://www.ons.gov.uk/peoplepopulationandcommunity/personalandhouseholdfinances/incomeandwealth/bulletins/householddisposableincomeandinequality/financialyearending2022), Household income inequality (https://www.ons.gov.uk/peoplepopulationandcommunity/personalandhouseholdfinances/incomeandwealth/bulletins/householdincomeinequalityfinancial/financialyearending2022) and Effects of taxes and benefits on UK household income (https://www.ons.gov.uk/peoplepopulationandcommunity/personalandhouseholdfinances/incomeandwealth/bulletins/theeffectsoftaxesandbenefitsonhouseholdincome/financialyearending2022) bulletins. The survey design and outputs are tailored to user needs.

The results of LCF are used by:

- HM Revenue and Customs (HMRC)

- the Department for Environment, Food and Rural Affairs (DEFRA)

- HM Treasury (HMT)

- Department for Work and Pensions (DWP)

- devolved governments of the UK

Many other government departments use LCF data as a basis for policymaking, for example, in areas of housing and transport. Within the ONS, LCF feeds into our Consumer Prices Index (CPI) (https://www.ons.gov.uk/economy/inflationandpriceindices/bulletins/consumerpriceinflation/previousReleases) and Retail Price Index (RPI), National Accounts and regional accounts of Consumer trends (https://www.ons.gov.uk/economy/nationalaccounts/satelliteaccounts/bulletins/consumertrends/januarytomarch2023), which are important macroeconomic measures of the UK economy. Users outside government include independent research institutes, academic researchers and business and market researchers.

The Household Finances Survey (HFS) expenditure steering group is used to engage with users and comprises of a group of important customers in the ONS and other government departments. Meetings are usually held biennially. The steering group is also consulted between meetings on proposals and developments, for example, on variable usage and questionnaire changes.

Strengths and limitations

Limitations

Experience of household surveys in the UK and in other countries indicates that reported expenditure on a few items (notably tobacco, alcohol and restaurants and catering) is below the levels that might be expected by comparison with other sources of information. National Lottery spending has also been under-recorded in the LCF, particularly for scratch cards.

Granularity

One of the key strengths of the LCF dataset is the level of detail within the collected information; the disaggregated levels of expenditure and person level information within the data can provide low level insights into expenditure trends over time. However, the survey sample is small, which can cause some volatility within the results depending on the level of detail the analysis is conducted.

In July 2021, the Office for Statistics Regulation carried out an Assessment of the LCF (https://osr.statisticsauthority.gov.uk/publication/assessment-report-the-living-costs-and-food-survey/#:~:text=In%20line%20with%20the%20Office%20for%20Statistics%20Regulation,the%20quality%20and%20public%20value%20of%20LCF%20data.). The ONS initiated a programme of work to meet the OSR recommendations, and in October 2022, OSR confirmed that LCF was to retain its national statistics status (https://osr.statisticsauthority.gov.uk/correspondence/ed-humpherson-to-alex-lambert-confirmation-of-national-statistics-for-the-living-costs-and-food-survey/) for our Family Spending in the UK bulletins (https://www.ons.gov.uk/peoplepopulationandcommunity/personalandhouseholdfinances/expenditure/bulletins/familyspendingintheuk/previousReleases).

Recent improvements

LCF has recently undertaken an uplift of the systems used to process the data from legacy statistical processing tools such as SPSS and SAS to R and Python. This has led to an improvement in the time taken to process the data to allow for more thorough quality assurance and scrutiny in the survey results.

5. Quality characteristics of the Living Costs and Food Survey (LCF) data

Accuracy and reliability

Multiple quality assurance methods ensure that the LCF data are as reliable as possible. These methods are applied during the interview and after collection through outlier detection and comparisons of the data between years. All data that are identified as possible errors are investigated and, where appropriate, adjusted.

Coherence and comparability

Comparability

A household expenditure survey has been conducted each year in the UK since 1957. From 1957 to March 2001, the Family Expenditure Survey (FES) and National Food Survey (NFS) provided information on household expenditure patterns and food consumption. Both surveys were well-established, important sources of information for government and the wider community, charting changes and patterns in the UK's spending and food consumption since the 1950s. In April 2001, these surveys were combined to form the Expenditure and Food Survey (EFS). The EFS was renamed to the Living Costs and Food (LCF) survey in January 2008.

A methodological discontinuity was introduced when the FES and NFS were combined to form the EFS in April 2001. At the same time, the survey adopted the Classification of Individual Consumption by Purpose (COICOP) (https://unstats.un.org/unsd/classifications/Family/Detail/5). This meant a significant change to the categorisation of expenditure.

Until 2005 to 2006, annual data were collected and published on a financial year basis. From 2006, data were collected on a calendar year basis.

In 2014 to 2015, the survey reverted to a financial year basis.

Other more minor changes to definitions used in the survey have been introduced. Changes made since 1991 are documented in the LCF User Guides (https://beta.ukdataservice.ac.uk/datacatalogue/studies/study?id=9022#!/documentation), which are available through the UK Data Service (UKDS).

Coherence

The main comparator for LCF estimates of expenditure data are the figures on final household consumption expenditure (HHFCE), published in our Consumer trends bulletin (https://www.ons.gov.uk/economy/nationalaccounts/satelliteaccounts/bulletins/consumertrends/januarytomarch2023) and used in UK National Accounts. LCF data feed into some of the estimates published in consumer trends, but other sources are also used. While differences occur in the estimates published, the differences are credible. Research is ongoing into the different estimates produced and their causes.

Accessibility and clarity

The UKDS at the University of Essex provides researchers with access to LCF microdata under an End User License.

Our recommended format for accessible content is a combination of HTML webpages for narrative, charts and graphs, with data being provided in usable formats such as CSV and Excel. Our website also offers users the option to download the narrative in PDF format. For further information, please refer to the contact details on our Accessibility statement (https://www.ons.gov.uk/help/accessibility).

Timeliness and punctuality

Quarterly datasets are provided to internal Office for National Statistics (ONS) customers and important government departments approximately four months after the end of each quarter.

Annual datasets are made available approximately one year after the end of the survey cycle.

For more details on related releases, the GOV.UK release calendar (https://www.gov.uk/government/statistics/announcements) provides advance notice of release dates. If there are any changes to the pre-announced release schedule, public attention will be drawn to the change and the reasons for the change will be explained fully at the same time, as set out in the Code of Practice for Official Statistics.

Concepts and definitions (including list of changes to definitions)

The LCF utilises a suite of standard concepts and definitions. Some of the main terms are defined in this section, while a list of definitions can be found in our Family spending bulletin (https://www.ons.gov.uk/peoplepopulationandcommunity/personalandhouseholdfinances/expenditure/bulletins/familyspendingintheuk/april2021tomarch2022#glossary).

Classification of Individual Consumption by Purpose (COICOP)

The COICOP (https://ec.europa.eu/eurostat/statistics-explained/index.php?title=Glossary:Classification_of_individual_consumption_by_purpose_(COICOP)) coding frame for expenditure items was introduced in 2001 to 2002. COICOP has been adapted to the needs of the Household Budget Survey (HBS) across the EU and is therefore compatible with similar national accounts and consumer prices indices. This allows the production of indicators which are comparable Europe-wide, such as the Harmonised Indices of Consumer Prices (CPI).

National Statistics Socio-economic classification (NS-SEC)

In 2001 to 2002, our NS-SEC (https://www.ons.gov.uk/methodology/classificationsandstandards/otherclassifications/thenationalstatisticssocioeconomicclassificationnssecrebasedonsoc2010) was adopted for all official surveys, replacing the social class based on occupation and socio-economic group. The long-term unemployed, which fall into a separate category, are defined as those unemployed and seeking work for 12 months or more. This group is derived from our UK Standard Occupation Classification (SOC2020) (https://www.ons.gov.uk/methodology/classificationsandstandards/standardoccupationalclassificationsoc/soc2020) coding frame.

Output quality

Response rates

Response rates are available in our Living Costs and Food Survey technical report: financial year ending (FYE) March 2022 (https://www.ons.gov.uk/peoplepopulationandcommunity/personalandhouseholdfinances/expenditure/methodologies/livingcostsandfoodsurveytechnicalreportfinancialyearendingmarch2022). In 2021 to 2022, the response rate was 27% in Great Britain (and 28% for the UK). This is lower than previously achieved because of the change to mode (from face-to-face to telephone mode) necessitated by the coronavirus (COVID-19) pandemic. A long-term decline in response has been observed for the LCF, in common with other social surveys. Non-response weighting is applied to help mitigate non-response bias.

The LCF is conducted with people who volunteer their time to answer questions about themselves and keep a diary for two weeks. The voluntary nature of the survey means that people who do not wish to take part in the survey can refuse to do so. Reasons for not participating in the survey include people who "cannot be bothered" and "refusal to headquarters after interviewer's visit". The sample is designed to ensure that the results of the survey represent the population of the UK. The risk of the survey not being representative may increase with every refusal or non-contact with a sampled household (survey non-response). One measure of the quality of survey results is therefore the response rate.

Sources of error

Survey results are subject to various sources of error. The total error in a survey estimate is the difference between the estimate derived from the data collected and the true value for the population. It is helpful to distinguish between systematic and random error.

Systematic error

Systematic error, or bias, covers those sources of error that will not be expected to average to zero over repeats of the survey. Bias may occur, for example, if a certain section of the population is excluded from the sampling frame, because non-respondents to the survey have different characteristics to respondents, or if interviewers systematically influence responses in one way or another.

Substantial efforts are made to avoid systematic errors, and these include:

- processes to ensure that households are selected in accordance with the sample design

- extensive measures to minimise non-response

- training to ensure that interviewers ask questions in such a way as to avoid biasing response

Additionally, the data are weighted to compensate for non-response (see Section 6: Methods used to produce the LCF data); each respondent is given a weight so that they represent the non-respondents that are like them in terms of the survey characteristics. The sample distribution is weighted so that it matches the population distribution in terms of region, age group and sex and tenure.

Random error

Random error is the difference from the estimates derived using the sample data from the true values for the population that occur through chance occurrences. Random error may result from sources such as variation in a respondent's interpretation of the survey questions, or interviewer inconsistencies in asking questions. Efforts are made to minimise these effects through pilot work to ensure questions are understood by respondents and through interviewer training emphasising the need for consistency in dealing with selected sample members.

Sampling error

An important component of random error is sampling error, which arises because the estimate is based on a sample rather than a full census of the population. The results obtained for any single sample may, by chance, vary from the true values for the population. Precision is usually estimated through the calculation of standard errors (for more information, see our Uncertainty and how we measure it for our surveys methodology (https://www.ons.gov.uk/methodology/methodologytopicsandstatisticalconcepts/uncertaintyandhowwemeasureit)). Standard errors are estimated for some of the main variables on LCF. These are published in our Living Costs and Food Survey: technical report data tables (https://www.ons.gov.uk/peoplepopulationandcommunity/personalandhouseholdfinances/expenditure/datasets/livingcostsandfoodsurveytechnicalreportdatatables).

The LCF uses a multi-stage stratified sample design. Consequently, it is inappropriate to estimate standard errors based on a simple random design, as this will not reflect the true sampling variation because of the complex sample design. The two-stage sample of addresses can lead to a substantial increase in standard error if the households or individuals within Primary Sampling Units (PSUs) are relatively homogeneous, but the PSUs differ from one another. Stratification tends to reduce sampling error and is most advantageous where the stratification factor is strongly related to characteristics of interest in the survey.

6. Methods used to produce the Living Costs and Food Survey (LCF) data

Sampling

Approximately 5,400 responding households in the UK per year are in the LCF survey sample.

Sampling frame

The sampling frame used for the LCF is the Royal Mail's Postcode Address File (PAF) (https://www.poweredbypaf.com/) of small users. The PAF is the most comprehensive address database in the UK. It is updated daily and contains approximately 30 million addresses.

Sample design

The LCF sample for Great Britain is a multi-stage stratified random sample. Addresses on the PAF with "small user" postcodes are used as the sample frame. Postal sectors are used as the Primary Sampling Units (PSUs), with 20 addresses selected from each PSU to form the monthly interviewer quota. Approximately 700 PSUs are selected annually after being arranged in 41 strata defined by Nomenclature of Territorial Units for Statistics Level 2 (NUTS2) areas and two 2011 Census variables: socio-economic group of the head of household or household reference person (https://analysisfunction.civilservice.gov.uk/policy-store/household-reference-person/) and ownership of cars.

During the coronavirus (COVID-19) pandemic, the sample sizes were increased to combat the impact of the change to interviewer mode from face-to-face to telephone. This fluctuated between 40 and 28 addresses per quota starting from June 2020 until it reduced to 25 addresses in January 2023 and returned to "normal" (20 addresses) in March 2023.

The Northern Ireland LCF (https://www.nisra.gov.uk/statistics/find-your-survey/northern-ireland-living-costs-and-food-survey#:~:text=The%20Living%20Costs%20and%20Food%20Survey%20%28LCF%29%20is,food%20consumption%20and%20nutrition.%20Details%20of%20the%20Survey), the companion survey to the Great Britain LCF, is conducted by the Central Survey Unit of the Northern Ireland Statistics and Research Agency (NISRA) (https://www.nisra.gov.uk/). A systematic random sample of private addresses is drawn from the NISRA Address Register (NAR). Addresses are sorted by district council and ward, so the sample is effectively stratified geographically.

Fieldwork

The fieldwork is conducted by the Office for National Statistics (ONS) in Great Britain and by NISRA for the Department of Finance and Personnel in Northern Ireland using largely identical questionnaires. Differences between the two questionnaires reflect the country-specific harmonised standards for ethnicity, nationality and national identity, and the different systems of local taxation used in Great Britain and Northern Ireland.

Households at the selected addresses receive an advance letter before being visited by an interviewer. They are asked to co-operate in the survey. The calling strategy which achieves the highest contact rate at the lowest cost is to vary calling times. Many households will be easily contacted within the first couple of calls, but for those which are not it is important to make sure that successive visits are at different times of the day (including evenings) and on different days of the week.

Interviews are conducted by Computer Assisted Personal Interviewing (CAPI) using laptop computers. Respondents complete a face-to-face interview and each individual aged 16 years or over in the visited household is asked to keep a record of daily expenditure for two weeks. Children aged between 7 and 15 years keep a simplified diary.

Response outcome categories

A full response denotes a household in which:

- all adults aged 16 years and over co-operated with the interview

- no income questions in the questionnaire were refused

- all adults kept a two-week record of their expenditure

- the information given was complete and usable

There are three types of partial responses on the LCF:

- one or more adults, that are not the main diary keeper (MDK), the main shopper in the household, refuse to keep the diary, but all adults complete the full income section of the interview

- one or more adults refuse the full income section but all adults in the household keep the diary and main income information is collected for all adults

- one or more adults (that are not the MDK) refuse to keep the diary and one or more adults refuse the full income section but main income information is collected for all adults

All partial responses must contain a diary from the MDK. If the MDK refuses to complete the diary, the household is classified as a refusal.

An outright refusal is a household that refuses to respond to the survey and the interviewer feels that there is no chance of an interview at the given time. In addition to outright refusals, there are also refusals when some of the information has not been collected. Refusals on the LCF are defined as:

- all adults complete the full income section, but the MDK of the household refuses to keep the diary

- one adult refuses to give the main income information in the questionnaire

A non-contact arises when an address is occupied but where it has not been possible to contact any member of the household in the field period.

44

Proxy interview

Ideally, all adult members of the household should be present during the interview, so that the income section can be asked personally. However, where a member of the household is not present during the interview, another member of the household (such as a spouse) may be able to provide documentary information about the absent person via a proxy interview.

How we process the data

Weighting

The weighting procedure comprises two stages. First, a non-response adjustment is made using weighting classes derived from an analysis of respondent and non-respondent LCF households using addresses linking LCF response status to the 2011 Census data for LCF addresses selected around the time of the census. Second, the non-response weights are calibrated to population totals. In response to the effects of the pandemic, tenure was introduced from financial year ending (FYE) 2021 as a further calibration control analogous to the changes for LFS with owning outright, owning through mortgage and renting as calibration groups, constructed from the numbers of males and females in different age groups and, separately, for regions.

Outliers

Extreme values in the data are identified and treated during the quarterly production process. For the annual file creation, to identify and treat outliers in household and person level datasets for income and expenditure, a draft run of the family spending tables is produced. From this, outliers are identified from a decimal representation of the expenditure influence, referred to as "most influence". Influence caps are set, and if the spending for the household exceeds the cap, then the expenditure can be classed as an outlier and different from the normal trend. The weight for that household is then treated accordingly to bring the weighted spending below the cap whilst attempting to minimise any additional impact to other spending categories. All the annual household weights are then scaled to account for the impact of the adjusted figures. This technique effectively reduces the impact of any outlying values without deleting them altogether.

How we quality assure and validate the data

Prior to publication LCF data are subjected to a rigorous process of quality assurance. An initial series of automatic checks are applied to raw household and income data as they are collected from respondents and entered onto the CAPI version of the questionnaire. These data are further checked by a team of editors within the ONS who also impute for missing values. Missing data are imputed using a combination of the following methods:

- by reference to tables based on external (non-LCF) data produced elsewhere
- by reference to tables based on LCF data from previous years showing average amounts according to household income
- by using information collected elsewhere in the questionnaire or by referring to the interviewers

Respondents' diaries are checked to ensure the process of recording daily expenditure has been understood and before they are returned to the ONS to ensure recorded information is complete. In manually entering diary data to the ONS systems, further checks are made to these data.

Once the data has been processed, detailed quality assurance is conducted on each of the stakeholder outputs during the processing and outputs stage. The LCF team also carries out a series of checks on the time series data to identify odd movements and extreme values or outliers in household and person level datasets.

How we disseminate the data

Our Statistical disclosure control methodology (https://www.ons.gov.uk/methodology/methodologytopicsandstatisticalconcepts/disclosurecontrol) is also applied to LCF data. This ensures that information attributable to an individual is not disclosed in any publication. The Code of Practice for Official Statistics (https://uksa.statisticsauthority.gov.uk/publication/code-of-practice/#:~:text=The%20Code%20of%20Practice%20for%20Official%20Statistics%20promotes,specific%20statement%20that%20requires%20sound%20judgement%20and%20interpretation.)and specifically, Principle 5: Confidentiality, sets out practices for how we protect data from being disclosed. The principle includes a guarantee to survey respondents to "ensure that official statistics do not reveal the identity of an individual or organisation, or any private information relating to them".

7. Related links

Living Costs and Food Survey

(https://www.ons.gov.uk/surveys/informationforhouseholdsandindividuals/householdandindividualsurveys/livin=
gcostsandfoodsurvey)

Survey | Updated regularly

An overview of the Living Costs and Food Survey study aimed at interested participants.

Household Finances Survey QMI

(https://www.ons.gov.uk/peoplepopulationandcommunity/personalandhouseholdfinances/incomeandwealth/m=
ethodologies/householdfinancessurveyqmi)

Methodology | Released 21 July 2023

Quality and Methodology Information (QMI) report for the Household Finances Survey (HFS), detailing the=
strengths and limitations of the data, methods used, and data uses and users.

Improving the measurement of household income

(https://www.ons.gov.uk/peoplepopulationandcommunity/personalandhouseholdfinances/incomeandwealth/m=
ethodologies/improvingthemeasurementofhouseholdincome)

Methodology | 26 November 2020

Headline measures of household income and inequality produced using the new Household Finances Survey
(HFS) data source, comparing them with previously published estimates published from the Living Costs and=
Food Survey (LCF).

Impact of increased cost of living on adults across Great Britain

(https://www.ons.gov.uk/peoplepopulationandcommunity/personalandhouseholdfinances/expenditure/articles/
impactofincreasedcostoflivingonadultsacrossgreatbritain/februarytomay2023)

Article | 14 July 2023

Analysis of the proportion of the population that are affected by an increase in their cost of living, and of the=
characteristics associated with financial vulnerability, using data from the Opinions and Lifestyle Survey.

Living Costs and Food Survey technical report: financial year ending March 2022

(https://www.ons.gov.uk/peoplepopulationandcommunity/personalandhouseholdfinances/expenditure/method=
ologies/livingcostsandfoodsurveytechnicalreportfinancialyearendingmarch2022)

Methodology | 1 August 2023

User guidance and technical information for the Living Costs and Food Survey for the financial year ending=
March 2022.

Family spending in the UK statistical bulletins
(https://www.ons.gov.uk/peoplepopulationandcommunity/personalandhouseholdfinances/expenditure/bulletin=
s/familyspendingintheuk/previousReleases)

Bulletin | Released annually

Average weekly household expenditure on goods and services in the UK, by age, income, economic status, socio-
economic class, household composition and region.

Family food statistics (https://www.gov.uk/government/collections/family-food-statistics#full-publication-update-
history)

Collection | Last updated 21 February 2023

Annual statistics about food and drink purchases in the UK.

Effects of taxes and benefits on UK household income: financial year ending 2022
(https://www.ons.gov.uk/peoplepopulationandcommunity/personalandhouseholdfinances/incomeandwealth/b=
ulletins/theeffectsoftaxesandbenefitsonhouseholdincome/financialyearending2022)

Bulletin | Released 18 July 2023

The redistribution effects of individuals and households of direct and indirect taxation and benefits received in=
cash or kind, analysed by household type.

Household income inequality, UK: financial year ending 2022
(https://www.ons.gov.uk/peoplepopulationandcommunity/personalandhouseholdfinances/incomeandwealth/b=
ulletins/householdincomeinequalityfinancial/financialyearending2022)

Bulletin | Released 25 January 2023

Initial insight into main estimates of household incomes and inequality in the UK, with analysis of how these=
measures have changed over time accounting for inflation and household composition.

Average household income, UK: financial year ending 2022
(https://www.ons.gov.uk/peoplepopulationandcommunity/personalandhouseholdfinances/incomeandwealth/b=
ulletins/householddisposableincomeandinequality/financialyearending2022)

Bulletin | Released 25 January 2023

Final estimates of average household income in the UK, with analysis of how these measures have changed over=
time, accounting for inflation and household composition.

Consumer price inflation, updating weights: 2023
(https://www.ons.gov.uk/economy/inflationandpriceindices/articles/consumerpriceinflationupdatingweights/202=
3)

Article | Released 13 March 2023

An overview of the latest annual update of Consumer Prices Index including owner occupiers' housing costs
(CPIH) weights.

Consumer trends, UK: January to March 2023

(https://www.ons.gov.uk/economy/nationalaccounts/satelliteaccounts/bulletins/consumertrends/januarytomarc=h2023)

Bulletin | 30 June 2023

Household final consumption expenditure (HHFCE) for the UK, as a measure of economic growth. Includes all spending on goods and services by members of UK households.

8. Cite this methodology

Office for National Statistics (ONS), released 1 August 2023, ONS website, methodology, Living Costs and Food Survey Quality and Methodology Information (QMI) (https://www.ons.gov.uk/peoplepopulationandcommunity/personalandhouseholdfinances/incomeandwealth/methodologies/livingcostsandfoodsurveyqmi)

Contact details for this methodology

Kate Pugh

lcf_enquiries@ons.gov.uk

Telephone: +44 1633 651836

Office for
National Statistics

Data and analysis from Census 2021

Living Costs and Food Survey technical report: financial year ending March 2022

User guidance and technical information for the Living Costs and Food Survey for the financial year ending March 2022.

Contact:
Alice Gallimore-Roberts

Last revised:
1 August 2023

Table of contents

1. Overview

This report provides an update on the sampling, fieldwork and data processing for the Living Costs and Food Survey (LCF) for the financial year ending (FYE) 2022 (April 2021 to March 2022). The survey is undertaken by Social Survey Collection, which is part of the Surveys Directorate within the Office for National Statistics (ONS).

This report contains response information, questionnaire changes and new or changed methodology for FYE 2022. It does not describe methodology that has changed prior to FYE 2022. For changes prior to FYE 2022, users should refer to our Living Costs and Food Survey technical report: financial year ending March 2021 (https://www.ons.gov.uk/peoplepopulationandcommunity/personalandhouseholdfinances/expenditure/methodolog ies/livingcostsandfoodsurveytechnicalreportfinancialyearendingmarch2021). For a more in-depth explanation of LCF processes and methodology, users should refer to the Living Costs and Food Survey QMI (https://www.ons.gov.uk/peoplepopulationandcommunity/personalandhouseholdfinances/incomeandwealth/metho dologies/livingcostsandfoodsurveyqmi).

The purpose of this report is to update the FYE 2021 technical report and accompanies our Family spending in the UK: March 2021 to April 2022 bulletin (https://www.ons.gov.uk/peoplepopulationandcommunity/personalandhouseholdfinances/expenditure/bulletins/fa milyspendingintheuk/april2021tomarch2022).

Alongside this report, we are publishing updated Living Costs and Food Survey: technical report data tables (https://www.ons.gov.uk/peoplepopulationandcommunity/personalandhouseholdfinances/expenditure/datasets/livi ngcostsandfoodsurveytechnicalreportdatatables) that provide information on response, characteristics of the sample, confidence intervals and interview metrics.

2. Response for FYE 2022

As shown in Table 4 of the accompanying dataset (https://www.ons.gov.uk/peoplepopulationandcommunity/personalandhouseholdfinances/expenditure/datasets/livingcostsandfoodsurveytechnicalreportdatatables), the overall response rate for the Living Costs and Food Survey (LCF) in Great Britain was 27% in the financial year ending (FYE) 2022. This is a 3% increase in comparison with FYE 2021.

Of the eligible sample for FYE 2022, it was not possible to contact 42% of addresses, a further 32% refused to take part and 5% had another reason for non-response. Of the 5,306 responding households in Great Britain, 5,227 cooperated fully, meaning they completed both interview and diary sections of the survey.

In FYE 2022, partial responses accounted for 1% of all co-operating households. Of these 79 partials, 76 occurred because one or more adults in the household refused to keep the diary but were happy to take part in the interview (Table 6 (https://www.ons.gov.uk/peoplepopulationandcommunity/personalandhouseholdfinances/expenditure/datasets/livingcostsandfoodsurveytechnicalreportdatatables)).

Interviewers record the main reason why people refuse before or during an interview from a list of pre-coded answers. In FYE 2022, the two most commonly cited reasons for refusing to take part in the survey were (Table 10 (https://www.ons.gov.uk/peoplepopulationandcommunity/personalandhouseholdfinances/expenditure/datasets/livingcostsandfoodsurveytechnicalreportdatatables)):

- cannot be bothered (31%), which was the top reason cited, as in the previous year
- refusal to headquarters after interviewer's visit (10%), which is a level similar to the previous year

3. Living Costs and Food Survey questionnaire changes for FYE 2022

Preparations for the April 2021 questionnaire changes began in September 2020. This allowed us to plan the changes and liaise with, and seek, stakeholder approval.

Changes for April 2021

Because of the UK still being under certain restrictions due to coronavirus (COVID-19), most of the changes for the April 2021 questionnaire were related to updating the time period within the questions related to the coronavirus pandemic.

Blocks or questions removed

Following interviewer feedback, a block of questions asking respondents to compare their spending during and before coronavirus was removed to reduce respondent burden and shorten the length of the questionnaire.

Addition of questions

A set of questions were introduced to measure the effectiveness of the Knock to Nudge (https://www.ons.gov.uk/peoplepopulationandcommunity/healthandsocialcare/conditionsanddiseases/methodologies/impactofcovid19ononssocialsurveydatacollection#:~:text=As%20a%20result%2C%20we%20introduced,put%20in%20place%20in%20July.) (KtN) trial that was introduced in October 2020. KtN involved interviewers visiting households to "nudge" those selected to participate in ONS surveys. Thus, offering survey participants an opportunity to schedule a telephone appointment with the interviewer at the doorstep, and for the interviewer to build a rapport with the respondent. For non-contacts, a call today card, indicating that the interviewer had visited the address, was posted through the door. These questions were included for Great Britain only, that is, not Northern Ireland.

The set of questions related to Health were reintroduced into the questionnaire at the request of users, following their removal in April 2020.

Other changes

An updated version of the UK Standard Occupation Classification (SOC) coding frame, SOC 2020, was implemented in July 2022. It was updated because of missing information in the coding frame version introduced in April 2021. This caused only marginal net change at the SOC Major Group level so the impact of the error on LCF outputs was minimal.

Steps were also taken at the data editing stage to check the data against the new SOC coding frame. For further information, users can refer to The impact of miscoding of occupational data in Office for National Statistics social surveys, UK (https://www.ons.gov.uk/employmentandlabourmarket/peopleinwork/employmentandemployeetypes/articles/thei

mpactofmiscodingofoccupationaldatainofficefornationalstatisticssocialsurveysuk/2022-09-
26#:~:text=Our%20research%20shows%20that%20around%20half%20of%20four-
digit,be%20affected%20has%20been%20produced%20with%20this%20article.).

The question wording of the coronavirus expenditure questions was updated following interviewer feedback, to improve the flow of the questionnaire.

Because of a change in the TV licensing laws, the routing to the question asking if anyone in the household has paid for a TV licence for the property in the last 12 months was amended to ask all households regardless of the ages of the respondents.

Previously all over-75s used to get a free TV licence, but the rules changed in August 2020, and free licences are now only available to over-75s who receive the pension credit benefit.

Changes made to the questionnaire in response to the pandemic

The actions implemented to continue the survey while coronavirus restrictions were in place were carried forward into 2021 -- please see Living Costs and Food Survey technical report: financial year ending March 2021 (https://www.ons.gov.uk/peoplepopulationandcommunity/personalandhouseholdfinances/expenditure/methodolog ies/livingcostsandfoodsurveytechnicalreportfinancialyearendingmarch2021) for more detail.

For the financial year ending (FYE) 2022, interviews continued to be held over the telephone to ensure data collection activities were carried out in line with the coronavirus restrictions over this period. The introduction of new questions and reintroduction of previously asked questions were kept to a minimum to make sure that the survey length was not increased significantly. The question prompts remained to continue to inform interviewers as to how the questions should be asked.

4. Terminology for FYE 2022

Design factor

The design factor, or deft, is the ratio of the standard error of an estimate calculated considering the complex design relative to the standard error that would have resulted had the survey design been a simple random sample of the same size. Design factors are estimated for some of the main variables on LCF. These are published in the technical report tables (https://www.ons.gov.uk/peoplepopulationandcommunity/personalandhouseholdfinances/expenditure/datasets/livingcostsandfoodsurveytechnicalreportdatatables).

The size of the deft varies between survey variables according to the degree to which a characteristic is clustered within primary sampling units (PSUs), or is distributed between strata, and the impact of the weighting. For a single variable, the size of the deft also varies according to the size of the subgroup on which the estimate is based and on the distribution of the subgroup between PSUs and strata.

Deft below 1.0 show that the standard errors associated with the complex design are lower than those associated with the simple random design probably because of the benefits of stratification. Deft greater than 1.0 show the survey has produced less precise estimates than would be obtained from a comparable simple random sample because of the effects of clustering and weighting.

5. Cite this methodology

Office for National Statistics (ONS), released 1 August 2023, ONS website, methodology, Living Costs and Food Survey technical report: financial year ending March 2022 (https://www.ons.gov.uk/peoplepopulationandcommunity/personalandhouseholdfinances/expenditure/methodologies/livingcostsandfoodsurveytechnicalreportfinancialyearendingmarch2022)

Contact details for this methodology

Alice Gallimore-Roberts
lcf_enquiries@ons.gov.uk
Telephone: +44 1633 580068

Office for
National Statistics

Data and analysis from Census 2021

Household Finances Survey QMI

Quality and Methodology Information (QMI) report for the Household
Finances Survey (HFS), detailing the strengths and limitations of the data,
methods used, and data uses and users.

Contact:
Vicky Parker and Georgina Thompson

Last revised:
21 July 2023

Table of contents

1. Output information

- Survey name: Household Finances Survey (HFS).

- Frequency: annual.

- How compiled: cross sectional and longitudinal sample survey.

- Geographic coverage: UK.

- Last revised: July 2023.

2. About this Quality and Methodology Information (QMI) report

This QMI report contains information on the quality characteristics of the data (including the European Statistical System's five dimensions of quality) as well as the methods used to create it. More information can be found in our Quality in official statistics methodology (https://www.ons.gov.uk/methodology/methodologytopicsandstatisticalconcepts/qualityinofficialstatistics).

The information in this report will help you to:

- understand the strengths and limitations of the data

- learn about existing uses and users of the data

- understand the methods used to create the data

- decide suitable uses for the data

- reduce the risk of misusing data

3. Important points

All reasonable attempts have been made to ensure that the data we collect are as accurate as possible. However, there are two potential sources of error that may affect the reliability of estimates and for which no adequate adjustments can be made, known as sampling and non-sampling errors. More information about these can be found in our Uncertainty and how we measure it for our surveys methodology (https://www.ons.gov.uk/methodology/methodologytopicsandstatisticalconcepts/uncertaintyandhowwemeasureit).

The Household Finances Survey (HFS) is a combination of the longitudinal Survey of Living Conditions (SLC) and the cross-sectional Living Costs and Food (LCF) survey.

HFS anonymised datasets will be made available through the UK Data Service, starting with the Financial Year Ending (FYE) 2021 annual dataset, which will be published in July 2023.

4. Quality summary

Overview

Over the past few years, the Office for National Statistics (ONS) has undertaken a programme of work to transform the production of its household financial statistics.

The Household Finances Survey (HFS) data source was launched in the financial year ending (FYE) 2020 to improve the quality of the ONS's income data. The HFS is a combination of the longitudinal Survey of Living Conditions (SLC) and the cross-sectional Living Costs and Food (LCF) survey. Both the SLC and LCF are conducted throughout the year and across the whole of the UK.

The ONS is responsible for conducting both the SLC and LCF survey in Great Britain. In Northern Ireland, the companion surveys to the Great Britain SLC and LCF are conducted by the Central Survey Unit Northern Ireland Statistics and Research agency (NISRA).

The SLC is an annual survey of approximately 12,000 UK households which provides both longitudinal and cross-sectional data on household income, housing, labour, education, and pensions. Respondents selected for the SLC remain in the survey for six years (or waves), with new wave one addresses introduced each year to maintain the size of the sample.

The LCF is the primary data source for household expenditure statistics. It is an annual survey of approximately 5,000 UK households.

The SLC and the LCF have harmonised questions and together they provide common variables on income, employment, benefits, and pensions. These harmonised variables create the "core" of the HFS output. LCF includes some additional expenditure questions, while SLC contains a policy-relevant module which is regularly reviewed.

The HFS follows a two-stage stratified cluster sampling design for selecting the new SLC panel and the annual LCF sample. In Great Britain, both the SLC and the LCF use the Postcode Address File (PAF) as a sampling frame. In Northern Ireland, a systematic random sample of private addresses is drawn from the Land and Property Services Agency's database. The total achieved sample size is around 17,000 households a year, including:

- April 2021 to March 2022: 17,796 households
- April 2020 to March 2021: 18,182 households

HFS data have been used since 2019 to obtain essential information on household income, its distribution across the population and how it is changing over time (see our Average household income, UK: financial year ending 2022 datasets (https://www.ons.gov.uk/peoplepopulationandcommunity/personalandhouseholdfinances/incomeandwealth/bulletins/householddisposableincomeandinequality/financialyearending2022/relateddata)). HFS data are used to produce our Household income inequality bulletin (https://www.ons.gov.uk/peoplepopulationandcommunity/personalandhouseholdfi

nances/incomeandwealth/bulletins/householdincomeinequalityfinancial/financialye
arending2022) and Effects of taxes and benefits on household income dataset
(https://www.ons.gov.uk/peoplepopulationandcommunity/personalandhouseholdfi
nances/incomeandwealth/datasets/theeffectsoftaxesandbenefitsonhouseholdinco
mefinancialyearending2014).

On 23 March 2020, the coronavirus (COVID-19) outbreak started officially, and the
UK was put into lockdown in an unprecedented attempt to reduce the spread of
infection. A full description of the impact of the coronavirus pandemic on HFS data
collection can be found in our Impact of COVID-19 on ONS social survey data
methodology
(https://www.ons.gov.uk/peoplepopulationandcommunity/healthandsocialcare/con
ditionsanddiseases/methodologies/impactofcovid19ononssocialsurveydatacollectio
n). Before the pandemic, the mode of collection for both the SLC and the LCF was
face-to-face interviewing.

As a result, all interviewing was paused in March 2020 and was restarted in April
2020 as telephone interviewing only. The length of the HFS questionnaire was
reduced to optimise for telephone interviewing and lessen burden on respondents.
Some questions were removed from the household section, such as material
deprivation, expenditure, and health questions. The questions which contribute to
important statistical publications produced by the Household Income and
Expenditure (HIE) branch at the ONS were retained on both surveys. The main
income section provides information on personal and household income from
different sources (for example, employment, benefits, self-employment).

From July 2020, during the period of telephone interviewing, a knock-to-nudge
exercise was undertaken. This involved interviewers visiting addresses to obtain
phone numbers and arrange a telephone appointment with respondents on the
doorstep. The interview itself would then take place on telephone.

In September 2022, the SLC and the LCF returned to face-to-face interviewing as the
default collection mode and the knock-to-nudge exercise was halted.

The HFS is HIE's principal data source for the period covering FYE 2020 onwards, as
well as revised timeseries data covering FYE 2017, FYE 2018 and FYE 2019.

Uses and users

The HFS data source is used in the production of nation statistics on household
disposable income and inequality (HDII), and the effects of taxes and benefits (ETB),
and associated statistical bulletins produced by the Household Income and
Expenditure Analysis (HIE) branch at the ONS. These statistics provide a greater
understanding of how income is distributed among UK households (broken down
by the main demographics) and resulting income inequality, as well as how these
measures change over time.

Users of the microdata include Think Tanks, Academics, and other Government
departments, who conduct income, taxes, and benefits research, for example using
micro-simulation models to predict policy changes.

Strengths and limitations

These income statistics were estimated from the LCF alone until FYE 2019, with a much smaller achieved sample of approximately 5,000 households. The larger HFS sample results in less volatility across the measured income distribution and enables greater precision in headline estimates, increased stability over time, and more granular statistics at regional levels and for different population subgroups.

Overall, the larger sample provided by the HFS leads to greater precision when analysing household income by UK regions. On the other hand, the HFS delivers little demonstrable improvement in precision for estimates of Scotland and Northern Ireland.

5. Quality characteristics of the Household Finances Survey data

Relevance

Prior to the launch of the HFS data source, extensive research was conducted to ensure there was a relevant and significant improvement to the measurement of household income and inequality statistics.

The HFS is an important source of income-based poverty statistics alongside other sources. A Government Statistical Service (GSS) Income and Earnings Coherence Steering Group was established in 2020, aimed at addressing the coherence and accessibility of income and earnings statistics.

ONS income statistics have been improved by moving from the LCF to the HFS as the primary data source. More detailed information on the combined HFS data source can be found in our Improving the measurement of household income methodology (https://www.ons.gov.uk/peoplepopulationandcommunity/personalandhouseholdfinances/incomeandwealth/methodologies/improvingthemeasurementofhouseholdincome).

See also, a Review of Income-based poverty statistics (https://osr.statisticsauthority.gov.uk/publication/review-of-income-based-poverty-statistics/pages/1/), produced by the Office for Statistics Regulation.

Accuracy and reliability

Multiple quality assurance methods ensure that the HFS data are as reliable as possible. These methods are applied during the interview and after collection through outlier detection and comparisons of the data between waves and rounds. All data that are identified as possible errors are investigated and, where appropriate, adjusted.

The longitudinal aspect of the SLC survey means that respondents are revisited in subsequent annual waves, which provides the opportunity to confirm the current round's data against that which has been collected previously.

Surveys, such as the SLC, provide estimates of population characteristics rather than exact measures. In principle, many random samples could be drawn and each would give different results, because of the fact that each sample would be made up of different people, who would give different answers to the questions asked. The spread of these results is the sampling variability, which generally reduces with increasing sample size.

Coherence and comparability

Major government surveys now use harmonised questions on important topics to ensure comparability of results. Where appropriate, HFS questions are harmonised with other government surveys. A list of harmonised questions is available in the

Harmonisation Programme
(https://webarchive.nationalarchives.gov.uk/ukgwa/20160105160709/http://www.on
s.gov.uk/ons/guide-method/harmonisation/harmonisation-index-page/index.html).
Further information on the Government Statistical Service (GSS) Harmonisation
Strategy (https://analysisfunction.civilservice.gov.uk/blog/harmonisation-an-
opportunity-to-build-inclusive-foundations/#harmonisation-strategy) can be found
on the GSS website.

Up until 2020, when the United Kingdom officially left the European Union,
questions were developed to meet Eurostat requirements. Therefore, results from
the HFS were internationally comparable. The core questions on the SLC and LCF
that make up the HFS are fully harmonised.

Accessibility and clarity

Our recommended format for accessible content is a combination of HTML
webpages for narrative, charts and graphs, with data being provided in usable
formats such as csv and excel. Our website also offers users the option to download
the narrative in PDF format. In some instances, other software may be used, or may
be available on request. Available formats for content published on our website but
not produced by us, or referenced on our website but stored elsewhere, may vary.

HFS anonymised datasets will be made available through the UK Data Service,
starting with the FYE 2021 annual dataset, which will be published in July 2023.

For further information please email us at SLCResearch@ONS.gov.uk.

Timeliness and punctuality

The HFS has been in existence since 2020 and has an annual financial year cycle.

Processed data are supplied to Household Income and Expenditure (HIE) Branch of
the ONS annually. Annual files are timetabled to be delivered approximately six
months after the end of the reporting period.

The data are used and available in the following releases from our HIE branch:

- Household income inequality UK: FYE 2022
  (https://www.ons.gov.uk/peoplepopulationandcommunity/personalandhouseho
  ldfinances/incomeandwealth/bulletins/householdincomeinequalityfinancial/fina
  ncialyearending2022), published January 2023

- All data related to Household income inequality UK: FYE 2022
  (https://www.ons.gov.uk/peoplepopulationandcommunity/personalandhouseho
  ldfinances/incomeandwealth/bulletins/householdincomeinequalityfinancial/fina
  ncialyearending2022/relateddata), published January 2023

- Household income inequality UK: FYE 2021
  (https://www.ons.gov.uk/peoplepopulationandcommunity/personalandhouseho
  ldfinances/incomeandwealth/bulletins/householdincomeinequalityfinancial/fina
  ncialyearending2021), published March 2022

- All data related to Household income inequality UK: FYE 2021
  (https://www.ons.gov.uk/peoplepopulationandcommunity/personalandhouseho
  ldfinances/incomeandwealth/bulletins/householdincomeinequalityfinancial/fina
  ncialyearending2021/relateddata), published March 2022

- Average household income UK: FYE 2022
  (https://www.ons.gov.uk/peoplepopulationandcommunity/personalandhouseho
  ldfinances/incomeandwealth/bulletins/householddisposableincomeandinequali
  ty/financialyearending2022), published January 2023

- All data related to Average household income UK: FYE 2022
  (https://www.ons.gov.uk/peoplepopulationandcommunity/personalandhouseho
  ldfinances/incomeandwealth/bulletins/householddisposableincomeandinequali
  ty/financialyearending2022/relateddata), published January 2023

- Average household income UK: FYE 2021
  (https://www.ons.gov.uk/peoplepopulationandcommunity/personalandhouseho
  ldfinances/incomeandwealth/bulletins/householddisposableincomeandinequali
  ty/financialyearending2021), published March 2022

- All data related to Average household income UK: FYE 2021
  (https://www.ons.gov.uk/peoplepopulationandcommunity/personalandhouseho
  ldfinances/incomeandwealth/bulletins/householddisposableincomeandinequali
  ty/financialyearending2021/relateddata), published March 2022

For more details on related releases, the Release calendar
(https://www.ons.gov.uk/releasecalendar) provides 12 months advance notice of
release dates. If there are any changes to the pre-announced release schedule,
public attention will be drawn to the change and the reasons for the change will be
explained fully at the same time, as set out in the Code of Practice for Official
Statistics (https://code.statisticsauthority.gov.uk/the-code/).

Concepts and definitions

The HFS utilises a suite of standard concepts and definitions. Some of the important
terms are defined in this section.

A household is defined as one person living alone or a group of people (not
necessarily related) living at the same address who share cooking facilities and
share a living room or sitting room or dining area.

The household reference person (HRP) is defined as the person who:

- owns the household accommodation
- is legally responsible for the rent of the accommodation
- has the household accommodation as an emolument or perquisite
- has the household accommodation by virtue of some relationship to the owner
  who is not a member of the household

If there are joint householders, the HRP is the one with the highest income; if the
income is the same, then the eldest householder is taken. The concept of the HRP
replaced the previous concept of the head of household in 2001 to 2002.

In 2001 to 2002, the National Statistics Socio-Economic classification (NS-SEC) was adopted for all official surveys, replacing the social class based on occupation and socio-economic group. The long-term unemployed, which fall into a separate category, are defined as those unemployed and seeking work for 12 months or more.

Geography

The fieldwork is conducted by ONS in Great Britain and by the Northern Ireland Statistics and Research Agency (NISRA) for the Department of Finance and Personnel in Northern Ireland using largely identical questionnaires. Differences between the two questionnaires reflect the country-specific harmonised standards for ethnicity, nationality and national identity, and the different systems of local taxation used in Great Britain and Northern Ireland.

Output quality

Prior to publication, HFS data are subjected to a rigorous process of quality assurance. An initial series of automatic checks are applied to raw household and income data as they are collected from respondents and entered onto the questionnaire. These data are further checked by a team of editors within the ONS and missing data are imputed where appropriate.

HIE carry out detailed checks on the HFS data. These checks include an automated process where variables are compared with annual variable guides. This ensures the correct types, naming conventions and acceptable values are provided; checking for missingness is also carried out. Suspicious data are further investigated by the HFS team and may be corrected if found to be in error. Automated checking is carried out at each stage of the production process and outputs are further quality assured using various techniques, for example, year on year analysis to check for dubious variations. Income estimates are compared with similar outputs and any movements in benefits data are assessed against known changes to the benefits system.

Sampling and non-sampling error

All reasonable attempts have been made to ensure that the data are as accurate as possible. However, there are two potential sources of error that may affect the accuracy of estimates and for which no adequate adjustments can be made: sampling and non-sampling errors.

Sampling error refers to the difference between the results obtained from the sample and the results that would be obtained if the entire population was fully enumerated. The survey estimates are therefore likely to differ from the figures that would have been produced if information had been collected for all households or individuals in the UK. The extent to which survey estimates vary from their population values can be estimated, to a given level of confidence, through the calculation of confidence intervals (https://www.ons.gov.uk/methodology/methodologytopicsandstatisticalconcepts/un

certaintyandhowwemeasureit#confidence-interval) via the standard error (https://www.ons.gov.uk/methodology/methodologytopicsandstatisticalconcepts/uncertaintyandhowwemeasureit#standard-error) of the estimate.

The standard error is a measure of sampling variability, which shows the extent to which the estimates are expected to vary over repeated random sampling. To estimate standard errors correctly, the complexity of the survey design needs to be accounted for.

Additional inaccuracies, which are not related to sampling variability, may occur for reasons such as errors in response and reporting. Inaccuracies of this kind are collectively referred to as non-sampling errors and may occur in a sample survey or a census. The main sources of non-sampling error are:

- response errors such as misleading questions, interviewer bias or respondent misreporting
- bias resulting from non-response, as the characteristics of non-responding persons may differ from responding persons
- data input errors or systematic mistakes in processing the data

Non-sampling errors are difficult to quantify in any collection. However, every effort was made to minimise their effect through careful design and testing of the questionnaire, training of interviewers, and extensive editing and quality control procedures at all stages of data processing. Imputation is another method used to improve accuracy resulting from missing observations in the dataset.

For more information on these terms, see our Uncertainty and how we measure it for our surveys methodology (https://www.ons.gov.uk/methodology/methodologytopicsandstatisticalconcepts/uncertaintyandhowwemeasureit#standard-error).

Response

The HFS is conducted with people who volunteer their time to answer questions. The voluntary nature of the survey means that people who do not wish to take part in the survey can refuse to do so. Where possible, we collect the reasons given for not participating in the survey. The sample is designed to ensure that the results of the survey represent the population of the UK. The risk of the survey not being representative may increase with every refusal or non-contact with a sampled household (survey non-response).

In 2020 to 2021, the HFS response rate was 42.5% in Great Britain. The response rate for the SLC was 44.2% for 2020 to 2021, while the LCF was 30.9%. Non-response weighting is applied to help mitigate non-response bias.

6. Methods used to produce the Household Finances Survey (HFS)

How the output is created

The HFS data source is a combination of data from the six waves of the longitudinal Survey of Living Conditions (SLC) data and the cross-sectional Living Costs and Food (LCF) survey data. Both the SLC and LCF are conducted throughout the year and across the whole of the UK. Both the SLC and LCF surveys are conducted by interviewers.

Together, the SLC and the LCF provide common variables on income, employment, benefits, and pensions. These harmonised variables create the "core" of the HFS output. LCF includes some additional expenditure questions, while SLC contains a policy-relevant module which is regularly reviewed.

HFS data provides essential information on household income, its distribution across the population and how it is changing over time, contributing to one of the most widely accessed bulletins produced by the ONS.

The LCF and SLC are voluntary sample surveys of private households. The basic unit of the survey is the household. The HFS (in line with other government social surveys) uses the harmonised definition of a household: a group of people (not necessarily related) living at the same address who share cooking facilities and share a living room or sitting room or dining area.

The household section should be completed for each household and must be answered by the household reference person (HRP) or their spouse or partner. Changes to the household composition between waves are also recorded. This allows new members of the household to be added and ineligible respondents who have left the household to be removed.

Detailed questions are asked about the different sources of income of each adult member of the household. In addition, personal information such as age, sex, marital status, and general health is recorded for each household member.

Editing

The fieldwork, and the editing and coding of data are carried out on a monthly basis. Interim monthly datasets are compiled and quality assured. Additional quality assurance checks are carried out at the completion of each quarter and quarterly datasets are produced. Once the field work for the calendar year has been completed, further quality assurance is carried out before producing the annual dataset for delivery to the Household Income and Expenditure (HIE) branch.

Imputation

Imputation is an adjustment process that is used to determine and assign replacement values to resolve problems of missing, invalid, or inconsistent data.

The problem of missing data in the HFS is approached via imputation. Statistical imputation is carried out using a nearest-neighbour imputation method where information from a donor record that has no errors or missing values is used to replace the missing values for a recipient record. In this approach, a donor is selected from a pool of potential donors with similar characteristics based on conditional probabilities.

Outliers

As part of the data cleaning process during the editing phase, outliers are identified. Outliers are checked through examination of other variables to find evidence to support or inform an edit to the outlier. Amendments are only made to data where sufficient evidence to support an amendment exists.

Additionally imputed data are quality assured to ensure no outliers are used as donors.

Weighting

Weighting for the annual LCF sample and the new SLC panel follows a procedure commonly used for cross-sectional surveys. All drawn households are first assigned their design (sampling) weight which equals the reciprocal of their selection probability. As not every drawn household will participate in the survey, a nonresponse adjustment factor is then multiplied onto the design weight. This factor is equal to the reciprocal of the household's response probability as obtained from a logistic regression model with survey participation as outcome and output area classification (OAC) and NUTS2 region as predictors. The adjustment therefore corrects for differential nonresponse rates across these two characteristics.

Finally, a calibration procedure is applied which ensures that weights sum up to known totals for specified population subgroups. Mathematically, this is done such that the input weights (nonresponse-adjusted design weights) are modified as little as possible. For HFS calibration, age and sex groups, regional totals at personal and household level, employment and tenure are used as control variables.

For the returning SLC panels, the weighting procedure starts from a "base weight" produced while weighting the sample of the previous year (for the former new panel, the base weight is the final calibrated weight while for the longer-running panels the base weight essentially equals the input to the final calibration stage).

To account for attrition between the previous and the current round, an attrition factor is applied which again is derived from a logistic regression model. In contrast to the model for the new panel, the attrition models contain a much wider range of predictors as information collected in previous rounds can be included. Currently, predictors in the attrition models include, for example, household composition (number of adults and children) as well as age, ethnicity, and health status of the HRP.

After incorporating new births and recent joiners to households, weights are calibrated using the same control groups as for the new panel. Finally, the weights for the new and the returning panels are combined in various ways to produce different sets of outputs, for example weights for the complete HFS sample or for the SLC part only.

It should be noted that a different scheme is applied when weighting LCF as an individual survey rather than as a part of HFS (see our Living Costs and Food Survey Technical Report (PDF, 688KB) (https://www.ons.gov.uk/file?uri=/peoplepopulationandcommunity/personalandhouseholdfinances/incomeandwealth/methodologies/livingcostsandfoodsurvey/livingcostsfoodtechnicalreport2015.pdf) for details).

7. Other information

Statistical disclosure control methodology is applied to Household Finances Survey (HFS) data. This ensures that information attributable to an individual or individual organisation is not identifiable in any published outputs. The Code of Practice for Official Statistics (https://code.statisticsauthority.gov.uk/the-code/) and specifically the Principle on Confidentiality set out practices for how we protect data from being disclosed. The principle includes the statement that the Office for National Statistics (ONS) outputs should "ensure that official statistics do not reveal the identity of an individual or organisation, or any private information relating to them, taking into account other relevant sources of information".

More information can be found in the National Statistician's guidance on the confidentiality of official statistics (https://analysisfunction.civilservice.gov.uk/policy-store/national-statisticians-guidance-confidentiality-of-official-statistics/) and on our Policy for social survey microdata methodology (https://www.ons.gov.uk/methodology/methodologytopicsandstatisticalconcepts/disclosurecontrol/policyforsocialsurveymicrodata).

8. Cite this methodology

Office for National Statistics (ONS), released 21 July 2023, ONS website, methodology, Household Finances Survey QMI (https://www.ons.gov.uk/peoplepopulationandcommunity/personalandhouseholdfinances/incomeandwealth/methodologies/householdfinancessurveyqmi)

Contact details for this methodology

Vicky Parker and Georgina Thompson
vicky.parker@ons.gov.uk
Telephone: +44 1633 455404

Office for
National Statistics

Family Spending

Contents:

ONS Social Surveys

Office for National Statistics

March 2023

A number of tables within the family spending workbooks have been placed under review to be removed from future publications. Tables under review are specified within the workbooks. If you use these for your analysis, please contact us via family.spending@ons.gov.uk**.**

Table A1

Components of household expenditure

UK, financial year ending 2022

			Average weekly expenditure all house-holds (£)	Total weekly expenditure (£ million)	Recording house-holds in sample	Percentage standard error (full method)
Total number of households					5,630	
Commodity or service						
1	**Food & non-alcoholic drinks**		**62.20**	**1,772**	**5,600**	*0.9*
1.1	Food		56.50	1,611	5,600	*0.9*
	1.1.1	Bread, rice and cereals	5.40	155	5,430	*1.2*
		1.1.1.1 Rice	0.40	11	1,660	*4.5*
		1.1.1.2 Bread	2.50	70	5,140	*1.3*
		1.1.1.3 Other breads and cereals	2.60	73	4,630	*1.6*
	1.1.2	Pasta products	0.40	13	2,270	*2.8*
	1.1.3	Buns, cakes, biscuits etc.	4.10	118	5,040	*1.7*
		1.1.3.1 Buns, crispbread and biscuits	2.40	69	4,710	*1.5*
		1.1.3.2 Cakes and puddings	1.70	49	3,610	*3.1*
	1.1.4	Pastry (savoury)	1.00	28	2,350	*2.3*
	1.1.5	Beef (fresh, chilled or frozen)	1.80	50	2,290	*2.9*
	1.1.6	Pork (fresh, chilled or frozen)	0.50	14	1,040	*4.0*
	1.1.7	Lamb (fresh, chilled or frozen)	0.50	14	600	*6.0*
	1.1.8	Poultry (fresh, chilled or frozen)	2.20	62	2,970	*2.0*
	1.1.9	Bacon and ham	0.70	21	2,260	*2.4*
	1.1.10	Other meats and meat preparations	6.80	194	4,880	*2.2*
		1.1.10.1 Sausages	0.90	26	2,530	*2.2*
		1.1.10.2 Offal, pate etc.	0.10	3	590	*6.3*
		1.1.10.3 Other preserved or processed meat and meat preparations	5.70	164	4,700	*2.5*
		1.1.10.4 Other fresh, chilled or frozen edible meat	0.00~	1	30	*37.4*
	1.1.11	Fish and fish products	3.00	84	3,540	*2.2*
		1.1.11.1 Fish (fresh, chilled or frozen)	1.00	28	1,470	*3.8*
		1.1.11.2 Seafood, dried, smoked or salted fish	0.70	19	1,280	*3.9*
		1.1.11.3 Other preserved or processed fish and seafood	1.30	37	2,720	*2.4*
	1.1.12	Milk	1.90	53	4,800	*1.6*
		1.1.12.1 Whole milk	0.40	11	1,290	*3.8*
		1.1.12.2 Low fat milk	1.40	39	4,100	*1.9*
		1.1.12.3 Preserved milk	0.10	4	240	*10.2*
	1.1.13	Cheese and curd	2.20	62	4,170	*1.7*
	1.1.14	Eggs	0.70	21	3,250	*2.0*
	1.1.15	Other milk products	2.50	71	4,540	*1.6*
		1.1.15.1 Other milk products	1.30	37	3,520	*2.1*
		1.1.15.2 Yoghurt	1.20	34	3,360	*2.0*
	1.1.16	Butter	0.50	13	1,680	*3.3*
	1.1.17	Margarine, other vegetable fats and peanut butter	0.60	17	2,280	*2.3*
	1.1.18	Cooking oils and fats	0.30	9	1,160	*4.3*
		1.1.18.1 Olive oil	0.10	4	480	*5.6*
		1.1.18.2 Edible oils and other edible animal fats	0.20	5	790	*5.8*
	1.1.19	Fresh fruit	3.80	109	4,890	*1.5*
		1.1.19.1 Citrus fruits (fresh)	0.60	17	2,760	*2.4*
		1.1.19.2 Bananas (fresh)	0.40	13	3,440	*1.9*
		1.1.19.3 Apples (fresh)	0.50	16	2,370	*2.5*
		1.1.19.4 Pears (fresh)	0.10	4	830	*4.5*
		1.1.19.5 Stone fruits (fresh)	0.50	15	2,050	*3.1*
		1.1.19.6 Berries (fresh)	1.60	45	3,350	*1.9*
	1.1.20	Other fresh, chilled or frozen fruits	0.50	13	1,870	*3.1*
	1.1.21	Dried fruit and nuts	0.90	25	2,130	*3.0*
	1.1.22	Preserved fruit and fruit based products	0.10	4	840	*4.9*
	1.1.23	Fresh vegetables	4.20	120	5,110	*1.6*
		1.1.23.1 Leaf and stem vegetables (fresh or chilled)	1.00	28	3,730	*2.1*
		1.1.23.2 Cabbages (fresh or chilled)	0.40	11	2,570	*2.6*
		1.1.23.3 Vegetables grown for their fruit (fresh, chilled or frozen)	1.50	43	4,340	*1.9*
		1.1.23.4 Root crops, non-starchy bulbs and mushrooms (fresh, chilled or frozen)	1.30	38	4,480	*2.3*

Note: The commodity and service categories are not comparable with those in publications before 2001-02
The numbering is sequential, it does not use actual COICOP codes.
Please see background notes for symbols and conventions used in this report.

Table A1

Components of household expenditure (cont.)

UK, financial year ending 2022

			Average weekly expenditure all house-holds (£)	Total weekly expenditure (£ million)	Recording house-holds in sample	Percentage standard error (full method)
Commodity or service						
1	**Food & non-alcoholic drinks (continued)**					
	1.1.24	Dried vegetables	0.10	2	280	*17.0*
	1.1.25	Other preserved or processed vegetables	2.00	56	4,320	*2.3*
	1.1.26	Potatoes	0.60	16	3,250	*2.0*
	1.1.27	Other tubers and products of tuber vegetables	1.90	55	4,210	*1.6*
	1.1.28	Sugar and sugar products	0.40	11	1,670	*3.5*
		1.1.28.1 Sugar	0.20	5	1,200	*4.3*
		1.1.28.2 Other sugar products	0.20	5	680	*5.4*
	1.1.29	Jams, marmalades	0.30	10	1,550	*4.2*
	1.1.30	Chocolate	2.30	65	3,850	*2.1*
	1.1.31	Confectionery products	0.80	24	2,670	*3.1*

Table A1

Components of household expenditure (cont.)

UK, financial year ending 2022

			Average weekly expenditure all house-holds (£)	Total weekly expenditure (£ million)	Recording house-holds in sample	Percentage standard error (full method)
	1.1.32	Edible ices and ice cream	0.80	24	2,070	2.9
	1.1.33	Other food products	2.80	80	4,610	2.0
		1.1.33.1 Sauces, condiments	1.40	39	3,820	1.8
		1.1.33.2 Baker's yeast, dessert preparations, soups	1.00	30	2,750	4.0
		1.1.33.3 Salt, spices, culinary herbs and other food products	0.40	12	1,580	6.1
1.2	Non-alcoholic drinks		5.60	160	5,040	1.6
	1.2.1	Coffee	1.10	33	2,060	3.4
	1.2.2	Tea	0.50	13	1,500	3.5
	1.2.3	Cocoa and powdered chocolate	0.10	4	400	7.6
	1.2.4	Fruit and vegetable juices	1.10	32	3,070	2.2
	1.2.5	Mineral or spring waters	0.40	11	1,400	4.5
	1.2.6	Soft drinks (inc. fizzy and ready to drink fruit drinks)	2.40	68	3,550	2.3
2	**Alcoholic drink, tobacco & narcotics**		**12.20**	**346**	**3,460**	**2.5**
2.1	Alcoholic drinks		9.30	265	3,200	2.6
	2.1.1	Spirits and liqueurs (brought home)	2.10	61	1,090	3.8
	2.1.2	Wines, fortified wines (brought home)	4.50	128	2,080	3.8
		2.1.2.1 Wine from grape or other fruit (brought home)	3.80	108	1,890	4.0
		2.1.2.2 Fortified wine (brought home)	0.10	4	130	11.5
		2.1.2.3 Champagne and sparkling wines (brought home)	0.60	17	420	10.2
	2.1.3	Beer, lager, ciders and perry (brought home)	2.60	75	1,780	4.4
		2.1.3.1 Beer and lager (brought home)	2.20	63	1,540	4.4
		2.1.3.2 Ciders and perry (brought home)	0.40	12	470	15.3
	2.1.4	Alcopops (brought home)	0.00~	1	80	16.4
2.2	Tobacco and narcotics		2.80	81	640	5.9
	2.2.1	Cigarettes	1.90	53	430	8.1
	2.2.2	Cigars, other tobacco products and narcotics	1.00	28	340	7.1
		2.2.2.1 Cigars	0.10	2	20	27.3
		2.2.2.2 Other tobacco	0.90	27	320	7.1
		2.2.2.3 Narcotics	0.00	0	0	0.0
3	**Clothing & footwear**		**17.60**	**501**	**3,120**	**3.4**
3.1	Clothing		14.40	411	2,950	3.6
	3.1.1	Men's outer garments	3.50	99	800	7.0
	3.1.2	Men's under garments	0.40	12	330	7.7
	3.1.3	Women's outer garments	6.40	182	1,620	4.9
	3.1.4	Women's under garments	1.10	32	800	5.0
	3.1.5	Boys' outer garments (5-15)	0.50	13	240	9.1
	3.1.6	Girls' outer garments (5-15)	0.90	25	330	9.4
	3.1.7	Infants' outer garments (under 5)	0.40	12	210	11.6
	3.1.8	Children's under garments (under 16)	0.30	9	310	7.9

Note: The commodity and service categories are not comparable with those in publications before 2001-02
The numbering is sequential, it does not use actual COICOP codes.
Please see background notes for symbols and conventions used in this report.

Table A1

Components of household expenditure (cont.)

UK, financial year ending 2022

			Average weekly expenditure all house-holds (£)	Total weekly expenditure (£ million)	Recording house-holds in sample	Percentage standard error (full method)
Commodity or service						
3	**Clothing & footwear (continued)**					
	3.1.9	Accessories	0.60	17	640	8.9
		3.1.9.1 Men's accessories	0.20	6	220	12.9
		3.1.9.2 Women's accessories	0.30	8	350	12.8
		3.1.9.3 Children's accessories	0.10	2	120	12.7
		3.1.9.4 Protective head gear (crash helmets)	0.10	2	10	50.4
	3.1.10	Haberdashery, clothing materials and clothing hire	0.20	7	210	13.4
	3.1.11	Dry cleaners, laundry and dyeing	0.10	4	80	21.4
		3.1.11.1 Dry cleaners and dyeing	0.10	3	60	22.6
		3.1.11.2 Laundry, launderettes	0.00~	1	30	58.3
3.2	Footwear		3.20	90	920	5.6
	3.2.1	Footwear for men	1.00	29	260	8.2
	3.2.2	Footwear for women	1.60	46	540	8.4
	3.2.3	Footwear for children (5 to 15 years) and infants (under 5)	0.50	14	200	11.2
	3.2.4	Repair and hire of footwear	0.00~	1	30	29.1
4	**Housing(net)[1], fuel & power**		**87.70**	**2,499**	**5,630**	**1.5**
4.1	Actual rentals for housing		51.60	1,472	1,500	2.4
	4.1.1	Gross rent	51.50	1,469	1,490	2.4
	4.1.2	less housing benefit, rebates and allowances received	9.70	276	860	6.0
	4.1.3	Net rent[2]	41.90	1,193	1,350	2.9
	4.1.4	Second dwelling - rent	0.10	3	10	49.2
4.2	Maintenance and repair of dwelling		9.70	276	2,260	5.3
	4.2.1	Central heating repairs	1.20	34	1,110	8.4
	4.2.2	House maintenance etc.	6.00	170	1,050	6.4
	4.2.3	Paint, wallpaper, timber	1.50	44	460	10.3
	4.2.4	Equipment hire, small materials	1.00	28	390	17.9
4.3	Water supply and miscellaneous services relating to the dwelling		10.40	295	5,310	2.1
	4.3.1	Water charges	8.20	232	5,250	1.0
	4.3.2	Other regular housing payments including service charge for rent	2.00	57	640	8.7
	4.3.3	Refuse collection, including skip hire	0.20	6	50	35.6
4.4	Electricity, gas and other fuels		25.70	732	5,590	0.8
	4.4.1	Electricity	13.70	391	5,580	1.0
	4.4.2	Gas	10.50	300	4,620	1.4
	4.4.3	Other fuels	1.40	40	450	8.4
		4.4.3.1 Coal and coke	0.10	4	90	20.8
		4.4.3.2 Oil for central heating	1.10	33	320	9.4

			Average weekly expenditure all house- holds (£)	Total weekly expenditure (£ million)	Recording house- holds in sample	Percentage standard error (full method)
	4.4.3.3	Paraffin, wood, peat, hot water etc.	0.10	4	80	21.9
5	**Household goods & services**		**34.70**	**989**	**5,270**	**3.1**
5.1	Furniture and furnishings, carpets and other floor coverings		17.80	508	1,940	5.1
	5.1.1	Furniture and furnishings	14.20	404	1,630	5.6
	5.1.1.1	Furniture	12.70	361	1,040	5.9
	5.1.1.2	Fancy, decorative goods	1.20	33	740	16.0
	5.1.1.3	Garden furniture	0.40	10	60	21.8
	5.1.2	Floor coverings	3.60	104	630	8.7
	5.1.2.1	Soft floor coverings	3.10	89	600	9.0
	5.1.2.2	Hard floor coverings	0.50	15	40	27.7
5.2	Household textiles		2.00	56	1,060	6.6
	5.2.1	Bedroom textiles, including duvets and pillows	0.80	24	420	7.0
	5.2.2	Other household textiles, including cushions, towels, curtains	1.20	33	1,060	9.6

Note: The commodity and service categories are not comparable with those in publications before 2001-02

The numbering is sequential, it does not use actual COICOP codes.

Please see background notes for symbols and conventions used in this report.

1 Excluding mortgage interest payments, council tax and NI rates. Mortgage interest payments can be found in category 13.

2 The figure included in total expenditure is net rent as opposed to gross rent.

Table A1

Components of household expenditure (cont.)

UK, financial year ending 2022

Commodity or service			Average weekly expenditure all house- holds (£)	Total weekly expenditure (£ million)	Recording house- holds in sample	Percentage standard error (full method)
5	**Household goods & services (continued)**					
5.3	Household appliances		3.20	92	410	12.3
	5.3.1	Gas cookers	0.00	0	0	66.0
	5.3.2	Electric cookers, combined gas/electric cookers	0.10	2	20	33.6
	5.3.3	Clothes washing machines and drying machines	0.40	10	40	31.9
	5.3.4	Refrigerators, freezers and fridge-freezers	0.40	12	30	24.5
	5.3.5	Other major electrical appliances, dishwashers, micro-waves vacuum cleaners, heaters etc.	1.50	42	140	24.1
	5.3.6	Fire extinguisher, water softener, safes etc	0.00~	1	10	73.4
	5.3.7	Small electric household appliances, excluding hairdryers	0.50	15	150	16.8
	5.3.8	Repairs to gas and electrical appliances and spare parts	0.40	10	50	21.4
	5.3.9	Rental/hire of major household appliances	0.00	0	10	50.0
5.4	Glassware, tableware and household utensils		1.90	55	1,700	3.7
	5.4.1	Glassware, china, pottery, cutlery and silverware	0.60	16	640	6.2
	5.4.2	Kitchen and domestic utensils	0.80	22	950	5.8
	5.4.3	Repair of glassware, tableware and household utensils	0.00	0	0	86.6
	5.4.4	Storage and other durable household articles	0.60	17	620	6.1
5.5	Tools and equipment for house and garden		3.00	85	1,600	5.3
	5.5.1	Electrical tools	0.40	11	80	16.4
	5.5.2	Garden tools, equipment and accessories e.g. lawn mowers etc.	0.60	16	300	10.2
	5.5.3	Small tools	0.40	13	380	11.4
	5.5.4	Door, electrical and other fittings	0.70	21	450	11.5
	5.5.5	Electrical consumables	0.80	24	870	7.9
5.6	Goods and services for routine household maintenance		6.80	193	4,930	4.3
	5.6.1	Cleaning materials	2.70	76	3,740	3.7
	5.6.1.1	Detergents, washing-up liquid, washing powder	1.00	27	2,120	2.7
	5.6.1.2	Disinfectants, polishes, other cleaning materials etc.	1.70	49	3,210	5.5
	5.6.2	Household goods and hardware	2.00	56	4,130	3.5
	5.6.2.1	Kitchen disposables	1.20	33	3,730	4.9
	5.6.2.2	Household hardware and appliances, matches	0.30	10	660	6.3
	5.6.2.3	Kitchen gloves, cloths etc.	0.20	5	840	4.7
	5.6.2.4	Pins, needles, tape measures, nails, nuts and bolts etc.	0.30	8	460	9.4
	5.6.3	Domestic services, carpet cleaning, hire/repair of furniture/furnishings	2.10	61	530	12.1
	5.6.3.1	Domestic services, including cleaners, gardeners, au pairs	1.50	42	290	12.0
	5.6.3.2	Carpet cleaning, ironing service, window cleaner	0.40	12	290	12.1
	5.6.3.3	Hire/repair of household furniture and furnishings	0.20	7	0	74.7
6	**Health**		**9.10**	**259**	**3,130**	**5.6**
6.1	Medical products, appliances and equipment		4.70	134	2,950	7.6
	6.1.1	Medicines, prescriptions and healthcare products	2.90	82	2,780	9.9
	6.1.1.1	NHS prescription charges and payments	0.20	6	200	8.8
	6.1.1.2	Medicines and medical goods (not NHS)	1.80	52	2,500	4.3
	6.1.1.3	Other medical products (e.g. plasters, condoms, hot water bottle etc.)	0.30	9	440	10.5
	6.1.1.4	Non-optical appliances and equipment (e.g. wheelchairs, batteries for hearing aids, shoe build-up)	0.50	15	70	50.9
	6.1.2	Spectacles, lenses, accessories and repairs	1.80	52	410	11.9
	6.1.2.1	Purchase of spectacles, lenses, prescription sunglasses	1.80	51	360	12.1
	6.1.2.2	Accessories/repairs to spectacles/lenses	0.00~	1	70	23.6
6.2	Hospital services		4.40	125	530	8.2
	6.2.1	Out patient services	4.20	121	520	8.3
	6.2.1.1	NHS medical, optical, dental and medical auxiliary services	0.80	23	170	14.3
	6.2.1.2	Private medical, optical, dental and medical auxiliary services	3.40	97	360	9.6
	6.2.1.3	Other services	0.00~	1	0	89.5
	6.2.2	In-patient hospital services	0.10	4	10	40.2

Note: The commodity and service categories are not comparable with those in publications before 2001-02

The numbering is sequential, it does not use actual COICOP codes.

Please see background notes for symbols and conventions used in this report.

Components of household expenditure (cont.)

UK, financial year ending 2022

			Average weekly expenditure all house-holds (£)	Total weekly expenditure (£ million)	Recording house-holds in sample	Percentage standard error (full method)
Commodity or service						
7	**Transport**		**74.40**	**2,121**	**4,950**	*2.6*
7.1	Purchase of vehicles		30.90	880	1,290	*5.4*
	7.1.1	Purchase of new cars and vans	9.80	280	330	*10.8*
		7.1.1.1 Outright purchases	4.50	128	70	*15.8*
		7.1.1.2 Loan/Hire Purchase of new car/van	5.30	152	260	*15.1*
	7.1.2	Purchase of second hand cars or vans	20.20	577	950	*6.1*
		7.1.2.1 Outright purchases	11.90	338	420	*8.1*
		7.1.2.2 Loan/Hire Purchase of second hand car/van	8.40	238	570	*8.4*
	7.1.3	Purchase of motorcycles	0.80	23	70	*22.7*
		7.1.3.1 Outright purchases of new or second hand motorcycles	0.20	7	20	*27.7*
		7.1.3.2 Loan/Hire Purchase of new or second hand motorcycles	0.10	3	10	*34.8*
		7.1.3.3 Purchase of bicycles and other vehicles	0.50	13	40	*35.0*
7.2	Operation of personal transport		30.70	876	4,400	*2.2*
	7.2.1	Spares and accessories	2.80	80	370	*12.8*
		7.2.1.1 Car/van accessories and fittings	0.30	9	90	*26.1*
		7.2.1.2 Car/van spare parts	2.10	59	210	*16.0*
		7.2.1.3 Motorcycle accessories and spare parts	0.00~	1	10	*48.8*
		7.2.1.4 Bicycle accessories, repairs and other costs	0.40	11	90	*28.9*
	7.2.2	Petrol, diesel and other motor oils	18.90	538	3,290	*2.0*
		7.2.2.1 Petrol	11.60	331	2,360	*2.4*
		7.2.2.2 Diesel oil	7.10	203	1,290	*3.8*
		7.2.2.3 Other motor oils	0.10	3	70	*17.2*
	7.2.3	Repairs and servicing	7.10	202	3,240	*4.1*
		7.2.3.1 Car or van repairs, servicing and other work	7.10	201	3,230	*4.1*
		7.2.3.2 Motorcycle repairs and servicing	0.00~	1	40	*22.4*
	7.2.4	Other motoring costs	2.00	56	1,710	*7.1*
		7.2.4.1 Motoring organisation subscription (e.g. AA and RAC)	0.30	10	560	*9.3*
		7.2.4.2 Garage rent, other costs (excluding fines), car washing etc.	0.70	20	260	*14.1*
		7.2.4.3 Parking fees, tolls, and permits (excluding motoring fines)	0.60	18	930	*7.2*
		7.2.4.4 Driving lessons	0.20	5	20	*29.5*
		7.2.4.5 Anti-freeze, battery water, cleaning materials	0.10	3	260	*12.8*
7.3	Transport services		12.80	365	2,180	*4.2*
	7.3.1	Rail and tube fares	1.70	48	530	*8.2*
		7.3.1.1 Season tickets	0.20	6	80	*24.6*
		7.3.1.2 Other than season tickets	1.40	41	470	*8.4*
	7.3.2	Bus and coach fares	0.80	22	500	*7.0*
		7.3.2.1 Season tickets	0.30	9	100	*10.7*
		7.3.2.2 Other than season tickets	0.40	13	430	*8.3*
	7.3.3	Combined fares	0.10	2	20	*36.4*
		7.3.3.1 Combined fares other than season tickets	0.00~	1	10	*35.0*
		7.3.3.2 Combined fares season tickets	0.00~	1	10	*63.0*
	7.3.4	Other travel and transport	10.30	293	1,660	*5.2*
		7.3.4.1 Air fares (within UK)	0.20	7	70	*42.5*
		7.3.4.2 Air fares (international)	2.20	63	260	*14.9*
		7.3.4.3 School travel	0.00~	0	10	*50.2*
		7.3.4.4 Taxis and hired cars with drivers	0.70	21	300	*8.9*
		7.3.4.5 Other personal travel and transport services	0.30	10	740	*8.1*
		7.3.4.6 Hire of self-drive cars, vans, bicycles	0.40	12	40	*28.6*
		7.3.4.7 Car leasing	6.20	177	520	*5.3*
		7.3.4.8 Water travel, ferries and season tickets	0.10	3	30	*34.3*

Note: The commodity and service categories are not comparable with those in publications before 2001-02
The numbering is sequential, it does not use actual COICOP codes.
Please see background notes for symbols and conventions used in this report.

Table A1

Components of household expenditure (cont.)

UK, financial year ending 2022

			Average weekly expenditure all house-holds (£)	Total weekly expenditure (£ million)	Recording house-holds in sample	Percentage standard error (full method)
Commodity or service						
8	**Communication**[3]		**21.20**	**605**	**5,550**	*1.2*
8.1	Postal services		0.70	21	940	*5.7*
8.2	Telephone and telefax equipment		1.10	32	230	*15.9*
	8.2.1	Telephone purchase	0.10	2	30	*32.8*
	8.2.2	Mobile phone purchase	1.10	30	210	*16.6*
	8.2.3	Answering machine, fax machine, modem purchase	0.00	0	0	*0.0*
8.3	Telephone and telefax services		8.60	245	4,580	*1.5*
	8.3.1	Telephone account (excluding combined payments)[4]	0.40	11	310	*7.1*
	8.3.2	Telephone coin and other payments	0.00~	0	0	*70.8*
	8.3.3	Mobile phone account (excluding combined payments)[5]	8.10	230	4,410	*1.5*
	8.3.4	Mobile phone - other payments	0.10	3	80	*17.0*
8.4	Internet subscription fees (ex. combined packages)[6]		0.80	24	680	*4.5*
8.5	Combined telecom services[7]		9.90	283	4,540	*1.2*
9	**Recreation & culture**		**56.10**	**1,598**	**5,570**	*3.0*
9.1	Audio-visual, photographic and information processing equipment		4.50	129	810	*13.1*
	9.1.1	Audio equipment and accessories, CD players	0.80	23	300	*12.3*
		9.1.1.1 Audio equipment, CD players including in car	0.30	7	40	*24.5*

			Average weekly expenditure all house- holds (£)	Total weekly expenditure (£ million)	Recording house- holds in sample	Percentage standard error (full method)
		9.1.1.2 Audio accessories e.g. tapes, headphones etc.	0.60	16	260	12.9
	9.1.2	TV, video and computers	3.60	102	550	16.4
		9.1.2.1 Purchase of TV and digital decoder	0.80	23	50	25.6
		9.1.2.2 Satellite dish purchase and installation	0.00~	0	0	100.4
		9.1.2.3 Cable TV connection	0.00	0	0	85.6
		9.1.2.4 Video recorder	0.00~	1	0	93.6
		9.1.2.5 DVD player/recorder	0.00~	0	10	45.4
		9.1.2.6 Blank, pre-recorded video cassettes, DVDs	0.10	4	110	13.6
		9.1.2.7 Personal computers, printers and calculators	2.50	73	380	21.9
		9.1.2.8 Spare parts for TV, video, audio	0.00~	1	30	38.3
		9.1.2.9 Repair of audio-visual, photographic and information processing	0.10	2	10	38.8
	9.1.3	Photographic, cine and optical equipment	0.10	4	40	21.5
		9.1.3.1 Photographic and cine equipment	0.10	3	40	24.0
		9.1.3.2 Camera films	0.00~	0	10	47.4
		9.1.3.3 Optical instruments, binoculars, telescopes, microscopes	0.00~	0	0	68.3
9.2	Other major durables for recreation and culture		4.00	114	130	23.8
	9.2.1	Purchase of boats, trailers and horses	0.20	7	10	45.6
	9.2.2	Purchase of caravans, mobile homes (including decoration)	2.20	64	30	39.8
	9.2.3	Accessories for boats, horses, caravans and motor caravans	0.10	3	10	46.5
	9.2.4	Musical instruments (purchase and hire)	0.20	5	30	30.7
	9.2.5	Major durables for indoor recreation	0.00~	1	0	77.1
	9.2.6	Maintenance and repair of other major durables	0.40	12	50	22.7
	9.2.7	Purchase of motor caravan (new and second-hand) - outright purchase	0.70	20	10	38.9
	9.2.8	Purchase of motor caravan (new and second-hand) - loan/HP	0.00~	1	0	70.7
9.3	Other recreational items and equipment, gardens and pets		16.80	478	3,940	4.8
	9.3.1	Games, toys and hobbies	3.00	84	1,400	5.4
	9.3.2	Computer software and games	1.00	28	330	12.0
		9.3.2.1 Computer software and game cartridges	0.60	16	300	10.7
		9.3.2.2 Computer games consoles	0.40	11	50	24.4
	9.3.3	Equipment for sport, camping and open-air recreation	2.20	62	410	22.9
	9.3.4	Horticultural goods, garden equipment and plants etc.	3.90	112	2,080	6.2
		9.3.4.1 BBQ and swings	0.20	6	50	31.9
		9.3.4.2 Plants, flowers, seeds, fertilisers, insecticides	3.40	98	2,000	6.4
		9.3.4.3 Garden decorative	0.20	6	140	21.9
		9.3.4.4 Artificial flowers, pot pourri	0.00~	1	70	18.8
	9.3.5	Pets and pet food	6.70	192	2,260	5.7
		9.3.5.1 Pet food	2.80	80	2,030	3.4
		9.3.5.2 Pet purchase and accessories	1.40	40	760	13.7
		9.3.5.3 Veterinary and other services for pets identified separately	2.50	71	350	11.9

Note: The commodity and service categories are not comparable with those in publications before 2001-02

The numbering is sequential, it does not use actual COICOP codes.

Please see background notes for symbols and conventions used in this report.

3 Changes to the questionnaire in FYE 2019 has resulted in the COICOP division "Communication" not being directly comparable with previous years. Please see the technical report for more information.

4 For FYE 2019 onwards, telephone payments made as part of a combined bill are excluded from this category and included in 8.5 instead.

5 For FYE 2019 onwards, mobile phone payments made as part of a combined bill are excluded from this category and included in 8.5 instead.

6 For FYE 2019 onwards, internet subscription fee payments made as part of a combined bill are excluded from this category and included in 8.5 instead.

7 New for FYE 2019. This encompasses all telecoms bills that include more than one service. Due to the nature of combined packages, this also includes packages that include television services. Television services reported as single bills are included in 9.4.3.

Table A1

Components of household expenditure (cont.)

UK, financial year ending 2022

			Average weekly expenditure all house- holds (£)	Total weekly expenditure (£ million)	Recording house- holds in sample	Percentage standard error (full method)
Commodity or service						
9	**Recreation & culture (continued)**					
9.4	Recreational and cultural services		15.90	455	5,420	2.6
	9.4.1	Sports admissions, subscriptions, leisure class fees and equipment hire	5.60	161	1,650	5.5
		9.4.1.1 Spectator sports: admission charges	0.40	11	110	16.8
		9.4.1.2 Participant sports (excluding subscriptions)	1.10	31	520	8.7
		9.4.1.3 Subscriptions to sports and social clubs	1.90	55	860	7.2
		9.4.1.4 Leisure class fees	2.20	62	540	10.5
		9.4.1.5 Hire of equipment for sport and open air recreation	0.10	2	30	31.6
	9.4.2	Cinema, theatre and museums etc.	1.90	53	530	10.3
		9.4.2.1 Cinemas	0.30	9	200	8.1
		9.4.2.2 Live entertainment: theatre, concerts, shows	0.90	24	160	12.1
		9.4.2.3 Museums, zoological gardens, theme parks, houses and gardens	0.70	20	210	22.1
	9.4.3	TV, video, satellite rental, cable subscriptions and TV licences	5.80	165	5,330	1.3
		9.4.3.1 TV licences	2.70	78	5,120	0.6
		9.4.3.2 Satellite subscriptions (excluding combined packages)[8]	1.40	40	660	4.1
		9.4.3.3 Rent for TV/Satellite/VCR (excluding combined packages)[9]	0.00~	0	0	78.4
		9.4.3.4 Cable subscriptions (excluding combined packages)[10]	0.20	5	180	11.1
		9.4.3.5 TV slot meter payments	0.00~	0	0	55.9
		9.4.3.6 Video, cassette and CD hire, including online entertainment packages	1.50	43	2,200	2.8
	9.4.4	Miscellaneous entertainments	1.40	39	1,000	7.4
		9.4.4.1 Admissions to clubs, dances, discos, bingo	0.40	12	220	11.5
		9.4.4.2 Social events and gatherings	0.20	6	90	20.8
		9.4.4.3 Subscriptions for leisure activities and other subscriptions	0.70	21	760	11.1
	9.4.5	Development of film, deposit for film development, passport photos, holiday and school photos	0.20	6	120	43.6
	9.4.6	Gambling payments	1.10	30	1,050	5.5
		9.4.6.1 Football pools stakes	0.00	0	10	45.4
		9.4.6.2 Bingo stakes excluding admission	0.10	2	30	25.6
		9.4.6.3 Lottery	0.80	24	950	5.6
		9.4.6.4 Bookmaker, tote, other betting stakes	0.20	4	120	17.9
9.5	Newspapers, books and stationery		4.40	124	3,760	2.7
	9.5.1	Books	1.10	30	940	5.6

Table A1

Components of household expenditure (cont.)

UK, financial year ending 2022

			Average weekly expenditure all house- holds (£)	Total weekly expenditure (£ million)	Recording house- holds in sample	Percentage standard error (full method)
	9.5.2	Stationery, diaries, address books, art materials	0.80	24	1,190	6.2
	9.5.3	Cards, calendars, posters and other printed matter	1.10	32	2,080	3.9
	9.5.4	Newspapers	0.90	25	1,270	4.2
	9.5.5	Magazines and periodicals	0.50	14	1,090	5.9
9.6	Package holidays[11]		10.50	299	570	7.1
	9.6.1	Package holidays - UK	1.80	50	190	10.0
	9.6.2	Package holidays - abroad	8.70	249	400	8.0
10	**Education**		**5.20**	**147**	**200**	**16.5**
10.1	Education fees		4.90	139	160	16.8
	10.1.1	Nursery and primary education	0.90	25	20	36.1
	10.1.2	Secondary education	1.30	37	20	26.8
	10.1.3	Sixth form college/college education	0.40	12	10	48.4
	10.1.4	University education	1.80	50	40	33.4
	10.1.5	Other education	0.60	16	70	17.9
10.2	Payments for school trips, other ad-hoc expenditure		0.30	8	40	32.4
	10.2.1	Nursery and primary education	0.10	3	20	40.1
	10.2.2	Secondary education	0.20	5	20	48.5
	10.2.3	Sixth form college/college education	0.00	0	0	88.6
	10.2.4	University education	0.00~	0	0	73.5
	10.2.5	Other education	0.00~	0	0	69.1

Note: The commodity and service categories are not comparable with those in publications before 2001-02
The numbering is sequential, it does not use actual COICOP codes.
Please see background notes for symbols and conventions used in this report.

8 For FYE 2019 onwards, satellite payments made as part of a combined bill are excluded from this category and included in 8.5 instead.

9 For FYE 2019 onwards, rent for TV/satellite/VCR payments made as part of a combined bill are excluded from this category and included in 8.5 instead.

10 For FYE 2019 onwards, cable subscription payments made as part of a combined bill are excluded from this category and included in 8.5 instead.

11 Recording of expenditure on package holidays was changed from 2011.

Table A1

Components of household expenditure (cont.)

UK, financial year ending 2022

			Average weekly expenditure all house- holds (£)	Total weekly expenditure (£ million)	Recording house- holds in sample	Percentage standard error (full method)
Commodity or service						
11	**Restaurants & hotels**		**34.80**	**992**	**4,270**	**2.3**
11.1	Catering services		25.40	724	4,070	2.4
	11.1.1	Restaurant and café meals	12.60	359	2,940	2.8
	11.1.2	Alcoholic drinks (away from home)	5.00	141	1,630	4.2
	11.1.3	Take away meals eaten at home	4.10	116	1,600	3.4
	11.1.4	Other take-away and snack food	2.90	83	2,030	3.3
		11.1.4.1 Hot and cold food	2.30	66	1,810	3.5
		11.1.4.2 Confectionery	0.10	3	350	8.6
		11.1.4.3 Ice cream	0.10	4	280	9.4
		11.1.4.4 Soft drinks	0.40	10	1,040	4.4
	11.1.5	Contract catering (food)	0.20	5	20	35.9
	11.1.6	Canteens	0.70	20	360	8.8
		11.1.6.1 School meals	0.60	16	230	10.6
		11.1.6.2 Meals bought and eaten at the workplace	0.10	4	140	13.1
11.2	Accommodation services		9.40	267	1,440	4.2
	11.2.1	Holiday in the UK	8.00	228	1,340	4.2
	11.2.2	Holiday abroad	1.30	38	130	15.3
	11.2.3	Room hire	0.00~	1	20	29.3
12	**Miscellaneous goods and services**		**40.60**	**1,158**	**5,560**	**2.0**
12.1	Personal care		11.20	319	4,800	2.5
	12.1.1	Hairdressing, beauty treatment	3.60	102	1,000	5.3
	12.1.2	Toilet paper	0.90	26	2,030	2.8
	12.1.3	Toiletries and soap	2.30	65	3,820	2.2
		12.1.3.1 Toiletries (disposable including tampons, lipsyl, toothpaste etc.)	1.30	37	3,190	2.2
		12.1.3.2 Bar of soap, liquid soap, shower gel etc.	0.50	14	1,780	4.2
		12.1.3.3 Toilet requisites (durable including razors, hairbrushes, toothbrushes etc.)	0.50	13	1,030	6.2
	12.1.4	Baby toiletries and accessories (disposable)	0.40	12	890	5.4
	12.1.5	Hair products, cosmetics and electrical appliances for personal care	4.00	114	2,770	3.6
		12.1.5.1 Hair products	0.80	24	1,450	4.7
		12.1.5.2 Cosmetics and related accessories	2.80	81	2,090	4.0
		12.1.5.3 Electrical appliances for personal care, including hairdryers, shavers etc.	0.30	9	110	17.6
12.2	Personal effects		3.50	99	980	18.4
	12.2.1	Jewellery, clocks and watches and other personal effects	2.50	72	700	22.6
	12.2.2	Leather and travel goods (excluding baby items)	0.60	16	320	13.9
	12.2.3	Sunglasses (non-prescription)	0.10	2	70	19.6
	12.2.4	Baby equipment (excluding prams and pushchairs)	0.10	2	20	34.6
	12.2.5	Prams, pram accessories and pushchairs	0.10	4	10	56.2
	12.2.6	Repairs to personal goods	0.10	2	10	66.9
12.3	Social protection		2.30	65	130	16.4
	12.3.1	Residential homes	0.00~	1	0	94.4
	12.3.2	Home help	0.50	15	20	50.7
	12.3.3	Nursery, crèche, playschools	0.80	23	50	18.4
	12.3.4	Child care payments	0.90	26	70	21.5

Note: The commodity and service categories are not comparable with those in publications before 2001-02
The numbering is sequential, it does not use actual COICOP codes.
Please see background notes for symbols and conventions used in this report.

Table A1

Components of household expenditure (cont.)

UK, financial year ending 2022

Commodity or service	Average weekly expenditure all house-holds (£)	Total weekly expenditure (£ million)	Recording house-holds in sample	Percentage standard error (full method)
12 Miscellaneous goods and services (continued)				
12.4 Insurance	18.10	515	5,210	1.8
12.4.1 Household insurances	5.00	143	4,630	2.3
12.4.1.1 Structure insurance	2.30	67	3,900	2.7
12.4.1.2 Contents insurance	2.30	66	4,440	2.6
12.4.1.3 Insurance for household appliances[12]	0.40	10	540	2.8
12.4.2 Medical insurance premiums[13]	2.50	70	950	7.4
12.4.3 Vehicle insurance including boat insurance	10.30	293	4,570	1.8
12.4.3.1 Vehicle insurance	10.30	293	4,570	1.8
12.4.3.2 Boat insurance (not home)	0.00	0	0	97.9
12.4.4 Non-package holiday, other travel insurance[14]	0.30	9	410	10.6
12.5 Other services	5.60	161	2,010	7.3
12.5.1 Moving house	2.90	82	310	9.2
12.5.1.1 Moving and storage of furniture	0.50	15	180	12.0
12.5.1.2 Property transaction - purchase and sale	1.20	34	100	12.4
12.5.1.3 Property transaction - sale only	0.50	14	40	20.8
12.5.1.4 Property transaction - purchase only	0.50	13	70	14.4
12.5.1.5 Property transaction - other payments	0.20	5	50	28.8
12.5.2 Bank, building society, post office, credit card charges	0.50	15	1,340	4.7
12.5.2.1 Bank and building society charges	0.50	13	1,220	4.8
12.5.2.2 Bank and Post Office counter charges	0.00~	0	0	78.3
12.5.2.3 Annual standing charge for credit cards	0.10	2	220	12.7
12.5.2.4 Commission travellers' cheques and currency	0.00	0	0	0.0
12.5.3 Other services and professional fees	2.20	64	710	14.1
12.5.3.1 Other professional fees including court fines	0.50	14	40	26.6
12.5.3.2 Legal fees	0.70	19	30	29.1
12.5.3.3 Funeral expenses	0.50	13	20	43.4
12.5.3.4 TU and professional organisations	0.50	15	600	7.7
12.5.3.5 Other payments for services e.g. photocopying	0.10	3	60	32.6
1-12 All expenditure groups	**455.70**	**12,987**	**5,630**	**1.2**
13 Other expenditure items	**73.10**	**2,084**	**5,480**	**2.7**
13.1 Housing: mortgage interest payments, council tax etc.	52.50	1,496	5,300	1.7
13.1.1 Mortgage interest payments	22.20	632	1,830	3.0
13.1.2 Mortgage protection premiums	0.70	21	520	5.6
13.1.3 Council tax, domestic rates	28.20	804	5,290	0.8
13.1.4 Council tax, mortgage (second dwelling)	1.40	39	40	27.1
13.2 Licences, fines and transfers	4.00	115	4,250	4.7
13.2.1 Stamp duty, licences and fines (excluding motoring fines)	0.60	16	70	32.6
13.2.2 Motoring fines	0.10	3	20	25.5
13.2.3 Motor vehicle road taxation payments less refunds	3.40	96	4,230	1.6
13.3 Holiday spending	1.40	40	60	16.5
13.3.1 Money spent abroad	1.40	40	60	16.5
13.3.2 Duty free goods bought in UK	0.00	0	0	0.0

Note: The commodity and service categories are not comparable with those in publications before 2001-02

The numbering is sequential, it does not use actual COICOP codes.

Please see background notes for symbols and conventions used in this report.

12 For FYE 2019, information about insurance for household appliances was collected in the questionnaire in addition to the diary. In previous years, this was based on diary data only.

13 For FYE 2019, critical illness cover, personal accident insurance and other medical insurance are included here. In previous years, these were included in other insurance.

14 For FYE 2019, information about insurance for non-package holiday and other travel insurance was collected in the questionnaire in addition to the diary. In previous years, this was based on diary data only.

Table A1

Components of household expenditure (cont.)

UK, financial year ending 2022

Commodity or service	Average weekly expenditure all house-holds (£)	Total weekly expenditure (£ million)	Recording house-holds in sample	Percentage standard error (full method)
13 Other expenditure items (continued)				
13.4 Money transfers and credit	15.20	433	2,410	11.0
13.4.1 Money, cash gifts given to children	0.30	9	60	29.5
13.4.1.1 Money given to children for specific purposes	0.20	6	50	29.9
13.4.1.2 Cash gifts to children (no specific purpose)	0.10	3	10	62.9
13.4.2 Cash gifts and donations	13.90	396	2,130	12.0
13.4.2.1 Money/presents given to those outside the household	5.10	146	690	19.3
13.4.2.2 Charitable donations and subscriptions	3.00	87	1,490	16.8
13.4.2.3 Money sent abroad	3.70	105	240	32.0
13.4.2.4 Maintenance allowance expenditure	2.10	59	160	13.3
13.4.3 Club instalment payments (child) and interest on credit cards	1.00	28	460	8.9
13.4.3.1 Club instalment payment	0.00	0	0	0.0
13.4.3.2 Interest on credit cards	1.00	28	460	8.9
Total expenditure	**528.80**	**15,072**	**5,630**	**1.2**
14 Other items recorded				

Table A1

Components of household expenditure (cont.)

UK, financial year ending 2022

		Average weekly expenditure all house-holds (£)	Total weekly expenditure (£ million)	Recording house-holds in sample	Percentage standard error (full method)
	Commodity or service				
14.1	Life assurance, contributions to pension funds	36.70	1,045	3,580	2.3
14.1.1	Life assurance premiums	3.20	91	1,700	4.9
14.1.2	Contributions to pension and superannuation funds etc.	29.30	835	2,830	2.3
14.1.3	Personal pensions	4.20	118	390	9.7
14.2	Other insurance including friendly societies	2.30	66	1,730	3.3
14.3	Income tax, payments less refunds	112.40	3,204	4,300	2.7
14.3.1	Income tax paid by employees under PAYE	87.50	2,493	3,020	2.7
14.3.2	Income tax paid direct e.g. by retired or unoccupied persons	4.50	128	230	23.0
14.3.3	Income tax paid direct by self-employed	3.70	106	210	11.7
14.3.4	Income tax deducted at source from income under covenant from investments or from annuities and pensions	14.60	417	1,400	6.5
14.3.5	Income tax on bonus earnings	3.00	85	670	11.8
14.3.6	Income tax refunds under PAYE	0.20	5	20	33.7
14.3.7	Income tax refunds other than PAYE	0.70	21	230	12.3
14.4	National insurance contribution	42.80	1,220	3,150	1.5
14.4.1	NI contributions paid by employees	42.60	1,215	3,120	1.5
14.4.2	NI contributions paid by non-employees	0.20	5	50	31.7
14.5	Purchase or alteration of dwellings (contracted out), mortgages	73.50	2,095	2,490	6.8
14.5.1	Outright purchase of houses, flats etc. including deposits	6.10	175	10	52.9
14.5.2	Capital repayment of mortgage	29.50	842	1,720	2.7
14.5.3	Central heating installation	1.50	41	160	10.9
14.5.4	DIY improvements: Double glazing, kitchen units, sheds etc.	1.40	40	80	31.7
14.5.5	Home improvements - contracted out	26.70	760	1,070	7.6
14.5.6	Bathroom fittings	0.50	15	90	26.4
14.5.7	Purchase of materials for Capital Improvements	0.80	22	40	46.1
14.5.8	Purchase of second dwelling	7.10	201	40	49.4
14.6	Savings and investments	4.20	120	500	9.5
14.6.1	Savings, investments (excluding AVCs)	3.50	99	410	10.6
14.6.2	Additional Voluntary Contributions	0.70	19	80	18.0
14.6.3	Food stamps, other food related expenditure	0.10	2	40	38.5
14.7	Pay off loan to clear other debt	2.00	57	210	10.1
14.8	Windfall receipts from gambling etc.[15]	0.20	5	100	17.8

Note: The commodity and service categories are not comparable with those in publications before 2001-02

The numbering is sequential, it does not use actual COICOP codes.

Please see background notes for symbols and conventions used in this report.

15 Expressed as an income figure as opposed to an expenditure figure.

Source: Office for National Statistics

Table A2

Expenditure on food and non-alcoholic drinks by place of purchase

UK, financial year ending 2022

		Large supermarket chains[1]			Other outlets			Internet expenditure[2]		
		Average weekly expenditure all households (£)	Total weekly expenditure (£ million)	Recording households in sample	Average weekly expenditure all households (£)	Total weekly expenditure (£ million)	Recording households in sample	Average weekly expenditure all households (£)	Total weekly expenditure (£ million)	Recording households in sample
1	**Food and non-alcoholic drinks**	**44.30**	**1,262**	**5,370**	**9.90**	**283**	**4,710**	**8.00**	**227**	**1,050**
1.1	Food	40.50	1,154	5,370	9.00	256	4,620	7.10	202	1,010
1.1.1	Bread, rice and cereals	4.00	115	5,040	0.70	20	1,750	0.70	19	820
1.1.2	Pasta products	0.30	9	1,880	0.10	2	230	0.10	2	320
1.1.3	Buns, cakes, biscuits etc.	3.00	86	4,590	0.70	20	1,590	0.40	12	690
1.1.4	Pastry (savoury)	0.80	23	2,040	0.00	1	130	0.10	4	290
1.1.5	Beef (fresh, chilled or frozen)	1.20	34	1,810	0.40	12	360	0.20	5	280
1.1.6	Pork (fresh, chilled or frozen)	0.30	9	790	0.10	3	170	0.10	2	120
1.1.7	Lamb (fresh, chilled or frozen)	0.30	8	410	0.20	6	150	0.00	1	50
1.1.8	Poultry (fresh, chilled or frozen)	1.60	45	2,470	0.30	9	390	0.30	8	380
1.1.9	Bacon and ham	0.50	16	1,820	0.10	3	280	0.10	3	280
1.1.10	Other meats and meat preparations	4.80	138	4,370	1.20	33	1,350	0.80	22	690
1.1.11	Fish and fish products	2.10	60	3,050	0.40	13	420	0.40	12	500
1.1.12	Milk	1.30	37	4,130	0.40	10	1,000	0.20	6	630
1.1.13	Cheese and curd	1.70	48	3,640	0.20	4	440	0.30	9	640
1.1.14	Eggs	0.50	15	2,610	0.10	2	400	0.10	3	440
1.1.15	Other milk products	2.00	56	4,060	0.20	4	560	0.40	11	670
1.1.16	Butter	0.40	11	1,370	0.00	1	150	0.10	2	240
1.1.17	Margarine, other vegetable fats and peanut butter	0.50	13	1,890	0.00	1	180	0.10	3	310
1.1.18	Cooking oils and fats	0.20	7	950	0.00	1	110	0.00	1	140
1.1.19	Fresh fruit	3.00	87	4,430	0.30	8	680	0.50	15	710
1.1.20	Other fresh, chilled or frozen fruits	0.40	10	1,560	0.00	1	150	0.10	2	270
1.1.21	Dried fruit and nuts	0.60	17	1,740	0.20	5	340	0.10	3	260
1.1.22	Preserved fruit and fruit based products	0.10	3	660	0.00	0	80	0.00	1	120
1.1.23	Fresh vegetables	3.10	90	4,660	0.50	13	880	0.60	17	780
1.1.24	Dried vegetables and other preserved and processed vegetables	0.70	20	2,840	1.20	33	3,100	0.20	5	520
1.1.25	Potatoes	0.40	12	2,680	0.10	2	350	0.10	2	450
1.1.26	Other tubers and products of tuber vegetables	1.50	43	3,720	0.20	6	820	0.20	7	550
1.1.27	Sugar and sugar products	0.30	7	1,290	0.10	2	260	0.10	1	210
1.1.28	Jams, marmalades	0.20	7	1,240	0.10	2	190	0.00	1	190
1.1.29	Chocolate	1.60	45	3,230	0.50	14	1,320	0.20	6	430
1.1.30	Confectionery products	0.50	13	2,010	0.30	9	1,090	0.10	2	210
1.1.31	Edible ices and ice cream	0.60	18	1,730	0.10	2	200	0.10	3	300
1.1.32	Other food products	1.90	53	4,030	0.40	13	1,010	0.50	14	710
1.2	Non-alcoholic drinks	3.80	108	4,500	0.90	27	1,750	0.90	25	810
1.2.1	Coffee	0.70	19	1,580	0.20	5	350	0.30	8	280
1.2.2	Tea	0.30	9	1,140	0.10	2	240	0.10	2	190
1.2.3	Cocoa and powdered chocolate	0.10	2	290	0.00	1	70	0.00	1	50
1.2.4	Fruit and vegetable juices (inc fruit squash)	0.90	25	2,630	0.10	2	370	0.20	5	470
1.2.5	Mineral or spring waters	0.30	7	1,110	0.10	2	280	0.10	1	130
1.2.6	Soft drinks	1.70	47	2,970	0.50	14	1,170	0.30	8	450

Note: The commodity and service categories are not comparable with those in publications before 2001-02.
The numbering is sequential, it does not use actual COICOP codes.
Please see background notes for symbols and conventions used in this report.
1 In 2011 the list of large supermarket chains was updated.
2 Includes internet expenditure from large supermarket chains.

Source: Office for National Statistics

Table A3

Expenditure on clothing and footwear by place of purchase

UK, financial year ending 2022

		Large supermarket chains[1]			Clothing chains			Other outlets[2]		
		Average weekly expenditure all house-holds (£)	Total weekly expenditure (£ million)	Recording house-holds in sample	Average weekly expenditure all house-holds (£)	Total weekly expenditure (£ million)	Recording house-holds in sample	Average weekly expenditure all house-holds (£)	Total weekly expenditure (£ million)	Recording house-holds in sample
3	**Clothing and footwear**	**1.70**	**49**	**1,040**	**4.70**	**133**	**1,200**	**11.00**	**313**	**2,140**
3.1	Clothing	1.60	45	990	4.20	120	1,160	8.50	241	1,920
3.1.1	Men's outer garments	0.20	5	130	0.90	25	250	2.40	69	520
3.1.2	Men's under garments	0.10	2	100	0.10	3	90	0.20	7	150
3.1.3	Women's outer garments	0.60	18	380	2.00	57	700	3.70	107	890
3.1.4	Women's under garments	0.20	6	250	0.50	14	370	0.40	12	250
3.1.5	Boys' outer garments	0.10	3	80	0.10	4	70	0.20	7	120
3.1.6	Girls' outer garments	0.10	3	90	0.30	7	100	0.50	14	180
3.1.7	Infants' outer garments	0.10	3	80	0.10	4	80	0.20	5	80
3.1.8	Children's under garments	0.10	4	140	0.10	3	100	0.10	3	100
3.1.9	Accessories	0.10	2	120	0.10	2	140	0.40	11	420
3.1.9.1	Men's accessories	0.00	1	40	0.00	1	30	0.20	5	160
3.1.9.2	Women's accessories	0.00	1	60	0.10	1	90	0.20	6	220
3.1.9.3	Children's accessories	0.00	0	20	0.00	0	30	0.00	1	80
3.1.10	Haberdashery and clothing hire	0.00	0	20	0.00	0	10	0.20	6	180
3.2	Footwear	0.10	4	150	0.50	14	200	2.50	72	620
3.2.1	Men's	0.00	1	30	0.10	3	40	0.90	25	190
3.2.2	Women's	0.10	2	90	0.30	8	130	1.30	36	360
3.2.3	Children's	0.00	1	30	0.10	2	40	0.40	10	130

Note: The commodity and service categories are not comparable with those in publications before 2001-02.
The numbering system is sequential, it does not use actual COICOP codes.
Please see background notes for symbols and conventions used in this report.

1 In 2011 the list of large supermarket chains was updated.

2 Includes internet expenditure from large supermarket chains.

Source: Office for National Statistics

Table A6

Detailed household expenditure by gross income decile group

UK, financial year ending 2022

This table is under review to be removed from future publications and replaced with disposable equivalised income tables. If you use this table for your analysis, please get in contact here.

	Lowest ten per cent	Second decile group	Third decile group	Fourth decile group	Fifth decile group	Sixth decile group	Seventh decile group	Eighth decile group	Ninth decile group	Highest ten per cent	All house-holds
Lower boundary of group (£ per week)		253	369	479	612	761	918	1,102	1,366	1,808	
Weighted number of households (thousands)	2,860	2,850	2,850	2,850	2,850	2,850	2,850	2,850	2,850	2,850	28,500
Total number of households in sample	530	540	560	580	580	570	570	580	560	560	5,630
Total number of persons in sample	710	830	990	1,170	1,310	1,400	1,460	1,590	1,650	1,750	12,850
Total number of adults in sample	630	720	850	950	1,060	1,110	1,160	1,250	1,240	1,310	10,260
Weighted average number of persons per household	1	2	2	2	2	3	3	3	3	3	2

Commodity or service	Average weekly household expenditure (£)										
1 Food & non-alcoholic drinks	**35.30**	**42.40**	**47.90**	**52.30**	**60.40**	**66.90**	**68.80**	**74.30**	**82.70**	**90.90**	**62.20**
1.1 Food	32.40	38.80	43.80	47.90	54.30	60.70	62.20	67.50	75.40	82.60	56.50
1.1.1 Bread, rice and cereals	3.00	3.70	4.50	4.20	5.10	5.60	6.10	6.70	7.40	8.00	5.40
1.1.2 Pasta products	0.20	0.30	0.30	0.30	0.40	0.50	0.50	0.50	0.60	0.70	0.40
1.1.3 Buns, cakes, biscuits etc.	2.30	3.00	3.30	3.60	4.00	4.40	4.50	4.80	6.10	5.30	4.10
1.1.4 Pastry (savoury)	0.50	0.60	0.70	0.70	1.00	1.00	1.20	1.30	1.40	1.50	1.00
1.1.5 Beef (fresh, chilled or frozen)	1.00	1.10	1.40	1.50	1.80	2.10	1.80	2.10	2.30	2.50	1.80
1.1.6 Pork (fresh, chilled or frozen)	0.30	0.40	0.40	0.40	0.50	0.50	0.60	0.70	0.60	0.50	0.50
1.1.7 Lamb (fresh, chilled or frozen)	0.30	0.40	0.40	0.50	0.50	0.50	0.50	0.50	0.70	0.80	0.50
1.1.8 Poultry (fresh, chilled or frozen)	1.10	1.30	1.60	1.70	1.90	2.30	2.60	2.60	3.00	3.50	2.20
1.1.9 Bacon and ham	0.40	0.60	0.50	0.60	0.80	0.80	0.80	1.00	0.90	0.90	0.70
1.1.10 Other meat and meat preparations	4.00	5.20	5.60	5.70	6.40	7.40	7.60	8.80	8.50	8.70	6.80
1.1.11 Fish and fish products	1.90	1.90	2.50	2.60	2.90	3.10	3.20	3.10	3.90	4.60	3.00
1.1.12 Milk	1.30	1.60	1.70	1.90	1.90	2.00	1.90	2.00	2.00	2.40	1.90
1.1.13 Cheese and curd	1.30	1.30	1.50	1.70	2.00	2.40	2.40	2.80	3.00	3.40	2.20
1.1.14 Eggs	0.50	0.50	0.50	0.70	0.60	0.80	0.80	0.90	0.90	1.00	0.70
1.1.15 Other milk products	1.50	1.50	2.00	2.30	2.30	2.90	2.60	2.80	3.30	3.50	2.50
1.1.16 Butter	0.30	0.30	0.30	0.40	0.40	0.50	0.50	0.60	0.50	0.80	0.50
1.1.17 Margarine, other vegetable fats and peanut butter	0.40	0.50	0.50	0.60	0.50	0.60	0.60	0.60	0.70	0.70	0.60
1.1.18 Cooking oils and fats	0.20	0.20	0.30	0.30	0.40	0.30	0.30	0.30	0.50	0.50	0.30
1.1.19 Fresh fruit	2.20	2.60	2.90	3.40	4.00	3.80	4.20	4.50	4.90	5.60	3.80
1.1.20 Other fresh, chilled or frozen fruits	0.20	0.30	0.30	0.30	0.50	0.50	0.50	0.60	0.70	0.80	0.50
1.1.21 Dried fruit and nuts	0.40	0.60	0.60	0.70	0.90	0.90	0.90	1.00	1.10	1.50	0.90
1.1.22 Preserved fruit and fruit based products	0.10	0.10	0.10	0.10	0.20	0.20	0.10	0.20	0.10	0.20	0.10
1.1.23 Fresh vegetables	2.40	2.60	2.90	3.50	3.90	4.30	4.50	4.90	5.80	7.20	4.20
1.1.24 Dried vegetables	[0.00]	[0.00]	0.00	0.00	0.10	0.10	0.00	0.10	0.10	0.10	0.10
1.1.25 Other preserved or processed vegetables	1.10	1.00	1.30	1.60	1.70	2.20	2.00	2.30	3.00	3.60	2.00
1.1.26 Potatoes	0.30	0.50	0.50	0.50	0.60	0.60	0.60	0.60	0.70	0.70	0.60
1.1.27 Other tubers and products of tuber vegetables	1.10	1.40	1.40	1.70	1.90	2.20	2.20	2.30	2.60	2.50	1.90
1.1.28 Sugar and sugar products	0.20	0.30	0.20	0.30	0.40	0.40	0.40	0.40	0.60	0.50	0.40
1.1.29 Jams, marmalades	0.20	0.30	0.30	0.20	0.40	0.30	0.40	0.30	0.50	0.50	0.30
1.1.30 Chocolate	1.30	1.60	1.70	2.00	2.10	2.50	2.60	3.00	2.80	3.20	2.30
1.1.31 Confectionery products	0.40	0.70	0.70	0.60	0.80	0.90	1.10	1.00	1.10	1.10	0.80
1.1.32 Edible ices and ice cream	0.40	0.60	0.60	0.70	0.90	0.80	0.90	1.00	1.20	1.10	0.80
1.1.33 Other food products	1.50	1.80	2.00	2.30	2.60	3.10	3.00	3.10	4.00	4.90	2.80
1.2 Non-alcoholic drinks	3.00	3.60	4.10	4.40	6.00	6.30	6.60	6.80	7.30	8.30	5.60
1.2.1 Coffee	0.60	0.70	1.00	1.00	1.20	1.10	1.10	1.30	1.40	1.90	1.10
1.2.2 Tea	0.30	0.40	0.30	0.40	0.40	0.50	0.50	0.50	0.50	0.50	0.50
1.2.3 Cocoa and powdered chocolate	0.10	0.10	0.10	0.10	0.10	0.10	0.20	0.10	0.10	0.10	0.10
1.2.4 Fruit and vegetable juices (inc. fruit squash)	0.60	0.60	0.70	0.80	1.10	1.10	1.20	1.40	1.70	2.10	1.10
1.2.5 Mineral or spring waters	0.20	0.20	0.30	0.30	0.50	0.40	0.40	0.40	0.50	0.60	0.40
1.2.6 Soft drinks (inc. fizzy and ready to drink fruit drinks	1.20	1.60	1.60	1.80	2.70	3.00	3.10	3.00	3.00	3.00	2.40

Note: The commodity and service categories are not comparable to those in publications before 2001-02.
The numbering system is sequential, it does not use actual COICOP codes.
Please see background notes for symbols and conventions used in this report.

Table A6

Detailed household expenditure by gross income decile group (cont.)

UK, financial year ending 2022

	Lowest ten per cent	Second decile group	Third decile group	Fourth decile group	Fifth decile group	Sixth decile group	Seventh decile group	Eighth decile group	Ninth decile group	Highest ten per cent	All house-holds
Commodity or service	Average weekly household expenditure (£)										
2 Alcoholic drink, tobacco & narcotics	**8.00**	**9.10**	**9.80**	**9.00**	**12.30**	**12.00**	**12.00**	**14.40**	**16.80**	**18.20**	**12.20**
2.1 Alcoholic drinks	4.80	5.30	6.90	6.50	8.60	10.00	9.40	12.00	14.10	15.50	9.30
2.1.1 Spirits and liqueurs (brought home)	1.40	1.50	1.80	1.70	2.30	2.40	2.20	2.60	2.80	2.80	2.10
2.1.2 Wines, fortified wines (brought home)	1.60	2.30	2.90	3.20	3.60	4.90	4.30	5.40	7.40	9.30	4.50
2.1.3 Beer, lager, ciders and perry (brought home)	1.80	1.50	2.20	1.60	2.70	2.60	2.80	4.00	3.90	3.30	2.60
2.1.4 Alcopops (brought home)	..	..	[0.00]	..	..	[0.00]	..	..	..	..	0.00
2.2 Tobacco and narcotics	3.20	3.80	2.90	2.50	3.70	2.00	2.70	2.40	2.70	2.70	2.80
2.2.1 Cigarettes	1.70	2.50	2.30	1.30	2.40	1.40	1.80	1.60	1.60	2.00	1.90
2.2.2 Cigars, other tobacco products and narcotics	1.40	1.30	0.60	1.20	1.30	0.60	0.80	0.80	1.10	0.80	1.00
3 Clothing & footwear	**6.80**	**7.50**	**10.20**	**12.40**	**15.00**	**18.00**	**18.30**	**26.60**	**26.70**	**34.30**	**17.60**
3.1 Clothing	6.20	6.40	8.40	10.30	12.30	15.50	14.60	22.00	21.10	27.60	14.40
3.1.1 Men's outer garments	1.40	1.10	1.50	1.80	3.10	3.40	3.30	5.30	5.20	8.70	3.50
3.1.2 Men's under garments	[0.10]	0.30	0.30	0.20	0.40	0.40	0.50	0.70	0.80	0.50	0.40
3.1.3 Women's outer garments	2.70	3.20	4.30	5.10	4.90	6.10	6.60	11.00	7.80	12.40	6.40
3.1.4 Women's under garments	0.50	0.70	0.60	0.60	1.10	1.40	1.40	1.70	1.50	1.50	1.10

82

Table A6
Detailed household expenditure by gross income decile group (cont.)
UK, financial year ending 2022

		Lowest ten per cent	Second decile group	Third decile group	Fourth decile group	Fifth decile group	Sixth decile group	Seventh decile group	Eighth decile group	Ninth decile group	Highest ten per cent	All house-holds
Commodity or service						Average weekly household expenditure (£)						
3.1.5	Boys' outer garments (5-15)	..	[0.10]	[0.20]	0.40	0.30	0.60	0.40	0.40	1.00	0.70	0.50
3.1.6	Girls' outer garments (5-15)	[0.20]	0.30	[0.40]	0.70	1.10	1.20	0.50	1.00	1.70	1.50	0.90
3.1.7	Infants' outer garments (under 5)	[0.20]	[0.10]	[0.50]	[0.40]	[0.30]	0.70	0.20	0.60	0.70	[0.40]	0.40
3.1.8	Children's under garments (under 16)	[0.10]	[0.10]	[0.10]	0.30	0.50	0.60	0.30	0.30	0.50	0.40	0.30
3.1.9	Accessories	0.30	0.20	0.30	0.50	0.40	0.80	0.80	0.50	1.30	0.80	0.60
3.1.10	Haberdashery and clothing hire	..	[0.10]	0.20	[0.10]	0.10	[0.10]	0.30	0.40	0.30	0.50	0.20
3.1.11	Dry cleaners, laundry and dyeing	[0.10]		..	..	..	..	[0.10]	..	[0.30]	[0.30]	0.10
3.2	Footwear	0.70	1.00	1.80	2.20	2.70	2.50	3.70	4.60	5.60	6.70	3.20
4	**Housing (net)[1], fuel & power**	**64.70**	**72.40**	**80.40**	**84.90**	**90.30**	**90.80**	**90.80**	**93.90**	**101.60**	**107.20**	**87.70**
4.1	Actual rentals for housing	68.40	65.50	57.40	49.90	52.70	49.70	46.40	40.90	46.50	39.10	51.60
4.1.1	Gross rent	68.40	65.50	57.00	49.90	52.50	49.70	46.40	40.90	46.30	38.80	51.50
4.1.2	less housing benefit, rebates & allowances rec'd	36.10	28.50	12.80	6.80	7.40	2.80	1.40	[0.30]	[0.50]	..	9.70
4.1.3	Net rent[2]	32.30	36.90	44.20	43.10	45.20	46.90	45.00	40.60	45.90	38.60	41.90
4.1.4	Second dwelling rent	:	..	..	:	..	..	:	:	..	..	..
4.2	Maintenance and repair of dwelling	3.40	5.50	4.70	8.50	9.30	7.70	10.20	13.90	13.70	20.00	9.70
4.3	Water supply and miscellaneous services relating to the dwelling	9.00	9.20	8.70	8.80	10.10	10.20	10.20	11.10	12.90	13.50	10.40
4.4	Electricity, gas and other fuels	20.00	20.70	22.30	24.40	25.70	26.00	25.40	28.30	28.90	34.90	25.70
4.4.1	Electricity	11.00	11.70	11.90	12.70	13.90	14.40	13.40	15.00	15.50	17.90	13.70
4.4.2	Gas	7.70	8.00	9.40	10.50	10.40	10.40	10.60	11.60	12.00	14.70	10.50
4.4.3	Other fuels	1.30	1.00	1.10	1.20	1.40	1.20	1.40	1.80	1.50	2.30	1.40

Note: The commodity and service categories are not comparable to those in publications before 2001-02.
The numbering system is sequential, it does not use actual COICOP codes.
Please see background notes for symbols and conventions used in this report.

1 Excluding mortgage interest payments, council tax and Northern Ireland rates. Mortgage interest payments can be found in category 13.

2 The figure included in total expenditure is net rent as opposed to gross rent.

Table A6
Detailed household expenditure by gross income decile group (cont.)
UK, financial year ending 2022

		Lowest ten per cent	Second decile group	Third decile group	Fourth decile group	Fifth decile group	Sixth decile group	Seventh decile group	Eighth decile group	Ninth decile group	Highest ten per cent	All house-holds
Commodity or service						Average weekly household expenditure (£)						
5	**Household goods & services**	**16.70**	**19.50**	**22.50**	**25.80**	**28.70**	**34.70**	**37.10**	**43.90**	**51.20**	**67.10**	**34.70**
5.1	Furniture and furnishings, carpets and other floor coverings	9.20	8.70	11.50	10.40	14.70	16.60	17.90	23.20	28.00	37.90	17.80
5.1.1	Furniture and furnishings	6.20	5.90	9.30	8.40	11.90	12.50	14.00	18.30	24.10	31.20	14.20
5.1.2	Floor coverings	3.00	2.80	2.20	2.00	2.80	4.20	3.90	4.90	3.90	6.70	3.60
5.2	Household textiles	0.80	1.40	1.30	1.60	1.50	2.60	1.70	2.60	3.60	2.70	2.00
5.3	Household appliances	0.60	2.20	1.30	3.30	2.10	3.70	4.90	4.90	4.00	5.20	3.20
5.4	Glassware, tableware and household utensils	0.90	1.10	1.10	1.70	1.50	2.30	2.50	2.30	3.00	3.00	1.90
5.5	Tools and equipment for house and garden	1.20	1.60	2.40	1.80	3.00	3.70	3.00	3.40	4.30	5.60	3.00
5.6	Goods and services for routine household maintenance	4.00	4.50	4.80	7.00	5.90	5.80	7.10	7.50	8.20	12.70	6.80
5.6.1	Cleaning materials	1.60	1.90	2.20	2.20	2.50	2.70	3.10	3.60	3.10	3.90	2.70
5.6.2	Household goods and hardware	0.90	1.20	1.40	1.70	1.90	2.00	2.20	2.20	3.20	2.80	2.00
5.6.3	Domestic services, carpet cleaning, hire/repair of furniture/furnishings	1.50	1.40	1.20	3.20	1.50	1.20	1.80	1.70	1.80	6.00	2.10
6	**Health**	**4.80**	**3.60**	**8.50**	**10.70**	**6.80**	**6.60**	**10.30**	**7.60**	**14.50**	**17.50**	**9.10**
6.1	Medical products, appliances and equipment	1.90	2.20	4.20	6.50	4.10	3.30	5.90	3.70	7.80	7.60	4.70
6.1.1	Medicines, prescriptions, healthcare products etc.	1.30	1.50	1.60	5.10	3.00	2.30	3.10	2.40	3.50	5.10	2.90
6.1.2	Spectacles, lenses, accessories and repairs	[0.60]	0.80	2.60	1.40	1.10	0.90	2.80	1.20	4.30	2.50	1.80
6.2	Hospital services	2.90	1.40	4.30	4.20	2.70	3.30	4.40	3.90	6.70	9.90	4.40
7	**Transport**	**24.40**	**27.80**	**38.90**	**51.30**	**66.60**	**71.40**	**82.80**	**99.50**	**112.70**	**168.80**	**74.40**
7.1	Purchase of vehicles	8.90	7.00	12.30	21.50	26.70	26.60	32.90	41.60	46.40	85.20	30.90
7.1.1	Purchase of new cars and vans	..	[2.20]	..	9.00	6.80	7.20	11.20	11.30	12.70	36.00	9.80
7.1.2	Purchase of second hand cars or vans	7.80	4.70	10.70	12.40	19.60	19.20	20.30	29.60	32.20	46.00	20.20
7.1.3	Purchase of motorcycles and other vehicles	..	..	..	..	..	..	[1.30]	[0.80]	[1.60]	[3.10]	0.80
7.2	Operation of personal transport	11.70	13.70	20.20	21.70	29.80	32.40	35.70	42.70	46.60	52.80	30.70
7.2.1	Spares and accessories	[1.20]	[0.90]	2.10	1.20	2.10	1.70	2.10	6.70	3.50	6.50	2.80
7.2.2	Petrol, diesel and other motor oils	7.10	8.30	11.80	14.50	18.70	21.00	22.30	25.60	28.20	31.30	18.90
7.2.3	Repairs and servicing	2.80	4.00	4.60	4.50	7.40	7.60	9.10	8.50	11.60	10.90	7.10
7.2.4	Other motoring costs	0.50	0.60	1.90	1.60	1.60	2.10	2.10	1.90	3.30	4.00	2.00
7.3	Transport services	3.90	7.10	6.30	8.10	10.20	12.50	14.20	15.20	19.60	30.90	12.80
7.3.1	Rail and tube fares	0.60	0.50	0.70	0.80	1.30	1.50	2.30	1.90	3.10	4.00	1.70
7.3.2	Bus and coach fares	0.60	0.70	0.60	0.80	0.90	1.00	1.00	0.70	0.70	0.70	0.80
7.3.3	Combined fares	..	:	:	..	..	..	:	:	..	..	[0.10]
7.3.4	Other travel and transport	2.50	5.90	5.00	6.50	7.90	9.90	11.00	12.60	15.60	26.00	10.30
8	**Communication**	**11.60**	**15.00**	**15.60**	**18.10**	**21.80**	**22.60**	**23.80**	**26.10**	**27.60**	**29.80**	**21.20**
8.1	Postal services	0.50	0.50	0.50	0.80	0.50	0.70	0.80	1.00	0.80	1.20	0.70
8.2	Telephone and telefax equipment	[0.30]	[1.20]	[0.40]	[0.40]	2.20	1.50	1.10	0.80	1.70	1.60	1.10
8.3	Telephone and telefax services[3]	4.10	4.70	5.00	6.20	8.00	9.20	9.90	12.20	13.00	13.70	8.60
8.4	Internet subscription fees (ex. combined packages)	0.80	0.60	0.70	0.80	0.90	0.80	1.00	1.00	0.80	1.10	0.80
8.5	Combined telecom services[4]	5.90	7.90	9.00	10.00	10.30	10.30	11.00	11.20	11.20	12.20	9.90

Note: The commodity and service categories are not comparable to those in publications before 2001-02.
The numbering system is sequential, it does not use actual COICOP codes.
Please see background notes for symbols and conventions used in this report.

3 For FYE 2019 onwards, excludes payments made as part of a combined bill.

4 New for FYE 2019. This encompasses all telecoms bills that include more than one service. Due to the nature of combined packages, this also includes packages that includes television services.

Detailed household expenditure by gross income decile group (cont.)

UK, financial year ending 2022

Commodity or service	Lowest ten per cent	Second decile group	Third decile group	Fourth decile group	Fifth decile group	Sixth decile group	Seventh decile group	Eighth decile group	Ninth decile group	Highest ten per cent	All house-holds
					Average weekly household expenditure (£)						
9 Recreation & culture	**25.00**	**23.80**	**32.40**	**39.20**	**52.10**	**54.10**	**67.40**	**61.20**	**81.00**	**124.60**	**56.10**
9.1 Audio-visual, photographic and information processing equipment	5.20	1.20	2.60	3.50	2.90	4.80	6.10	3.40	5.20	10.60	4.50
9.1.1 Audio equipment and accessories, CD players	[0.40]	[0.40]	[0.20]	0.40	0.70	0.50	1.10	1.00	1.60	1.90	0.80
9.1.2 TV, video and computers	4.50	0.70	2.30	3.10	2.20	4.20	4.90	2.20	3.50	8.30	3.60
9.1.3 Photographic, cine and optical equipment	..	..	..	..	..	..	..	..	..	[0.40]	0.10
9.2 Other major durables for recreation and culture	..	..	[1.60]	..	..	[4.00]	[6.60]	3.70	4.50	7.50	4.00
9.3 Other recreational items and equipment, gardens and pets	7.00	7.80	11.60	11.90	15.30	16.00	18.60	21.30	21.70	36.50	16.80
9.3.1 Games, toys and hobbies	0.80	1.90	2.30	2.30	4.20	3.20	2.30	3.50	4.90	4.20	3.00
9.3.2 Computer software and games	..	0.70	0.30	0.70	0.60	0.70	0.80	1.20	2.00	2.70	1.00
9.3.3 Equipment for sport, camping and open-air recreation	[0.70]	[0.20]	[1.10]	0.70	1.00	1.80	1.00	3.20	2.30	9.70	2.20
9.3.4 Horticultural goods, garden equipment and plants	1.90	2.40	3.00	3.50	4.00	4.30	5.30	4.00	4.60	6.20	3.90
9.3.5 Pets and pet food	3.50	2.70	4.80	4.70	5.60	5.90	9.10	9.40	7.90	13.70	6.70
9.4 Recreational and cultural services	6.50	6.70	10.00	12.20	13.20	15.50	16.10	19.30	25.00	35.00	15.90
9.4.1 Sports admissions, subscriptions, leisure class fees and equipment hire	1.30	1.00	2.00	3.90	3.70	4.90	5.60	6.30	9.50	18.20	5.60
9.4.2 Cinema, theatre and museums etc.	0.30	[0.40]	0.80	0.90	1.10	2.30	1.90	3.50	3.60	3.70	1.90
9.4.3 TV, video, satellite rental, cable subscriptions and TV licences[5]	3.50	3.80	4.80	5.00	6.30	5.80	6.10	6.90	7.30	8.50	5.80
9.4.4 Miscellaneous entertainments	0.50	0.60	1.00	0.90	0.90	1.10	1.30	1.60	2.30	3.50	1.40
9.4.5 Development of film, deposit for film development, passport photos, holiday and school photos	..	..	..	..	[0.10]	[0.10]	[0.10]	[0.20]	[1.10]	[0.20]	0.20
9.4.6 Gambling payments	0.90	0.80	1.30	1.30	1.20	1.20	1.00	0.90	1.10	0.90	1.10
9.5 Newspapers, books and stationery	2.70	2.80	3.40	4.10	3.90	4.70	4.40	5.30	5.50	6.90	4.40
9.5.1 Books	0.50	0.50	0.50	0.80	1.00	1.10	1.20	1.40	1.50	2.20	1.10
9.5.2 Diaries, address books, cards etc.	0.90	1.10	1.30	1.70	1.60	2.30	2.10	2.50	2.80	3.10	1.90
9.5.3 Newspapers	0.90	0.80	1.10	1.10	0.90	0.80	0.70	0.80	0.60	0.80	0.90
9.5.4 Magazines and periodicals	0.40	0.40	0.50	0.40	0.50	0.40	0.40	0.50	0.60	0.70	0.50
9.6 Package holidays	2.90	3.10	3.30	6.60	8.60	9.20	15.70	8.30	19.10	28.00	10.50
9.6.1 Package holidays - UK	[0.80]	[1.20]	[0.90]	[1.30]	[1.10]	2.40	1.80	[2.10]	3.40	2.70	1.80
9.6.2 Package holidays - abroad	[2.10]	1.90	2.30	5.30	7.60	6.80	14.00	6.20	15.70	25.30	8.70
10 Education	**[2.10]**	**..**	**[4.10]**	**[3.70]**	**[1.60]**	**[1.70]**	**[4.00]**	**[7.20]**	**6.70**	**20.00**	**5.20**
10.1 Education fees	..	..	[4.10]	[3.60]	[1.20]	[1.60]	[3.70]	[7.00]	6.10	19.00	4.90
10.2 Payments for school trips, other ad-hoc expenditure	..	..	..	..	..	..	..	..	..	..	0.30
11 Restaurants & hotels	**10.40**	**13.20**	**16.80**	**22.30**	**30.50**	**35.40**	**37.70**	**46.60**	**52.80**	**82.20**	**34.80**
11.1 Catering services	8.70	10.00	12.30	16.20	22.20	27.20	28.20	33.70	39.60	56.20	25.40
11.1.1 Restaurant and café meals	4.40	4.90	6.70	8.90	10.50	13.10	13.10	17.10	19.10	28.10	12.60
11.1.2 Alcoholic drinks (away from home)	1.70	2.30	2.00	2.70	3.70	4.40	5.80	6.70	8.30	12.10	5.00
11.1.3 Take away meals eaten at home	1.50	1.70	1.90	2.20	3.70	5.30	4.50	5.60	6.20	8.30	4.10
11.1.4 Other take-away and snack food	0.90	0.90	1.60	1.90	2.90	3.60	3.70	3.50	4.70	5.20	2.90
11.1.5 Contract catering (food) and canteens	..	..	[0.20]	0.50	1.40	0.80	1.00	0.80	1.20	2.60	0.90
11.2 Accommodation services	1.80	3.20	4.50	6.10	8.30	8.20	9.60	12.90	13.30	26.00	9.40
11.2.1 Holiday in the UK	1.30	2.90	4.40	5.70	6.80	6.50	8.00	12.10	11.90	20.30	8.00
11.2.2 Holiday abroad	..	..	..	..	[1.50]	[1.60]	[1.50]	[0.80]	1.20	5.60	1.30
11.2.3 Room hire	:	..	:	..	..	..	..	..	..	..	[0.00]

Note: The commodity and service categories are not comparable to those in publications before 2001-02

The numbering system is sequential, it does not use actual COICOP codes.

Please see background notes for symbols and conventions used in this report.

5 For FYE 2019 onwards, excludes payments made as part of a combined bill.

Table A6

Detailed household expenditure by gross income decile group (cont.)

UK, financial year ending 2022

Commodity or service	Lowest ten per cent	Second decile group	Third decile group	Fourth decile group	Fifth decile group	Sixth decile group	Seventh decile group	Eighth decile group	Ninth decile group	Highest ten per cent	All house-holds
					Average weekly household expenditure (£)						
12 Miscellaneous goods & services	**18.40**	**18.50**	**25.90**	**33.40**	**34.90**	**37.00**	**44.90**	**50.10**	**61.50**	**82.00**	**40.60**
12.1 Personal care	4.80	6.10	8.00	9.10	10.30	11.20	12.60	12.70	17.50	19.40	11.20
12.1.1 Hairdressing, beauty treatment	1.40	1.80	1.80	2.90	3.50	3.10	3.90	3.90	6.40	7.00	3.60
12.1.2 Toilet paper	0.60	0.60	0.70	0.80	0.90	1.20	0.90	1.00	1.30	1.10	0.90
12.1.3 Toiletries and soap	1.20	1.60	1.80	2.10	2.40	2.40	2.50	2.50	2.90	3.30	2.30
12.1.4 Baby toiletries and accessories (disposable)	0.20	0.20	0.20	0.50	0.40	0.50	0.50	0.50	0.60	0.50	0.40
12.1.5 Hair products, cosmetics and related electrical appliances	1.50	1.90	3.40	2.80	3.10	4.10	4.80	4.70	6.30	7.40	4.00
12.2 Personal effects	1.30	0.60	1.90	2.10	1.90	3.20	3.20	4.10	4.50	11.90	3.50
12.3 Social protection	..	..	..	[0.90]	[3.40]	[1.40]	[3.30]	[1.50]	[2.80]	7.00	2.30
12.4 Insurance	7.70	9.30	11.30	15.40	16.50	18.30	21.50	22.20	26.60	32.00	18.10
12.4.1 Household insurances - structural, contents and appliances	2.90	3.50	3.60	4.80	4.50	5.00	4.90	5.90	6.50	8.40	5.00
12.4.2 Medical insurance premiums[6]	0.30	0.50	1.10	2.10	2.20	2.50	2.20	3.20	4.40	6.10	2.50
12.4.3 Vehicle insurance including boat insurance	4.30	5.10	6.50	8.10	9.60	10.50	13.70	12.80	15.20	17.10	10.30
12.4.4 Non-package holiday, other travel insurance[7]	[0.20]	[0.20]	0.20	0.40	0.20	0.30	0.60	0.30	0.50	0.50	0.30
12.5 Other services	4.00	2.00	3.20	6.00	2.70	3.00	4.30	9.50	10.10	11.60	5.60

Detailed household expenditure by gross income decile group (cont.)

UK, financial year ending 2022

		Lowest ten per cent	Second decile group	Third decile group	Fourth decile group	Fifth decile group	Sixth decile group	Seventh decile group	Eighth decile group	Ninth decile group	Highest ten per cent	All house-holds
Commodity or service		Average weekly household expenditure (£)										
12.5.1	Moving house	2.70	[1.50]	2.00	1.70	1.20	[1.30]	2.40	4.40	5.20	6.30	2.90
12.5.2	Bank, building society, post office, credit card charges	0.20	0.20	0.30	0.40	0.40	0.60	0.50	0.70	0.80	1.00	0.50
12.5.3	Other services and professional fees	1.10	[0.30]	0.80	4.00	1.00	1.10	1.40	4.40	4.10	4.20	2.20
1-12	**All expenditure groups**	**228.50**	**253.30**	**312.80**	**363.20**	**421.00**	**451.20**	**498.00**	**551.40**	**635.70**	**842.70**	**455.70**
13	**Other expenditure items**	**23.60**	**30.30**	**36.70**	**50.60**	**68.10**	**62.40**	**73.40**	**109.70**	**116.70**	**160.00**	**73.10**
13.1	Housing: mortgage interest payments, council tax etc.	17.90	20.80	27.00	35.90	41.20	47.60	56.10	70.60	86.50	121.30	52.50
13.2	Licences, fines and transfers	1.80	1.90	2.40	2.90	3.60	4.00	4.80	4.90	5.40	8.60	4.00
13.3	Holiday spending	..	..	..	..	[2.30]	..	..	..	..	..	1.40
13.4	Money transfers and credit	3.80	7.00	7.10	10.50	21.00	10.00	11.80	31.80	21.60	27.60	15.20
13.4.1	Money, cash gifts given to children	..	:	..	..	..	..	..	..	[1.10]	[1.10]	0.30
13.4.2	Cash gifts and donations	3.30	6.70	6.60	8.80	19.70	9.00	10.50	30.30	18.90	25.20	13.90
13.4.3	Club instalment payments (child) and interest on credit cards	0.50	0.30	0.40	1.60	1.00	1.00	1.20	1.10	1.60	1.30	1.00
Total expenditure		**252.00**	**283.60**	**349.60**	**413.70**	**489.00**	**513.70**	**571.40**	**661.10**	**752.40**	**1002.70**	**528.80**
14	**Other items recorded**											
14.1	Life assurance and contributions to pension funds	3.40	3.60	7.40	9.70	17.10	24.80	36.90	51.20	75.00	137.50	36.70
14.2	Other insurance inc. friendly societies	0.90	1.10	1.80	1.80	1.90	2.10	2.60	3.40	3.50	4.10	2.30
14.3	Income tax, payments *less* refunds	1.50	7.70	20.90	32.30	51.50	70.10	102.00	133.30	195.50	509.60	112.40
14.4	National insurance contributions	0.60	2.20	6.70	11.90	22.70	34.60	51.20	69.10	94.00	135.20	42.80
14.5	Purchase or alteration of dwellings, mortgages	26.90	12.80	49.90	24.90	38.30	52.20	59.60	80.40	127.80	262.60	73.50
14.6	Savings and investments	[0.50]	0.40	1.00	3.50	3.10	3.70	3.10	4.00	9.20	13.40	4.20
14.7	Pay off loan to clear other debt	..	..	[0.70]	[1.30]	2.20	2.20	2.30	4.50	3.30	3.30	2.00
14.8	Windfall receipts from gambling etc[8]	..	[0.20]	[0.20]	[0.10]	[0.30]	[0.30]	..	..	..	..	0.20

Note: The commodity and service categories are not comparable to those in publications before 2001-02.
The numbering system is sequential, it does not use actual COICOP codes.
Please see background notes for symbols and conventions used in this report.
6 For FYE 2019 onwards, critical illness cover, personal accident insurance and other medical insurance are included here. They were not included in previous years
7 For FYE 2019 onwards, information about insurance for non-package holiday and other travel insurance was collected in the questionnaire in addition to the diary. In previous years, this was based on diary data only.
8 Expressed as an income figure as opposed to an expenditure figure.

Source: Office for National Statistics

Table A11

Detailed household expenditure by age of household reference person

UK, financial year ending 2022

	Less than 30	30 to 49	50 to 64	65 to 74	75 or over	All house- holds
Weighted number of households (thousands)	2,610	9,410	7,890	4,490	4,100	28,500
Total number of households in sample	360	1,820	1,640	1,140	670	5,630
Total number of persons in sample	760	5,410	3,660	1,970	1,050	12,850
Total number of adults in sample	630	3,380	3,270	1,950	1,040	10,260
Weighted average number of persons per household	2.2	3.1	2.3	1.7	1.5	2.3

Commodity or service	Average weekly household expenditure (£)					
1 Food & non-alcoholic drinks	**44.50**	**69.80**	**68.00**	**56.90**	**50.20**	**62.20**
1.1 Food	39.90	63.10	61.70	52.40	46.60	56.50
1.1.1 Bread, rice and cereals	3.80	6.50	6.10	4.50	3.80	5.40
1.1.2 Pasta products	0.50	0.60	0.40	0.30	0.20	0.40
1.1.3 Buns, cakes, biscuits etc.	3.00	4.80	4.40	3.70	3.50	4.10
1.1.4 Pastry (savoury)	0.80	1.40	1.10	0.60	0.50	1.00
1.1.5 Beef (fresh, chilled or frozen)	1.10	1.70	2.10	1.80	1.50	1.80
1.1.6 Pork (fresh, chilled or frozen)	0.20	0.50	0.50	0.50	0.50	0.50
1.1.7 Lamb (fresh, chilled or frozen)	[0.20]	0.50	0.60	0.50	0.60	0.50
1.1.8 Poultry (fresh, chilled or frozen)	2.00	2.60	2.50	1.70	1.20	2.20
1.1.9 Bacon and ham	0.40	0.70	1.00	0.80	0.60	0.70
1.1.10 Other meat and meat preparations	4.40	7.60	7.60	6.30	5.70	6.80
1.1.11 Fish and fish products	1.80	2.60	3.30	3.50	3.30	3.00
1.1.12 Milk	1.20	2.00	1.90	2.00	1.90	1.90
1.1.13 Cheese and curd	1.70	2.50	2.40	2.00	1.50	2.20
1.1.14 Eggs	0.50	0.80	0.70	0.60	0.70	0.70
1.1.15 Other milk products	2.00	2.70	2.60	2.30	2.20	2.50
1.1.16 Butter	0.20	0.40	0.60	0.50	0.50	0.50
1.1.17 Margarine, other vegetable fats and peanut butter	0.40	0.60	0.60	0.60	0.70	0.60
1.1.18 Cooking oils and fats	0.20	0.40	0.30	0.30	0.30	0.30
1.1.19 Fresh fruit	2.50	4.00	3.90	3.90	4.00	3.80
1.1.20 Other fresh, chilled or frozen fruits	0.30	0.60	0.50	0.40	0.30	0.50
1.1.21 Dried fruit and nuts	0.40	0.90	0.90	1.00	1.00	0.90
1.1.22 Preserved fruit and fruit based products	0.10	0.10	0.10	0.10	0.20	0.10
1.1.23 Fresh vegetables	3.20	4.50	4.60	4.10	3.40	4.20
1.1.24 Dried vegetables	[0.00]	0.10	0.10	0.10	0.00	0.10
1.1.25 Other preserved or processed vegetables	1.80	2.30	2.30	1.60	1.20	2.00
1.1.26 Potatoes	0.30	0.50	0.60	0.70	0.60	0.60
1.1.27 Other tubers and products of tuber vegetables	1.50	2.50	2.10	1.40	1.10	1.90
1.1.28 Sugar and sugar products	0.30	0.50	0.30	0.30	0.30	0.40
1.1.29 Jams, marmalades	0.20	0.30	0.30	0.40	0.40	0.30
1.1.30 Chocolate	1.40	2.60	2.60	2.00	1.60	2.30
1.1.31 Confectionery products	0.70	1.10	0.80	0.60	0.50	0.80
1.1.32 Edible ices and ice cream	0.50	1.00	0.90	0.80	0.60	0.80
1.1.33 Other food products	2.30	3.30	3.10	2.30	2.00	2.80
1.2 Non-alcoholic drinks	4.60	6.70	6.30	4.60	3.60	5.60
1.2.1 Coffee	0.60	1.10	1.20	1.30	1.20	1.10
1.2.2 Tea	0.20	0.40	0.50	0.70	0.50	0.50
1.2.3 Cocoa and powdered chocolate	0.20	0.10	0.10	0.10	0.10	0.10
1.2.4 Fruit and vegetable juices (inc. fruit squash)	1.00	1.50	1.20	0.80	0.70	1.10
1.2.5 Mineral or spring waters	0.30	0.50	0.40	0.30	0.20	0.40
1.2.6 Soft drinks (inc. fizzy and ready to drink fruit drinks)	2.40	3.10	2.90	1.50	0.90	2.40

Note: The commodity and service categories are not comparable to those in publications before 2001-02
The numbering system is sequential, it does not use actual COICOP codes.
Please see background notes for symbols and conventions used in this report.

Table A11   Detailed household expenditure by age of household reference person (cont.)

UK, financial year ending 2022

Commodity or service			Less than 30	30 to 49	50 to 64	65 to 74	75 or over	All house-holds
			Average weekly household expenditure (£)					
2	**Alcoholic drink, tobacco & narcotics**		**5.80**	**10.90**	**16.00**	**14.80**	**8.70**	**12.20**
2.1	Alcoholic drinks		4.40	8.30	12.00	11.90	6.70	9.30
	2.1.1	Spirits and liqueurs (brought home)	1.30	1.80	2.70	2.60	1.90	2.10
	2.1.2	Wines, fortified wines (brought home)	1.40	3.40	5.90	6.90	3.70	4.50
	2.1.3	Beer, lager, ciders and perry (brought home)	1.70	3.00	3.40	2.40	1.10	2.60
	2.1.4	Alcopops (brought home)	..	0.00	0.00	[0.00]	..	0.00
2.2	Tobacco and narcotics		1.40	2.60	4.00	2.90	2.00	2.80
	2.2.1	Cigarettes	[0.50]	1.40	2.80	2.30	1.60	1.90
	2.2.2	Cigars, other tobacco products and narcotics	0.90	1.20	1.20	0.70	[0.40]	1.00
3	**Clothing & footwear**		**12.40**	**22.50**	**19.90**	**14.60**	**8.50**	**17.60**
3.1	Clothing		10.90	18.20	16.40	12.00	6.90	14.40
	3.1.1	Men's outer garments	2.80	4.20	4.30	3.10	1.20	3.50
	3.1.2	Men's under garments	[0.20]	0.50	0.50	0.40	0.30	0.40
	3.1.3	Women's outer garments	4.60	7.30	7.80	5.60	3.70	6.40
	3.1.4	Women's under garments	0.90	1.20	1.40	0.90	0.70	1.10
	3.1.5	Boys' outer garments (5-15)	[0.20]	0.90	0.50	0.10	..	0.50
	3.1.6	Girls' outer garments (5-15)	[0.50]	2.00	0.40	0.30	..	0.90
	3.1.7	Infants' outer garments (under 5)	1.00	0.70	0.20	0.20	..	0.40
	3.1.8	Children's under garments (under 16)	0.40	0.70	0.20	0.10	..	0.30
	3.1.9	Accessories	0.30	0.60	0.70	0.80	0.20	0.60
	3.1.10	Haberdashery, clothing materials and clothing hire	..	0.30	0.20	0.30	0.20	0.20
	3.1.11	Dry cleaners, laundry and dyeing	..	[0.10]	0.20	0.20	[0.20]	0.10
3.2	Footwear		1.50	4.20	3.50	2.60	1.60	3.20
4	**Housing (net)[1], fuel & power**		**138.10**	**106.50**	**81.50**	**59.50**	**54.90**	**87.70**
4.1	Actual rentals for housing		111.20	70.50	40.00	28.10	18.60	51.60
	4.1.1	Gross rent	111.10	70.50	39.80	27.80	18.50	51.50
	4.1.2	less housing benefit, rebates & allowances rec'd	7.60	9.30	9.10	13.10	9.30	9.70
	4.1.3	Net rent[2]	103.50	61.20	30.70	14.80	9.30	41.90
	4.1.4	Second dwelling rent	..	:	..	..	..	..
4.2	Maintenance and repair of dwelling		5.00	8.40	12.60	10.00	9.60	9.70
4.3	Water supply and miscellaneous services relating to the dwelling		10.20	10.70	10.10	9.60	11.00	10.40
4.4	Electricity, gas and other fuels		19.30	26.20	27.90	24.90	24.90	25.70
	4.4.1	Electricity	11.40	14.40	14.80	12.80	12.70	13.70
	4.4.2	Gas	7.60	10.90	11.40	10.30	10.00	10.50
	4.4.3	Other fuels	..	0.90	1.70	1.80	2.20	1.40

Note: The commodity and service categories are not comparable to those in publications before 2001-02

The numbering system is sequential, it does not use actual COICOP codes.

Please see background notes for symbols and conventions used in this report.

1 Excluding mortgage interest payments, council tax and Northern Ireland rates. Mortgage interest payments can be found in category 13.

2 The figure included in total expenditure is net rent as opposed to gross rent.

Table A11

Detailed household expenditure by age of household reference person (cont.)

UK, financial year ending 2022

Commodity or service			Less than 30	30 to 49	50 to 64	65 to 74	75 or over	All house-holds
			Average weekly household expenditure (£)					
5	**Household goods & services**		**26.40**	**35.30**	**39.50**	**38.60**	**25.10**	**34.70**
5.1	Furniture and furnishings and floor coverings		16.70	18.90	22.40	16.00	9.30	17.80
	5.1.1	Furniture and furnishings	14.10	15.20	17.60	12.90	6.70	14.20
	5.1.2	Floor coverings	2.60	3.70	4.80	3.10	2.50	3.60
5.2	Household textiles		1.40	1.90	2.30	2.40	1.50	2.00
5.3	Household appliances		[1.00]	3.30	2.80	6.20	2.00	3.20
5.4	Glassware, tableware and household utensils		1.70	2.30	2.00	1.70	1.30	1.90
5.5	Tools and equipment for house and garden		1.80	2.90	3.20	4.10	2.10	3.00
5.6	Goods and services for routine household maintenance		3.90	6.10	6.70	8.20	8.80	6.80
	5.6.1	Cleaning materials	1.60	2.80	3.20	2.80	2.00	2.70
	5.6.2	Household goods and hardware	1.80	2.20	2.00	1.90	1.50	2.00
	5.6.3	Domestic services, carpet cleaning, hire of furniture/furnishings	[0.50]	1.00	1.50	3.50	5.40	2.10
6	**Health**		**3.40**	**7.60**	**10.30**	**12.40**	**10.20**	**9.10**

UK, financial year ending 2022	Less than 30	30 to 49	50 to 64	65 to 74	75 or over	All house-holds
Commodity or service	Average weekly household expenditure (£)					
6.1 Medical products, appliances and equipment	1.90	3.80	4.90	7.40	5.20	4.70
6.1.1 Medicines, prescriptions and healthcare products	1.20	2.60	3.10	4.40	2.80	2.90
6.1.2 Spectacles, lenses, accessories and repairs	[0.70]	1.30	1.90	3.00	2.40	1.80
6.2 Hospital services	1.50	3.80	5.30	5.00	5.00	4.40
7 Transport	**61.60**	**84.90**	**94.60**	**61.70**	**33.50**	**74.40**
7.1 Purchase of vehicles	22.50	34.40	42.10	26.00	12.10	30.90
7.1.1 Purchase of new cars and vans	[6.30]	8.40	14.60	10.90	[5.00]	9.80
7.1.2 Purchase of second hand cars or vans	15.60	25.00	26.10	14.70	7.10	20.20
7.1.3 Purchase of motorcycles and other vehicles	..	1.00	1.40	..	:	0.80
7.2 Operation of personal transport	24.20	34.40	37.20	27.00	17.60	30.70
7.2.1 Spares and accessories	1.70	3.40	3.10	2.50	1.90	2.80
7.2.2 Petrol, diesel and other motor oils	15.40	21.40	23.50	15.70	9.80	18.90
7.2.3 Repairs and servicing	6.10	7.60	8.30	6.90	4.50	7.10
7.2.4 Other motoring costs	1.00	2.30	2.20	1.90	1.40	2.00
7.3 Transport services	14.80	15.90	15.40	8.70	3.80	12.80
7.3.1 Rail and tube fares	3.00	1.90	2.00	0.90	0.50	1.70
7.3.2 Bus and coach fares	1.20	1.00	1.00	0.30	[0.20]	0.80
7.3.4 Combined fares	..	..	..	..	:	[0.10]
7.3.5 Other travel and transport	10.60	12.90	12.30	7.40	3.20	10.30
8 Communication	**19.00**	**23.70**	**23.80**	**18.40**	**15.20**	**21.20**
8.1 Postal services	0.30	0.60	0.90	0.90	1.00	0.70
8.2 Telephone and telefax equipment	[0.10]	1.70	1.10	1.00	[0.60]	1.10
8.3 Telephone and telefax services[3]	10.80	10.90	9.60	5.20	3.80	8.60
8.4 Internet subscription fees (ex. combined packages)	2.00	1.20	0.60	0.40	0.20	0.80
8.5 Combined telecom services[4]	5.70	9.30	11.60	10.90	9.60	9.90

Note: The commodity and service categories are not comparable to those in publications before 2001-02

The numbering system is sequential, it does not use actual COICOP codes.

Please see background notes for symbols and conventions used in this report.

3 For FYE 2019 onwards, excludes payments made as part of a combined bill.

4 For FYE 2019 onwards telecoms bills can include more than one service. Due to the nature of combined packages, this also includes packages that includes television services.

Table A11

Detailed household expenditure by age of household reference person (cont.)

UK, financial year ending 2022

	Less than 30	30 to 49	50 to 64	65 to 74	75 or over	All house-holds
Commodity or service	Average weekly household expenditure (£)					
9 Recreation & culture	**38.30**	**60.80**	**67.20**	**53.90**	**37.50**	**56.10**
9.1 Audio-visual, photographic and information processing equipment	6.00	5.00	4.80	4.30	2.30	4.50
9.1.1 Audio equipment and accessories, CD players	0.80	0.80	1.00	0.90	[0.40]	0.80
9.1.2 TV, video and computers	5.10	4.10	3.70	3.30	1.90	3.60
9.1.3 Photographic, cine and optical equipment	..	[0.20]	[0.20]	[0.10]	..	0.10
9.2 Other major durables for recreation and culture	..	2.20	8.60	5.10	[0.50]	4.00
9.3 Other recreational items and equipment, gardens and pets	10.50	20.60	18.30	14.70	11.20	16.80
9.3.1 Games, toys and hobbies	3.40	5.00	2.00	1.70	1.10	3.00
9.3.2 Computer software and games	0.60	1.50	1.00	0.30	..	1.00
9.3.3 Equipment for sport, camping and open-air recreation	1.10	3.60	2.30	0.70	[0.80]	2.20
9.3.4 Horticultural goods, garden equipment and plants	1.60	3.00	4.50	5.10	5.10	3.90
9.3.5 Pets and pet food	3.90	7.40	8.40	6.90	3.70	6.70
9.4 Recreational and cultural services	14.20	19.50	16.70	14.00	9.60	15.90
9.4.1 Sports admissions, subscriptions, leisure class fees and equipment hire	4.60	8.60	5.70	3.30	1.80	5.60
9.4.2 Cinema, theatre and museums etc.	2.10	2.00	2.40	1.70	0.60	1.90
9.4.3 TV, video, satellite rental, cable subscriptions and TV licences[5]	5.30	6.40	6.20	5.50	4.40	5.80
9.4.4 Miscellaneous entertainments	0.70	1.70	1.10	1.50	1.30	1.40
9.4.5 Development of film, deposit for film development, passport photos, holiday and school photos	..	0.20	0.10	0.10	[0.10]	0.20
9.4.6 Gambling payments	0.40	0.60	1.10	1.80	1.40	1.10
9.5 Newspapers, books and stationery	2.10	4.00	4.20	5.50	5.70	4.40
9.5.1 Books	0.40	1.20	1.20	1.20	0.80	1.10

UK, financial year ending 2022	Less than 30	30 to 49	50 to 64	65 to 74	75 or over	All house-holds
Commodity or service	Average weekly household expenditure (£)					
9.5.2 Diaries, address books, cards etc.	1.60	2.20	2.00	1.80	1.60	1.90
9.5.3 Newspapers	..	0.20	0.60	1.90	2.40	0.90
9.5.4 Magazines and periodicals	[0.00]	0.40	0.50	0.60	0.90	0.50
9.6 Package holidays	5.20	9.50	14.60	10.40	8.30	10.50
9.6.1 Package holidays - UK	..	1.60	1.80	1.80	2.80	1.80
9.6.2 Package holidays - abroad	4.80	7.90	12.80	8.50	5.50	8.70
10 Education	**[7.10]**	**8.50**	**5.20**	**[1.50]**	**..**	**5.20**
10.1 Education fees	[6.90]	7.90	4.90	[1.50]	..	4.90
10.2 Payments for school trips, other ad-hoc expenditure	..	0.60	[0.30]	:	:	0.30
11 Restaurants & hotels	**32.00**	**39.20**	**40.70**	**32.00**	**18.20**	**34.80**
11.1 Catering services	26.90	29.00	29.20	22.30	12.50	25.40
11.1.1 Restaurant and café meals	11.70	12.80	14.40	13.70	8.10	12.60
11.1.2 Alcoholic drinks (away from home)	5.50	4.70	6.40	5.20	2.20	5.00
11.1.3 Take away meals eaten at home	5.60	5.80	4.10	1.90	1.50	4.10
11.1.4 Other take-away and snack food	3.20	4.20	3.40	1.40	0.60	2.90
11.1.5 Contract catering (food) and canteens	[1.00]	1.40	0.90	..	..	0.90
11.2 Accommodation services	5.10	10.20	11.50	9.70	5.70	9.40
11.2.1 Holiday in the UK	3.60	8.50	10.00	8.30	5.40	8.00
11.2.2 Holiday abroad	[1.50]	1.70	1.40	1.30	..	1.30
11.2.3 Room hire	..	..	..	..	..	[0.00]

Note: The commodity and service categories are not comparable to those in publications before 2001-02

The numbering system is sequential, it does not use actual COICOP codes.

Please see background notes for symbols and conventions used in this report.

5 For FYE 2019 onwards, excludes payments made as part of a combined bill.

Table A11

Detailed household expenditure by age of household reference person (cont.)

UK, financial year ending 2022

	Less than 30	30 to 49	50 to 64	65 to 74	75 or over	All house-holds
Commodity or service	Average weekly household expenditure (£)					
12 Miscellaneous goods & services	**31.00**	**47.80**	**41.60**	**34.30**	**35.40**	**40.60**
12.1 Personal care	9.40	12.20	12.60	10.10	8.50	11.20
12.1.1 Hairdressing, beauty treatment	3.10	3.30	4.20	3.70	3.00	3.60
12.1.2 Toilet paper	0.70	1.00	1.00	0.80	0.70	0.90
12.1.3 Toiletries and soap	1.60	2.50	2.40	2.20	1.90	2.30
12.1.4 Baby toiletries and accessories (disposable)	0.70	0.80	0.20	0.10	0.10	0.40
12.1.5 Hair products, cosmetics and related electrical appliances	3.20	4.60	4.60	3.20	2.80	4.00
12.2 Personal effects	3.50	5.10	3.10	2.80	1.10	3.50
12.3 Social protection	..	4.90	[0.30]	..	[3.60]	2.30
12.4 Insurance	13.70	18.20	20.30	17.50	16.90	18.10
12.4.1 Household insurances - structural, contents and appliances	2.20	4.30	5.70	6.10	5.90	5.00
12.4.2 Medical insurance premiums[6]	0.40	1.70	3.00	3.00	3.80	2.50
12.4.3 Vehicle insurance including boat insurance	11.00	12.00	11.20	7.70	6.90	10.30
12.4.4 Non-package holiday, other travel insurance[7]	[0.20]	0.20	0.50	0.60	0.30	0.30
12.5 Other services	4.00	7.30	5.40	3.80	5.30	5.60
12.5.1 Moving house	2.50	3.80	2.50	2.00	[2.60]	2.90
12.5.2 Bank, building society, post office, credit card charges	0.20	0.60	0.60	0.60	0.30	0.50
12.5.3 Other services and professional fees	1.30	2.90	2.30	1.20	2.50	2.20
1-12 All expenditure groups	**419.70**	**517.70**	**508.20**	**398.70**	**297.70**	**455.70**
13 Other expenditure items	**56.90**	**90.70**	**74.50**	**56.60**	**58.60**	**73.10**
13.1 Housing: mortgage interest payments, council tax etc.	49.00	74.60	50.80	32.80	28.80	52.50
13.2 Licences, fines and transfers	2.90	4.20	5.30	3.50	2.50	4.00
13.3 Holiday spending	..	1.50	2.00	..	..	1.40
13.4 Money transfers and credit	2.80	10.40	16.40	19.40	27.20	15.20
13.4.1 Money, cash gifts given to children	:	0.20	[0.50]	..	..	0.30
13.4.2 Cash gifts and donations	2.10	9.00	14.60	17.80	27.00	13.90
13.4.3 Club instalment payments (child) and interest on credit cards	0.70	1.20	1.30	0.90	[0.20]	1.00

Table A11

Detailed household expenditure by age of household reference person (cont.)

UK, financial year ending 2022

Commodity or service	Less than 30	30 to 49	50 to 64	65 to 74	75 or over	All house-holds
	Average weekly household expenditure (£)					
Total expenditure	**476.60**	**608.40**	**582.70**	**455.30**	**356.30**	**528.80**
14 Other items recorded						
14.1 Life assurance & contributions to pension funds	33.30	55.30	47.10	10.20	4.80	36.70
14.2 Other insurance inc. friendly societies	0.80	2.20	3.20	2.40	1.80	2.30
14.3 Income tax, payments *less* refunds	91.30	153.90	138.50	53.80	44.50	112.40
14.4 National insurance contributions	52.20	67.30	51.60	6.90	2.80	42.80
14.5 Purchase or alteration of dwellings, mortgages	36.50	111.50	85.50	45.10	18.10	73.50
14.6 Savings and investments	4.10	5.10	5.00	3.80	1.00	4.20
14.7 Pay off loan to clear other debt	[1.70]	3.40	2.40	..	:	2.00
14.8 Windfall receipts from gambling etc[8]	..	0.10	0.20	0.40	[0.10]	0.20

Note: The commodity and service categories are not comparable to those in publications before 2001-02

The numbering system is sequential, it does not use actual COICOP codes.

Please see background notes for symbols and conventions used in this report.

6 For FYE 2019 onwards, critical illness cover, personal accident insurance and other medical insurance are included here. They were not included in previous years

7 For FYE 2019 onwards, information about insurance for non-package holiday and other travel insurance was collected in the questionnaire in addition to the diary. In previous years, this was based on diary data only.

8 Expressed as an income figure as opposed to an expenditure figure.

Source: Office for National Statistics

Table 3.1

Detailed household expenditure by disposable income decile group

UK, financial year ending 2022

This table is under review to be removed from future publications and replaced with disposable equivalised income tables. If you use this table for your analysis, please get in contact here.

	Lowest ten per cent	Second decile group	Third decile group	Fourth decile group	Fifth decile group	Sixth decile group	Seventh decile group	Eighth decile group	Ninth decile group	Highest ten per cent	All house-holds
Lower boundary of group (£ per week)		247	349	443	555	668	795	928	1127	1438	
Weighted number of households (thousands)	2,850	2,850	2,850	2,850	2,850	2,850	2,850	2,850	2,850	2,850	28,500
Total number of households in sample	540	540	560	580	570	580	570	580	570	560	5,630
Total number of persons in sample	720	780	950	1,160	1,300	1,400	1,480	1,630	1,680	1,750	12,850
Total number of adults in sample	640	680	820	940	1,040	1,100	1,170	1,250	1,280	1,340	10,260
Weighted average number of persons per household	1.4	1.5	1.7	2.1	2.4	2.5	2.7	2.9	3.0	3.2	2.3

Commodity or service	Average weekly household expenditure (£)										
1 Food & non-alcoholic drinks	**35.50**	**41.40**	**45.50**	**53.60**	**58.40**	**66.90**	**71.00**	**74.10**	**83.60**	**91.80**	**62.20**
1.1 Food	32.50	38.00	41.70	48.80	52.70	60.50	64.30	67.20	76.40	83.40	56.50
1.1.1 Bread, rice and cereals	3.00	3.60	4.10	4.50	5.00	5.60	6.30	6.60	7.40	8.20	5.40
1.1.2 Pasta products	0.20	0.30	0.30	0.40	0.40	0.50	0.50	0.50	0.60	0.70	0.40
1.1.3 Buns, cakes, biscuits etc.	2.40	2.80	3.10	3.80	4.00	4.50	4.60	4.90	5.80	5.60	4.10
1.1.4 Pastry (savoury)	0.50	0.60	0.60	0.80	1.00	1.00	1.30	1.30	1.30	1.50	1.00
1.1.5 Beef (fresh, chilled or frozen)	1.10	1.10	1.30	1.50	1.60	2.10	1.80	2.10	2.30	2.60	1.80
1.1.6 Pork (fresh, chilled or frozen)	0.30	0.40	0.40	0.40	0.50	0.60	0.70	0.60	0.60	0.50	0.50
1.1.7 Lamb (fresh, chilled or frozen)	0.30	0.40	0.40	0.40	0.50	0.60	0.50	0.50	0.60	0.80	0.50
1.1.8 Poultry (fresh, chilled or frozen)	1.10	1.30	1.40	1.70	2.10	2.20	2.60	2.70	2.90	3.50	2.20
1.1.9 Bacon and ham	0.40	0.50	0.60	0.60	0.70	0.80	0.90	0.90	1.00	0.90	0.70
1.1.10 Other meat and meat preparations	4.00	5.10	5.40	5.90	6.10	7.60	7.60	8.90	8.40	9.00	6.80
1.1.11 Fish and fish products	1.80	2.00	2.20	2.70	2.90	3.00	3.10	3.30	4.10	4.50	3.00
1.1.12 Milk	1.20	1.60	1.50	2.10	1.80	2.00	2.00	2.10	2.10	2.40	1.90
1.1.13 Cheese and curd	1.30	1.20	1.50	1.60	2.10	2.30	2.60	2.60	3.20	3.40	2.20
1.1.14 Eggs	0.50	0.50	0.60	0.70	0.60	0.80	0.80	0.90	1.00	1.00	0.70
1.1.15 Other milk products	1.50	1.70	1.70	2.30	2.30	2.80	2.80	2.80	3.30	3.50	2.50
1.1.16 Butter	0.30	0.30	0.30	0.40	0.40	0.60	0.50	0.50	0.60	0.80	0.50
1.1.17 Margarine, other vegetable fats and peanut butter	0.40	0.50	0.60	0.50	0.60	0.60	0.70	0.60	0.70	0.70	0.60
1.1.18 Cooking oils and fats	0.20	0.20	0.30	0.30	0.30	0.30	0.30	0.30	0.50	0.50	0.30
1.1.19 Fresh fruit	2.20	2.50	2.90	3.30	3.60	4.20	4.20	4.40	5.20	5.60	3.80
1.1.20 Other fresh, chilled or frozen fruits	0.20	0.30	0.30	0.30	0.40	0.60	0.50	0.50	0.70	0.80	0.50
1.1.21 Dried fruit and nuts	0.40	0.60	0.60	0.60	0.90	0.90	1.10	0.90	1.20	1.50	0.90
1.1.22 Preserved fruit and fruit based products	0.10	0.10	0.10	0.10	0.10	0.20	0.20	0.20	0.20	0.20	0.10
1.1.23 Fresh vegetables	2.40	2.50	2.90	3.40	3.70	4.30	4.70	4.80	6.00	7.10	4.20
1.1.24 Dried vegetables	[0.00]	[0.10]	[0.00]	0.10	[0.10]	0.10	0.10	0.10	0.10	0.10	0.10
1.1.25 Other preserved or processed vegetables	1.00	1.00	1.30	1.70	1.60	1.90	2.30	2.30	3.10	3.50	2.00
1.1.26 Potatoes	0.30	0.40	0.50	0.50	0.50	0.60	0.60	0.60	0.70	0.70	0.60
1.1.27 Other tubers and products of tuber vegetables	1.10	1.40	1.40	1.70	1.80	2.10	2.30	2.60	2.50	2.50	1.90
1.1.28 Sugar and sugar products	0.20	0.30	0.20	0.30	0.40	0.40	0.50	0.40	0.60	0.50	0.40
1.1.29 Jams, marmalades	0.20	0.30	0.20	0.30	0.30	0.30	0.40	0.30	0.50	0.50	0.30
1.1.30 Chocolate	1.30	1.60	1.60	2.00	2.10	2.50	2.80	2.70	2.90	3.30	2.30
1.1.31 Confectionery products	0.40	0.70	0.60	0.70	0.80	0.90	1.10	1.10	1.10	1.10	0.80
1.1.32 Edible ices and ice cream	0.40	0.50	0.70	0.70	0.80	0.90	0.90	1.10	1.20	1.10	0.80
1.1.33 Other food products	1.50	1.80	1.90	2.30	2.60	2.90	3.20	3.10	4.10	4.80	2.80
1.2 Non-alcoholic drinks	3.00	3.40	3.90	4.80	5.60	6.30	6.70	6.90	7.20	8.40	5.60
1.2.1 Coffee	0.60	0.70	0.90	1.10	1.10	1.20	1.10	1.50	1.30	1.90	1.10
1.2.2 Tea	0.30	0.40	0.30	0.40	0.40	0.50	0.60	0.40	0.60	0.60	0.50
1.2.3 Cocoa and powdered chocolate	0.10	0.10	0.10	0.20	0.10	0.10	0.20	0.10	0.20	0.20	0.10
1.2.4 Fruit and vegetable juices (inc. fruit squash)	0.60	0.60	0.70	0.80	1.00	1.20	1.20	1.40	1.60	2.10	1.10
1.2.5 Mineral or spring waters	0.20	0.20	0.30	0.40	0.40	0.40	0.40	0.40	0.50	0.60	0.40
1.2.6 Soft drinks (inc. fizzy and ready to drink fruit drinks)	1.20	1.40	1.60	1.90	2.60	2.90	3.30	3.00	3.00	3.10	2.40

Note: The commodity and service categories are not comparable to those in publications before 2001-02.
The numbering system is sequential, it does not use actual COICOP codes.
Please see background notes for symbols and conventions used in this report.

Table 3.1

Detailed household expenditure by disposable income decile group (cont.)

UK, financial year ending 2022

	Lowest ten per cent	Second decile group	Third decile group	Fourth decile group	Fifth decile group	Sixth decile group	Seventh decile group	Eighth decile group	Ninth decile group	Highest ten per cent	All house-holds
Commodity or service	Average weekly household expenditure (£)										
2 Alcoholic drink, tobacco & narcotics	**8.70**	**8.90**	**9.60**	**8.90**	**11.50**	**12.40**	**11.90**	**14.90**	**16.20**	**18.70**	**12.20**
2.1 Alcoholic drinks	5.40	5.00	6.80	6.60	8.10	9.90	9.40	12.00	13.90	15.90	9.30
2.1.1 Spirits and liqueurs (brought home)	1.50	1.30	1.70	1.80	2.10	2.60	2.20	2.40	2.90	2.90	2.10
2.1.2 Wines, fortified wines (brought home)	2.00	2.30	2.90	3.20	3.60	4.30	4.50	5.40	7.50	9.40	4.50
2.1.3 Beer, lager, ciders and perry (brought home)	1.90	1.30	2.20	1.60	2.40	2.90	2.80	4.10	3.50	3.60	2.60
2.1.4 Alcopops (brought home)	..	..	..	..	..	[0.00]	..	..	..	[0.00]	0.00
2.2 Tobacco and narcotics	3.20	3.90	2.80	2.20	3.40	2.40	2.50	2.90	2.20	2.80	2.80
2.2.1 Cigarettes	1.80	2.70	2.10	1.10	2.30	1.70	1.70	2.00	1.20	2.10	1.90
2.2.2 Cigars, other tobacco products and narcotics	1.50	1.20	0.70	1.10	1.10	0.70	0.80	0.90	1.00	0.80	1.00
3 Clothing & footwear	**6.70**	**7.90**	**9.50**	**12.60**	**14.60**	**17.40**	**17.20**	**28.10**	**26.00**	**35.90**	**17.60**
3.1 Clothing	6.10	6.70	7.80	10.40	12.10	14.90	13.60	23.30	20.50	29.00	14.40

Table 3.1
Detailed household expenditure by disposable income decile group (cont.)
UK, financial year ending 2022

Commodity or service	Lowest ten per cent	Second decile group	Third decile group	Fourth decile group	Fifth decile group	Sixth decile group	Seventh decile group	Eighth decile group	Ninth decile group	Highest ten per cent	All house-holds
					Average weekly household expenditure (£)						
3.1.1 Men's outer garments	1.30	1.30	1.60	1.80	2.90	3.50	2.90	5.70	4.80	9.10	3.50
3.1.2 Men's under garments	[0.10]	0.30	0.20	0.20	0.40	0.40	0.50	0.60	0.80	0.50	0.40
3.1.3 Women's outer garments	2.70	3.30	3.80	5.20	4.90	6.00	5.40	11.60	8.10	12.70	6.40
3.1.4 Women's under garments	0.60	0.70	0.60	0.60	1.20	1.40	1.10	1.80	1.40	1.70	1.10
3.1.5 Boys' outer garments (5-15)	..	[0.20]	..	0.50	[0.30]	0.70	0.30	0.50	1.00	0.70	0.50
3.1.6 Girls' outer garments (5-15)	[0.20]	[0.30]	[0.20]	1.00	0.80	1.00	0.80	1.20	1.50	1.60	0.90
3.1.7 Infants' outer garments (under 5)	[0.20]	..	[0.50]	[0.30]	0.40	0.50	0.50	0.60	0.70	[0.40]	0.40
3.1.8 Children's under garments (under 16)	..	[0.10]	[0.10]	0.30	0.40	0.50	0.60	0.30	0.50	0.40	0.30
3.1.9 Accessories	0.30	0.20	0.30	0.30	0.60	0.60	1.00	0.50	1.10	1.00	0.60
3.1.10 Haberdashery and clothing hire	[0.10]	[0.10]	0.20	[0.00]	0.10	[0.20]	0.30	[0.30]	0.40		0.20
3.1.11 Dry cleaners, laundry and dyeing	[0.10]	..	[0.10]	..	..	..	..	[0.20]	..	[0.30]	0.10
3.2 Footwear	0.60	1.20	1.60	2.30	2.50	2.60	3.60	4.80	5.50	6.90	3.20
4 Housing (net)[1], fuel & power	**65.20**	**70.20**	**80.20**	**86.60**	**89.60**	**93.30**	**89.80**	**91.60**	**94.50**	**116.00**	**87.70**
4.1 Actual rentals for housing	67.00	62.20	56.30	53.80	52.30	51.20	47.00	41.90	36.30	48.30	51.60
4.1.1 Gross rent	66.50	62.20	56.30	53.80	52.20	51.20	47.00	41.90	36.30	47.90	51.50
4.1.2 less housing benefit, rebates & allowances rec'd	34.60	27.30	12.20	7.20	9.50	1.80	2.90	[0.70]	..	..	9.70
4.1.3 Net rent[2]	31.90	34.90	44.10	46.60	42.70	49.40	44.20	41.20	36.20	47.50	41.90
4.1.4 Second dwelling rent	..	:	:	:	..	:	..	:	:	..	..
4.2 Maintenance and repair of dwelling	3.60	5.60	5.50	7.00	10.50	8.30	9.40	12.20	15.30	19.50	9.70
4.3 Water supply and miscellaneous services relating to the dwelling	9.00	9.10	8.40	8.90	10.80	10.10	9.80	11.20	12.80	13.60	10.40
4.4 Electricity, gas and other fuels	20.20	20.70	22.00	24.10	25.50	25.50	26.40	27.00	30.20	34.90	25.70
4.4.1 Electricity	11.10	11.80	11.50	12.60	13.90	14.10	14.30	14.10	15.90	18.00	13.70
4.4.2 Gas	7.60	8.00	9.30	10.40	10.40	10.40	10.50	11.60	12.50	14.60	10.50
4.4.3 Other fuels	1.60	0.90	1.20	1.20	1.20	1.00	1.60	1.30	1.80	2.40	1.40

Note: The commodity and service categories are not comparable to those in publications before 2001-02.

The numbering system is sequential, it does not use actual COICOP codes.

Please see background notes for symbols and conventions used in this report.

1 Excluding mortgage interest payments, council tax and Northern Ireland rates. Mortgage interest payments can be found in category 13.

2 The figure included in total expenditure is net rent as opposed to gross rent.

Table 3.1
Detailed household expenditure by disposable income decile group (cont.)
UK, financial year ending 2022

Commodity or service	Lowest ten per cent	Second decile group	Third decile group	Fourth decile group	Fifth decile group	Sixth decile group	Seventh decile group	Eighth decile group	Ninth decile group	Highest ten per cent	All house-holds
					Average weekly household expenditure (£)						
5 Household goods & services	**17.00**	**19.60**	**23.80**	**24.50**	**29.60**	**35.80**	**34.90**	**42.10**	**54.00**	**65.90**	**34.70**
5.1 Furniture and furnishings, carpets and other floor coverings	9.10	8.90	12.90	9.70	16.20	17.10	16.40	22.60	29.40	35.90	17.80
5.1.1 Furniture and furnishings	6.80	5.60	10.70	7.40	13.70	12.00	12.80	18.30	25.70	28.90	14.20
5.1.2 Floor coverings	2.30	3.30	2.20	2.30	2.50	5.10	3.60	4.30	3.70	7.00	3.60
5.2 Household textiles	0.80	1.60	1.20	1.50	1.40	2.50	2.10	2.50	3.40	2.90	2.00
5.3 Household appliances	0.60	2.20	2.00	2.40	2.10	3.90	4.70	4.40	4.80	5.10	3.20
5.4 Glassware, tableware and household utensils	0.90	1.00	1.10	1.70	1.30	2.10	2.60	2.40	2.90	3.10	1.90
5.5 Tools and equipment for house and garden	1.40	1.30	1.80	2.30	2.50	4.00	3.00	3.70	4.10	5.60	3.00
5.6 Goods and services for routine household maintenance	4.00	4.50	4.70	6.80	6.00	6.20	6.20	6.50	9.30	13.30	6.80
5.6.1 Cleaning materials	1.60	1.90	2.00	2.30	2.40	2.90	2.80	2.90	4.00	3.90	2.70
5.6.2 Household goods and hardware	1.00	1.10	1.40	1.60	1.90	2.10	2.10	2.30	2.90	3.20	2.00
5.6.3 Domestic services, carpet cleaning, hire/repair of furniture/furnishings	1.50	1.40	1.30	2.90	1.70	1.10	1.30	1.30	2.40	6.30	2.10
6 Health	**4.80**	**3.80**	**8.30**	**8.50**	**8.20**	**8.50**	**8.60**	**7.80**	**12.80**	**19.60**	**9.10**
6.1 Medical products, appliances and equipment	2.00	1.90	4.50	4.00	6.10	4.10	5.50	3.70	7.60	7.80	4.70
6.1.1 Medicines, prescriptions, healthcare products etc.	1.40	1.40	1.60	2.40	5.30	2.80	3.00	2.60	3.40	5.00	2.90
6.1.2 Spectacles, lenses, accessories and repairs	[0.60]	[0.50]	2.90	1.60	0.80	1.30	2.50	1.10	4.20	2.80	1.80
6.2 Hospital services	2.80	1.90	3.80	4.60	2.10	4.40	3.10	4.10	5.30	11.80	4.40
7 Transport	**25.90**	**28.30**	**34.90**	**54.70**	**63.10**	**73.80**	**82.20**	**99.10**	**120.20**	**161.90**	**74.40**
7.1 Purchase of vehicles	9.70	7.00	10.40	23.80	22.80	31.70	27.60	43.30	55.80	77.00	30.90
7.1.1 Purchase of new cars and vans	..	[2.60]	..	7.60	7.50	7.10	8.50	10.00	19.50	33.60	9.80
7.1.2 Purchase of second hand cars or vans	8.50	4.40	8.80	16.10	14.90	24.60	17.70	32.10	34.00	41.20	20.20
7.1.3 Purchase of motorcycles and other vehicles	..	:	..	:	..	[1.40]	[1.10]	[2.30]	[2.10]		0.80
7.2 Operation of personal transport	12.60	13.50	18.70	22.90	28.80	31.40	39.50	40.00	44.80	55.00	30.70
7.2.1 Spares and accessories	1.30	[1.00]	1.80	1.10	2.30	1.70	5.00	3.50	2.90	7.40	2.80
7.2.2 Petrol, diesel and other motor oils	7.50	8.20	11.10	14.70	18.20	20.80	23.30	25.60	27.10	32.40	18.90
7.2.3 Repairs and servicing	3.30	3.50	4.50	5.40	6.40	7.10	9.20	8.80	11.50	11.40	7.10
7.2.4 Other motoring costs	0.50	0.80	1.30	1.70	1.90	1.90	2.10	2.10	3.30	3.90	2.00
7.3 Transport services	3.60	7.80	5.80	8.00	11.50	10.60	15.10	15.90	19.60	29.90	12.80
7.3.1 Rail and tube fares	0.60	0.60	0.70	0.70	1.80	1.20	2.10	2.00	3.20	3.70	1.70
7.3.2 Bus and coach fares	0.60	0.80	0.60	0.70	0.80	0.80	1.30	0.60	0.80	0.60	0.80
7.3.3 Combined fares	..	:	..	:	..	..	..	..	..	..	[0.10]
7.3.4 Other travel and transport	2.30	6.40	4.50	6.60	8.80	8.50	11.60	13.30	15.40	25.40	10.30
8 Communication	**12.70**	**13.80**	**15.70**	**17.90**	**21.20**	**23.30**	**23.60**	**27.10**	**27.00**	**30.00**	**21.20**
8.1 Postal services	0.40	0.50	0.50	0.80	0.70	0.70	0.70	1.00	1.00	1.10	0.70
8.2 Telephone and telefax equipment	[1.30]	[0.30]	[0.40]	[0.40]	1.50	2.20	1.00	1.50	1.50	1.50	1.10
8.3 Telephone and telefax services[3]	4.20	4.60	5.00	6.10	8.20	8.80	10.30	12.10	12.80	14.00	8.60
8.4 Internet subscription fees (ex. combined packages)	0.70	0.70	0.80	0.70	0.70	1.00	1.00	0.90	0.70	1.20	0.80
8.5 Combined telecom services[4]	6.10	7.70	9.10	9.80	10.00	10.50	10.60	11.70	11.50	12.10	9.90

Note: The commodity and service categories are not comparable to those in publications before 2001-02.

The numbering system is sequential, it does not use actual COICOP codes.

Please see background notes for symbols and conventions used in this report.

3 For FYE 2019 onwards, excludes payments made as part of a combined bill.

4 New for FYE 2019. This encompasses all telecoms bills that include more than one service. Due to the nature of combined packages, this also includes packages that includes television services.

Table 3.1
Detailed household expenditure by disposable income decile group (cont.)
UK, financial year ending 2022

Commodity or service	Lowest ten per cent	Second decile group	Third decile group	Fourth decile group	Fifth decile group	Sixth decile group	Seventh decile group	Eighth decile group	Ninth decile group	Highest ten per cent	All house-holds
	Average weekly household expenditure (£)										
9 **Recreation & culture**	**26.20**	**23.70**	**31.00**	**45.10**	**44.30**	**54.60**	**67.30**	**60.10**	**88.60**	**119.80**	**56.10**
9.1 Audio-visual, photographic and information processing equipment	5.20	1.30	1.90	3.80	3.00	5.00	6.30	3.30	9.10	6.50	4.50
9.1.1 Audio equipment and accessories, CD players	[0.40]	[0.40]	[0.20]	0.40	0.60	0.60	0.90	1.40	1.20	2.10	0.80
9.1.2 TV, video and computers	4.50	0.80	1.70	3.40	2.40	4.40	5.40	1.70	7.80	4.00	3.60
9.1.3 Photographic, cine and optical equipment	..	..	..	..	..	..	..	..	..	[0.40]	0.10
9.2 Other major durables for recreation and culture	..	..	..	..	..	..	[6.90]	5.20	3.10	7.50	4.00
9.3 Other recreational items and equipment, gardens and pets	6.80	7.60	11.40	13.10	13.70	15.80	18.70	21.70	23.20	35.60	16.80
9.3.1 Games, toys and hobbies	0.80	1.70	2.40	2.70	2.70	3.90	3.40	3.30	4.30	4.40	3.00
9.3.2 Computer software and games	[0.10]	[0.60]	[0.30]	1.00	0.40	0.40	1.30	1.00	2.30	2.30	1.00
9.3.3 Equipment for sport, camping and open-air recreation	[0.70]	[0.20]	[1.10]	0.80	0.90	1.50	1.50	3.30	2.20	9.60	2.20
9.3.4 Horticultural goods, garden equipment and plants	1.90	2.30	2.90	3.70	4.20	3.80	5.50	4.00	5.10	5.70	3.90
9.3.5 Pets and pet food	3.30	2.70	4.70	4.90	5.50	6.30	7.10	10.00	9.20	13.60	6.70
9.4 Recreational and cultural services	6.50	6.40	9.80	12.30	13.70	14.90	16.70	17.30	27.10	34.80	15.90
9.4.1 Sports admissions, subscriptions, leisure class fees and equipment hire	1.40	0.90	2.00	3.90	3.90	4.90	5.30	6.50	9.90	17.60	5.60
9.4.2 Cinema, theatre and museums etc.	0.30	[0.40]	0.90	0.70	1.50	1.90	1.80	2.00	5.30	3.80	1.90
9.4.3 TV, video, satellite rental, cable subscriptions and TV licences[5]	3.40	3.90	4.60	5.20	6.20	5.70	6.70	6.40	7.40	8.50	5.80
9.4.4 Miscellaneous entertainments	0.50	0.50	0.70	1.00	1.10	1.00	1.60	1.40	2.20	3.70	1.40
9.4.5 Development of film, deposit for film development, passport photos, holiday and school photos	..	..	..	[0.20]	..	[0.10]	[0.10]	[0.20]	[1.20]	[0.20]	0.20
9.4.6 Gambling payments	0.90	0.60	1.50	1.30	0.90	1.20	1.20	0.90	1.00	0.90	1.10
9.5 Newspapers, books and stationery	2.80	2.90	3.50	3.70	3.80	4.60	4.60	4.50	6.30	6.70	4.40
9.5.1 Books	0.50	0.50	0.60	0.70	0.90	1.10	1.40	1.10	1.90	2.00	1.10
9.5.2 Diaries, address books, cards etc.	1.00	1.10	1.40	1.50	1.60	2.30	2.20	2.30	2.90	3.20	1.90
9.5.3 Newspapers	0.80	0.80	1.10	1.10	0.80	0.90	0.70	0.70	0.70	0.90	0.90
9.5.4 Magazines and periodicals	0.50	0.40	0.40	0.40	0.40	0.40	0.40	0.40	0.80	0.70	0.50
9.6 Package holidays	2.70	3.80	4.30	4.10	8.70	10.60	14.00	8.10	19.80	28.70	10.50
9.6.1 Package holidays - UK	..	1.50	[1.10]	[0.60]	1.40	2.60	[1.50]	[2.30]	3.00	3.00	1.80
9.6.2 Package holidays - abroad	[2.00]	2.20	3.30	3.60	7.30	8.00	12.50	5.80	16.90	25.70	8.70
10 **Education**	**[2.20]**	**..**	**[4.10]**	**[2.70]**	**[2.70]**	**[2.00]**	**[4.20]**	**[3.60]**	**10.30**	**19.50**	**5.20**
10.1 Education fees	..	..	[4.10]	[2.60]	[2.30]	..	[4.00]	[3.50]	9.70	18.60	4.90
10.2 Payments for school trips, other ad-hoc expenditure	..	..	:	..	..	..	..	..	..	..	0.30
11 **Restaurants & hotels**	**10.70**	**12.80**	**17.60**	**21.50**	**29.70**	**34.90**	**38.80**	**45.90**	**52.90**	**83.40**	**34.80**
11.1 Catering services	8.80	9.90	12.80	15.90	21.20	26.90	29.20	33.50	38.40	57.70	25.40
11.1.1 Restaurant and café meals	4.50	5.00	6.80	8.40	10.00	13.30	13.80	16.60	18.70	28.90	12.60
11.1.2 Alcoholic drinks (away from home)	1.70	2.30	2.40	2.60	3.40	4.40	5.60	7.30	7.50	12.60	5.00
11.1.3 Take away meals eaten at home	1.50	1.50	2.00	2.10	3.90	5.00	4.80	5.40	6.40	8.20	4.10
11.1.4 Other take-away and snack food	0.90	1.00	1.40	2.10	2.90	3.20	4.00	3.30	4.90	5.30	2.90
11.1.5 Contract catering (food) and canteens	..	[0.20]	[0.20]	0.60	1.10	1.10	1.00	1.00	0.90	2.60	0.90
11.2 Accommodation services	1.90	2.90	4.80	5.60	8.50	8.10	9.60	12.40	14.50	25.70	9.40
11.2.1 Holiday in the UK	1.50	2.60	4.80	4.90	6.20	7.60	7.90	11.60	13.00	20.00	8.00
11.2.2 Holiday abroad	..	..	..	[0.70]	[2.30]	..	[1.60]	[0.70]	1.40	5.70	1.30
11.2.3 Room hire	:	..	:	..	..	..	..	..	..	..	[0.00]

Note: The commodity and service categories are not comparable to those in publications before 2001-02.
The numbering system is sequential, it does not use actual COICOP codes.
Please see background notes for symbols and conventions used in this report.

5 For FYE 2019 onwards, excludes payments made as part of a combined bill.

Table 3.1
Detailed household expenditure by disposable income decile group (cont.)
UK, financial year ending 2022

Commodity or service	Lowest ten per cent	Second decile group	Third decile group	Fourth decile group	Fifth decile group	Sixth decile group	Seventh decile group	Eighth decile group	Ninth decile group	Highest ten per cent	All house-holds
	Average weekly household expenditure (£)										
12 **Miscellaneous goods & services**	**18.70**	**18.20**	**25.30**	**33.60**	**31.40**	**41.50**	**43.30**	**49.40**	**62.70**	**82.30**	**40.60**
12.1 Personal care	5.00	5.80	8.10	9.40	9.20	11.90	12.10	13.40	17.40	19.70	11.20
12.1.1 Hairdressing, beauty treatment	1.50	1.60	2.10	2.70	2.80	3.80	3.80	3.60	6.60	7.20	3.60
12.1.2 Toilet paper	0.60	0.60	0.70	0.70	1.00	1.10	1.10	0.90	1.30	1.20	0.90
12.1.3 Toiletries and soap	1.20	1.60	1.70	2.10	2.20	2.60	2.30	2.90	2.80	3.30	2.30
12.1.4 Baby toiletries and accessories (disposable)	0.20	0.20	0.30	0.50	0.50	0.50	0.60	0.50	0.70	0.50	0.40
12.1.5 Hair products, cosmetics and related electrical appliances	1.50	1.90	3.20	3.40	2.70	4.00	4.40	5.50	6.00	7.40	4.00
12.2 Personal effects	1.40	0.70	1.50	2.20	2.40	2.90	3.00	3.60	4.90	12.20	3.50
12.3 Social protection	..	..	..	..	[0.80]	[4.00]	[3.20]	[2.10]	[2.00]	7.20	2.30
12.4 Insurance	7.80	9.20	11.50	15.20	15.70	18.80	21.30	22.30	27.00	32.10	18.10
12.4.1 Household insurances - structural, contents and appliances	3.00	3.50	3.90	4.20	4.60	5.10	5.20	5.70	6.50	8.40	5.00

Table 3.1
Detailed household expenditure by disposable income decile group (cont.)
UK, financial year ending 2022

		Lowest ten per cent	Second decile group	Third decile group	Fourth decile group	Fifth decile group	Sixth decile group	Seventh decile group	Eighth decile group	Ninth decile group	Highest ten per cent	All house-holds
	Commodity or service	Average weekly household expenditure (£)										
12.4.2	Medical insurance premiums[6]	0.30	0.60	0.90	2.30	1.70	2.90	2.40	2.70	5.10	5.50	2.50
12.4.3	Vehicle insurance including boat insurance	4.20	5.00	6.40	8.40	9.20	10.50	13.00	13.60	14.90	17.70	10.30
12.4.4	Non-package holiday, other travel insurance[7]	0.20	[0.10]	0.30	0.30	0.20	0.30	0.60	0.30	0.50	0.50	0.30
12.5	Other services	4.00	2.10	3.30	5.50	3.40	3.80	3.70	7.90	11.40	11.20	5.60
12.5.1	Moving house	2.70	[1.60]	1.80	1.60	1.80	1.90	1.50	3.40	6.30	6.10	2.90
12.5.2	Bank, building society, post office, credit card charges	0.20	0.20	0.30	0.40	0.50	0.50	0.60	0.60	1.00	1.00	0.50
12.5.3	Other services and professional fees	1.10	[0.30]	1.20	3.50	1.20	1.40	1.60	3.90	4.10	4.10	2.20
1-12	**All expenditure groups**	**234.20**	**249.00**	**305.40**	**370.30**	**404.20**	**464.30**	**492.60**	**543.70**	**648.60**	**844.70**	**455.70**
13	**Other expenditure items**	**25.20**	**29.80**	**40.40**	**49.20**	**68.00**	**62.80**	**70.80**	**92.80**	**138.70**	**153.60**	**73.10**
13.1	Housing: mortgage interest payments, council tax etc.	18.60	21.10	29.30	35.00	42.30	47.60	55.90	72.30	89.00	113.80	52.50
13.2	Licences, fines and transfers	1.90	1.70	2.30	2.80	3.50	4.20	4.60	4.90	5.30	8.90	4.00
13.3	Holiday spending	..	..	..	..	[1.90]	..	..	..	..	..	1.40
13.4	Money transfers and credit	4.10	6.90	8.50	9.70	20.20	10.10	9.80	14.30	40.00	28.30	15.20
13.4.1	Money, cash gifts given to children	..	:	..	..	..	..	..	..	[0.40]	[1.80]	0.30
13.4.2	Cash gifts and donations	3.60	6.60	7.60	8.50	18.70	9.00	8.70	12.90	38.00	25.30	13.90
13.4.3	Club instalment payments (child) and interest on credit cards	0.50	0.30	0.80	1.10	1.40	0.80	1.00	1.10	1.60	1.30	1.00
	Total expenditure	**259.50**	**278.90**	**345.80**	**419.50**	**472.20**	**527.10**	**563.50**	**636.50**	**787.30**	**998.30**	**528.80**
14	**Other items recorded**											
14.1	Life assurance and contributions to pension funds	3.50	4.70	8.40	10.30	18.90	25.90	34.90	52.50	74.90	132.50	36.70
14.2	Other insurance inc. friendly societies	1.00	1.10	1.60	1.90	1.80	2.30	2.60	3.30	3.90	3.90	2.30
14.3	Income tax, payments less refunds	15.50	10.50	25.10	36.80	56.90	75.50	104.70	142.90	197.00	459.30	112.40
14.4	National insurance contributions	0.90	3.30	10.30	13.10	26.60	36.30	49.80	69.50	89.20	129.10	42.80
14.5	Purchase or alteration of dwellings, mortgages	27.70	18.20	22.10	51.20	36.00	46.30	72.60	74.50	131.30	255.30	73.50
14.6	Savings and investments	[0.50]	0.50	2.80	2.10	2.90	3.60	1.90	6.20	8.80	12.70	4.20
14.7	Pay off loan to clear other debt	..	..	[0.90]	[1.20]	2.50	1.90	1.90	4.40	3.40	3.30	2.00
14.8	Windfall receipts from gambling etc[8]	..	..	[0.20]	[0.10]	[0.20]	[0.40]	..	[0.20]	..	..	0.20

Note: The commodity and service categories are not comparable to those in publications before 2001-02.

The numbering system is sequential, it does not use actual COICOP codes.

Please see background notes for symbols and conventions used in this report.

6 For FYE 2019, critical illness cover, personal accident insurance and other medical insurance are included here. They were not included in previous years.

7 For FYE 2019, information about insurance for non-package holiday and other travel insurance was collected in the questionnaire in addition to the diary. In previous years, this was based on diary data only.

8 Expressed as an income figure as opposed to an expenditure figure.

Source: Office for National Statistics

Table 3.1E
Detailed household expenditure by equivalised disposable income decile group (OECD-modified scale)
UK, financial year ending 2022

		Lowest ten per cent	Second decile group	Third decile group	Fourth decile group	Fifth decile group	Sixth decile group	Seventh decile group	Eighth decile group	Ninth decile group	Highest ten per cent	All house-holds
Lower boundary of group (£ per week)			196	263	315	369	429	494	569	663	829	
Weighted number of households (thousands)		2,850	2,850	2,850	2,850	2,850	2,850	2,850	2,850	2,850	2,850	28,500
Total number of households in sample		520	540	540	550	590	600	570	580	560	590	5,630
Total number of persons in sample		1,040	1,190	1,220	1,240	1,350	1,440	1,360	1,350	1,320	1,330	12,850
Total number of adults in sample		780	880	930	970	1,080	1,130	1,110	1,130	1,110	1,140	10,260
Weighted average number of persons per household		2.1	2.3	2.3	2.3	2.3	2.4	2.4	2.4	2.4	2.3	2.3

Commodity or service						Average weekly household expenditure (£)						
1	**Food & non-alcoholic drinks**	**46.70**	**50.70**	**56.40**	**60.20**	**58.20**	**68.00**	**65.00**	**67.70**	**73.10**	**75.80**	**62.20**
1.1	Food	42.50	46.30	50.80	54.80	52.80	62.20	58.90	61.50	66.80	68.80	56.50
1.1.1	Bread, rice and cereals	4.20	4.70	4.90	5.10	5.50	5.90	5.80	5.70	6.60	6.00	5.40
1.1.2	Pasta products	0.40	0.40	0.40	0.40	0.40	0.50	0.50	0.50	0.50	0.60	0.40
1.1.3	Buns, cakes, biscuits etc.	3.10	3.60	4.10	4.10	4.10	4.70	4.30	4.30	4.90	4.30	4.10
1.1.4	Pastry (savoury)	0.70	0.80	0.90	1.00	1.00	1.10	1.10	1.10	1.30	1.00	1.00
1.1.5	Beef (fresh, chilled or frozen)	1.50	1.30	1.50	1.90	1.70	1.90	1.50	2.20	2.00	2.10	1.80
1.1.6	Pork (fresh, chilled or frozen)	0.50	0.40	0.50	0.50	0.50	0.50	0.50	0.60	0.50	0.40	0.50
1.1.7	Lamb (fresh, chilled or frozen)	0.40	0.50	0.50	0.40	0.40	0.60	0.50	0.60	0.50	0.70	0.50
1.1.8	Poultry (fresh, chilled or frozen)	1.60	1.70	1.90	2.20	2.00	2.40	2.30	2.40	2.60	2.70	2.20
1.1.9	Bacon and ham	0.50	0.60	0.70	0.80	0.70	0.80	0.90	0.90	0.80	0.80	0.70
1.1.10	Other meat and meat preparations	4.70	5.90	6.70	6.90	6.30	7.30	7.20	7.20	8.00	7.60	6.80
1.1.11	Fish and fish products	2.10	2.40	2.40	2.90	2.30	3.30	2.80	3.40	3.60	4.50	3.00
1.1.12	Milk	1.70	1.90	1.90	2.10	1.80	2.00	1.90	1.80	1.90	1.90	1.90
1.1.13	Cheese and curd	1.70	1.50	1.90	2.10	2.00	2.40	2.30	2.50	2.60	3.00	2.20
1.1.14	Eggs	0.60	0.60	0.60	0.70	0.70	0.70	0.70	0.80	0.90	0.90	0.70
1.1.15	Other milk products	1.80	2.00	2.20	2.40	2.40	2.80	2.60	2.70	2.90	3.00	2.50
1.1.16	Butter	0.40	0.40	0.40	0.40	0.40	0.50	0.50	0.50	0.70	0.60	0.50
1.1.17	Margarine, other vegetable fats and peanut butter	0.50	0.60	0.60	0.60	0.70	0.60	0.60	0.60	0.60	0.60	0.60
1.1.18	Cooking oils and fats	0.40	0.30	0.30	0.30	0.30	0.30	0.30	0.30	0.40	0.40	0.30
1.1.19	Fresh fruit	2.70	2.90	3.40	3.60	3.50	4.30	4.10	4.40	4.40	5.00	3.80
1.1.20	Other fresh, chilled or frozen fruits	0.30	0.30	0.40	0.40	0.40	0.50	0.50	0.50	0.60	0.60	0.50
1.1.21	Dried fruit and nuts	0.70	0.50	0.70	0.70	0.80	1.10	0.80	1.00	1.10	1.30	0.90
1.1.22	Preserved fruit and fruit based products	0.10	0.10	0.10	0.10	0.20	0.20	0.20	0.10	0.10	0.20	0.10
1.1.23	Fresh vegetables	3.10	3.10	3.20	3.70	3.50	4.40	4.50	4.70	5.60	6.20	4.20
1.1.24	Dried vegetables	0.10	0.20	[0.00]	0.00	0.00	0.10	0.00	0.00	0.10	0.10	0.10
1.1.25	Other preserved or processed vegetables	1.30	1.20	1.40	1.60	1.80	2.20	2.20	2.30	2.70	3.00	2.00
1.1.26	Potatoes	0.40	0.50	0.60	0.60	0.60	0.60	0.60	0.50	0.50	0.60	0.60
1.1.27	Other tubers and products of tuber vegetables	1.60	1.80	2.00	2.00	2.00	2.10	2.00	2.00	2.00	1.80	1.90
1.1.28	Sugar and sugar products	0.30	0.30	0.40	0.40	0.40	0.50	0.40	0.40	0.40	0.30	0.40
1.1.29	Jams, marmalades	0.20	0.20	0.30	0.40	0.40	0.30	0.30	0.40	0.30	0.50	0.30
1.1.30	Chocolate	1.70	1.90	2.30	2.20	2.10	2.60	2.50	2.30	2.20	2.90	2.30
1.1.31	Confectionery products	0.70	0.80	0.90	0.90	0.80	0.80	0.90	0.80	0.90	0.80	0.80
1.1.32	Edible ices and ice cream	0.70	0.70	0.70	0.90	0.90	0.90	0.80	0.90	0.90	0.90	0.80
1.1.33	Other food products	2.10	2.10	2.30	2.50	2.40	3.20	2.80	3.00	3.90	3.70	2.80
1.2	Non-alcoholic drinks	4.20	4.40	5.60	5.40	5.30	5.80	6.10	6.20	6.30	6.90	5.60
1.2.1	Coffee	0.70	0.80	0.90	1.00	1.00	1.20	1.40	1.30	1.40	1.80	1.10
1.2.2	Tea	0.40	0.40	0.40	0.40	0.40	0.40	0.50	0.60	0.50	0.60	0.50
1.2.3	Cocoa and powdered chocolate	0.10	0.10	0.10	0.20	0.20	0.10	0.10	0.10	0.10	0.20	0.10
1.2.4	Fruit and vegetable juices (inc. fruit squash)	0.80	0.90	0.90	1.10	0.90	1.20	1.20	1.20	1.40	1.60	1.10
1.2.5	Mineral or spring waters	0.30	0.30	0.40	0.40	0.40	0.30	0.40	0.40	0.40	0.50	0.40
1.2.6	Soft drinks (inc. fizzy and ready to drink fruit drinks)	1.90	1.90	2.90	2.40	2.40	2.60	2.40	2.70	2.50	2.30	2.40

Note: The commodity and service categories are not comparable to those in publications before 2001-02.
The numbering system is sequential, it does not use actual COICOP codes.
Please see background notes for symbols and conventions used in this report.

Table 3.1E
Detailed household expenditure by equivalised disposable income decile group (OECD-modified scale) (cont.)
UK, financial year ending 2022

		Lowest ten per cent	Second decile group	Third decile group	Fourth decile group	Fifth decile group	Sixth decile group	Seventh decile group	Eighth decile group	Ninth decile group	Highest ten per cent	All house-holds
Commodity or service						Average weekly household expenditure (£)						
2	**Alcoholic drink, tobacco & narcotics**	**9.50**	**7.90**	**10.30**	**9.60**	**12.50**	**13.70**	**11.90**	**13.00**	**13.90**	**19.40**	**12.20**
2.1	Alcoholic drinks	5.70	4.60	6.60	7.10	9.50	10.60	9.60	10.70	12.20	16.30	9.30
2.1.1	Spirits and liqueurs (brought home)	1.60	1.30	1.60	1.80	2.60	2.20	2.20	2.60	2.50	3.00	2.10
2.1.2	Wines, fortified wines (brought home)	2.00	1.90	2.60	3.10	4.20	4.90	4.60	4.80	6.50	10.30	4.50
2.1.3	Beer, lager, ciders and perry (brought home)	2.10	1.50	2.30	2.20	2.50	3.50	2.80	3.20	3.20	3.00	2.60
2.1.4	Alcopops (brought home)	..	..	[0.00]	..	..	..	..	..	..	[0.00]	0.00
2.2	Tobacco and narcotics	3.80	3.20	3.70	2.50	3.00	3.10	2.20	2.30	1.60	3.10	2.80
2.2.1	Cigarettes	2.00	2.10	2.60	1.70	1.90	2.00	1.40	1.50	1.10	2.30	1.90
2.2.2	Cigars, other tobacco products and narcotics	1.80	1.20	1.10	0.80	1.10	1.10	0.80	0.80	0.50	0.80	1.00
3	**Clothing & footwear**	**9.50**	**12.00**	**10.80**	**15.10**	**14.50**	**17.50**	**19.30**	**22.50**	**25.00**	**29.50**	**17.60**
3.1	Clothing	8.20	9.90	9.00	13.30	12.30	14.30	14.70	18.10	20.00	24.60	14.40
3.1.1	Men's outer garments	1.50	1.70	1.70	2.70	2.10	3.20	3.50	5.80	4.80	7.80	3.50
3.1.2	Men's under garments	[0.10]	0.40	0.30	0.40	0.40	0.30	0.50	0.70	0.50	0.50	0.40
3.1.3	Women's outer garments	4.00	3.30	3.80	6.40	5.20	6.50	6.00	7.90	10.00	10.80	6.40
3.1.4	Women's under garments	0.60	0.80	0.70	1.10	1.30	1.30	1.40	0.90	1.60	1.40	1.10
3.1.5	Boys' outer garments (5-15)	[0.50]	0.60	0.30	0.40	0.50	0.40	0.50	0.50	0.40	0.50	0.50

95

Table 3.1E

Table 3.1E
Detailed household expenditure by equivalised disposable income decile group (OECD-modified scale) (cont.)
UK, financial year ending 2022

	Lowest ten per cent	Second decile group	Third decile group	Fourth decile group	Fifth decile group	Sixth decile group	Seventh decile group	Eighth decile group	Ninth decile group	Highest ten per cent	All house-holds
Commodity or service	Average weekly household expenditure (£)										
3.1.6 Girls' outer garments (5-15)	0.40	1.30	0.60	1.10	1.00	1.00	0.80	0.70	0.90	0.80	0.90
3.1.7 Infants' outer garments (under 5)	[0.30]	[0.70]	[0.40]	[0.30]	0.40	0.40	0.50	[0.20]	0.50	[0.40]	0.40
3.1.8 Children's under garments (under 16)	[0.20]	0.50	0.30	0.40	0.50	0.40	0.30	0.30	0.30	0.30	0.30
3.1.9 Accessories	0.30	0.30	0.60	0.40	0.60	0.50	0.70	0.80	0.60	1.10	0.60
3.1.10 Haberdashery and clothing hire	[0.10]	[0.10]	[0.10]	[0.10]	0.20	0.20	0.50	[0.20]	0.30	0.50	0.20
3.1.11 Dry cleaners, laundry and dyeing	..	..	[0.10]	..	..	..	..	..	..	[0.50]	0.10
3.2 Footwear	1.40	2.20	1.80	1.90	2.20	3.20	4.60	4.50	5.00	4.90	3.20
4 Housing (net)[1], fuel & power	**79.50**	**87.50**	**80.40**	**88.80**	**85.10**	**80.90**	**92.10**	**77.20**	**97.80**	**107.30**	**87.70**
4.1 Actual rentals for housing	83.40	73.20	61.00	55.00	45.20	34.10	48.60	29.50	43.90	42.70	51.60
4.1.1 Gross rent	83.00	73.10	61.00	55.00	45.00	34.10	48.60	29.50	43.60	42.50	51.50
4.1.2 less housing benefit, rebates & allowances rec'd	39.30	22.90	19.80	8.10	3.30	0.70	1.10	0.50	0.50	0.60	9.70
4.1.3 Net rent[2]	43.70	50.20	41.10	46.90	41.80	33.40	47.50	29.00	43.10	41.90	41.90
4.1.4 Second dwelling rent	..	..	:	..	..	:	:	..	..	:	..
4.2 Maintenance and repair of dwelling	3.90	4.00	6.80	6.20	8.60	13.10	8.20	11.70	15.30	19.10	9.70
4.3 Water supply and miscellaneous services relating to the dwelling	8.40	9.30	9.10	10.10	9.60	10.00	9.90	11.10	12.20	13.90	10.40
4.4 Electricity, gas and other fuels	23.10	24.00	23.40	25.60	25.10	24.40	26.60	25.50	26.90	32.20	25.70
4.4.1 Electricity	12.80	13.00	12.40	14.00	13.30	13.10	13.80	13.60	14.20	17.00	13.70
4.4.2 Gas	9.00	9.50	9.70	10.40	10.50	10.60	10.90	10.80	11.20	12.70	10.50
4.4.3 Other fuels	1.30	1.50	1.30	1.20	1.30	0.80	1.80	1.10	1.60	2.40	1.40

Note: The commodity and service categories are not comparable to those in publications before 2001-02.
The numbering system is sequential, it does not use actual COICOP codes.
Please see background notes for symbols and conventions used in this report.

1 Excluding mortgage interest payments, council tax and Northern Ireland rates. Mortgage interest payments can be found in category 13.

2 The figure included in total expenditure is net rent as opposed to gross rent.

Table 3.1E
Detailed household expenditure by equivalised disposable income decile group (OECD-modified scale) (cont.)
UK, financial year ending 2022

	Lowest ten per cent	Second decile group	Third decile group	Fourth decile group	Fifth decile group	Sixth decile group	Seventh decile group	Eighth decile group	Ninth decile group	Highest ten per cent	All house-holds
Commodity or service	Average weekly household expenditure (£)										
5 Household goods & services	**19.70**	**21.40**	**23.30**	**25.30**	**28.40**	**35.90**	**38.90**	**46.00**	**44.50**	**63.70**	**34.70**
5.1 Furniture and furnishings, carpets and other floor coverings	10.70	9.60	12.90	10.70	14.50	19.10	15.10	25.70	22.40	37.70	17.80
5.1.1 Furniture and furnishings	7.90	6.50	10.60	7.80	12.50	13.80	12.40	21.10	18.90	30.30	14.20
5.1.2 Floor coverings	2.80	3.10	2.30	2.80	2.00	5.30	2.70	4.50	3.40	7.40	3.60
5.2 Household textiles	1.10	1.30	1.20	1.70	1.60	2.40	2.80	2.30	2.70	2.70	2.00
5.3 Household appliances	1.10	2.20	0.90	3.50	2.70	1.70	8.30	2.50	4.90	4.50	3.20
5.4 Glassware, tableware and household utensils	1.10	1.20	1.10	1.70	1.70	2.20	2.40	2.50	2.50	2.80	1.90
5.5 Tools and equipment for house and garden	1.50	2.30	1.80	1.90	3.00	3.30	2.80	4.10	4.00	5.10	3.00
5.6 Goods and services for routine household maintenance	4.20	4.80	5.40	5.80	4.80	7.20	7.40	9.00	8.00	10.90	6.80
5.6.1 Cleaning materials	2.00	2.20	2.50	2.80	2.30	3.40	2.80	2.50	2.50	3.50	2.70
5.6.2 Household goods and hardware	1.10	1.50	1.60	1.60	1.70	2.10	2.10	2.40	2.30	3.00	2.00
5.6.3 Domestic services, carpet cleaning, hire/repair of furniture/furnishings	1.00	1.10	1.30	1.40	0.80	1.60	2.50	4.10	3.20	4.30	2.10
6 Health	**3.70**	**7.30**	**4.10**	**9.60**	**10.00**	**8.80**	**8.60**	**8.90**	**13.90**	**15.90**	**9.10**
6.1 Medical products, appliances and equipment	1.60	3.00	3.40	3.80	7.90	4.30	4.50	5.30	5.40	7.80	4.70
6.1.1 Medicines, prescriptions, healthcare products etc.	1.30	1.70	2.00	2.40	5.80	2.60	2.70	2.70	3.20	4.60	2.90
6.1.2 Spectacles, lenses, accessories and repairs	[0.30]	1.30	1.40	1.40	2.20	1.70	1.80	2.60	2.20	3.20	1.80
6.2 Hospital services	[2.10]	4.30	[0.80]	5.90	2.00	4.40	4.10	3.60	8.50	8.20	4.40
7 Transport	**33.90**	**38.60**	**41.80**	**57.60**	**62.10**	**80.10**	**78.70**	**97.50**	**106.50**	**147.50**	**74.40**
7.1 Purchase of vehicles	11.80	12.30	13.40	21.80	22.70	37.20	31.20	42.40	44.70	71.30	30.90
7.1.1 Purchase of new cars and vans	[2.10]	[1.80]	[3.60]	4.20	5.10	10.40	8.80	14.20	12.30	35.90	9.80
7.1.2 Purchase of second hand cars or vans	9.10	10.30	9.40	17.50	17.30	26.60	21.80	26.90	30.30	33.10	20.20
7.1.3 Purchase of motorcycles and other vehicles	..	..	..	..	..	..	..	[1.30]	[2.10]	[2.20]	0.80
7.2 Operation of personal transport	15.70	18.10	20.20	26.10	30.90	32.60	33.90	38.60	43.30	47.80	30.70
7.2.1 Spares and accessories	1.40	1.50	1.10	1.30	2.40	1.60	3.00	5.10	4.10	6.40	2.80
7.2.2 Petrol, diesel and other motor oils	9.90	12.00	12.80	17.80	18.90	20.50	20.80	23.80	25.80	26.30	18.90
7.2.3 Repairs and servicing	3.70	3.30	5.00	5.60	7.70	7.90	7.60	8.00	10.70	11.50	7.10
7.2.4 Other motoring costs	0.70	1.20	1.30	1.50	1.90	2.60	2.40	1.70	2.70	3.50	2.00
7.3 Transport services	6.30	8.20	8.10	9.60	8.50	10.30	13.60	16.50	18.50	28.30	12.80
7.3.1 Rail and tube fares	0.60	1.20	0.80	1.20	1.10	1.40	1.60	2.40	3.00	3.40	1.70
7.3.2 Bus and coach fares	1.00	0.80	0.80	1.20	0.90	0.60	0.90	0.70	0.50	0.40	0.80
7.3.3 Combined fares	..	:	..	..	:	..	..	..	..	..	[0.10]
7.3.4 Other travel and transport	4.60	6.20	6.50	7.10	6.50	8.40	11.10	13.40	14.90	24.20	10.30
8 Communication	**15.20**	**15.60**	**18.20**	**21.30**	**21.90**	**23.00**	**23.50**	**23.40**	**24.30**	**25.70**	**21.20**
8.1 Postal services	0.50	0.50	0.70	0.60	0.60	0.90	0.80	0.70	1.00	1.30	0.70
8.2 Telephone and telefax equipment	[1.40]	[0.60]	[0.70]	2.10	0.90	1.30	[1.00]	0.90	0.90	1.30	1.10
8.3 Telephone and telefax services[3]	5.70	6.00	6.90	7.80	9.20	9.10	9.70	10.30	10.70	10.70	8.60
8.4 Internet subscription fees (ex. combined packages)	1.00	0.70	0.70	0.70	0.70	0.90	0.70	0.90	0.90	1.10	0.80
8.5 Combined telecom services[4]	6.70	7.80	9.30	10.10	10.50	10.80	11.30	10.60	10.80	11.40	9.90

Note: The commodity and service categories are not comparable to those in publications before 2001-02.
The numbering system is sequential, it does not use actual COICOP codes.
Please see background notes for symbols and conventions used in this report.

3 For FYE 2019 onwards, excludes payments made as part of a combined bill.

4 New for FYE 2019. This encompasses all telecoms bills that include more than one service. Due to the nature of combined packages, this also includes packages that includes television services.

Table 3.1E
Detailed household expenditure by equivalised disposable income decile group (OECD-modified scale) (cont.)
UK, financial year ending 2022

Commodity or service	Lowest ten per cent	Second decile group	Third decile group	Fourth decile group	Fifth decile group	Sixth decile group	Seventh decile group	Eighth decile group	Ninth decile group	Highest ten per cent	All house-holds
	Average weekly household expenditure (£)										
9 **Recreation & culture**	**31.60**	**27.10**	**35.10**	**39.20**	**43.00**	**58.50**	**73.40**	**68.00**	**70.10**	**114.90**	**56.10**
9.1 Audio-visual, photographic and information processing equipment	5.70	1.90	2.00	3.40	2.60	5.60	4.00	6.30	4.10	9.70	4.50
9.1.1 Audio equipment and accessories, CD players	[0.40]	[0.40]	0.40	0.40	0.40	0.60	0.80	1.60	1.50	1.80	0.80
9.1.2 TV, video and computers	5.10	1.40	1.60	3.10	2.10	4.90	3.10	4.70	2.40	7.60	3.60
9.1.3 Photographic, cine and optical equipment	..	..	..	..	..	..	..	..	..	[0.30]	0.10
9.2 Other major durables for recreation and culture	..	..	..	..	[1.90]	..	15.60	[4.60]	5.80	5.50	4.00
9.3 Other recreational items and equipment, gardens and pets	8.90	9.70	14.20	13.20	14.10	17.40	17.00	21.40	18.10	33.60	16.80
9.3.1 Games, toys and hobbies	1.90	2.90	4.30	2.70	2.20	3.30	3.00	2.90	2.70	3.60	3.00
9.3.2 Computer software and games	[0.50]	0.30	0.50	0.80	0.70	1.50	1.10	1.70	1.10	1.60	1.00
9.3.3 Equipment for sport, camping and open-air recreation	[0.60]	0.40	1.40	0.70	1.10	1.30	1.50	3.30	2.10	9.40	2.20
9.3.4 Horticultural goods, garden equipment and plants	1.80	2.60	2.70	3.90	3.50	3.90	4.20	6.00	4.50	6.20	3.90
9.3.5 Pets and pet food	4.00	3.50	5.30	5.20	6.70	7.50	7.20	7.50	7.80	12.80	6.70
9.4 Recreational and cultural services	8.00	7.90	10.70	12.60	12.70	19.50	15.90	18.90	22.40	30.70	15.90
9.4.1 Sports admissions, subscriptions, leisure class fees and equipment hire	2.20	1.70	2.90	3.70	3.20	6.70	6.30	6.50	8.00	15.20	5.60
9.4.2 Cinema, theatre and museums etc.	[0.30]	[0.40]	0.80	1.30	1.50	3.60	1.60	2.80	3.10	3.20	1.90
9.4.3 TV, video, satellite rental, cable subscriptions and TV licences[5]	4.00	4.30	4.90	5.30	5.90	5.90	5.90	7.20	6.80	7.90	5.80
9.4.4 Miscellaneous entertainments	0.60	0.40	1.20	1.00	0.90	1.70	0.70	1.40	2.30	3.40	1.40
9.4.5 Development of film, deposit for film development, passport photos, holiday and school photos	..	[0.00]	..	[0.10]	[0.10]	[0.10]	[0.30]	[0.10]	[1.20]	[0.10]	0.20
9.4.6 Gambling payments	0.90	1.10	0.90	1.20	1.00	1.50	1.10	1.00	1.10	0.80	1.10
9.5 Newspapers, books and stationery	2.70	3.20	3.30	4.00	3.50	4.80	5.20	4.70	5.90	6.30	4.40
9.5.1 Books	0.50	0.50	0.80	0.80	0.90	1.00	1.30	1.30	2.00	1.70	1.10
9.5.2 Diaries, address books, cards etc.	1.20	1.10	1.30	1.90	1.50	2.60	2.50	2.10	2.40	2.70	1.90
9.5.3 Newspapers	0.60	1.00	0.80	1.00	0.70	0.80	0.90	0.60	1.10	1.10	0.90
9.5.4 Magazines and periodicals	0.40	0.50	0.40	0.30	0.40	0.40	0.50	0.60	0.50	0.70	0.50
9.6 Package holidays	3.00	3.40	4.60	5.00	8.10	10.20	15.60	12.00	13.70	29.10	10.50
9.6.1 Package holidays - UK	[1.00]	[1.40]	[1.10]	[1.10]	[1.20]	2.20	2.70	[1.00]	2.30	3.50	1.80
9.6.2 Package holidays - abroad	[2.00]	[2.00]	3.40	3.90	6.90	8.10	12.80	11.00	11.40	25.60	8.70
10 **Education**	**[3.30]**	**[1.50]**	**[1.90]**	**[2.60]**	**[4.50]**	**[3.60]**	**[6.40]**	**[4.00]**	**8.00**	**15.80**	**5.20**
10.1 Education fees	[3.30]	..	[1.70]	[2.50]	[4.30]	[3.30]	[6.20]	[3.60]	7.90	15.00	4.90
10.2 Payments for school trips, other ad-hoc expenditure	..	..	..	..	..	..	..	..	..	..	0.30
11 **Restaurants & hotels**	**13.30**	**16.10**	**21.40**	**24.60**	**27.20**	**32.90**	**37.70**	**47.00**	**57.10**	**70.60**	**34.80**
11.1 Catering services	10.80	12.90	15.30	19.70	20.00	25.60	27.70	34.20	41.70	46.40	25.40
11.1.1 Restaurant and café meals	4.70	6.00	6.90	9.40	10.20	13.30	13.70	16.90	21.10	23.50	12.60
11.1.2 Alcoholic drinks (away from home)	1.90	1.80	2.50	2.90	3.10	4.10	5.80	7.70	8.70	11.20	5.00
11.1.3 Take away meals eaten at home	2.10	2.50	2.70	3.70	3.40	4.20	4.30	4.90	5.90	7.10	4.10
11.1.4 Other take-away and snack food	1.80	2.00	2.20	3.00	2.70	3.00	2.90	3.50	3.90	3.90	2.90
11.1.5 Contract catering (food) and canteens	[0.30]	0.60	1.00	0.60	0.60	1.00	1.00	1.20	1.90	0.60	0.90
11.2 Accommodation services	2.60	3.20	6.10	5.00	7.30	7.30	10.00	12.80	15.50	24.20	9.40
11.2.1 Holiday in the UK	2.10	3.00	5.40	4.70	6.30	6.60	8.90	10.20	13.10	19.70	8.00
11.2.2 Holiday abroad	..	..	..	..	..	[0.60]	[1.00]	[2.60]	2.40	4.40	1.30
11.2.3 Room hire	..	:	..	..	..	..	..	:	..	..	[0.00]

Note: The commodity and service categories are not comparable to those in publications before 2001-02.
The numbering system is sequential, it does not use actual COICOP codes.
Please see background notes for symbols and conventions used in this report.

5 For FYE 2019 onwards, excludes payments made as part of a combined bill.

Table 3.1E

Detailed household expenditure by equivalised disposable income decile group (OECD-modified scale) (cont.)
UK, financial year ending 2022

Commodity or service	Lowest ten per cent	Second decile group	Third decile group	Fourth decile group	Fifth decile group	Sixth decile group	Seventh decile group	Eighth decile group	Ninth decile group	Highest ten per cent	All house-holds
	Average weekly household expenditure (£)										
12 **Miscellaneous goods & services**	**19.20**	**26.40**	**26.80**	**31.70**	**34.10**	**48.30**	**41.80**	**48.40**	**53.70**	**76.20**	**40.60**
12.1 Personal care	5.60	8.50	8.20	10.40	10.00	12.60	12.10	13.60	14.30	16.60	11.20
12.1.1 Hairdressing, beauty treatment	1.20	1.60	2.20	3.20	2.70	4.20	3.90	4.60	5.20	7.00	3.60
12.1.2 Toilet paper	0.80	0.80	0.90	1.10	1.00	0.90	0.90	1.00	0.90	1.10	0.90
12.1.3 Toiletries and soap	1.50	2.10	2.10	2.20	2.10	2.50	2.50	2.40	2.40	2.80	2.30
12.1.4 Baby toiletries and accessories (disposable)	0.40	0.60	0.40	0.30	0.40	0.60	0.40	0.30	0.60	0.30	0.40
12.1.5 Hair products, cosmetics and related electrical appliances	1.80	3.40	2.60	3.60	3.80	4.50	4.40	5.20	5.20	5.50	4.00
12.2 Personal effects	1.40	1.80	1.70	2.20	2.30	2.50	2.90	3.50	4.20	12.00	3.50
12.3 Social protection	..	[1.40]	[1.00]	[1.00]	[1.00]	[6.00]	[2.10]	[1.90]	[2.80]	5.60	2.30
12.4 Insurance	9.10	11.60	12.70	14.90	17.40	19.80	18.90	22.20	23.60	30.60	18.10
12.4.1 Household insurances - structural, contents and appliances	2.80	3.30	4.00	4.00	5.00	5.30	5.00	6.30	5.90	8.50	5.00
12.4.2 Medical insurance premiums[6]	[0.30]	0.70	0.80	1.70	2.30	2.20	1.80	2.90	4.50	7.40	2.50
12.4.3 Vehicle insurance including boat insurance	5.80	7.30	7.70	9.00	9.90	12.10	11.70	12.50	12.60	14.10	10.30
12.4.4 Non-package holiday, other travel insurance[7]	[0.20]	0.30	0.10	0.30	0.20	0.30	0.40	0.50	0.60	0.50	0.30
12.5 Other services	3.10	3.10	3.20	3.10	3.40	7.40	5.80	7.10	8.80	11.30	5.60
12.5.1 Moving house	[1.80]	1.60	[2.00]	1.70	2.00	2.90	1.30	2.90	6.40	6.10	2.90
12.5.2 Bank, building society, post office, credit card charges	0.20	0.30	0.30	0.50	0.40	0.50	0.60	0.60	0.80	1.00	0.50

	Lowest ten per cent	Second decile group	Third decile group	Fourth decile group	Fifth decile group	Sixth decile group	Seventh decile group	Eighth decile group	Ninth decile group	Highest ten per cent	All house-holds
Commodity or service	Average weekly household expenditure (£)										
12.5.3 Other services and professional fees	1.10	1.10	0.90	1.00	1.00	4.00	3.80	3.60	1.60	4.20	2.20
1-12 All expenditure groups	**285.10**	**312.40**	**330.60**	**385.70**	**401.50**	**471.30**	**497.20**	**523.60**	**588.00**	**762.20**	**455.70**
13 Other expenditure items	**28.00**	**34.10**	**36.60**	**49.30**	**61.70**	**70.70**	**74.10**	**104.60**	**118.90**	**153.50**	**73.10**
13.1 Housing: mortgage interest payments, council tax etc.	21.10	24.90	28.90	35.70	46.00	53.50	55.20	73.60	80.30	105.90	52.50
13.2 Licences, fines and transfers	2.10	2.70	2.80	3.50	3.70	4.10	4.60	6.20	4.70	6.00	4.00
13.3 Holiday spending	..	..	..	..	..	..	..	..	..	..	1.40
13.4 Money transfers and credit	4.20	6.40	4.70	9.80	10.40	11.20	12.80	22.00	31.10	39.40	15.20
13.4.1 Money, cash gifts given to children	..	..	..	..	..	..	..	..	[1.00]	..	0.30
13.4.2 Cash gifts and donations	3.80	5.00	4.00	8.40	8.80	10.30	11.90	20.50	28.80	37.30	13.90
13.4.3 Club instalment payments (child) and interest on credit cards	0.30	1.20	0.50	1.20	1.40	0.90	0.90	1.10	1.20	1.10	1.00
Total expenditure	**313.10**	**346.40**	**367.10**	**435.00**	**463.10**	**542.00**	**571.30**	**628.30**	**706.90**	**915.70**	**528.80**
14 Other items recorded											
14.1 Life assurance and contributions to pension funds	4.40	7.40	8.50	13.90	22.00	29.20	37.90	49.50	70.70	123.40	36.70
14.2 Other insurance inc. friendly societies	1.00	1.10	1.70	1.70	2.00	2.90	2.90	2.90	3.20	3.90	2.30
14.3 Income tax, payments *less* refunds	17.00	13.10	21.50	40.90	60.60	83.50	112.40	136.90	204.90	433.60	112.40
14.4 National insurance contributions	3.00	6.40	11.40	18.90	31.00	40.70	50.40	66.60	87.30	112.30	42.80
14.5 Purchase or alteration of dwellings, mortgages	29.00	41.00	28.20	38.20	38.50	58.30	89.10	87.20	108.90	217.10	73.50
14.6 Savings and investments	[0.30]	1.60	1.10	1.20	5.70	3.10	3.10	4.30	8.50	13.00	4.20
14.7 Pay off loan to clear other debt	[0.30]	..	[1.20]	[1.10]	2.30	2.00	2.20	3.90	4.00	[2.20]	2.00
14.8 Windfall receipts from gambling etc [8]	..	[0.40]	[0.10]	..	[0.30]	[0.30]	..	..	..	..	0.20

Note: The commodity and service categories are not comparable to those in publications before 2001-02.

The numbering system is sequential, it does not use actual COICOP codes.

Please see background notes for symbols and conventions used in this report.

6 For FYE 2019, critical illness cover, personal accident insurance and other medical insurance are included here. They were not included in previous years.

7 For FYE 2019, information about insurance for non-package holiday and other travel insurance was collected in the questionnaire in addition to the diary. In previous years, this was based on diary data only.

8 Expressed as an income figure as opposed to an expenditure figure.

Source: Office for National Statistics

Table 3.1E5
Detailed household expenditure by disposable equivalised income quintile group (OECD-modified scale)
UK, financial year ending 2022

	Lowest twenty per cent	Second quintile group	Third quintile group	Fourth quintile group	Highest twenty per cent	All house- holds
Lower boundary of group (£ per week)		263	369	494	663	
Weighted number of households (thousands)	5,710	5,690	5,700	5,700	5,700	28,500
Total number of households in sample	1,060	1,100	1,190	1,150	1,150	5,630
Total number of persons in sample	2,230	2,460	2,800	2,710	2,660	12,850
Total number of adults in sample	1,660	1,900	2,220	2,240	2,250	10,260
Weighted average number of persons per household	2.2	2.3	2.4	2.4	2.3	2.3
Commodity or service			Average Weekly Expenditure (£)			
1 Food & non-alcoholic drinks	**48.70**	**58.30**	**63.10**	**66.30**	**74.40**	**62.20**
1.1 Food	44.40	52.80	57.50	60.20	67.80	56.50
1.1.1 Bread, rice and cereals	4.50	5.00	5.70	5.70	6.30	5.40
1.1.2 Pasta products	0.40	0.40	0.40	0.50	0.50	0.40
1.1.3 Buns, cakes, biscuits etc.	3.40	4.10	4.40	4.30	4.60	4.10
1.1.4 Pastry (savoury)	0.80	0.90	1.00	1.10	1.10	1.00
1.1.5 Beef (fresh, chilled or frozen)	1.40	1.70	1.80	1.90	2.00	1.80
1.1.6 Pork (fresh, chilled or frozen)	0.40	0.50	0.50	0.60	0.50	0.50
1.1.7 Lamb (fresh, chilled or frozen)	0.40	0.40	0.50	0.50	0.60	0.50
1.1.8 Poultry (fresh, chilled or frozen)	1.60	2.00	2.20	2.30	2.60	2.20
1.1.9 Bacon and ham	0.50	0.70	0.70	0.90	0.80	0.70
1.1.10 Other meat and meat preparations	5.30	6.80	6.80	7.20	7.80	6.80
1.1.11 Fish and fish products	2.20	2.60	2.80	3.10	4.10	3.00
1.1.12 Milk	1.80	2.00	1.90	1.90	1.90	1.90
1.1.13 Cheese and curd	1.60	2.00	2.20	2.40	2.80	2.20
1.1.14 Eggs	0.60	0.70	0.70	0.80	0.90	0.70
1.1.15 Other milk products	1.90	2.30	2.60	2.70	3.00	2.50
1.1.16 Butter	0.40	0.40	0.40	0.50	0.60	0.50
1.1.17 Margarine, other vegetable fats and peanut butter	0.50	0.60	0.60	0.60	0.60	0.60
1.1.18 Cooking oils and fats	0.30	0.30	0.30	0.30	0.40	0.30
1.1.19 Fresh fruit	2.80	3.50	3.90	4.30	4.70	3.80
1.1.20 Other fresh, chilled or frozen fruits	0.30	0.40	0.50	0.50	0.60	0.50
1.1.21 Dried fruit and nuts	0.60	0.70	0.90	0.90	1.20	0.90
1.1.22 Preserved fruit and fruit based products	0.10	0.10	0.20	0.20	0.20	0.10
1.1.23 Fresh vegetables	3.10	3.40	3.90	4.60	5.90	4.20
1.1.24 Dried vegetables	0.10	0.00	0.10	0.00	0.10	0.10
1.1.25 Other preserved or processed vegetables	1.20	1.50	2.00	2.30	2.80	2.00
1.1.26 Potatoes	0.50	0.60	0.60	0.60	0.60	0.60
1.1.27 Other tubers and products of tuber vegetables	1.70	2.00	2.10	2.00	1.90	1.90
1.1.28 Sugar and sugar products	0.30	0.40	0.40	0.40	0.40	0.40
1.1.29 Jams, marmalades	0.20	0.30	0.30	0.40	0.40	0.30
1.1.30 Chocolate	1.80	2.30	2.40	2.40	2.50	2.30
1.1.31 Confectionery products	0.80	0.90	0.80	0.90	0.80	0.80
1.1.32 Edible ices and ice cream	0.70	0.80	0.90	0.80	0.90	0.80
1.1.33 Other food products	2.10	2.40	2.80	2.90	3.80	2.80
1.2 Non-alcoholic drinks	4.30	5.50	5.60	6.20	6.60	5.60
1.2.1 Coffee	0.80	0.90	1.10	1.30	1.60	1.10
1.2.2 Tea	0.40	0.40	0.40	0.50	0.50	0.50
1.2.3 Cocoa and powdered chocolate	0.10	0.10	0.20	0.10	0.20	0.10
1.2.4 Fruit and vegetable juices (inc. fruit squash)	0.80	1.00	1.10	1.20	1.50	1.10
1.2.5 Mineral or spring waters	0.30	0.40	0.30	0.40	0.40	0.40
1.2.6 Soft drinks (inc. fizzy and ready to drink fruit drinks)	1.90	2.60	2.50	2.60	2.40	2.40

Note: The commodity and service categories are not comparable to those in publications before 2001-02.
The numbering system is sequential, it does not use actual COICOP codes.
Please see background notes for symbols and conventions used in this report.

ONS, Family Spending, © Crown copyright

Table 3.1E5
Detailed household expenditure by disposable equivalised income quintile group (OECD-modified scale)
United Kingdom financial year ending 2022

	Lowest twenty per cent	Second quintile group	Third quintile group	Fourth quintile group	Highest twenty per cent	All house- holds
Commodity or service			Average Weekly Expenditure (£)			
2 Alcoholic drink, tobacco & narcotics	**8.70**	**9.90**	**13.10**	**12.40**	**16.60**	**12.20**
2.1 Alcoholic drinks	5.20	6.90	10.00	10.20	14.30	9.30
2.1.1 Spirits and liqueurs (brought home)	1.40	1.70	2.40	2.40	2.80	2.10
2.1.2 Wines, fortified wines (brought home)	2.00	2.90	4.60	4.70	8.40	4.50
2.1.3 Beer, lager, ciders and perry (brought home)	1.80	2.20	3.00	3.00	3.10	2.60
2.1.4 Alcopops (brought home)	[0.00]	[0.00]	[0.00]	[0.00]	[0.00]	0.00
2.2 Tobacco and narcotics	3.50	3.10	3.10	2.30	2.30	2.80
2.2.1 Cigarettes	2.00	2.10	1.90	1.50	1.70	1.90
2.2.2 Cigars, other tobacco products and narcotics	1.50	0.90	1.10	0.80	0.60	1.00
3 Clothing & footwear	**10.80**	**13.00**	**16.00**	**20.90**	**27.20**	**17.60**
3.1 Clothing	9.00	11.10	13.30	16.40	22.30	14.40
3.1.1 Men's outer garments	1.60	2.20	2.70	4.70	6.30	3.50
3.1.2 Men's under garments	0.30	0.40	0.30	0.60	0.50	0.40
3.1.3 Women's outer garments	3.70	5.10	5.90	7.00	10.40	6.40

United Kingdom financial year ending 2022	Lowest twenty per cent	Second quintile group	Third quintile group	Fourth quintile group	Highest twenty per cent	All house-holds
Commodity or service			Average Weekly Expenditure (£)			
3.1.4 Women's under garments	0.70	0.90	1.30	1.20	1.50	1.10
3.1.5 Boys' outer garments (5-15)	0.50	0.40	0.50	0.50	0.40	0.50
3.1.6 Girls' outer garments (5-15)	0.90	0.80	1.00	0.70	0.90	0.90
3.1.7 Infants' outer garments (under 5)	0.50	0.30	0.40	0.40	0.50	0.40
3.1.8 Children's under garments (under 16)	0.30	0.30	0.40	0.30	0.30	0.30
3.1.9 Accessories	0.30	0.50	0.50	0.70	0.90	0.60
3.1.10 Haberdashery and clothing hire	0.10	0.10	0.20	0.30	0.40	0.20
3.1.11 Dry cleaners, laundry and dyeing	[0.10]	[0.10]	[0.10]	[0.10]	0.30	0.10
3.2 Footwear	1.80	1.80	2.70	4.50	5.00	3.20
4 Housing (net)[1], fuel & power	**83.50**	**84.60**	**83.00**	**84.70**	**102.60**	**87.70**
4.1 Actual rentals for housing	78.30	58.00	39.60	39.00	43.30	51.60
4.1.1 Gross rent	78.10	58.00	39.60	39.00	43.10	51.50
4.1.2 *less housing benefit, rebates & allowances rec'd*	31.10	14.00	2.00	0.80	0.50	9.70
4.1.3 Net rent[2]	47.00	44.00	37.60	38.20	42.50	41.90
4.1.4 Second dwelling rent	..	:	..	:	..	..
4.2 Maintenance and repair of dwelling	3.90	6.50	10.80	9.90	17.20	9.70
4.3 Water supply and miscellaneous services relating to the dwelling	8.90	9.60	9.80	10.50	13.00	10.40
4.4 Electricity, gas and other fuels	23.50	24.50	24.70	26.00	29.60	25.70
4.4.1 Electricity	12.90	13.20	13.20	13.70	15.60	13.70
4.4.2 Gas	9.20	10.10	10.50	10.90	11.90	10.50
4.4.3 Other fuels	1.40	1.20	1.00	1.50	2.00	1.40

Note: The commodity and service categories are not comparable to those in publications before 2001-02.

The numbering system is sequential, it does not use actual COICOP codes.

Please see background notes for symbols and conventions used in this report.

1 Excluding mortgage interest payments, council tax and Northern Ireland rates. Mortgage interest payments can be found in category 13

2 The figure included in total expenditure is net rent as opposed to gross rent.

ONS, Family Spending, © Crown copyright

Table 3.1E5

Detailed household expenditure by disposable equivalised income quintile group (OECD-modified scale)
United Kingdom financial year ending 2022

Commodity or service	Lowest twenty per cent	Second quintile group	Third quintile group	Fourth quintile group	Highest twenty per cent	All house-holds
			Average Weekly Expenditure (£)			
5 Household goods & services	**20.50**	**24.30**	**32.10**	**42.50**	**54.10**	**34.70**
5.1 Furniture and furnishings, carpets and other floor coverings	10.10	11.80	16.80	20.40	30.00	17.80
5.1.1 Furniture and furnishings	7.20	9.20	13.10	16.80	24.60	14.20
5.1.2 Floor coverings	2.90	2.50	3.70	3.60	5.40	3.60
5.2 Household textiles	1.20	1.50	2.00	2.50	2.70	2.00
5.3 Household appliances	1.60	2.20	2.20	5.40	4.70	3.20
5.4 Glassware, tableware and household utensils	1.20	1.40	1.90	2.50	2.60	1.90
5.5 Tools and equipment for house and garden	1.90	1.90	3.20	3.50	4.60	3.00
5.6 Goods and services for routine household maintenance	4.50	5.60	6.00	8.20	9.40	6.80
5.6.1 Cleaning materials	2.10	2.70	2.90	2.70	3.00	2.70
5.6.2 Household goods and hardware	1.30	1.60	1.90	2.20	2.70	2.00
5.6.3 Domestic services, carpet cleaning, hire/repair of furniture/furnishings	1.00	1.30	1.20	3.30	3.70	2.10
6 Health	**5.50**	**6.90**	**9.40**	**8.80**	**14.90**	**9.10**
6.1 Medical products, appliances and equipment	2.30	3.60	6.10	4.90	6.60	4.70
6.1.1 Medicines, prescriptions, healthcare products etc.	1.50	2.20	4.20	2.70	3.90	2.90
6.1.2 Spectacles, lenses, accessories and repairs	0.80	1.40	2.00	2.20	2.70	1.80
6.2 Hospital services	3.20	3.30	3.20	3.80	8.30	4.40
7 Transport	**36.20**	**49.70**	**71.10**	**88.10**	**127.00**	**74.40**
7.1 Purchase of vehicles	12.10	17.60	30.00	36.80	58.00	30.90
7.1.1 Purchase of new cars and vans	2.00	3.90	7.70	11.50	24.10	9.80
7.1.2 Purchase of second hand cars or vans	9.70	13.40	22.00	24.30	31.70	20.20
7.1.3 Purchase of motorcycles and other vehicles	..	..	[0.30]	1.00	2.20	0.80
7.2 Operation of personal transport	16.90	23.20	31.70	36.20	45.60	30.70
7.2.1 Spares and accessories	1.50	1.20	2.00	4.10	5.30	2.80
7.2.2 Petrol, diesel and other motor oils	11.00	15.30	19.70	22.30	26.10	18.90
7.2.3 Repairs and servicing	3.50	5.30	7.80	7.80	11.10	7.10
7.2.4 Other motoring costs	0.90	1.40	2.30	2.10	3.10	2.00
7.3 Transport services	7.30	8.90	9.40	15.00	23.40	12.80
7.3.1 Rail and tube fares	0.90	1.00	1.20	2.00	3.20	1.70
7.3.2 Bus and coach fares	0.90	1.00	0.70	0.80	0.40	0.80
7.3.3 Combined fares	..	..	..	[0.20]	[0.10]	
7.3.4 Other travel and transport	5.40	6.80	7.40	12.20	19.60	10.30
8 Communication[3]	**15.40**	**19.80**	**22.50**	**23.40**	**25.00**	**21.20**
8.1 Postal services	0.50	0.60	0.80	0.80	1.10	0.70
8.2 Telephone and telefax equipment	1.00	1.40	1.10	0.90	1.10	1.10
8.3 Telephone and telefax services	5.90	7.30	9.10	10.00	10.70	8.60
8.4 Internet subscription fees	0.80	0.70	0.80	0.80	1.00	0.80
8.5 Combined telecom services	7.20	9.70	10.60	10.90	11.10	9.90

Note: The commodity and service categories are not comparable to those in publications before 2001-02.

The numbering system is sequential, it does not use actual COICOP codes.

Please see background notes for symbols and conventions used in this report.

3 Recording of expenditure on internet, telephone and television services via combined payment packages was changed from 2011.

Table 3.1E5
Detailed household expenditure by disposable equivalised income quintile group (OECD-modified scale)
United Kingdom financial year ending 2022

Commodity or service	Lowest twenty per cent	Second quintile group	Third quintile group	Fourth quintile group	Highest twenty per cent	All house-holds
	Average Weekly Expenditure (£)					
9 Recreation & culture[3]	**29.30**	**37.20**	**50.80**	**70.70**	**92.50**	**56.10**
9.1 Audio-visual, photographic and information processing equipment	3.80	2.70	4.10	5.20	6.90	4.50
9.1.1 Audio equipment and accessories, CD players	0.40	0.40	0.50	1.20	1.60	0.80
9.1.2 TV, video and computers	3.30	2.30	3.50	3.90	5.00	3.60
9.1.3 Photographic, cine and optical equipment	..	..	..	..	[0.30]	0.10
9.2 Other major durables for recreation and culture	[2.20]	[0.60]	[1.40]	10.10	5.70	4.00
9.3 Other recreational items and equipment, gardens and pets	9.30	13.70	15.80	19.20	25.90	16.80
9.3.1 Games, toys and hobbies	2.40	3.50	2.70	3.00	3.20	3.00
9.3.2 Computer software and games	0.40	0.70	1.10	1.40	1.30	1.00
9.3.3 Equipment for sport, camping and open-air recreation	0.50	1.00	1.20	2.40	5.70	2.20
9.3.4 Horticultural goods, garden equipment and plants	2.20	3.30	3.70	5.10	5.30	3.90
9.3.5 Pets and pet food	3.70	5.20	7.10	7.40	10.30	6.70
9.4 Recreational and cultural services	8.00	11.70	16.10	17.40	26.60	15.90
9.4.1 Sports admissions, subscriptions, leisure class fees and equipment hire	1.90	3.30	5.00	6.40	11.60	5.60
9.4.2 Cinema, theatre and museums etc.	0.30	1.10	2.60	2.20	3.10	1.90
9.4.3 TV, video, satellite rental, cable subscriptions and TV licences	4.20	5.10	5.90	6.50	7.40	5.80
9.4.4 Miscellaneous entertainments	0.50	1.10	1.30	1.10	2.80	1.40
9.4.5 Development of film, deposit for film development, passport photos, holiday and school photos	[0.00]	0.10	0.10	0.20	0.70	0.20
9.4.6 Gambling payments	1.00	1.00	1.20	1.00	1.00	1.10
9.5 Newspapers, books and stationery	3.00	3.70	4.20	4.90	6.10	4.40
9.5.1 Books	0.50	0.80	0.90	1.30	1.90	1.10
9.5.2 Diaries, address books, cards etc.	1.20	1.60	2.00	2.30	2.50	1.90
9.5.3 Newspapers	0.80	0.90	0.80	0.80	1.10	0.90
9.5.4 Magazines and periodicals	0.40	0.40	0.40	0.60	0.60	0.50
9.6 Package holidays[4]	3.20	4.80	9.20	13.80	21.40	10.50
9.6.1 Package holidays - UK	1.20	1.10	1.70	1.80	2.90	1.80
9.6.2 Package holidays - abroad	2.00	3.70	7.50	11.90	18.50	8.70
10 Education	**2.40**	**2.20**	**4.00**	**5.20**	**11.90**	**5.20**
10.1 Education fees	[2.20]	2.10	3.80	4.90	11.40	4.90
10.2 Payments for school trips, other ad-hoc expenditure	[0.20]	..	..	..	..	0.30
11 Restaurants & hotels	**14.70**	**23.00**	**30.10**	**42.30**	**63.90**	**34.80**
11.1 Catering services	11.90	17.50	22.80	30.90	44.00	25.40
11.1.1 Restaurant and café meals	5.30	8.20	11.80	15.30	22.30	12.60
11.1.2 Alcoholic drinks (away from home)	1.80	2.70	3.60	6.70	10.00	5.00
11.1.3 Take away meals eaten at home	2.30	3.20	3.80	4.60	6.50	4.10
11.1.4 Other take-away and snack food	1.90	2.60	2.90	3.20	3.90	2.90
11.1.5 Contract catering (food) and canteens	0.50	0.80	0.80	1.10	1.30	0.90
11.2 Accommodation services	2.90	5.50	7.30	11.40	19.80	9.40
11.2.1 Holiday in the UK	2.60	5.10	6.40	9.50	16.40	8.00
11.2.2 Holiday abroad	..	..	[0.80]	1.80	3.40	1.30
11.2.3 Room hire	..	..	..	..	..	[0.00]

Note: The commodity and service categories are not comparable to those in publications before 2001-02
The numbering system is sequential, it does not use actual COICOP codes
Please see background notes for symbols and conventions used in this report.
3 Recording of expenditure on internet, telephone and television services via combined payment packages was changed from 2011
4 Recording of expenditure on package holidays was changed from 2011

ONS, Family Spending, © Crown copyright

Table 3.1E5
Detailed household expenditure by disposable equivalised income quintile group (OECD-modified scale)
United Kingdom financial year ending 2022

Commodity or service	Lowest twenty per cent	Second quintile group	Third quintile group	Fourth quintile group	Highest twenty per cent	All house-holds
	Average Weekly Expenditure (£)					
12 Miscellaneous goods & services	**22.80**	**29.30**	**41.20**	**45.10**	**64.90**	**40.60**
12.1 Personal care	7.00	9.30	11.30	12.90	15.40	11.20
12.1.1 Hairdressing, beauty treatment	1.40	2.70	3.40	4.20	6.10	3.60
12.1.2 Toilet paper	0.80	1.00	0.90	1.00	1.00	0.90
12.1.3 Toiletries and soap	1.80	2.20	2.30	2.50	2.60	2.30
12.1.4 Baby toiletries and accessories (disposable)	0.50	0.30	0.50	0.40	0.40	0.40
12.1.5 Hair products, cosmetics and related electrical appliances	2.60	3.10	4.10	4.80	5.40	4.00
12.2 Personal effects	1.60	2.00	2.40	3.20	8.10	3.50
12.3 Social protection	[0.70]	1.00	3.50	2.00	4.20	2.30
12.4 Insurance	10.40	13.80	18.60	20.50	27.10	18.10
12.4.1 Household insurances - structural, contents and appliances	3.00	4.00	5.10	5.70	7.20	5.00
12.4.2 Medical insurance premiums	0.50	1.20	2.20	2.30	6.00	2.50

Table 3.1E5

Detailed household expenditure by disposable equivalised income quintile group (OECD-modified scale)
United Kingdom financial year ending 2022

		Lowest twenty per cent	Second quintile group	Third quintile group	Fourth quintile group	Highest twenty per cent	All house-holds
Commodity or service		Average Weekly Expenditure (£)					
	12.4.3 Vehicle insurance including boat insurance	6.60	8.40	11.00	12.10	13.30	10.30
	12.4.4 Non-package holiday, other travel insurance	..	..	..	..	..	0.10
12.5	Other services	3.10	3.20	5.40	6.50	10.10	5.60
	12.5.1 Moving house	1.70	1.80	2.50	2.10	6.20	2.90
	12.5.2 Bank, building society, post office, credit card charges	0.30	0.40	0.50	0.60	0.90	0.50
	12.5.3 Other services and professional fees	1.10	1.00	2.50	3.70	2.90	2.20
1-12	**All expenditure groups**	**298.70**	**358.20**	**436.40**	**510.40**	**675.00**	**455.70**
13	**Other expenditure items**	**31.00**	**42.90**	**66.20**	**89.40**	**136.20**	**73.10**
13.1	Housing: mortgage interest payments, council tax etc.	23.00	32.30	49.80	64.40	93.10	52.50
	13.1.1 Mortgage interest payments	4.70	7.90	18.50	29.10	50.80	22.20
	13.1.2 Mortgage protection premiums	0.20	0.30	0.80	1.10	1.20	0.70
	13.1.3 Council tax, domestic rates	17.60	24.00	30.10	32.50	37.00	28.20
	13.1.4 Council tax, mortgage (second dwelling)	..	..	..	..	4.10	1.40
13.2	Licences, fines and transfers	2.40	3.20	3.90	5.40	5.40	4.00
13.3	Holiday spending	..	..	[1.70]	[2.20]	[2.50]	1.40
13.4	Money transfers and credit	5.30	7.30	10.80	17.40	35.20	15.20
	13.4.1 Money, cash gifts given to children	..	[0.10]	..	[0.20]	[1.00]	0.30
	13.4.2 Cash gifts and donations	4.40	6.20	9.60	16.20	33.10	13.90
	13.4.3 Club instalment payments (child) and interest on credit cards	0.80	0.90	1.20	1.00	1.20	1.00
Total expenditure		**329.80**	**401.10**	**502.50**	**599.80**	**811.20**	**528.80**
14	**Other items recorded**						
14.1	Life assurance and contributions to pension funds	5.90	11.20	25.60	43.70	97.00	36.70
14.2	Other insurance inc. friendly societies	1.00	1.70	2.50	2.90	3.60	2.30
14.3	Income tax, payments *less* refunds	15.10	31.20	72.00	124.70	319.20	112.40
14.4	National insurance contributions	4.70	15.10	35.90	58.50	99.80	42.80
14.5	Purchase or alteration of dwellings, mortgages	35.00	33.20	48.40	88.20	163.00	73.50
14.6	Savings and investments	1.00	1.20	4.40	3.70	10.70	4.20
14.7	Pay off loan to clear other debt	0.70	1.20	2.10	3.00	3.10	2.00
14.8	Windfall receipts from gambling etc[5]	0.20	0.10	0.30	[0.10]	[0.30]	0.20

Note: The commodity and service categories are not comparable to those in publications before 2001-02.
The numbering system is sequential, it does not use actual COICOP codes.
Please see background notes for symbols and conventions used in this report.
5 Expressed as an income figure as opposed to an expenditure figure.

Source: Office for National Statistics

Table 3.2

Detailed household expenditure as a percentage of total expenditure by disposable income decile group

UK, financial year ending 2022

> **This table is under review to be removed from future publications and replaced with disposable equivalised income tables.**
> **If you use this table for your analysis, please get in contact here.**

	Lowest ten per cent	Second decile group	Third decile group	Fourth decile group	Fifth decile group	Sixth decile group	Seventh decile group	Eighth decile group	Ninth decile group	Highest ten per cent	All house-holds
Lower boundary of group (£ per week)		247	349	443	555	668	795	928	1127	1438	
Weighted number of households (thousands)	2,850	2,850	2,850	2,850	2,850	2,850	2,850	2,850	2,850	2,850	28,500
Total number of households in sample	540	540	560	580	570	580	570	580	570	560	5,630
Total number of persons in sample	720	780	950	1,160	1,300	1,400	1,480	1,630	1,680	1,750	12,850
Total number of adults in sample	640	680	820	940	1,040	1,100	1,170	1,250	1,280	1,340	10,260
Weighted average number of persons per household	1.4	1.5	1.7	2.1	2.4	2.5	2.7	2.9	3.0	3.2	2.3

Commodity or service					Percentage of total expenditure						
1 Food & non-alcoholic drinks	**13.7**	**14.8**	**13.2**	**12.8**	**12.4**	**12.7**	**12.6**	**11.6**	**10.6**	**9.2**	**11.8**
1.1 Food	12.5	13.6	12.1	11.6	11.2	11.5	11.4	10.6	9.7	8.4	10.7
1.1.1 Bread, rice and cereals	1.2	1.3	1.2	1.1	1.1	1.1	1.1	1.0	0.9	0.8	1.0
1.1.2 Pasta products	0.1	0.1	0.1	0.1	0.1	0.1	0.1	0.1	0.1	0.1	0.1
1.1.3 Buns, cakes, biscuits etc.	0.9	1.0	0.9	0.9	0.8	0.8	0.8	0.8	0.7	0.6	0.8
1.1.4 Pastry (savoury)	0.2	0.2	0.2	0.2	0.2	0.2	0.2	0.2	0.2	0.2	0.2
1.1.5 Beef (fresh, chilled or frozen)	0.4	0.4	0.4	0.4	0.3	0.4	0.3	0.3	0.3	0.3	0.3
1.1.6 Pork (fresh, chilled or frozen)	0.1	0.1	0.1	0.1	0.1	0.1	0.1	0.1	0.1	0.1	0.1
1.1.7 Lamb (fresh, chilled or frozen)	0.1	0.1	0.1	0.1	0.1	0.1	0.1	0.1	0.1	0.1	0.1
1.1.8 Poultry (fresh, chilled or frozen)	0.4	0.5	0.4	0.4	0.5	0.4	0.5	0.4	0.4	0.4	0.4
1.1.9 Bacon and ham	0.2	0.2	0.2	0.1	0.2	0.2	0.2	0.1	0.1	0.1	0.1
1.1.10 Other meat and meat preparations	1.5	1.8	1.6	1.4	1.3	1.4	1.3	1.4	1.1	0.9	1.3
1.1.11 Fish and fish products	0.7	0.7	0.6	0.6	0.6	0.6	0.6	0.5	0.5	0.5	0.6
1.1.12 Milk	0.5	0.6	0.4	0.5	0.4	0.4	0.3	0.3	0.3	0.2	0.4
1.1.13 Cheese and curd	0.5	0.4	0.4	0.4	0.4	0.4	0.5	0.4	0.4	0.3	0.4
1.1.14 Eggs	0.2	0.2	0.2	0.2	0.1	0.1	0.2	0.1	0.1	0.1	0.1
1.1.15 Other milk products	0.6	0.6	0.5	0.6	0.5	0.5	0.5	0.4	0.4	0.4	0.5
1.1.16 Butter	0.1	0.1	0.1	0.1	0.1	0.1	0.1	0.1	0.1	0.1	0.1
1.1.17 Margarine, other vegetable fats and peanut butter	0.2	0.2	0.2	0.1	0.1	0.1	0.1	0.1	0.1	0.1	0.1
1.1.18 Cooking oils and fats	0.1	0.1	0.1	0.1	0.1	0.1	0.1	0.1	0.1	0.1	0.1
1.1.19 Fresh fruit	0.9	0.9	0.9	0.8	0.8	0.8	0.7	0.7	0.7	0.6	0.7
1.1.20 Other fresh, chilled or frozen fruits	0.1	0.1	0.1	0.1	0.1	0.1	0.1	0.1	0.1	0.1	0.1
1.1.21 Dried fruit and nuts	0.1	0.2	0.2	0.1	0.2	0.2	0.2	0.1	0.1	0.2	0.2
1.1.22 Preserved fruit and fruit based products	0.0	0.0	0.0	0.0	0.0	0.0	0.0	0.0	0.0	0.0	0.0
1.1.23 Fresh vegetables	0.9	0.9	0.8	0.8	0.8	0.8	0.8	0.8	0.8	0.7	0.8
1.1.24 Dried vegetables	[0.0]	[0.0]	[0.0]	0.0	[0.0]	0.0	0.0	0.0	0.0	0.0	0.0
1.1.25 Other preserved or processed vegetables	0.4	0.4	0.4	0.4	0.3	0.4	0.4	0.4	0.4	0.4	0.4
1.1.26 Potatoes	0.1	0.2	0.1	0.1	0.1	0.1	0.1	0.1	0.1	0.1	0.1
1.1.27 Other tubers and products of tuber vegetables	0.4	0.5	0.4	0.4	0.4	0.4	0.4	0.4	0.3	0.2	0.4
1.1.28 Sugar and sugar products	0.1	0.1	0.1	0.1	0.1	0.1	0.1	0.1	0.1	0.0	0.1
1.1.29 Jams, marmalades	0.1	0.1	0.1	0.1	0.1	0.1	0.1	0.1	0.1	0.0	0.1
1.1.30 Chocolate	0.5	0.6	0.5	0.5	0.4	0.5	0.5	0.4	0.4	0.3	0.4
1.1.31 Confectionery products	0.2	0.2	0.2	0.2	0.2	0.2	0.2	0.2	0.1	0.1	0.2
1.1.32 Edible ices and ice cream	0.2	0.2	0.2	0.2	0.2	0.2	0.2	0.2	0.2	0.1	0.2
1.1.33 Other food products	0.6	0.6	0.5	0.5	0.6	0.6	0.6	0.5	0.5	0.5	0.5
1.2 Non-alcoholic drinks	1.2	1.2	1.1	1.1	1.2	1.2	1.2	1.1	0.9	0.8	1.1
1.2.1 Coffee	0.2	0.3	0.3	0.3	0.2	0.2	0.2	0.2	0.2	0.2	0.2
1.2.2 Tea	0.1	0.1	0.1	0.1	0.1	0.1	0.1	0.1	0.1	0.1	0.1
1.2.3 Cocoa and powdered chocolate	0.0	0.0	0.0	0.0	0.0	0.0	0.0	0.0	0.0	0.0	0.0
1.2.4 Fruit and vegetable juices (inc. fruit squash)	0.2	0.2	0.2	0.2	0.2	0.2	0.2	0.2	0.2	0.2	0.2
1.2.5 Mineral or spring waters	0.1	0.1	0.1	0.1	0.1	0.1	0.1	0.1	0.1	0.1	0.1
1.2.6 Soft drinks (inc. fizzy and ready to drink fruit drinks)	0.5	0.5	0.5	0.5	0.6	0.6	0.6	0.5	0.4	0.3	0.5

Note: The commodity and service categories are not comparable to those in publications before 2001-02.
The numbering system is sequential, it does not use actual COICOP codes.
Please see background notes for symbols and conventions used in this report.

Table 3.2

Detailed household expenditure as a percentage of total expenditure by disposable income decile group (cont.)

UK, financial year ending 2022

	Lowest ten per cent	Second decile group	Third decile group	Fourth decile group	Fifth decile group	Sixth decile group	Seventh decile group	Eighth decile group	Ninth decile group	Highest ten per cent	All house-holds
Commodity or service					Percentage of total expenditure						
2 Alcoholic drink, tobacco & narcotics	**3.3**	**3.2**	**2.8**	**2.1**	**2.4**	**2.3**	**2.1**	**2.3**	**2.1**	**1.9**	**2.3**
2.1 Alcoholic drinks	2.1	1.8	2.0	1.6	1.7	1.9	1.7	1.9	1.8	1.6	1.8
2.1.1 Spirits and liqueurs (brought home)	0.6	0.5	0.5	0.4	0.5	0.5	0.4	0.4	0.4	0.3	0.4
2.1.2 Wines, fortified wines (brought home)	0.8	0.8	0.8	0.8	0.8	0.8	0.8	0.9	1.0	0.9	0.9
2.1.3 Beer, lager, ciders and perry (brought home)	0.7	0.5	0.6	0.4	0.5	0.6	0.5	0.6	0.4	0.4	0.5
2.1.4 Alcopops (brought home)	..	..	..	..	..	[0.0]	..	..	..	[0.0]	0.0
2.2 Tobacco and narcotics	1.3	1.4	0.8	0.5	0.7	0.5	0.4	0.5	0.3	0.3	0.5
2.2.1 Cigarettes	0.7	1.0	0.6	0.3	0.5	0.3	0.3	0.3	0.2	0.2	0.4
2.2.2 Cigars, other tobacco products and narcotics	0.6	0.4	0.2	0.3	0.2	0.1	0.1	0.1	0.1	0.1	0.2
3 Clothing & footwear	**2.6**	**2.8**	**2.7**	**3.0**	**3.1**	**3.3**	**3.1**	**4.4**	**3.3**	**3.6**	**3.3**
3.1 Clothing	2.3	2.4	2.3	2.5	2.6	2.8	2.4	3.7	2.6	2.9	2.7

Table 3.2
Detailed household expenditure as a percentage of total expenditure by disposable income decile group (cont.)
UK, financial year ending 2022

	Lowest ten per cent	Second decile group	Third decile group	Fourth decile group	Fifth decile group	Sixth decile group	Seventh decile group	Eighth decile group	Ninth decile group	Highest ten per cent	All house-holds
Commodity or service						Percentage of total expenditure					
3.1.1 Men's outer garments	0.5	0.5	0.5	0.4	0.6	0.7	0.5	0.9	0.6	0.9	0.7
3.1.2 Men's under garments	[0.0]	0.1	0.1	0.0	0.1	0.1	0.1	0.1	0.1	0.1	0.1
3.1.3 Women's outer garments	1.0	1.2	1.1	1.3	1.0	1.1	1.0	1.8	1.0	1.3	1.2
3.1.4 Women's under garments	0.2	0.2	0.2	0.1	0.3	0.3	0.2	0.3	0.2	0.2	0.2
3.1.5 Boys' outer garments (5-15)	..	[0.1]	..	0.1	[0.1]	0.1	0.1	0.1	0.1	0.1	0.1
3.1.6 Girls' outer garments (5-15)	[0.1]	[0.1]	[0.1]	0.2	0.2	0.2	0.2	0.2	0.2	0.2	0.2
3.1.7 Infants' outer garments (under 5)	[0.1]		..	[0.2]	[0.1]	0.1	0.1	0.1	0.1	[0.0]	0.1
3.1.8 Children's under garments (under 16)	..	[0.0]	[0.0]	0.1	0.1	0.1	0.1	0.1	0.1	0.0	0.1
3.1.9 Accessories	0.1	0.1	0.1	0.1	0.1	0.1	0.2	0.1	0.1	0.1	0.1
3.1.10 Haberdashery and clothing hire	[0.0]	[0.0]	0.1	[0.0]	0.0	[0.0]	0.1	[0.0]	0.0	0.1	0.0
3.1.11 Dry cleaners, laundry and dyeing	[0.1]	..	[0.0]	..	..	..	..	[0.0]	..	[0.0]	0.0
3.2 Footwear	0.2	0.4	0.5	0.5	0.5	0.5	0.6	0.8	0.7	0.7	0.6
4 Housing (net)[1], fuel & power	**25.1**	**25.2**	**23.2**	**20.6**	**19.0**	**17.7**	**15.9**	**14.4**	**12.0**	**11.6**	**16.6**
4.1 Actual rentals for housing	25.8	22.3	16.3	12.8	11.1	9.7	8.3	6.6	4.6	4.8	9.8
4.1.1 Gross rent	25.6	22.3	16.3	12.8	11.1	9.7	8.3	6.6	4.6	4.8	9.7
4.1.2 less housing benefit, rebates & allowances rec'd	13.3	9.8	3.5	1.7	2.0	0.3	0.5	[0.1]	..	..	1.8
4.1.3 Net rent[2]	12.3	12.5	12.8	11.1	9.0	9.4	7.8	6.5	4.6	4.8	7.9
4.1.4 Second dwelling rent	..	:	:	:	..	:	:	:	:	..	..
4.2 Maintenance and repair of dwelling	1.4	2.0	1.6	1.7	2.2	1.6	1.7	1.9	1.9	2.0	1.8
4.3 Water supply and miscellaneous services relating to the dwelling	3.5	3.3	2.4	2.1	2.3	1.9	1.7	1.8	1.6	1.4	2.0
4.4 Electricity, gas and other fuels	7.8	7.4	6.4	5.7	5.4	4.8	4.7	4.2	3.8	3.5	4.9
4.4.1 Electricity	4.3	4.2	3.3	3.0	2.9	2.7	2.5	2.2	2.0	1.8	2.6
4.4.2 Gas	2.9	2.9	2.7	2.5	2.2	2.0	1.9	1.8	1.6	1.5	2.0
4.4.3 Other fuels	0.6	0.3	0.4	0.3	0.3	0.2	0.3	0.2	0.2	0.2	0.3

Note: The commodity and service categories are not comparable to those in publications before 2001-02.
The numbering system is sequential, it does not use actual COICOP codes.
Please see background notes for symbols and conventions used in this report.

1 Excluding mortgage interest payments, council tax and Northern Ireland rates. Mortgage interest payments can be found in category 13.

2 The figure included in total expenditure is net rent as opposed to gross rent.

Table 3.2
Detailed household expenditure as a percentage of total expenditure by disposable income decile group (cont.)
UK, financial year ending 2022

	Lowest ten per cent	Second decile group	Third decile group	Fourth decile group	Fifth decile group	Sixth decile group	Seventh decile group	Eighth decile group	Ninth decile group	Highest ten per cent	All house-holds
Commodity or service						Percentage of total expenditure					
5 Household goods & services	**6.5**	**7.0**	**6.9**	**5.8**	**6.3**	**6.8**	**6.2**	**6.6**	**6.9**	**6.6**	**6.6**
5.1 Furniture and furnishings, carpets and other floor coverings	3.5	3.2	3.7	2.3	3.4	3.2	2.9	3.5	3.7	3.6	3.4
5.1.1 Furniture and furnishings	2.6	2.0	3.1	1.8	2.9	2.3	2.3	2.9	3.3	2.9	2.7
5.1.2 Floor coverings	0.9	1.2	0.6	0.5	0.5	1.0	0.6	0.7	0.5	0.7	0.7
5.2 Household textiles	0.3	0.6	0.3	0.4	0.3	0.5	0.4	0.4	0.4	0.3	0.4
5.3 Household appliances	0.2	0.8	0.6	0.6	0.5	0.7	0.8	0.7	0.6	0.5	0.6
5.4 Glassware, tableware and household utensils	0.4	0.4	0.3	0.4	0.3	0.4	0.5	0.4	0.4	0.3	0.4
5.5 Tools and equipment for house and garden	0.5	0.5	0.5	0.6	0.5	0.8	0.5	0.6	0.5	0.6	0.6
5.6 Goods and services for routine household maintenance	1.6	1.6	1.4	1.6	1.3	1.2	1.1	1.0	1.2	1.3	1.3
5.6.1 Cleaning materials	0.6	0.7	0.6	0.6	0.5	0.6	0.5	0.5	0.5	0.4	0.5
5.6.2 Household goods and hardware	0.4	0.4	0.4	0.4	0.4	0.4	0.4	0.4	0.4	0.3	0.4
5.6.3 Domestic services, carpet cleaning, hire/repair of furniture/furnishings	0.6	0.5	0.4	0.7	0.4	0.2	0.2	0.2	0.3	0.6	0.4
6 Health	**1.8**	**1.4**	**2.4**	**2.0**	**1.7**	**1.6**	**1.5**	**1.2**	**1.6**	**2.0**	**1.7**
6.1 Medical products, appliances and equipment	0.8	0.7	1.3	1.0	1.3	0.8	1.0	0.6	1.0	0.8	0.9
6.1.1 Medicines, prescriptions, healthcare products etc.	0.5	0.5	0.5	0.6	1.1	0.5	0.5	0.4	0.4	0.5	0.5
6.1.2 Spectacles, lenses, accessories and repairs	[0.2]	[0.2]	0.8	0.4	0.2	0.2	0.4	0.2	0.5	0.3	0.3
6.2 Hospital services	1.1	0.7	1.1	1.1	0.4	0.8	0.5	0.6	0.7	1.2	0.8
7 Transport	**10.0**	**10.1**	**10.1**	**13.0**	**13.4**	**14.0**	**14.6**	**15.6**	**15.3**	**16.2**	**14.1**
7.1 Purchase of vehicles	3.7	2.5	3.0	5.7	4.8	6.0	4.9	6.8	7.1	7.7	5.8
7.1.1 Purchase of new cars and vans	..	[0.9]	..	1.8	1.6	1.3	1.5	1.6	2.5	3.4	1.9
7.1.2 Purchase of second hand cars or vans	3.3	1.6	2.5	3.8	3.2	4.7	3.1	5.0	4.3	4.1	3.8
7.1.3 Purchase of motorcycles and other vehicles	..	:	..	..	..	..	[0.3]	[0.2]	[0.3]	[0.2]	0.2
7.2 Operation of personal transport	4.9	4.8	5.4	5.5	6.1	6.0	7.0	6.3	5.7	5.5	5.8
7.2.1 Spares and accessories	0.5	[0.4]	0.5	0.3	0.5	0.3	0.9	0.5	0.4	0.7	0.5
7.2.2 Petrol, diesel and other motor oils	2.9	2.9	3.2	3.5	3.9	3.9	4.1	4.0	3.4	3.2	3.6
7.2.3 Repairs and servicing	1.3	1.2	1.3	1.3	1.4	1.3	1.6	1.4	1.5	1.1	1.3
7.2.4 Other motoring costs	0.2	0.3	0.4	0.4	0.4	0.4	0.4	0.3	0.4	0.4	0.4
7.3 Transport services	1.4	2.8	1.7	1.9	2.4	2.0	2.7	2.5	2.5	3.0	2.4
7.3.1 Rail and tube fares	0.2	0.2	0.2	0.2	0.4	0.2	0.4	0.3	0.4	0.4	0.3
7.3.2 Bus and coach fares	0.2	0.3	0.2	0.2	0.2	0.2	0.2	0.1	0.1	0.1	0.1
7.3.3 Combined fares	..	:	..	..	..	..	..	..	..	..	[0.0]
7.3.4 Other travel and transport	0.9	2.3	1.3	1.6	1.9	1.6	2.1	2.1	2.0	2.5	1.9
8 Communication	**4.9**	**4.9**	**4.6**	**4.3**	**4.5**	**4.4**	**4.2**	**4.3**	**3.4**	**3.0**	**4.0**
8.1 Postal services	0.2	0.2	0.1	0.2	0.1	0.1	0.1	0.1	0.1	0.1	0.1
8.2 Telephone and telefax equipment	[0.5]	[0.1]	[0.1]	[0.1]	0.3	0.4	0.2	0.2	0.1	0.1	0.2
8.3 Telephone and telefax services[3]	1.6	1.6	1.4	1.5	1.7	1.7	1.8	1.9	1.6	1.4	1.6
8.4 Internet subscription fees (ex. combined packages)	0.3	0.2	0.2	0.2	0.2	0.2	0.2	0.1	0.1	0.1	0.2
8.5 Combined telecom services[4]	2.3	2.8	2.6	2.3	2.1	2.0	1.9	1.8	1.5	1.2	1.9

Note: The commodity and service categories are not comparable to those in publications before 2001-02.
The numbering system is sequential, it does not use actual COICOP codes.
Please see background notes for symbols and conventions used in this report.

3 For FYE 2019 onwards, excludes payments made as part of a combined bill.

4 New for FYE 2019 onwards. This encompasses all telecoms bills that include more than one service. Due to the nature of combined packages, this also includes packages that includes television services.

Table 3.2
Detailed household expenditure as a percentage of total expenditure by disposable income decile group (cont.)
UK, financial year ending 2022

Commodity or service	Lowest ten per cent	Second decile group	Third decile group	Fourth decile group	Fifth decile group	Sixth decile group	Seventh decile group	Eighth decile group	Ninth decile group	Highest ten per cent	All house-holds
	Percentage of total expenditure										
9 Recreation & culture	**10.1**	**8.5**	**9.0**	**10.8**	**9.4**	**10.4**	**11.9**	**9.4**	**11.3**	**12.0**	**10.6**
9.1 Audio-visual, photographic and information processing equipment	2.0	0.5	0.6	0.9	0.6	1.0	1.1	0.5	1.2	0.6	0.9
9.1.1 Audio equipment and accessories, CD players	[0.1]	[0.1]	[0.1]	0.1	0.1	0.1	0.2	0.2	0.2	0.2	0.2
9.1.2 TV, video and computers	1.7	0.3	0.5	0.8	0.5	0.8	1.0	0.3	1.0	0.4	0.7
9.1.3 Photographic, cine and optical equipment	..	..	..	..	..	..	..	..	..	[0.0]	0.0
9.2 Other major durables for recreation and culture	..	..	..	..	..	..	[1.2]	0.8	0.4	0.8	0.8
9.3 Other recreational items and equipment, gardens and pets	2.6	2.7	3.3	3.1	2.9	3.0	3.3	3.4	2.9	3.6	3.2
9.3.1 Games, toys and hobbies	0.3	0.6	0.7	0.6	0.6	0.7	0.6	0.5	0.6	0.4	0.6
9.3.2 Computer software and games	[0.0]	[0.2]	[0.1]	0.2	0.1	0.1	0.2	0.2	0.3	0.2	0.2
9.3.3 Equipment for sport, camping and open-air recreation	[0.3]	[0.1]	[0.3]	0.2	0.2	0.3	0.3	0.5	0.3	1.0	0.4
9.3.4 Horticultural goods, garden equipment and plants	0.7	0.8	0.8	0.9	0.9	0.7	1.0	0.6	0.6	0.6	0.7
9.3.5 Pets and pet food	1.3	1.0	1.4	1.2	1.2	1.2	1.3	1.6	1.2	1.4	1.3
9.4 Recreational and cultural services	2.5	2.3	2.8	2.9	2.9	2.8	3.0	2.7	3.4	3.5	3.0
9.4.1 Sports admissions, subscriptions, leisure class fees and equipment hire	0.5	0.3	0.6	0.9	0.8	0.9	0.9	1.0	1.3	1.8	1.1
9.4.2 Cinema, theatre and museums etc.	0.1	[0.1]	0.3	0.2	0.3	0.4	0.3	0.3	0.7	0.4	0.4
9.4.3 TV, video, satellite rental, cable subscriptions and TV licences[5]	1.3	1.4	1.3	1.2	1.3	1.1	1.2	1.0	0.9	0.9	1.1
9.4.4 Miscellaneous entertainments	0.2	0.2	0.2	0.2	0.2	0.2	0.3	0.2	0.3	0.4	0.3
9.4.5 Development of film, deposit for film development, passport photos, holiday and school photos	..	..	..	[0.0]	..	[0.0]	[0.0]	[0.0]	[0.2]	[0.0]	0.0
9.4.6 Gambling payments	0.3	0.2	0.4	0.3	0.2	0.2	0.2	0.1	0.1	0.1	0.2
9.5 Newspapers, books and stationery	1.1	1.0	1.0	0.9	0.8	0.9	0.8	0.7	0.8	0.7	0.8
9.5.1 Books	0.2	0.2	0.2	0.2	0.2	0.2	0.2	0.2	0.2	0.2	0.2
9.5.2 Diaries, address books, cards etc.	0.4	0.4	0.4	0.4	0.3	0.4	0.4	0.4	0.4	0.3	0.4
9.5.3 Newspapers	0.3	0.3	0.3	0.3	0.2	0.2	0.1	0.1	0.1	0.1	0.2
9.5.4 Magazines and periodicals	0.2	0.2	0.1	0.1	0.1	0.1	0.1	0.1	0.1	0.1	0.1
9.6 Package holidays	1.0	1.4	1.3	1.0	1.8	2.0	2.5	1.3	2.5	2.9	2.0
9.6.1 Package holidays - UK	..	0.5	[0.3]	[0.1]	0.3	0.5	[0.3]	[0.4]	0.4	0.3	0.3
9.6.2 Package holidays - abroad	[0.8]	0.8	0.9	0.8	1.5	1.5	2.2	0.9	2.1	2.6	1.6
10 Education	**[0.8]**	**..**	**[1.2]**	**[0.6]**	**[0.6]**	**[0.4]**	**[0.7]**	**[0.6]**	**1.3**	**2.0**	**1.0**
10.1 Education fees	..	..	[1.2]	[0.6]	[0.5]	..	[0.7]	[0.5]	1.2	1.9	0.9
10.2 Payments for school trips, other ad-hoc expenditure	..	..	:	..	..	..	..	..	..	..	0.1
11 Restaurants & hotels	**4.1**	**4.6**	**5.1**	**5.1**	**6.3**	**6.6**	**6.9**	**7.2**	**6.7**	**8.4**	**6.6**
11.1 Catering services	3.4	3.5	3.7	3.8	4.5	5.1	5.2	5.3	4.9	5.8	4.8
11.1.1 Restaurant and café meals	1.7	1.8	2.0	2.0	2.1	2.5	2.4	2.6	2.4	2.9	2.4
11.1.2 Alcoholic drinks (away from home)	0.6	0.8	0.7	0.6	0.7	0.8	1.0	1.1	1.0	1.3	0.9
11.1.3 Take away meals eaten at home	0.6	0.6	0.6	0.5	0.8	1.0	0.9	0.8	0.8	0.8	0.8
11.1.4 Other take-away and snack food	0.3	0.3	0.4	0.5	0.6	0.6	0.7	0.5	0.6	0.5	0.5
11.1.5 Contract catering (food) and canteens	..	[0.1]	[0.1]	0.1	0.2	0.2	0.2	0.2	0.1	0.3	0.2
11.2 Accommodation services	0.7	1.0	1.4	1.3	1.8	1.5	1.7	1.9	1.8	2.6	1.8
11.2.1 Holiday in the UK	0.6	0.9	1.4	1.2	1.3	1.4	1.4	1.8	1.6	2.0	1.5
11.2.2 Holiday abroad	..	..	..	[0.2]	[0.5]	..	[0.3]	[0.1]	0.2	0.6	0.3
11.2.3 Room hire	:	..	..	:	..	..	..	..	..	..	[0.0]

Note: The commodity and service categories are not comparable to those in publications before 2001-02.
The numbering system is sequential, it does not use actual COICOP codes.
Please see background notes for symbols and conventions used in this report.

5 For FYE 2019 onwards, excludes payments made as part of a combined bill.

Table 3.2
Detailed household expenditure as a percentage of total expenditure by disposable income decile group (cont.)
UK, financial year ending 2022

Commodity or service	Lowest ten per cent	Second decile group	Third decile group	Fourth decile group	Fifth decile group	Sixth decile group	Seventh decile group	Eighth decile group	Ninth decile group	Highest ten per cent	All house-holds
	Percentage of total expenditure										
12 Miscellaneous goods & services	**7.2**	**6.5**	**7.3**	**8.0**	**6.7**	**7.9**	**7.7**	**7.8**	**8.0**	**8.2**	**7.7**
12.1 Personal care	1.9	2.1	2.3	2.2	1.9	2.3	2.2	2.1	2.2	2.0	2.1
12.1.1 Hairdressing, beauty treatment	0.6	0.6	0.6	0.6	0.6	0.7	0.7	0.6	0.8	0.7	0.7
12.1.2 Toilet paper	0.2	0.2	0.2	0.2	0.2	0.2	0.2	0.1	0.2	0.1	0.2
12.1.3 Toiletries and soap	0.5	0.6	0.5	0.5	0.5	0.5	0.4	0.5	0.4	0.3	0.4
12.1.4 Baby toiletries and accessories (disposable)	0.1	0.1	0.1	0.1	0.1	0.1	0.1	0.1	0.1	0.0	0.1
12.1.5 Hair products, cosmetics and related electrical appliances	0.6	0.7	0.9	0.8	0.6	0.8	0.8	0.9	0.8	0.7	0.8
12.2 Personal effects	0.5	0.2	0.4	0.5	0.5	0.6	0.5	0.6	0.6	1.2	0.7
12.3 Social protection	..	..	..	..	[0.2]	[0.8]	[0.6]	[0.3]	[0.3]	0.7	0.4
12.4 Insurance	3.0	3.3	3.3	3.6	3.3	3.6	3.8	3.5	3.4	3.2	3.4
12.4.1 Household insurances - structural, contents and appliances	1.2	1.3	1.1	1.0	1.0	1.0	0.9	0.9	0.8	0.8	0.9

Table 3.2

Detailed household expenditure as a percentage of total expenditure by disposable income decile group (cont.)
UK, financial year ending 2022

Commodity or service		Lowest ten per cent	Second decile group	Third decile group	Fourth decile group	Fifth decile group	Sixth decile group	Seventh decile group	Eighth decile group	Ninth decile group	Highest ten per cent	All house-holds
						Percentage of total expenditure						
12.4.2	Medical insurance premiums[6]	0.1	0.2	0.3	0.6	0.4	0.5	0.4	0.4	0.7	0.6	0.5
12.4.3	Vehicle insurance including boat insurance	1.6	1.8	1.8	2.0	1.9	2.0	2.3	2.1	1.9	1.8	1.9
12.4.4	Non-package holiday, other travel insurance[7]	0.1	[0.0]	0.1	0.1	0.0	0.1	0.1	0.1	0.1	0.0	0.1
12.5	Other services	1.5	0.8	1.0	1.3	0.7	0.7	0.7	1.2	1.4	1.1	1.1
12.5.1	Moving house	1.0	[0.6]	0.5	0.4	0.4	0.4	0.3	0.5	0.8	0.6	0.5
12.5.2	Bank, building society, post office, credit card charges	0.1	0.1	0.1	0.1	0.1	0.1	0.1	0.1	0.1	0.1	0.1
12.5.3	Other services and professional fees	0.4	[0.1]	0.4	0.8	0.3	0.3	0.3	0.6	0.5	0.4	0.4
1-12	All expenditure groups	90.3	89.3	88.3	88.3	85.6	88.1	87.4	85.4	82.4	84.6	86.2
13	Other expenditure items	9.7	10.7	11.7	11.7	14.4	11.9	12.6	14.6	17.6	15.4	13.8
13.1	Housing: mortgage interest payments, council tax etc.	7.2	7.6	8.5	8.3	9.0	9.0	9.9	11.4	11.3	11.4	9.9
13.2	Licences, fines and transfers	0.8	0.6	0.7	0.7	0.8	0.8	0.8	0.8	0.7	0.9	0.8
13.3	Holiday spending	..	..	..	..	[0.4]	..	..	..	..	..	0.3
13.4	Money transfers and credit	1.6	2.5	2.5	2.3	4.3	1.9	1.7	2.3	5.1	2.8	2.9
13.4.1	Money, cash gifts given to children	..	:	..	..	..	..	..	..	[0.1]	[0.2]	0.1
13.4.2	Cash gifts and donations	1.4	2.4	2.2	2.0	4.0	1.7	1.5	2.0	4.8	2.5	2.6
13.4.3	Club instalment payments (child) and interest on credit cards	0.2	0.1	0.2	0.3	0.3	0.2	0.2	0.2	0.2	0.1	0.2
Total expenditure		100.0	100.0	100.0	100.0	100.0	100.0	100.0	100.0	100.0	100.0	100.0

Note: The commodity and service categories are not comparable to those in publications before 2001-02.

The numbering system is sequential, it does not use actual COICOP codes.

Please see background notes for symbols and conventions used in this report.

6 For FYE 2019 onwards, critical illness cover, personal accident insurance and other medical insurance are included here. They were not included in previous years.

7 For FYE 2019 onwards, information about insurance for non-package holiday and other travel insurance was collected in the questionnaire in addition to the diary. In previous years, this was based on diary data only.

Source: Office for National Statistics

Table 3.2E
Detailed household expenditure as a percentage of total expenditure by equivalised disposable income decile group (OECD-modified scale)

UK, financial year ending 2022

	Lowest ten per cent	Second decile group	Third decile group	Fourth decile group	Fifth decile group	Sixth decile group	Seventh decile group	Eighth decile group	Ninth decile group	Highest ten per cent	All house-holds
Lower boundary of group (£ per week)		196	263	315	369	429	494	569	663	829	
Weighted number of households (thousands)	2,850	2,850	2,850	2,850	2,850	2,850	2,850	2,850	2,850	2,850	28,500
Total number of households in sample	520	540	540	550	590	600	570	580	560	590	5,630
Total number of persons in sample	1,040	1,190	1,220	1,240	1,350	1,440	1,360	1,350	1,320	1,330	12,850
Total number of adults in sample	780	880	930	970	1,080	1,130	1,110	1,130	1,110	1,140	10,260
Weighted average number of persons per household	2.1	2.3	2.3	2.3	2.3	2.4	2.4	2.4	2.4	2.3	2.3

Commodity or service					Percentage of total expenditure						
1 Food & non-alcoholic drinks	**14.9**	**14.6**	**15.4**	**13.8**	**12.6**	**12.5**	**11.4**	**10.8**	**10.3**	**8.3**	**11.8**
1.1 Food	13.6	13.4	13.8	12.6	11.4	11.5	10.3	9.8	9.5	7.5	10.7
1.1.1 Bread, rice and cereals	1.3	1.4	1.3	1.2	1.2	1.1	1.0	0.9	0.9	0.7	1.0
1.1.2 Pasta products	0.1	0.1	0.1	0.1	0.1	0.1	0.1	0.1	0.1	0.1	0.1
1.1.3 Buns, cakes, biscuits etc.	1.0	1.0	1.1	0.9	0.9	0.9	0.8	0.7	0.7	0.5	0.8
1.1.4 Pastry (savoury)	0.2	0.2	0.2	0.2	0.2	0.2	0.2	0.2	0.2	0.1	0.2
1.1.5 Beef (fresh, chilled or frozen)	0.5	0.4	0.4	0.4	0.4	0.4	0.3	0.3	0.3	0.2	0.3
1.1.6 Pork (fresh, chilled or frozen)	0.1	0.1	0.1	0.1	0.1	0.1	0.1	0.1	0.1	0.0	0.1
1.1.7 Lamb (fresh, chilled or frozen)	0.1	0.1	0.1	0.1	0.1	0.1	0.1	0.1	0.1	0.1	0.1
1.1.8 Poultry (fresh, chilled or frozen)	0.5	0.5	0.5	0.5	0.4	0.4	0.4	0.4	0.4	0.3	0.4
1.1.9 Bacon and ham	0.2	0.2	0.2	0.2	0.2	0.1	0.2	0.1	0.1	0.1	0.1
1.1.10 Other meat and meat preparations	1.5	1.7	1.8	1.6	1.4	1.4	1.3	1.2	1.1	0.8	1.3
1.1.11 Fish and fish products	0.7	0.7	0.7	0.7	0.5	0.6	0.5	0.5	0.5	0.5	0.6
1.1.12 Milk	0.5	0.5	0.5	0.5	0.4	0.4	0.3	0.3	0.3	0.2	0.4
1.1.13 Cheese and curd	0.5	0.4	0.5	0.5	0.4	0.4	0.4	0.4	0.4	0.3	0.4
1.1.14 Eggs	0.2	0.2	0.2	0.2	0.1	0.1	0.1	0.1	0.1	0.1	0.1
1.1.15 Other milk products	0.6	0.6	0.6	0.6	0.5	0.5	0.5	0.4	0.4	0.3	0.5
1.1.16 Butter	0.1	0.1	0.1	0.1	0.1	0.1	0.1	0.1	0.1	0.1	0.1
1.1.17 Margarine, other vegetable fats and peanut butter	0.1	0.2	0.2	0.1	0.1	0.1	0.1	0.1	0.1	0.1	0.1
1.1.18 Cooking oils and fats	0.1	0.1	0.1	0.1	0.1	0.1	0.1	0.1	0.1	0.0	0.1
1.1.19 Fresh fruit	0.9	0.8	0.9	0.8	0.8	0.8	0.7	0.7	0.6	0.5	0.7
1.1.20 Other fresh, chilled or frozen fruits	0.1	0.1	0.1	0.1	0.1	0.1	0.1	0.1	0.1	0.1	0.1
1.1.21 Dried fruit and nuts	0.2	0.2	0.2	0.2	0.2	0.2	0.1	0.2	0.1	0.1	0.2
1.1.22 Preserved fruit and fruit based products	0.0	0.0	0.0	0.0	0.0	0.0	0.0	0.0	0.0	0.0	0.0
1.1.23 Fresh vegetables	1.0	0.9	0.9	0.8	0.8	0.8	0.8	0.8	0.8	0.7	0.8
1.1.24 Dried vegetables	0.0	0.1	[0.0]	0.0	0.0	0.0	0.0	0.0	0.0	0.0	0.0
1.1.25 Other preserved or processed vegetables	0.4	0.4	0.4	0.4	0.4	0.4	0.4	0.4	0.4	0.3	0.4
1.1.26 Potatoes	0.1	0.1	0.2	0.1	0.1	0.1	0.1	0.1	0.1	0.1	0.1
1.1.27 Other tubers and products of tuber vegetables	0.5	0.5	0.5	0.4	0.4	0.4	0.3	0.3	0.3	0.2	0.4
1.1.28 Sugar and sugar products	0.1	0.1	0.1	0.1	0.1	0.1	0.1	0.1	0.1	0.0	0.1
1.1.29 Jams, marmalades	0.1	0.1	0.1	0.1	0.1	0.1	0.1	0.1	0.0	0.1	0.1
1.1.30 Chocolate	0.5	0.6	0.6	0.5	0.5	0.5	0.4	0.4	0.3	0.3	0.4
1.1.31 Confectionery products	0.2	0.2	0.2	0.2	0.2	0.2	0.2	0.1	0.1	0.1	0.2
1.1.32 Edible ices and ice cream	0.2	0.2	0.2	0.2	0.2	0.2	0.1	0.1	0.1	0.1	0.2
1.1.33 Other food products	0.7	0.6	0.6	0.6	0.5	0.6	0.5	0.5	0.5	0.4	0.5
1.2 Non-alcoholic drinks	1.3	1.3	1.5	1.3	1.2	1.1	1.1	1.0	0.9	0.8	1.1
1.2.1 Coffee	0.2	0.2	0.2	0.2	0.2	0.2	0.2	0.2	0.2	0.2	0.2
1.2.2 Tea	0.1	0.1	0.1	0.1	0.1	0.1	0.1	0.1	0.1	0.1	0.1
1.2.3 Cocoa and powdered chocolate	0.0	0.0	0.0	0.0	0.0	0.0	0.0	0.0	0.0	0.0	0.0
1.2.4 Fruit and vegetable juices (inc. fruit squash)	0.2	0.3	0.2	0.3	0.2	0.2	0.2	0.2	0.2	0.2	0.2
1.2.5 Mineral or spring waters	0.1	0.1	0.1	0.1	0.1	0.1	0.1	0.1	0.1	0.1	0.1
1.2.6 Soft drinks (inc. fizzy and ready to drink fruit drinks)	0.6	0.5	0.8	0.6	0.5	0.5	0.4	0.4	0.3	0.3	0.5

Note: The commodity and service categories are not comparable to those in publications before 2001-02.
The numbering system is sequential, it does not use actual COICOP codes.
Please see background notes for symbols and conventions used in this report.

Table 3.2E
Detailed household expenditure as a percentage of total expenditure by equivalised disposable income decile group (OECD-modified scale) (cont)

UK, financial year ending 2022

	Lowest ten per cent	Second decile group	Third decile group	Fourth decile group	Fifth decile group	Sixth decile group	Seventh decile group	Eighth decile group	Ninth decile group	Highest ten per cent	All house-holds
Commodity or service					Percentage of total expenditure						
2 Alcoholic drink, tobacco & narcotics	**3.0**	**2.3**	**2.8**	**2.2**	**2.7**	**2.5**	**2.1**	**2.1**	**2.0**	**2.1**	**2.3**
2.1 Alcoholic drinks	1.8	1.3	1.8	1.6	2.0	2.0	1.7	1.7	1.7	1.8	1.8
2.1.1 Spirits and liqueurs (brought home)	0.5	0.4	0.4	0.4	0.6	0.4	0.4	0.4	0.4	0.3	0.4
2.1.2 Wines, fortified wines (brought home)	0.7	0.5	0.7	0.7	0.9	0.9	0.8	0.8	0.9	1.1	0.9
2.1.3 Beer, lager, ciders and perry (brought home)	0.7	0.4	0.6	0.5	0.5	0.6	0.5	0.5	0.5	0.3	0.5
2.1.4 Alcopops (brought home)	..	..	[0.0]	..	..	..	..	..	..	[0.0]	0.0
2.2 Tobacco and narcotics	1.2	0.9	1.0	0.6	0.7	0.6	0.4	0.4	0.2	0.3	0.5
2.2.1 Cigarettes	0.6	0.6	0.7	0.4	0.4	0.4	0.3	0.2	0.2	0.3	0.4
2.2.2 Cigars, other tobacco products and narcotics	0.6	0.3	0.3	0.2	0.2	0.2	0.1	0.1	0.1	0.1	0.2
3 Clothing & footwear	**3.0**	**3.5**	**2.9**	**3.5**	**3.1**	**3.2**	**3.4**	**3.6**	**3.5**	**3.2**	**3.3**
3.1 Clothing	2.6	2.9	2.5	3.1	2.7	2.6	2.6	2.9	2.8	2.7	2.7
3.1.1 Men's outer garments	0.5	0.5	0.5	0.6	0.5	0.6	0.6	0.9	0.7	0.9	0.7
3.1.2 Men's under garments	[0.0]	0.1	0.1	0.1	0.1	0.1	0.1	0.1	0.1	0.1	0.1

107

UK, financial year ending 2022	Lowest ten per cent	Second decile group	Third decile group	Fourth decile group	Fifth decile group	Sixth decile group	Seventh decile group	Eighth decile group	Ninth decile group	Highest ten per cent	All house-holds
Commodity or service						Percentage of total expenditure					
3.1.3 Women's outer garments	1.3	1.0	1.0	1.5	1.1	1.2	1.1	1.3	1.4	1.2	1.2
3.1.4 Women's under garments	0.2	0.2	0.2	0.3	0.3	0.2	0.2	0.1	0.2	0.2	0.2
3.1.5 Boys' outer garments (5-15)	[0.2]	0.2	0.1	0.1	0.1	0.1	0.1	0.1	0.1	0.1	0.1
3.1.6 Girls' outer garments (5-15)	0.1	0.4	0.2	0.2	0.2	0.2	0.1	0.1	0.1	0.1	0.2
3.1.7 Infants' outer garments (under 5)	[0.1]	[0.2]	[0.1]	[0.1]	0.1	0.1	0.1	[0.0]	0.1	[0.0]	0.1
3.1.8 Children's under garments (under 16)	[0.1]	0.1	0.1	0.1	0.1	0.1	0.1	0.0	0.0	0.0	0.1
3.1.9 Accessories	0.1	0.1	0.2	0.1	0.1	0.1	0.1	0.1	0.1	0.1	0.1
3.1.10 Haberdashery and clothing hire	[0.0]	[0.0]	[0.0]	[0.0]	0.0	0.0	0.1	[0.0]	0.0	0.1	0.0
3.1.11 Dry cleaners, laundry and dyeing	..	..	[0.0]	..	..	..	..	..	..	[0.1]	0.0
3.2 Footwear	0.4	0.6	0.5	0.4	0.5	0.6	0.8	0.7	0.7	0.5	0.6
4 Housing (net)[1], fuel & power	**25.4**	**25.3**	**21.9**	**20.4**	**18.4**	**14.9**	**16.1**	**12.3**	**13.8**	**11.7**	**16.6**
4.1 Actual rentals for housing	26.6	21.1	16.6	12.6	9.8	6.3	8.5	4.7	6.2	4.7	9.8
4.1.1 Gross rent	26.5	21.1	16.6	12.6	9.7	6.3	8.5	4.7	6.2	4.6	9.7
4.1.2 less housing benefit, rebates & allowances rec'd	12.5	6.6	5.4	1.9	0.7	0.1	0.2	0.1	0.1	0.1	1.8
4.1.3 Net rent[2]	14.0	14.5	11.2	10.8	9.0	6.2	8.3	4.6	6.1	4.6	7.9
4.1.4 Second dwelling rent	..	..	:	:	..	..	:	:	..	..	..
4.2 Maintenance and repair of dwelling	1.2	1.1	1.9	1.4	1.9	2.4	1.4	1.9	2.2	2.1	1.8
4.3 Water supply and miscellaneous services relating to the dwelling	2.7	2.7	2.5	2.3	2.1	1.9	1.7	1.8	1.7	1.5	2.0
4.4 Electricity, gas and other fuels	7.4	6.9	6.4	5.9	5.4	4.5	4.7	4.1	3.8	3.5	4.9
4.4.1 Electricity	4.1	3.8	3.4	3.2	2.9	2.4	2.4	2.2	2.0	1.9	2.6
4.4.2 Gas	2.9	2.7	2.6	2.4	2.3	2.0	1.9	1.7	1.6	1.4	2.0
4.4.3 Other fuels	0.4	0.4	0.3	0.3	0.3	0.1	0.3	0.2	0.2	0.3	0.3

Note: The commodity and service categories are not comparable to those in publications before 2001-02.

The numbering system is sequential, it does not use actual COICOP codes.

Please see background notes for symbols and conventions used in this report.

1 Excluding mortgage interest payments, council tax and Northern Ireland rates. Mortgage interest payments can be found in category 13.

2 The figure included in total expenditure is net rent as opposed to gross rent.

Table 3.2E

Detailed household expenditure as a percentage of total expenditure by equivalised disposable income decile group (OECD-modified scale) (cont)

UK, financial year ending 2022

Commodity or service	Lowest ten per cent	Second decile group	Third decile group	Fourth decile group	Fifth decile group	Sixth decile group	Seventh decile group	Eighth decile group	Ninth decile group	Highest ten per cent	All house-holds
						Percentage of total expenditure					
5 Household goods & services	**6.3**	**6.2**	**6.3**	**5.8**	**6.1**	**6.6**	**6.8**	**7.3**	**6.3**	**7.0**	**6.6**
5.1 Furniture and furnishings, carpets and other floor coverings	3.4	2.8	3.5	2.5	3.1	3.5	2.6	4.1	3.2	4.1	3.4
5.1.1 Furniture and furnishings	2.5	1.9	2.9	1.8	2.7	2.5	2.2	3.4	2.7	3.3	2.7
5.1.2 Floor coverings	0.9	0.9	0.6	0.7	0.4	1.0	0.5	0.7	0.5	0.8	0.7
5.2 Household textiles	0.3	0.4	0.3	0.4	0.4	0.5	0.5	0.4	0.4	0.3	0.4
5.3 Household appliances	0.3	0.6	0.2	0.8	0.6	0.3	1.5	0.4	0.7	0.5	0.6
5.4 Glassware, tableware and household utensils	0.4	0.3	0.3	0.4	0.4	0.4	0.4	0.4	0.3	0.3	0.4
5.5 Tools and equipment for house and garden	0.5	0.7	0.5	0.4	0.7	0.6	0.5	0.7	0.6	0.6	0.6
5.6 Goods and services for routine household maintenance	1.3	1.4	1.5	1.3	1.0	1.3	1.3	1.4	1.1	1.2	1.3
5.6.1 Cleaning materials	0.7	0.6	0.7	0.7	0.5	0.6	0.5	0.4	0.4	0.4	0.5
5.6.2 Household goods and hardware	0.4	0.4	0.4	0.4	0.4	0.4	0.4	0.4	0.3	0.3	0.4
5.6.3 Domestic services, carpet cleaning, hire/repair of furniture/furnishings	0.3	0.3	0.3	0.3	0.2	0.3	0.4	0.6	0.4	0.5	0.4
6 Health	**1.2**	**2.1**	**1.1**	**2.2**	**2.2**	**1.6**	**1.5**	**1.4**	**2.0**	**1.7**	**1.7**
6.1 Medical products, appliances and equipment	0.5	0.9	0.9	0.9	1.7	0.8	0.8	0.8	0.8	0.8	0.9
6.1.1 Medicines, prescriptions, healthcare products etc.	0.4	0.5	0.5	0.5	1.2	0.5	0.5	0.4	0.4	0.5	0.5
6.1.2 Spectacles, lenses, accessories and repairs	[0.1]	0.4	0.4	0.3	0.5	0.3	0.3	0.4	0.3	0.3	0.3
6.2 Hospital services	[0.7]	1.2	[0.2]	1.3	0.4	0.8	0.7	0.6	1.2	0.9	0.8
7 Transport	**10.8**	**11.1**	**11.4**	**13.2**	**13.4**	**14.8**	**13.8**	**15.5**	**15.1**	**16.1**	**14.1**
7.1 Purchase of vehicles	3.8	3.6	3.7	5.0	4.9	6.9	5.5	6.7	6.3	7.8	5.8
7.1.1 Purchase of new cars and vans	[0.7]	[0.5]	[1.0]	1.0	1.1	1.9	1.5	2.3	1.7	3.9	1.9
7.1.2 Purchase of second hand cars or vans	2.9	3.0	2.6	4.0	3.7	4.9	3.8	4.3	4.3	3.6	3.8
7.1.3 Purchase of motorcycles and other vehicles	..	..	..	..	..	..	..	[0.2]	[0.3]	[0.2]	0.2
7.2 Operation of personal transport	5.0	5.2	5.5	6.0	6.7	6.0	5.9	6.1	6.1	5.2	5.8
7.2.1 Spares and accessories	0.5	0.4	0.3	0.3	0.5	0.3	0.5	0.8	0.6	0.7	0.5
7.2.2 Petrol, diesel and other motor oils	3.2	3.5	3.5	4.1	4.1	3.8	3.6	3.8	3.6	2.9	3.6
7.2.3 Repairs and servicing	1.2	1.0	1.4	1.3	1.7	1.5	1.3	1.3	1.5	1.3	1.3
7.2.4 Other motoring costs	0.2	0.3	0.4	0.3	0.4	0.5	0.4	0.3	0.4	0.4	0.4
7.3 Transport services	2.0	2.4	2.2	2.2	1.8	1.9	2.4	2.6	2.6	3.1	2.4
7.3.1 Rail and tube fares	0.2	0.3	0.2	0.3	0.2	0.3	0.3	0.4	0.4	0.4	0.3
7.3.2 Bus and coach fares	0.3	0.2	0.2	0.3	0.2	0.1	0.1	0.1	0.1	0.0	0.1
7.3.3 Combined fares	..	:	..	..	:	..	..	..	..	..	[0.0]
7.3.4 Other travel and transport	1.5	1.8	1.8	1.6	1.4	1.5	1.9	2.1	2.1	2.6	1.9
8 Communication	**4.9**	**4.5**	**5.0**	**4.9**	**4.7**	**4.2**	**4.1**	**3.7**	**3.4**	**2.8**	**4.0**
8.1 Postal services	0.1	0.1	0.2	0.1	0.1	0.2	0.1	0.1	0.1	0.1	0.1
8.2 Telephone and telefax equipment	[0.4]	[0.2]	[0.2]	0.5	0.2	0.2	[0.2]	0.1	0.1	0.1	0.2
8.3 Telephone and telefax services[3]	1.8	1.7	1.9	1.8	2.0	1.7	1.7	1.6	1.5	1.2	1.6
8.4 Internet subscription fees (ex. combined packages)	0.3	0.2	0.2	0.2	0.1	0.2	0.1	0.1	0.1	0.1	0.2
8.5 Combined telecom services[4]	2.1	2.2	2.5	2.3	2.3	2.0	2.0	1.7	1.5	1.2	1.9

Note: The commodity and service categories are not comparable to those in publications before 2001-02.

The numbering system is sequential, it does not use actual COICOP codes.

Please see background notes for symbols and conventions used in this report.

3 For FYE 2019 onwards, excludes payments made as part of a combined bill.

4 New for FYE 2019. This encompasses all telecoms bills that include more than one service. Due to the nature of combined packages, this also includes packages that includes television services.

Table 3.2E
Detailed household expenditure as a percentage of total expenditure by equivalised disposable income decile group (OECD-modified scale) (cont)
UK, financial year ending 2022

Commodity or service	Lowest ten per cent	Second decile group	Third decile group	Fourth decile group	Fifth decile group	Sixth decile group	Seventh decile group	Eighth decile group	Ninth decile group	Highest ten per cent	All house-holds
					Percentage of total expenditure						
9 Recreation & culture	**10.1**	**7.8**	**9.6**	**9.0**	**9.3**	**10.8**	**12.8**	**10.8**	**9.9**	**12.5**	**10.6**
9.1 Audio-visual, photographic and information processing equipment	1.8	0.5	0.5	0.8	0.6	1.0	0.7	1.0	0.6	1.1	0.9
9.1.1 Audio equipment and accessories, CD players	[0.1]	[0.1]	0.1	0.1	0.1	0.1	0.1	0.3	0.2	0.2	0.2
9.1.2 TV, video and computers	1.6	0.4	0.4	0.7	0.5	0.9	0.5	0.7	0.3	0.8	0.7
9.1.3 Photographic, cine and optical equipment	..	..	..	..	..	..	..	..	..	[0.0]	0.0
9.2 Other major durables for recreation and culture	..	..	..	..	[0.4]	..	2.7	[0.7]	0.8	0.6	0.8
9.3 Other recreational items and equipment, gardens and pets	2.8	2.8	3.9	3.0	3.0	3.2	3.0	3.4	2.6	3.7	3.2
9.3.1 Games, toys and hobbies	0.6	0.8	1.2	0.6	0.5	0.6	0.5	0.5	0.4	0.4	0.6
9.3.2 Computer software and games	[0.2]	0.1	0.1	0.2	0.1	0.3	0.2	0.3	0.2	0.2	0.2
9.3.3 Equipment for sport, camping and open-air recreation	[0.2]	0.1	0.4	0.2	0.2	0.2	0.3	0.5	0.3	1.0	0.4
9.3.4 Horticultural goods, garden equipment and plants	0.6	0.8	0.7	0.9	0.7	0.7	0.7	0.9	0.6	0.7	0.7
9.3.5 Pets and pet food	1.3	1.0	1.4	1.2	1.4	1.4	1.3	1.2	1.1	1.4	1.3
9.4 Recreational and cultural services	2.6	2.3	2.9	2.9	2.7	3.6	2.8	3.0	3.2	3.4	3.0
9.4.1 Sports admissions, subscriptions, leisure class fees and equipment hire	0.7	0.5	0.8	0.8	0.7	1.2	1.1	1.0	1.1	1.7	1.1
9.4.2 Cinema, theatre and museums etc.	[0.1]	[0.1]	0.2	0.3	0.3	0.7	0.3	0.4	0.4	0.3	0.4
9.4.3 TV, video, satellite rental, cable subscriptions and TV licences[5]	1.3	1.3	1.3	1.2	1.3	1.1	1.0	1.1	1.0	0.9	1.1
9.4.4 Miscellaneous entertainments	0.2	0.1	0.3	0.2	0.2	0.3	0.1	0.2	0.3	0.4	0.3
9.4.5 Development of film, deposit for film development, passport photos, holiday and school photos	..	[0.0]	..	[0.0]	[0.0]	[0.0]	[0.0]	[0.0]	[0.2]	[0.0]	0.0
9.4.6 Gambling payments	0.3	0.3	0.2	0.3	0.2	0.3	0.2	0.2	0.2	0.1	0.2
9.5 Newspapers, books and stationery	0.9	0.9	0.9	0.9	0.8	0.9	0.9	0.7	0.8	0.7	0.8
9.5.1 Books	0.2	0.2	0.2	0.2	0.2	0.2	0.2	0.2	0.3	0.2	0.2
9.5.2 Diaries, address books, cards etc.	0.4	0.3	0.4	0.4	0.3	0.5	0.4	0.3	0.3	0.3	0.4
9.5.3 Newspapers	0.2	0.3	0.2	0.2	0.2	0.2	0.2	0.1	0.2	0.1	0.2
9.5.4 Magazines and periodicals	0.1	0.1	0.1	0.1	0.1	0.1	0.1	0.1	0.1	0.1	0.1
9.6 Package holidays[4]	0.9	1.0	1.2	1.2	1.8	1.9	2.7	1.9	1.9	3.2	2.0
9.6.1 Package holidays - UK	[0.3]	[0.4]	[0.3]	[0.3]	[0.3]	0.4	0.5	[0.2]	0.3	0.4	0.3
9.6.2 Package holidays - abroad	[0.6]	[0.6]	0.9	0.9	1.5	1.5	2.2	1.8	1.6	2.8	1.6
10 Education	**[1.1]**	**[0.4]**	**[0.5]**	**[0.6]**	**[1.0]**	**[0.7]**	**[1.1]**	**[0.6]**	**1.1**	**1.7**	**1.0**
10.1 Education fees	[1.0]	..	[0.5]	[0.6]	[0.9]	[0.6]	[1.1]	[0.6]	1.1	1.6	0.9
10.2 Payments for school trips, other ad-hoc expenditure	..	..	..	..	..	..	..	..	..	..	0.1
11 Restaurants & hotels	**4.3**	**4.7**	**5.8**	**5.7**	**5.9**	**6.1**	**6.6**	**7.5**	**8.1**	**7.7**	**6.6**
11.1 Catering services	3.4	3.7	4.2	4.5	4.3	4.7	4.8	5.4	5.9	5.1	4.8
11.1.1 Restaurant and café meals	1.5	1.7	1.9	2.2	2.2	2.5	2.4	2.7	3.0	2.6	2.4
11.1.2 Alcoholic drinks (away from home)	0.6	0.5	0.7	0.7	0.7	0.8	1.0	1.2	1.2	1.2	0.9
11.1.3 Take away meals eaten at home	0.7	0.7	0.7	0.9	0.7	0.8	0.8	0.8	0.8	0.8	0.8
11.1.4 Other take-away and snack food	0.6	0.6	0.6	0.7	0.6	0.6	0.5	0.6	0.6	0.4	0.5
11.1.5 Contract catering (food) and canteens	[0.1]	0.2	0.3	0.1	0.1	0.2	0.2	0.2	0.3	0.1	0.2
11.2 Accommodation services	0.8	0.9	1.7	1.1	1.6	1.4	1.7	2.0	2.2	2.6	1.8
11.2.1 Holiday in the UK	0.7	0.9	1.5	1.1	1.4	1.2	1.6	1.6	1.9	2.2	1.5
11.2.2 Holiday abroad	..	..	..	..	..	[0.1]	[0.2]	[0.4]	0.3	0.5	0.3
11.2.3 Room hire	..	:	..	..	..	..	..	:	..	..	[0.0]

Note: The commodity and service categories are not comparable to those in publications before 2001-02.
The numbering system is sequential, it does not use actual COICOP codes.
Please see background notes for symbols and conventions used in this report.

5 For FYE 2019 onwards, excludes payments made as part of a combined bill.

Table 3.2E
Detailed household expenditure as a percentage of total expenditure by equivalised disposable income decile group (OECD-modified scale) (cont)
UK, financial year ending 2022

Commodity or service	Lowest ten per cent	Second decile group	Third decile group	Fourth decile group	Fifth decile group	Sixth decile group	Seventh decile group	Eighth decile group	Ninth decile group	Highest ten per cent	All house-holds
					Percentage of total expenditure						
12 Miscellaneous goods & services	**6.1**	**7.6**	**7.3**	**7.3**	**7.4**	**8.9**	**7.3**	**7.7**	**7.6**	**8.3**	**7.7**
12.1 Personal care	1.8	2.4	2.2	2.4	2.2	2.3	2.1	2.2	2.0	1.8	2.1
12.1.1 Hairdressing, beauty treatment	0.4	0.5	0.6	0.7	0.6	0.8	0.7	0.7	0.7	0.8	0.7
12.1.2 Toilet paper	0.3	0.2	0.2	0.3	0.2	0.2	0.2	0.2	0.1	0.1	0.2
12.1.3 Toiletries and soap	0.5	0.6	0.6	0.5	0.5	0.5	0.4	0.4	0.3	0.3	0.4
12.1.4 Baby toiletries and accessories (disposable)	0.1	0.2	0.1	0.1	0.1	0.1	0.1	0.1	0.1	0.0	0.1
12.1.5 Hair products, cosmetics and related electrical appliances	0.6	1.0	0.7	0.8	0.8	0.8	0.8	0.8	0.7	0.6	0.8
12.2 Personal effects	0.5	0.5	0.5	0.5	0.5	0.5	0.5	0.6	0.6	1.3	0.7
12.3 Social protection	..	[0.4]	[0.3]	[0.2]	[0.2]	[1.1]	[0.4]	[0.3]	[0.4]	0.6	0.4

Table 3.2E

Detailed household expenditure as a percentage of total expenditure by equivalised disposable income decile group (OECD-modified scale) (cont)

UK, financial year ending 2022

	Lowest ten per cent	Second decile group	Third decile group	Fourth decile group	Fifth decile group	Sixth decile group	Seventh decile group	Eighth decile group	Ninth decile group	Highest ten per cent	All house-holds
Commodity or service						Percentage of total expenditure					
12.4 Insurance	2.9	3.4	3.5	3.4	3.8	3.7	3.3	3.5	3.3	3.3	3.4
12.4.1 Household insurances - structural, contents and appliances	0.9	0.9	1.1	0.9	1.1	1.0	0.9	1.0	0.8	0.9	0.9
12.4.2 Medical insurance premiums[6]	[0.1]	0.2	0.2	0.4	0.5	0.4	0.3	0.5	0.6	0.8	0.5
12.4.3 Vehicle insurance including boat insurance	1.9	2.1	2.1	2.1	2.1	2.2	2.1	2.0	1.8	1.5	1.9
12.4.4 Non-package holiday, other travel insurance[7]	[0.1]	0.1	0.0	0.1	0.0	0.1	0.1	0.1	0.1	0.1	0.1
12.5 Other services	1.0	0.9	0.9	0.7	0.7	1.4	1.0	1.1	1.2	1.2	1.1
12.5.1 Moving house	[0.6]	0.5	[0.5]	0.4	0.4	0.5	0.2	0.5	0.9	0.7	0.5
12.5.2 Bank, building society, post office, credit card charges	0.1	0.1	0.1	0.1	0.1	0.1	0.1	0.1	0.1	0.1	0.1
12.5.3 Other services and professional fees	0.3	0.3	0.3	0.2	0.2	0.7	0.7	0.6	0.2	0.5	0.4
1-12 All expenditure groups	**91.1**	**90.2**	**90.0**	**88.7**	**86.7**	**87.0**	**87.0**	**83.3**	**83.2**	**83.2**	**86.2**
13 Other expenditure items	**8.9**	**9.8**	**10.0**	**11.3**	**13.3**	**13.0**	**13.0**	**16.7**	**16.8**	**16.8**	**13.8**
13.1 Housing: mortgage interest payments, council tax etc.	6.7	7.2	7.9	8.2	9.9	9.9	9.7	11.7	11.4	11.6	9.9
13.2 Licences, fines and transfers	0.7	0.8	0.8	0.8	0.8	0.8	0.8	1.0	0.7	0.7	0.8
13.3 Holiday spending	..	..	..	..	..	..	..	..	..	..	0.3
13.4 Money transfers and credit	1.3	1.8	1.3	2.3	2.2	2.1	2.2	3.5	4.4	4.3	2.9
13.4.1 Money, cash gifts given to children	..	..	..	..	..	..	..	..	[0.1]	..	0.1
13.4.2 Cash gifts and donations	1.2	1.4	1.1	1.9	1.9	1.9	2.1	3.3	4.1	4.1	2.6
13.4.3 Club instalment payments (child) and interest on credit cards	0.1	0.4	0.1	0.3	0.3	0.2	0.2	0.2	0.2	0.1	0.2
Total expenditure	**100.0**	**100.0**	**100.0**	**100.0**	**100.0**	**100.0**	**100.0**	**100.0**	**100.0**	**100.0**	**100.0**

Note: The commodity and service categories are not comparable to those in publications before 2001-02.

The numbering system is sequential, it does not use actual COICOP codes.

Please see background notes for symbols and conventions used in this report.

6 For FYE 2019, critical illness cover, personal accident insurance and other medical insurance are included here. They were not included in previous years.

7 For FYE 2019, information about insurance for non-package holiday and other travel insurance was collected in the questionnaire in addition to the diary. In previous years, this was based on diary data only.

Source: Office for National Statistics

Table 3.2E5

Detailed household expenditure as a percentage of total expenditure by disposable equivalised income quintile group (OECD-modified scale)

UK, financial year ending 2022

	Lowest twenty per cent	Second quintile group	Third quintile group	Fourth quintile group	Highest twenty per cent	All house-holds
Lower boundary of group (£ per week)		263	369	494	663	
Weighted number of households (thousands)	5,710	5,690	5,700	5,700	5,700	28,500
Total number of households in sample	1,060	1,100	1,190	1,150	1,150	5,630
Total number of persons in sample	2,230	2,460	2,800	2,710	2,660	12,850
Total number of adults in sample	1,660	1,900	2,220	2,240	2,250	10,260
Weighted average number of persons per household	2.2	2.3	2.4	2.4	2.3	2.3
Commodity or service	Percentage of total expenditure (%)					
1 Food & non-alcoholic drinks	**14.8**	**14.5**	**12.5**	**11.1**	**9.2**	**11.8**
1.1 Food	13.5	13.2	11.4	10.0	8.4	10.7
1.1.1 Bread, rice and cereals	1.4	1.2	1.1	1.0	0.8	1.0
1.1.2 Pasta products	0.1	0.1	0.1	0.1	0.1	0.1
1.1.3 Buns, cakes, biscuits etc.	1.0	1.0	0.9	0.7	0.6	0.8
1.1.4 Pastry (savoury)	0.2	0.2	0.2	0.2	0.1	0.2
1.1.5 Beef (fresh, chilled or frozen)	0.4	0.4	0.4	0.3	0.2	0.3
1.1.6 Pork (fresh, chilled or frozen)	0.1	0.1	0.1	0.1	0.1	0.1
1.1.7 Lamb (fresh, chilled or frozen)	0.1	0.1	0.1	0.1	0.1	0.1
1.1.8 Poultry (fresh, chilled or frozen)	0.5	0.5	0.4	0.4	0.3	0.4
1.1.9 Bacon and ham	0.2	0.2	0.1	0.1	0.1	0.1
1.1.10 Other meat and meat preparations	1.6	1.7	1.4	1.2	1.0	1.3
1.1.11 Fish and fish products	0.7	0.7	0.6	0.5	0.5	0.6
1.1.12 Milk	0.5	0.5	0.4	0.3	0.2	0.4
1.1.13 Cheese and curd	0.5	0.5	0.4	0.4	0.3	0.4
1.1.14 Eggs	0.2	0.2	0.1	0.1	0.1	0.1
1.1.15 Other milk products	0.6	0.6	0.5	0.4	0.4	0.5
1.1.16 Butter	0.1	0.1	0.1	0.1	0.1	0.1
1.1.17 Margarine, other vegetable fats and peanut butter	0.2	0.1	0.1	0.1	0.1	0.1
1.1.18 Cooking oils and fats	0.1	0.1	0.1	0.1	0.1	0.1
1.1.19 Fresh fruit	0.8	0.9	0.8	0.7	0.6	0.7
1.1.20 Other fresh, chilled or frozen fruits	0.1	0.1	0.1	0.1	0.1	0.1
1.1.21 Dried fruit and nuts	0.2	0.2	0.2	0.2	0.1	0.2
1.1.22 Preserved fruit and fruit based products	0.0	0.0	0.0	0.0	0.0	0.0
1.1.23 Fresh vegetables	0.9	0.9	0.8	0.8	0.7	0.8
1.1.24 Dried vegetables	0.0	0.0	0.0	0.0	0.0	0.0
1.1.25 Other preserved or processed vegetables	0.4	0.4	0.4	0.4	0.3	0.4
1.1.26 Potatoes	0.1	0.1	0.1	0.1	0.1	0.1
1.1.27 Other tubers and products of tuber vegetables	0.5	0.5	0.4	0.3	0.2	0.4
1.1.28 Sugar and sugar products	0.1	0.1	0.1	0.1	0.0	0.1
1.1.29 Jams, marmalades	0.1	0.1	0.1	0.1	0.1	0.1
1.1.30 Chocolate	0.5	0.6	0.5	0.4	0.3	0.4
1.1.31 Confectionery products	0.2	0.2	0.2	0.1	0.1	0.2
1.1.32 Edible ices and ice cream	0.2	0.2	0.2	0.1	0.1	0.2
1.1.33 Other food products	0.6	0.6	0.6	0.5	0.5	0.5
1.2 Non-alcoholic drinks	1.3	1.4	1.1	1.0	0.8	1.1
1.2.1 Coffee	0.2	0.2	0.2	0.2	0.2	0.2
1.2.2 Tea	0.1	0.1	0.1	0.1	0.1	0.1
1.2.3 Cocoa and powdered chocolate	0.0	0.0	0.0	0.0	0.0	0.0
1.2.4 Fruit and vegetable juices (inc. fruit squash)	0.3	0.3	0.2	0.2	0.2	0.2
1.2.5 Mineral or spring waters	0.1	0.1	0.1	0.1	0.1	0.1
1.2.6 Soft drinks (inc. fizzy and ready to drink fruit drinks)	0.6	0.7	0.5	0.4	0.3	0.5

Note: The commodity and service categories are not comparable to those in publications before 2001-02
The numbering system is sequential, it does not use actual COICOP codes.
Please see background notes for symbols and conventions used in this report.

Source: Office for National Statistics

Table 3.2E5

Detailed household expenditure as a percentage of total expenditure by disposable equivalised income quintile group (OECD-modified scale)

UK, financial year ending 2022

	Lowest twenty per cent	Second quintile group	Third quintile group	Fourth quintile group	Highest twenty per cent	All house-holds
Commodity or service	Percentage of total expenditure (%)					
2 Alcoholic drink, tobacco & narcotics	**2.6**	**2.5**	**2.6**	**2.1**	**2.0**	**2.3**
2.1 Alcoholic drinks	1.6	1.7	2.0	1.7	1.8	1.8
2.1.1 Spirits and liqueurs (brought home)	0.4	0.4	0.5	0.4	0.3	0.4
2.1.2 Wines, fortified wines (brought home)	0.6	0.7	0.9	0.8	1.0	0.9
2.1.3 Beer, lager, ciders and perry (brought home)	0.5	0.6	0.6	0.5	0.4	0.5
2.1.4 Alcopops (brought home)	[0.00]	[0.00]	[0.00]	[0.00]	[0.00]	0.0
2.2 Tobacco and narcotics	1.1	0.8	0.6	0.4	0.3	0.5
2.2.1 Cigarettes	0.6	0.5	0.4	0.2	0.2	0.4
2.2.2 Cigars, other tobacco products and narcotics	0.5	0.2	0.2	0.1	0.1	0.2
3 Clothing & footwear	**3.3**	**3.2**	**3.2**	**3.5**	**3.4**	**3.3**
3.1 Clothing	2.7	2.8	2.6	2.7	2.7	2.7

Table 3.2E5

Detailed household expenditure as a percentage of total expenditure by disposable equivalised income quintile group (OECD-modified scale)

UK, financial year ending 2022

Commodity or service		Lowest twenty per cent	Second quintile group	Third quintile group	Fourth quintile group	Highest twenty per cent	All house-holds
		Percentage of total expenditure (%)					
3.1.1	Men's outer garments	0.5	0.6	0.5	0.8	0.8	0.7
3.1.2	Men's under garments	0.1	0.1	0.1	0.1	0.1	0.1
3.1.3	Women's outer garments	1.1	1.3	1.2	1.2	1.3	1.2
3.1.4	Women's under garments	0.2	0.2	0.2	0.2	0.2	0.2
3.1.5	Boys' outer garments (5-15)	0.2	0.1	0.1	0.1	0.1	0.1
3.1.6	Girls' outer garments (5-15)	0.3	0.2	0.2	0.1	0.1	0.2
3.1.7	Infants' outer garments (under 5)	0.1	0.1	0.1	0.1	0.1	0.1
3.1.8	Children's under garments (under 16)	0.1	0.1	0.1	0.0	0.0	0.1
3.1.9	Accessories	0.1	0.1	0.1	0.1	0.1	0.1
3.1.10	Haberdashery and clothing hire	0.0	0.0	0.0	0.1	0.0	0.0
3.1.11	Dry cleaners, laundry and dyeing	[0.00]	[0.00]	[0.00]	[0.00]	0.0	0.0
3.2	Footwear	0.5	0.5	0.5	0.8	0.6	0.6
4	**Housing (net)[1], fuel & power**	**25.3**	**21.1**	**16.5**	**14.1**	**12.6**	**16.6**
4.1	Actual rentals for housing	23.7	14.5	7.9	6.5	5.3	9.8
4.1.1	Gross rent	23.7	14.5	7.9	6.5	5.3	9.7
4.1.2	*less housing benefit, rebates & allowances rec'd*	9.4	3.5	0.4	0.1	0.1	1.8
4.1.3	Net rent[2]	14.2	11.0	7.5	6.4	5.2	7.9
4.1.4	Second dwelling rent	..	:	..	:	..	..
4.2	Maintenance and repair of dwelling	1.2	1.6	2.2	1.7	2.1	1.8
4.3	Water supply and miscellaneous services relating to the dwelling	2.7	2.4	2.0	1.8	1.6	2.0
4.4	Electricity, gas and other fuels	7.1	6.1	4.9	4.3	3.6	4.9
4.4.1	Electricity	3.9	3.3	2.6	2.3	1.9	2.6
4.4.2	Gas	2.8	2.5	2.1	1.8	1.5	2.0
4.4.3	Other fuels	0.4	0.3	0.2	0.2	0.2	0.3

Note: The commodity and service categories are not comparable to those in publications before 2001-02.
The numbering system is sequential, it does not use actual COICOP codes.
Please see background notes for symbols and conventions used in this report.
1 Excluding mortgage interest payments, council tax and Northern Ireland rates. Mortgage interest payments can be found in category 14.
2 The figure included in total expenditure is net rent as opposed to gross rent.

Source: Office for National Statistics

Table 3.2E5

Detailed household expenditure as a percentage of total expenditure by disposable equivalised income quintile group (OECD-modified scale)

UK, financial year ending 2022

Commodity or service		Lowest twenty per cent	Second quintile group	Third quintile group	Fourth quintile group	Highest twenty per cent	All house-holds
		Percentage of total expenditure (%)					
5	**Household goods & services**	**6.2**	**6.1**	**6.4**	**7.1**	**6.7**	**6.6**
5.1	Furniture and furnishings, carpets and other floor coverings	3.1	2.9	3.3	3.4	3.7	3.4
5.1.1	Furniture and furnishings	2.2	2.3	2.6	2.8	3.0	2.7
5.1.2	Floor coverings	0.9	0.6	0.7	0.6	0.7	0.7
5.2	Household textiles	0.4	0.4	0.4	0.4	0.3	0.4
5.3	Household appliances	0.5	0.5	0.4	0.9	0.6	0.6
5.4	Glassware, tableware and household utensils	0.3	0.4	0.4	0.4	0.3	0.4
5.5	Tools and equipment for house and garden	0.6	0.5	0.6	0.6	0.6	0.6
5.6	Goods and services for routine household maintenance	1.4	1.4	1.2	1.4	1.2	1.3
5.6.1	Cleaning materials	0.6	0.7	0.6	0.4	0.4	0.5
5.6.2	Household goods and hardware	0.4	0.4	0.4	0.4	0.3	0.4
5.6.3	Domestic services, carpet cleaning, hire/repair of furniture/furnishings	0.3	0.3	0.2	0.6	0.5	0.4
6	**Health**	**1.7**	**1.7**	**1.9**	**1.5**	**1.8**	**1.7**
6.1	Medical products, appliances and equipment	0.7	0.9	1.2	0.8	0.8	0.9
6.1.1	Medicines, prescriptions, healthcare products etc.	0.5	0.5	0.8	0.4	0.5	0.5
6.1.2	Spectacles, lenses, accessories and repairs	0.2	0.4	0.4	0.4	0.3	0.3
6.2	Hospital services	1.0	0.8	0.6	0.6	1.0	0.8
7	**Transport**	**11.0**	**12.4**	**14.2**	**14.7**	**15.7**	**14.1**
7.1	Purchase of vehicles	3.7	4.4	6.0	6.1	7.1	5.8
7.1.1	Purchase of new cars and vans	0.6	1.0	1.5	1.9	3.0	1.9
7.1.2	Purchase of second hand cars or vans	2.9	3.4	4.4	4.1	3.9	3.8
7.1.3	Purchase of motorcycles and other vehicles	..	..	[0.10]	0.2	0.3	0.2
7.2	Operation of personal transport	5.1	5.8	6.3	6.0	5.6	5.8
7.2.1	Spares and accessories	0.4	0.3	0.4	0.7	0.6	0.5
7.2.2	Petrol, diesel and other motor oils	3.3	3.8	3.9	3.7	3.2	3.6
7.2.3	Repairs and servicing	1.1	1.3	1.5	1.3	1.4	1.3
7.2.4	Other motoring costs	0.3	0.4	0.4	0.3	0.4	0.4
7.3	Transport services	2.2	2.2	1.9	2.5	2.9	2.4
7.3.1	Rail and tube fares	0.3	0.2	0.2	0.3	0.4	0.3
7.3.2	Bus and coach fares	0.3	0.3	0.1	0.1	0.1	0.1
7.3.3	Combined fares	..	..			[0.00]	[0.00]
7.3.4	Other travel and transport	1.6	1.7	1.5	2.0	2.4	1.9
8	**Communication[3]**	**4.7**	**4.9**	**4.5**	**3.9**	**3.1**	**4.0**
8.1	Postal services	0.1	0.2	0.2	0.1	0.1	0.1
8.2	Telephone and telefax equipment	0.3	0.3	0.2	0.2	0.1	0.2
8.3	Telephone and telefax services	1.8	1.8	1.8	1.7	1.3	1.6
8.4	Internet subscription fees	0.3	0.2	0.2	0.1	0.1	0.2
8.5	Combined telecom services	2.2	2.4	2.1	1.8	1.4	1.9

Table 3.2E5

Detailed household expenditure as a percentage of total expenditure by disposable equivalised income quintile group (OECD-modified scale)

UK, financial year ending 2022

Commodity or service		Lowest twenty per cent	Second quintile group	Third quintile group	Fourth quintile group	Highest twenty per cent	All house-holds
		Percentage of total expenditure (%)					
9	**Recreation & culture**[3]	**8.9**	**9.3**	**10.1**	**11.8**	**11.4**	**10.6**
9.1	Audio-visual, photographic and information processing equipment	1.1	0.7	0.8	0.9	0.9	0.9
9.1.1	Audio equipment and accessories, CD players	0.1	0.1	0.1	0.2	0.2	0.2
9.1.2	TV, video and computers	1.0	0.6	0.7	0.6	0.6	0.7
9.1.3	Photographic, cine and optical equipment	..	..	..	..	[0.00]	0.0
9.2	Other major durables for recreation and culture	[0.70]	[0.10]	[0.30]	1.7	0.7	0.8
9.3	Other recreational items and equipment, gardens and pets	2.8	3.4	3.1	3.2	3.2	3.2
9.3.1	Games, toys and hobbies	0.7	0.9	0.5	0.5	0.4	0.6
9.3.2	Computer software and games	0.1	0.2	0.2	0.2	0.2	0.2
9.3.3	Equipment for sport, camping and open-air recreation	0.2	0.3	0.2	0.4	0.7	0.4
9.3.4	Horticultural goods, garden equipment and plants	0.7	0.8	0.7	0.8	0.7	0.7
9.3.5	Pets and pet food	1.1	1.3	1.4	1.2	1.3	1.3
9.4	Recreational and cultural services	2.4	2.9	3.2	2.9	3.3	3.0
9.4.1	Sports admissions, subscriptions, leisure class fees and equipment hire	0.6	0.8	1.0	1.1	1.4	1.1
9.4.2	Cinema, theatre and museums etc.	0.1	0.3	0.5	0.4	0.4	0.4
9.4.3	TV, video, satellite rental, cable subscriptions and TV licences	1.3	1.3	1.2	1.1	0.9	1.1
9.4.4	Miscellaneous entertainments	0.2	0.3	0.3	0.2	0.3	0.3
9.4.5	Development of film, deposit for film development, passport photos, holiday and school photos	[0.00]	0.0	0.0	0.0	0.1	0.0
9.4.6	Gambling payments	0.3	0.3	0.2	0.2	0.1	0.2
9.5	Newspapers, books and stationery	0.9	0.9	0.8	0.8	0.8	0.8
9.5.1	Books	0.2	0.2	0.2	0.2	0.2	0.2
9.5.2	Diaries, address books, cards etc.	0.4	0.4	0.4	0.4	0.3	0.4
9.5.3	Newspapers	0.2	0.2	0.2	0.1	0.1	0.2
9.5.4	Magazines and periodicals	0.1	0.1	0.1	0.1	0.1	0.1
9.6	Package holidays[4]	1.0	1.2	1.8	2.3	2.6	2.0
9.6.1	Package holidays - UK	0.4	0.3	0.3	0.3	0.4	0.3
9.6.2	Package holidays - abroad	0.6	0.9	1.5	2.0	2.3	1.6
10	**Education**	**0.7**	**0.6**	**0.8**	**0.9**	**1.5**	**1.0**
10.1	Education fees	[0.70]	0.5	0.8	0.8	1.4	0.9
10.2	Payments for school trips, other ad-hoc expenditure	[0.10]	..	..	..	..	0.1
11	**Restaurants & hotels**	**4.5**	**5.7**	**6.0**	**7.1**	**7.9**	**6.6**
11.1	Catering services	3.6	4.4	4.5	5.2	5.4	4.8
11.1.1	Restaurant and café meals	1.6	2.0	2.3	2.6	2.8	2.4
11.1.2	Alcoholic drinks (away from home)	0.6	0.7	0.7	1.1	1.2	0.9
11.1.3	Take away meals eaten at home	0.7	0.8	0.8	0.8	0.8	0.8
11.1.4	Other take-away and snack food	0.6	0.6	0.6	0.5	0.5	0.5
11.1.5	Contract catering (food) and canteens	0.1	0.2	0.1	0.2	0.2	0.2
11.2	Accommodation services	0.9	1.4	1.5	1.9	2.4	1.8
11.2.1	Holiday in the UK	0.8	1.3	1.3	1.6	2.0	1.5
11.2.2	Holiday abroad	..	..	[0.20]	0.3	0.4	0.3
11.2.3	Room hire	..	..	..	..	..	[0.00]

Table 3.2E5

Detailed household expenditure as a percentage of total expenditure by disposable equivalised income quintile group (OECD-modified scale)

UK, financial year ending 2022

Commodity or service		Lowest twenty per cent	Second quintile group	Third quintile group	Fourth quintile group	Highest twenty per cent	All house-holds
		Percentage of total expenditure (%)					
12	**Miscellaneous goods & services**	**6.9**	**7.3**	**8.2**	**7.5**	**8.0**	**7.7**
12.1	Personal care	2.1	2.3	2.2	2.1	1.9	2.1
12.1.1	Hairdressing, beauty treatment	0.4	0.7	0.7	0.7	0.7	0.7
12.1.2	Toilet paper	0.2	0.2	0.2	0.2	0.1	0.2
12.1.3	Toiletries and soap	0.5	0.5	0.5	0.4	0.3	0.4
12.1.4	Baby toiletries and accessories (disposable)	0.1	0.1	0.1	0.1	0.1	0.1

Table 3.2E5

Detailed household expenditure as a percentage of total expenditure by disposable equivalised income quintile group (OECD-modified scale)

UK, financial year ending 2022

		Lowest twenty per cent	Second quintile group	Third quintile group	Fourth quintile group	Highest twenty per cent	All house-holds
Commodity or service		Percentage of total expenditure (%)					
	12.1.5 Hair products, cosmetics and related electrical appliances	0.8	0.8	0.8	0.8	0.7	0.8
12.2	Personal effects	0.5	0.5	0.5	0.5	1.0	0.7
12.3	Social protection	[0.20]	0.2	0.7	0.3	0.5	0.4
12.4	Insurance	3.1	3.4	3.7	3.4	3.3	3.4
	12.4.1 Household insurances - structural, contents						
	and appliances	0.9	1.0	1.0	0.9	0.9	0.9
	12.4.2 Medical insurance premiums	0.2	0.3	0.4	0.4	0.7	0.5
	12.4.3 Vehicle insurance including boat insurance	2.0	2.1	2.2	2.0	1.6	1.9
	12.4.4 Non-package holiday, other travel insurance	..	..	..	..	..	0.0
12.5	Other services	0.9	0.8	1.1	1.1	1.2	1.1
	12.5.1 Moving house	0.5	0.5	0.5	0.4	0.8	0.5
	12.5.2 Bank, building society, post office, credit card charges	0.1	0.1	0.1	0.1	0.1	0.1
	12.5.3 Other services and professional fees	0.3	0.2	0.5	0.6	0.4	0.4
1-12	**All expenditure groups**	**90.6**	**89.3**	**86.8**	**85.1**	**83.2**	**86.2**
13	**Other expenditure items**	**9.4**	**10.7**	**13.2**	**14.9**	**16.8**	**13.8**
13.1	Housing: mortgage interest payments,						
	council tax etc.	7.0	8.0	9.9	10.7	11.5	9.9
	13.1.1 Mortgage interest payments	1.4	2.0	3.7	4.8	6.3	4.2
	13.1.2 Mortgage protection premiums	0.1	0.1	0.2	0.2	0.1	0.1
	13.1.3 Council tax, domestic rates	5.3	6.0	6.0	5.4	4.6	5.3
	13.1.4 Council tax, mortgage (second dwelling)	..	..	..	..	0.5	0.3
13.2	Licences, fines and transfers	0.7	0.8	0.8	0.9	0.7	0.8
13.3	Holiday spending	..	..	[0.30]	[0.40]	[0.30]	0.3
13.4	Money transfers and credit	1.6	1.8	2.1	2.9	4.3	2.9
	13.4.1 Money, cash gifts given to children	..	[0.00]	..	[0.00]	[0.10]	0.1
	13.4.2 Cash gifts and donations	1.3	1.6	1.9	2.7	4.1	2.6
	13.4.3 Club instalment payments (child) and interest on						
	credit cards	0.2	0.2	0.2	0.2	0.1	0.2
Total expenditure		**100.0**	**100.0**	**100.0**	**100.0**	**100.0**	**100.0**
14	**Other items recorded**						
14.1	Life assurance and contributions to pension funds	4.6	7.8	14.3	20.8	39.3	21.3
14.2	Other insurance inc. friendly societies	1.4	3.8	7.1	9.8	12.3	8.1
14.3	Income tax, payments *less* refunds	10.6	8.3	9.6	14.7	20.1	13.9
14.4	National insurance contributions	0.3	0.3	0.9	0.6	1.3	0.8
14.5	Purchase or alteration of dwellings, mortgages	0.2	0.3	0.4	0.5	0.4	0.4
14.6	Savings and investments	0.1	0.0	0.1	0.0	0.0	0.0
14.7	Pay off loan to clear other debt	0.0	0.0	0.0	0.0	0.0	0.0
14.8	Windfall receipts from gambling etc[5]	0.0	0.0	0.0	[0.00]	[0.00]	0.0

Note: The commodity and service categories are not comparable to those in publications before 2001-02.
The numbering system is sequential, it does not use actual COICOP codes.
Please see background notes for symbols and conventions used in this report.
5 Expressed as an income figure as opposed to an expenditure figure.

Source: Office for National Statistics

Table 4.1

Household expenditure based on COICOP classification, 2001-02 to 2021-22 at 2022 prices[1]

United Kingdom

	2001-02	2002-03	2003-04	2004-05	2005-06	2006[2]	2006[3]	2007	2008	2009	2010	2011	2012
Weighted number of households (thousands)	24,450	24,350	24,670	24,430	24,800	24,790	25,440	25,350	25,690	25,980	26,320	26,110	26,410
Total number of households in sample	7,470	6,930	7,050	6,800	6,790	6,650	6,650	6,140	5,850	5,830	5,260	5,690	5,600
Total number of persons in sample	18,120	16,590	16,970	16,260	16,090	15,850	15,850	14,650	13,830	13,740	12,180	13,430	13,180
Total number of adults in sample	13,450	12,450	12,620	12,260	12,170	12,000	12,000	11,220	10,640	10,650	9,430	10,330	10,200
Weighted average number of persons per household	2.4	2.4	2.4	2.4	2.4	2.4	2.3	2.4	2.4	2.3	2.3	2.4	2.3
Commodity or service					Average weekly household expenditure (£)								
1 Food & non-alcoholic drinks	63.70	65.30	65.30	66.80	66.70	67.50	66.60	66.30	64.00	62.50	61.60	60.20	60.40
2 Alcoholic drinks, tobacco & narcotics	23.50	23.10	23.40	22.20	20.70	20.80	20.80	20.30	18.80	18.70	18.70	17.50	17.20
3 Clothing & footwear	16.00	16.80	17.70	19.60	19.70	20.70	20.40	20.40	21.40	22.50	25.30	23.00	24.60
4 Housing (net)[4], fuel & power	70.30	70.60	73.20	72.70	74.50	74.60	74.60	77.40	73.00	75.60	79.40	78.90	80.70
5 Household goods & services	40.40	40.10	41.70	42.20	40.20	40.70	40.30	40.60	39.00	35.00	38.20	31.70	32.20
6 Health	7.60	7.90	8.00	7.70	8.30	8.70	8.60	8.20	7.10	7.10	6.60	8.40	7.80
7 Transport	106.90	107.70	107.20	101.70	101.00	99.80	97.80	96.30	93.80	85.70	87.80	82.60	78.70
8 Communication[5]	13.50	13.70	14.40	15.30	15.80	15.60	15.40	16.30	16.80	16.30	17.30	16.90	16.90
9 Recreation & culture	61.20	62.80	64.80	67.50	66.70	68.40	67.30	67.80	71.40	67.90	66.90	73.50	70.60
10 Education	20.80	18.30	17.30	20.50	19.70	20.40	19.80	16.90	13.80	14.50	19.70	13.10	11.60
11 Restaurants & hotels	59.70	61.20	58.50	58.80	57.80	58.30	57.80	55.40	54.00	53.70	53.40	51.60	51.10
12 Miscellaneous goods & services	44.40	46.70	46.20	46.30	44.10	44.60	44.10	42.80	42.20	40.60	40.60	42.60	41.40
1-12 All expenditure groups	528.00	534.20	537.70	541.30	535.20	540.00	533.60	528.50	515.10	499.90	515.50	500.00	493.50
13 Other expenditure items[6]	85.70	82.60	84.00	84.90	88.60	86.70	84.60	79.90	83.60	85.20	78.90	79.50	77.00
Total expenditure[7]	613.70	616.80	621.70	626.10	623.90	626.70	618.20	608.40	598.80	585.10	594.40	579.50	570.50
Average weekly expenditure per person (£)													
Total expenditure	258.30	259.00	263.80	262.30	264.60	265.10	264.40	258.20	254.00	250.00	254.90	246.20	243.50

Table 4.1

Household expenditure based on COICOP classification, 2001-02 to 2021-22 at 2022 prices1

United Kingdom

	2013	2014	2014-15	2015-16	2016-17	2017-18	2018-19	2019-20	2020-21	2021-22
Weighted number of households (thousands)	26,840	26,600	26,760	27,220	27,210	27,150	27,480	27,820	28,200	28,500
Total number of households in sample	5,140	5,130	5,170	4,920	5,040	5,410	5,480	5,440	5,400	5,630
Total number of persons in sample	12,120	12,120	12,160	11,620	11,960	12,780	12,790	12,670	12,240	12,850
Total number of adults in sample	9,350	9,440	9,510	8,950	9,260	9,940	9,980	9,880	9,880	10,260
Weighted average number of persons per household	2.4	2.4	2.4	2.4	2.4	2.4	2.4	2.4	2.3	2.3
Commodity or service										
1 Food & non-alcoholic drinks	60.30	60.40	60.30	60.30	62.60	64.00	64.00	64.90	70.40	62.20
2 Alcoholic drinks, tobacco & narcotics	15.50	15.20	14.70	13.70	14.10	14.20	14.10	13.70	14.50	12.20
3 Clothing & footwear	23.50	24.60	24.50	24.20	25.90	24.70	24.50	23.60	15.00	17.60
4 Housing (net)[4], fuel & power	84.80	80.50	80.50	79.80	79.60	81.80	83.60	85.70	88.30	87.70
5 Household goods & services	37.20	39.40	40.80	39.40	43.70	44.00	43.70	38.60	36.40	34.70
6 Health	7.50	8.30	8.20	8.20	8.20	7.60	8.50	8.50	6.80	9.10
7 Transport	85.60	90.60	89.40	90.20	96.80	94.90	95.20	89.90	66.60	74.40
8 Communication[5]	17.30	18.20	18.20	18.50	19.30	19.90	23.30	22.40	21.20	21.20
9 Recreation & culture	72.70	77.50	78.10	77.10	82.70	82.40	82.30	78.60	46.80	56.10
10 Education	12.90	13.00	11.80	8.50	6.70	9.70	6.20	4.80	8.60	5.20
11 Restaurants & hotels	49.60	51.00	50.70	52.90	57.10	55.70	55.50	55.60	19.10	34.80
12 Miscellaneous goods & services	41.80	42.70	43.20	42.10	43.80	45.40	47.40	46.60	37.60	40.60
1-12 All expenditure groups	508.70	521.30	520.30	515.00	540.60	544.40	548.30	532.80	431.40	455.70
13 Other expenditure items[6]	81.20	77.10	73.80	80.60	79.40	83.20	81.90	73.80	68.60	73.10
Total expenditure[7]	**589.90**	**598.40**	**594.10**	**595.60**	**620.00**	**627.60**	**630.20**	**606.60**	**500.00**	**528.80**
Average weekly expenditure per person (£)										
Total expenditure	**250.20**	**249.80**	**249.20**	**252.80**	**261.60**	**261.90**	**264.80**	**256.60**	**213.20**	**226.70**

Note: The commodity and service categories are not comparable to those in publications before 2001-02.

1 Figures have been deflated to 2022 prices using deflators specific to the COICOP category.

2 From 2001-02 to this version of 2006, figures shown are based on weighted data using non-response weights based on the 1991 Census and population figures from the 1991 and 2001 Censuses.

3 From this version of 2006, figures shown are based on weighted data using updated weights, with non-response weights and population figures based on the 2001 Census.

4 Excluding mortgage interest payments, council tax and Northern Ireland rates. Mortgage interest payments can be found in category 13.

5 Changes to the questionnaire from FYE 2019 has resulted in the COICOP division "Communication" not being directly comparable with previous years. Please see the technical report for more information.

6 An improvement to the imputation of mortgage interest payments has been implemented for 2006 data onwards. This means there is a slight discontinuity between 2006 and earlier years.

7 Due to changes to collection approach for COVID19 pandemic in 2020/21, the weighting method was adjusted to include a tenure calibration constraint. See the Methodology section of the bulletin for more details

Source: Office for National Statistics

Table 4.2

Household expenditure as a percentage of total expenditure based on COICOP classification, 2001-02 to 2021-22 at 2022 prices1

United Kingdom

	2001-02	2002-03	2003-04	2004-05	2005-06	2006[2]	2006[3]	2007	2008	2009	2010	2011	2012
Weighted number of households (thousands)	24,450	24,350	24,670	24,430	24,800	24,790	25,440	25,350	25,690	25,980	26,320	26,110	26,410
Total number of households in sample	7,470	6,930	7,050	6,800	6,790	6,650	6,650	6,140	5,850	5,830	5,260	5,690	5,600
Total number of persons in sample	18,120	16,590	16,970	16,260	16,090	15,850	15,850	14,650	13,830	13,740	12,180	13,430	13,180
Total number of adults in sample	13,450	12,450	12,620	12,260	12,170	12,000	12,000	11,220	10,640	10,650	9,430	10,330	10,200
Weighted average number of persons per household	2.4	2.4	2.4	2.4	2.4	2.4	2.3	2.4	2.4	2.3	2.3	2.4	2.3
Commodity or service	Percentage of total expenditure (%)												
1 Food & non-alcoholic drinks	10	11	10	11	11	11	11	11	11	11	10	10	11
2 Alcoholic drinks, tobacco & narcotics	4	4	4	4	3	3	3	3	3	3	3	3	3
3 Clothing & footwear	3	3	3	3	3	3	3	3	4	4	4	4	4
4 Housing (net)[4], fuel & power	11	11	12	12	12	12	12	13	12	13	13	14	14
5 Household goods & services	7	7	7	7	6	6	7	7	7	6	6	5	6
6 Health	1	1	1	1	1	1	1	1	1	1	1	1	1
7 Transport	17	17	17	16	16	16	16	16	16	15	15	14	14
8 Communication[5]	2	2	2	2	3	2	2	3	3	3	3	3	3
9 Recreation & culture	10	10	10	11	11	11	11	11	12	12	11	13	12
10 Education	3	3	3	3	3	3	3	3	2	2	3	2	2
11 Restaurants & hotels	10	10	9	9	9	9	9	9	9	9	9	9	9
12 Miscellaneous goods & services	7	8	7	7	7	7	7	7	7	7	7	7	7
1-12 All expenditure groups	86	87	86	86	86	86	86	87	86	85	87	86	87
13 Other expenditure items[6]	14	13	14	14	14	14	14	13	14	15	13	14	13
Total expenditure[7]	**100**	**100**	**100**	**100**	**100**	**100**	**100**	**100**	**100**	**100**	**100**	**100**	**100**

Note: The commodity and service categories are not comparable to those in publications before 2001-02.

1 Figures have been deflated to 2022 prices using deflators specific to the COICOP category.

2 From 2001-02 to this version of 2006, figures shown are based on weighted data using non-response weights based on the 1991 Census and population figures from the 1991 and 2001 Censuses.

3 From this version of 2006, figures shown are based on weighted data using updated weights, with non-response weights and population figures based on the 2001 Census.

4 Excluding mortgage interest payments, council tax and Northern Ireland rates. Mortgage interest payments can be found in category 13.

5 Changes to the questionnaire from FYE 2019 has resulted in the COICOP division "Communication" not being directly comparable with previous years. Please see the technical report for more information.

6 An improvement to the imputation of mortgage interest payments has been implemented for 2006 data onwards. This means there is a slight discontinuity between 2006 and earlier years.

7 Due to changes to collection approach for COVID19 pandemic in 2020/21, the weighting method was adjusted to include a tenure calibration constraint. See the Methodology section of the bulletin for more details

Source: Office for National Statistics

Table 4.2

Household expenditure as a percentage of total expenditure based on COICOP classification, 2001-02 to 2021-22 at 2022 prices[1]

United Kingdom

	2013	2014	2014-15	2015-16	2016-17	2017-18	2018-19	2019-20	2020-21	2021-22
Weighted number of households (thousands)	26,840	26,600	26,760	27,220	27,210	27,150	27,480	27,820	28,200	28,500
Total number of households in sample	5,140	5,130	5,170	4,920	5,040	5,410	5,480	5,440	5,400	5,630
Total number of persons in sample	12,120	12,120	12,160	11,620	11,960	12,780	12,790	12,670	12,240	12,850
Total number of adults in sample	9,350	9,440	9,510	8,950	9,260	9,940	9,980	9,880	9,880	10,260
Weighted average number of persons per household	2.4	2.4	2.4	2.4	2.4	2.4	2.4	2.4	2.3	2.3
Commodity or service										
1 Food & non-alcoholic drinks	10	10	10	10	10	10	10	11	14	12
2 Alcoholic drinks, tobacco & narcotics	3	3	2	2	2	2	2	2	3	2
3 Clothing & footwear	4	4	4	4	4	4	4	4	3	3
4 Housing (net)[4], fuel & power	14	13	14	13	13	13	13	14	18	17
5 Household goods & services	6	7	7	7	7	7	7	6	7	7
6 Health	1	1	1	1	1	1	1	1	1	2
7 Transport	15	15	15	15	16	15	15	15	13	14
8 Communication[5]	3	3	3	3	3	3	4	4	4	4
9 Recreation & culture	12	13	13	13	13	13	13	13	9	11
10 Education	2	2	2	1	1	2	1	1	2	1
11 Restaurants & hotels	8	9	9	9	9	9	9	9	4	7
12 Miscellaneous goods & services	7	7	7	7	7	7	8	8	8	8
1-12 All expenditure groups	86	87	88	86	87	87	87	88	86	86
13 Other expenditure items[6]	14	13	12	14	13	13	13	12	14	14
Total expenditure[7]	**100**	**100**	**100**	**100**	**100**	**100**	**100**	**100**	**100**	**100**

Note: The commodity and service categories are not comparable to those in publications before 2001-02.

1 Figures have been deflated to 2022 prices using deflators specific to the COICOP category.

2 From 2001-02 to this version of 2006, figures shown are based on weighted data using non-response weights based on the 1991 Census and population figures from the 1991 and 2001 Censuses.

3 From this version of 2006, figures shown are based on weighted data using updated weights, with non-response weights and population figures based on the 2001 Census.

4 Excluding mortgage interest payments, council tax and Northern Ireland rates. Mortgage interest payments can be found in category 13.

5 Changes to the questionnaire from FYE 2019 has resulted in the COICOP division "Communication" not being directly comparable with previous years. Please see the technical report for more information.

6 An improvement to the imputation of mortgage interest payments has been implemented for 2006 data onwards. This means there is a slight discontinuity between 2006 and earlier years.

7 Due to changes to collection approach for COVID19 pandemic in 2020/21, the weighting method was adjusted to include a tenure calibration constraint. See the Methodology section of the bulletin for more details

Source: Office for National Statistics

Table 4.3

Household expenditure at current[1] prices
UK, financial year ending March 2002 to financial year ending March 2022

	2001-02	2002-03	2003-04	2004-05	2005-06	2006[2]	2006[3]	2007	2008	2009	2010	2011	2012	2013	2014
Weighted number of households (thousands)	24,450	24,350	24,670	24,430	24,800	24,790	25,440	25,350	25,690	25,980	26,320	26,110	26,410	26,840	26,600
Total number of households in sample	7,470	6,930	7,050	6,800	6,790	6,650	6,650	6,140	5,850	5,830	5,260	5,690	5,600	5,140	5,130
Total number of persons in sample	18,120	16,590	16,970	16,260	16,090	15,850	15,850	14,650	13,830	13,740	12,180	13,430	13,180	12,120	12,120
Total number of adults in sample	13,450	12,450	12,620	12,260	12,170	12,000	12,000	11,220	10,640	10,650	9,430	10,330	10,200	9,350	9,440
Weighted average number of persons per household	2.4	2.4	2.4	2.4	2.4	2.4	2.3	2.4	2.4	2.3	2.3	2.4	2.3	2.4	2.4
Commodity or service						Average weekly household expenditure (£)									
1 Food & non-alcoholic drinks	41.80	42.70	43.50	44.70	45.30	46.90	46.30	48.10	50.70	52.20	53.20	54.80	56.80	58.80	58.80
2 Alcoholic drinks, tobacco & narcotics	11.40	11.40	11.70	11.30	10.80	11.10	11.10	11.20	10.80	11.20	11.80	12.00	12.60	12.00	12.30
3 Clothing & footwear	22.90	22.30	22.70	23.90	22.70	23.20	23.00	22.00	21.60	20.90	23.40	21.70	23.40	22.60	23.70
4 Housing(net)[4], fuel & power	35.90	36.90	39.00	40.40	44.20	47.60	47.50	51.80	53.00	57.30	60.40	63.30	68.00	74.40	72.70
5 Household goods & services	30.50	30.20	31.30	31.60	30.00	30.30	29.90	30.70	30.10	27.90	31.40	27.30	28.50	33.10	35.40
6 Health	4.50	4.80	5.00	4.90	5.50	5.90	5.80	5.70	5.10	5.30	5.00	6.60	6.40	6.20	7.10
7 Transport	57.80	59.20	60.70	59.60	61.70	62.00	60.80	61.70	63.40	58.40	64.90	65.70	64.10	70.40	74.80
8 Communication[5]	10.40	10.60	11.20	11.70	11.90	11.70	11.60	11.90	12.00	11.70	13.00	13.30	13.80	14.50	15.50
9 Recreation & culture	54.10	56.40	57.30	59.00	57.50	58.50	57.60	57.40	60.10	57.90	58.10	63.90	61.50	63.90	68.80
10 Education	5.60	5.20	5.20	6.50	6.60	7.20	7.00	6.80	6.20	7.00	10.00	7.00	6.80	8.80	9.80
11 Restaurants & hotels	33.40	35.40	34.90	36.10	36.70	37.90	37.60	37.20	37.70	38.40	39.20	39.70	40.50	40.40	42.50
12 Miscellaneous goods & services	30.70	33.10	33.60	34.90	34.60	36.00	35.70	35.30	35.60	35.00	35.90	38.60	38.40	39.10	40.00
1-12 All expenditure groups	338.80	348.30	356.20	364.70	367.60	378.30	373.80	379.80	386.30	383.10	406.30	413.90	420.70	444.30	461.20
13 Other expenditure items[6]	59.50	57.90	61.90	69.70	75.80	77.60	75.10	79.30	84.60	71.80	67.30	69.70	68.30	73.00	70.10
Total expenditure[7]	398.30	406.20	418.10	434.40	443.40	455.90	449.00	459.20	471.00	455.00	473.60	483.60	489.00	517.30	531.30
Average weekly expenditure per person (£)															
Total expenditure	167.60	170.50	177.40	182.00	188.00	192.80	192.00	194.80	199.80	194.40	203.10	205.40	208.70	219.40	221.80

Note: The commodity and service categories are not comparable to those in publications before 2001-02
1 Data in Table 4.3 have not been deflated to 2022 prices and therefore show the actual expenditure for the year they were collected.
Because inflation is not taken into account, comparisons between the years should be made with caution.
2 From 2002-03 to this version of 2006, figures shown are based on weighted data using non-response weights based on the
1991 Census and population figures from the 1991 and 2001 Censuses.
3 From this version of 2006, figures shown are based on weighted data using updated weights, with non-response weights
and population figures based on the 2001 Census.
4 Excluding mortgage interest payments, council tax and Northern Ireland rates. Mortgage interest payments can be found in category 13.
5 Changes to the questionnaire from FYE 2019 has resulted in the COICOP division "Communication" not being directly comparable with previous years. Please see the technical report for more information.
6 An error was discovered in the derivation of mortgage capital repayments which was leading to double counting. This has
been amended for the 2006 data onwards.
7 Due to changes to collection approach for COVID19 pandemic in 2020/21, the weighting method was adjusted to include a tenure calibration constraint. See the Methodology section of the bulletin for more details

Source: Office for National Statistics

Table 4.3

Household expenditure at current[1] prices

UK, financial year ending March 2002 to financial year ending March 2022

		2014-15	2015-16	2016-17	2017-18	2018-19	2019-20	2020-21	2021-22
Weighted number of households (thousands)		26,760	27,220	27,210	27,150	27,480	27,820	28,200	28,500
Total number of households in sample		5,170	4,920	5,040	5,410	5,480	5,440	5,400	5,630
Total number of persons in sample		12,160	11,620	11,960	12,780	12,790	12,670	12,240	12,850
Total number of adults in sample		9,510	8,950	9,260	9,940	9,980	9,880	9,880	10,260
Weighted average number of persons per household		2.4	2.4	2.4	2.4	2.4	2.4	2.3	2.3
Commodity or service									
1	Food & non-alcoholic drinks	58.30	56.80	58.00	61.00	61.90	63.70	69.20	62.20
2	Alcoholic drinks, tobacco & narcotics	12.00	11.40	11.90	12.60	13.00	12.90	14.10	12.20
3	Clothing & footwear	23.70	23.50	25.10	24.70	24.50	23.40	14.50	17.60
4	Housing(net)[4], fuel & power	72.80	72.50	72.60	76.20	79.40	83.00	84.60	87.70
5	Household goods & services	36.70	35.50	39.30	40.90	41.00	36.50	34.50	34.70
6	Health	7.00	7.20	7.30	7.00	8.00	8.20	6.70	9.10
7	Transport	73.30	72.70	79.70	81.20	85.00	81.60	60.80	74.40
8	Communication[5]	15.50	16.00	17.20	17.90	21.30	21.40	20.90	21.20
9	Recreation & culture	69.30	68.00	73.50	75.00	77.20	74.80	45.50	56.10
10	Education	9.00	7.00	5.70	8.70	5.70	4.50	8.30	5.20
11	Restaurants & hotels	42.50	45.10	50.10	50.30	51.40	52.90	18.30	34.80
12	Miscellaneous goods & services	40.40	39.70	41.80	43.80	45.70	45.70	37.20	40.60
1-12	All expenditure groups	460.50	455.30	482.20	499.20	514.10	508.50	414.60	455.70
13	Other expenditure items[6]	66.90	73.60	72.00	76.50	77.90	79.30	66.90	73.10
	Total expenditure[7]	**527.30**	**528.90**	**554.20**	**575.70**	**592.00**	**587.90**	**481.50**	**528.80**
Average weekly expenditure per person (£)									
	Total expenditure	**221.20**	**224.50**	**233.80**	**240.20**	**248.80**	**248.70**	**205.30**	**226.70**

Note. The commodity and service categories are not comparable to those in publications before 2001-02

1 Data in Table 4.3 have not been deflated to 2022 prices and therefore show the actual expenditure for the year they were collected. Because inflation is not taken into account, comparisons between the years should be made with caution.

2 From 2002-03 to this version of 2006, figures shown are based on weighted data using non-response weights based on the 1991 Census and population figures from the 1991 and 2001 Censuses.

3 From this version of 2006, figures shown are based on weighted data using updated weights, with non-response weights and population figures based on the 2001 Census.

4 Excluding mortgage interest payments, council tax and Northern Ireland rates. Mortgage interest payments can be found in category 13.

5 Changes to the questionnaire from FYE 2019 has resulted in the COICOP division "Communication" not being directly comparable with previous years. Please see the technical report for more information.

6 An error was discovered in the derivation of mortgage capital repayments which was leading to double counting. This has been amended for the 2006 data onwards.

7 Due to changes to collection approach for COVID19 pandemic in 2020/21, the weighting method was adjusted to include a tenure calibration constraint. See the Methodology section of the bulletin for more details

Source: Office for National Statistics

Background notes

Symbols and conventions used in Family Spending tables

[]   Figures should be used with extra caution because they are based on fewer than 20 reporting households.

..   The data is suppressed if the unweighted sample counts are less than 10 reporting households.

..   No figures are available because there are no reporting households.

~   The figure is greater than 0 but rounds to 0.

Rounding: Individual figures have been rounded independently. The sum of component items does not therefore necessarily add to the totals shown.

Averages: These are averages (means) for all households included in the column or row, and unless specified, are not restricted to those households reporting expenditure on a particular item or income of a particular type.

Impact of the coronavirus (COVID-19) pandemic on the Living Costs and Food Survey (LCF) for the financial year ending 2020

Following Government guidance in relation to the coronavirus (COVID-19) pandemic, a pause in data collection led to interviews being conducted for 13 fewer days in March 2020 than planned. Final March interviews took place on Monday March 16th. All households that were not interviewed as a result were treated as non-responders and data were weighted to account for reduced data collection in March 2020 compared to previous years.

Data collected in March 2020 may have covered changes to spending habits around the start of the first UK lockdown on March 23rd, for example panic buying beforehand and reduced spending during lockdown when people were advised to stay at home and many businesses were closed. However, due to reduced data collection in the latter half of March data may not accurately reflect the impact of lockdown on spending and the annual estimates reported in this release will not be significantly impacted.

Family Spending

Contents:

ONS Social Surveys

Office for National Statistics

March 2023

A number of tables within the family spending workbooks have been placed under review to be removed from future publications. Tables under review are specified within the workbooks. If you use these for your analysis, please contact us via

family.spending@ons.gov.uk**.**

Table A4

Household expenditure by gross income decile group

UK, financial year ending 2022

> **This table is under review to be removed from future publications and replaced with disposable equivalised income tables.**
> **If you use this table for your analysis, please get in contact here.**

	Lowest ten per cent	Second decile group	Third decile group	Fourth decile group	Fifth decile group	Sixth decile group	Seventh decile group	Eighth decile group	Ninth decile group	Highest ten per cent	All house-holds
Lower boundary of group (£ per week)		253	369	479	612	761	918	1,102	1,366	1,808	
Weighted number of households (thousands)	2,860	2,850	2,850	2,850	2,850	2,850	2,850	2,850	2,850	2,850	28,500
Total number of households in sample	530	540	560	580	580	570	570	580	560	560	5,630
Total number of persons in sample	710	830	990	1,170	1,310	1,400	1,460	1,590	1,650	1,750	12,850
Total number of adults in sample	630	720	850	950	1,060	1,110	1,160	1,250	1,240	1,310	10,260
Weighted average number of persons per household	1.4	1.5	1.8	2.1	2.4	2.6	2.6	2.8	3.0	3.2	2.3

Commodity or service						Average weekly household expenditure (£)					
1 Food & non-alcoholic drinks	35.30	42.40	47.90	52.30	60.40	66.90	68.80	74.30	82.70	90.90	62.20
2 Alcoholic drinks, tobacco & narcotics	8.00	9.10	9.80	9.00	12.30	12.00	12.00	14.40	16.80	18.20	12.20
3 Clothing & footwear	6.80	7.50	10.20	12.40	15.00	18.00	18.30	26.60	26.70	34.30	17.60
4 Housing(net)[1], fuel & power	64.70	72.40	80.40	84.90	90.30	90.80	90.80	93.90	101.60	107.20	87.70
5 Household goods & services	16.70	19.50	22.50	25.80	28.70	34.70	37.10	43.90	51.20	67.10	34.70
6 Health	4.80	3.60	8.50	10.70	6.80	6.60	10.30	7.60	14.50	17.50	9.10
7 Transport	24.40	27.80	38.90	51.30	66.60	71.40	82.80	99.50	112.70	168.80	74.40
8 Communication	11.60	15.00	15.60	18.10	21.80	22.60	23.80	26.10	27.60	29.80	21.20
9 Recreation & culture	25.00	23.80	32.40	39.20	52.10	54.10	67.40	61.20	81.00	124.60	56.10
10 Education	[2.10]	..	[4.10]	[3.70]	[1.60]	[1.70]	[4.00]	[7.20]	6.70	20.00	5.20
11 Restaurants & hotels	10.40	13.20	16.80	22.30	30.50	35.40	37.70	46.60	52.80	82.20	34.80
12 Miscellaneous goods & services	18.40	18.50	25.90	33.40	34.90	37.00	44.90	50.10	61.50	82.00	40.60
1-12 All expenditure groups	228.50	253.30	312.80	363.20	421.00	451.20	498.00	551.40	635.70	842.70	455.70
13 Other expenditure items	23.60	30.30	36.70	50.60	68.10	62.40	73.40	109.70	116.70	160.00	73.10
Total expenditure	**252.00**	**283.60**	**349.60**	**413.70**	**489.00**	**513.70**	**571.40**	**661.10**	**752.40**	**1002.70**	**528.80**
Average weekly expenditure per person (£)											
Total expenditure	**184.00**	**184.70**	**193.30**	**195.60**	**206.60**	**201.40**	**219.00**	**239.20**	**247.80**	**315.90**	**226.70**

Note: The commodity and service categories are not comparable to those in publications before 2001-02.
Please see background notes for symbols and conventions used in this report.

1 Excluding mortgage interest payments, council tax and Northern Ireland rates. Mortgage interest payments can be found in Category 13.

Source: Office for National Statistics

Table A5

Household expenditure as a percentage of total expenditure by gross income decile group

UK, financial year ending 2022

> This table is under review to be removed from future publications and replaced with disposable equivalised income tables.
> If you use this table for your analysis, please get in contact here.

	Lowest ten per cent	Second decile group	Third decile group	Fourth decile group	Fifth decile group	Sixth decile group	Seventh decile group	Eighth decile group	Ninth decile group	Highest ten per cent	All house-holds
Lower boundary of group (£ per week)		253	369	479	612	761	918	1,102	1,366	1,808	
Weighted number of households (thousands)	2,860	2,850	2,850	2,850	2,850	2,850	2,850	2,850	2,850	2,850	28,500
Total number of households in sample	530	540	560	580	580	570	570	580	560	560	5,630
Total number of persons in sample	710	830	990	1,170	1,310	1,400	1,460	1,590	1,650	1,750	12,850
Total number of adults in sample	630	720	850	950	1,060	1,110	1,160	1,250	1,240	1,310	10,260
Weighted average number of persons per household	1.4	1.5	1.8	2.1	2.4	2.6	2.6	2.8	3.0	3.2	2.3

Commodity or service	Percentage of total expenditure										
1 Food & non-alcoholic drinks	14	15	14	13	12	13	12	11	11	9	12
2 Alcoholic drinks, tobacco & narcotics	3	3	3	2	3	2	2	2	2	2	2
3 Clothing & footwear	3	3	3	3	3	4	3	4	4	3	3
4 Housing(net)[1], fuel & power	26	26	23	21	18	18	16	14	13	11	17
5 Household goods & services	7	7	6	6	6	7	7	7	7	7	7
6 Health	2	1	2	3	1	1	2	1	2	2	2
7 Transport	10	10	11	12	14	14	14	15	15	17	14
8 Communication	5	5	4	4	4	4	4	4	4	3	4
9 Recreation & culture	10	8	9	9	11	11	12	9	11	12	11
10 Education	[1]	..	[1]	[1]	[0]	[0]	[1]	[1]	1	2	1
11 Restaurants & hotels	4	5	5	5	6	7	7	7	7	8	7
12 Miscellaneous goods & services	7	7	7	8	7	7	8	8	8	8	8
1-12 All expenditure groups	91	89	89	88	86	88	87	83	84	84	86
13 Other expenditure items	9	11	11	12	14	12	13	17	16	16	14
Total expenditure	100	100	100	100	100	100	100	100	100	100	100

Note: The commodity and service categories are not comparable to those in publications before 2001-02.
Please see background notes for symbols and conventions used in this report.

1 Excluding mortgage interest payments, council tax and Northern Ireland rates. Mortgage interest payments can be found in Category 13.

Source: Office for National Statistics

Table A7

Household expenditure by disposable income decile group

UK, financial year ending 2022

> **This table is under review to be removed from future publications and replaced with disposable equivalised income tables.**
> **If you use this table for your analysis, please get in contact here.**

	Lowest ten per cent	Second decile group	Third decile group	Fourth decile group	Fifth decile group	Sixth decile group	Seventh decile group	Eighth decile group	Ninth decile group	Highest ten per cent	All house-holds
Lower boundary of group (£ per week)		247	349	443	555	668	795	928	1,127	1,438	
Weighted number of households (thousands)	2,850	2,850	2,850	2,850	2,850	2,850	2,850	2,850	2,850	2,850	28,500
Total number of households in sample	540	540	560	580	570	580	570	580	570	560	5,630
Total number of persons in sample	720	780	950	1,160	1,300	1,400	1,480	1,630	1,680	1,750	12,850
Total number of adults in sample	640	680	820	940	1,040	1,100	1,170	1,250	1,280	1,340	10,260
Weighted average number of persons per household	1.4	1.5	1.7	2.1	2.4	2.5	2.7	2.9	3.0	3.2	2.3

Commodity or service	Average weekly household expenditure (£)										
1 Food & non-alcoholic drinks	35.50	41.40	45.50	53.60	58.40	66.90	71.00	74.10	83.60	91.80	62.20
2 Alcoholic drinks, tobacco & narcotics	8.70	8.90	9.60	8.90	11.50	12.40	11.90	14.90	16.20	18.70	12.20
3 Clothing & footwear	6.70	7.90	9.50	12.60	14.60	17.40	17.20	28.10	26.00	35.90	17.60
4 Housing(net)[1], fuel & power	65.20	70.20	80.20	86.60	89.60	93.30	89.80	91.60	94.50	116.00	87.70
5 Household goods & services	17.00	19.60	23.80	24.50	29.60	35.80	34.90	42.10	54.00	65.90	34.70
6 Health	4.80	3.80	8.30	8.50	8.20	8.50	8.60	7.80	12.80	19.60	9.10
7 Transport	25.90	28.30	34.90	54.70	63.10	73.80	82.20	99.10	120.20	161.90	74.40
8 Communication	12.70	13.80	15.70	17.90	21.20	23.30	23.60	27.10	27.00	30.00	21.20
9 Recreation & culture	26.20	23.70	31.00	45.10	44.30	54.60	67.30	60.10	88.60	119.80	56.10
10 Education	[2.20]	..	[4.10]	[2.70]	[2.70]	[2.00]	[4.20]	[3.60]	10.30	19.50	5.20
11 Restaurants & hotels	10.70	12.80	17.60	21.50	29.70	34.90	38.80	45.90	52.90	83.40	34.80
12 Miscellaneous goods & services	18.70	18.20	25.30	33.60	31.40	41.50	43.30	49.40	62.70	82.30	40.60
1-12 All expenditure groups	234.20	249.00	305.40	370.30	404.20	464.30	492.60	543.70	648.60	844.70	455.70
13 Other expenditure items	25.20	29.80	40.40	49.20	68.00	62.80	70.80	92.80	138.70	153.60	73.10
Total expenditure	**259.50**	**278.90**	**345.80**	**419.50**	**472.20**	**527.10**	**563.50**	**636.50**	**787.30**	**998.30**	**528.80**
Average weekly expenditure per person (£) **Total expenditure**	**191.30**	**191.80**	**198.10**	**200.20**	**197.30**	**210.00**	**209.80**	**223.00**	**263.40**	**307.70**	**226.70**

Note: The commodity and service categories are not comparable to those in publications before 2001-02.
Please see background notes for symbols and conventions used in this report.
1 Excluding mortgage interest payments, council tax and Northern Ireland rates. Mortgage interest payments can be found in category 13.

Source: Office for National Statistics

Table A8

Household expenditure as a percentage of total expenditure by disposable income decile group

UK, financial year ending 2022

> This table is under review to be removed from future publications and replaced with disposable equivalised income tables.
> If you use this table for your analysis, please get in contact here.

	Lowest ten per cent	Second decile group	Third decile group	Fourth decile group	Fifth decile group	Sixth decile group	Seventh decile group	Eighth decile group	Ninth decile group	Highest ten per cent	All house-holds
Lower boundary of group (£ per week)		247	349	443	555	668	795	928	1,127	1,438	
Weighted number of households (thousands)	2,850	2,850	2,850	2,850	2,850	2,850	2,850	2,850	2,850	2,850	28,500
Total number of households in sample	540	540	560	580	570	580	570	580	570	560	5,630
Total number of persons in sample	720	780	950	1,160	1,300	1,400	1,480	1,630	1,680	1,750	12,850
Total number of adults in sample	640	680	820	940	1,040	1,100	1,170	1,250	1,280	1,340	10,260
Weighted average number of persons per household	1.4	1.5	1.7	2.1	2.4	2.5	2.7	2.9	3.0	3.2	2.3

Commodity or service					Percentage of total expenditure						
1 Food & non-alcoholic drinks	14	15	13	13	12	13	13	12	11	9	12
2 Alcoholic drinks, tobacco & narcotics	3	3	3	2	2	2	2	2	2	2	2
3 Clothing & footwear	3	3	3	3	3	3	3	4	3	4	3
4 Housing(net)[1], fuel & power	25	25	23	21	19	18	16	14	12	12	17
5 Household goods & services	7	7	7	6	6	7	6	7	7	7	7
6 Health	2	1	2	2	2	2	2	1	2	2	2
7 Transport	10	10	10	13	13	14	15	16	15	16	14
8 Communication	5	5	5	4	4	4	4	4	3	3	4
9 Recreation & culture	10	9	9	11	9	10	12	9	11	12	11
10 Education	[1]	..	[1]	[1]	[1]	[0]	[1]	[1]	1	2	1
11 Restaurants & hotels	4	5	5	5	6	7	7	7	7	8	7
12 Miscellaneous goods & services	7	7	7	8	7	8	8	8	8	8	8
1-12 All expenditure groups	90	89	88	88	86	88	87	85	82	85	86
13 Other expenditure items	10	11	12	12	14	12	13	15	18	15	14
Total expenditure	**100**	**100**	**100**	**100**	**100**	**100**	**100**	**100**	**100**	**100**	**100**

Note: The commodity and service categories are not comparable to those in publications before 2001-02.
Please see background notes for symbols and conventions used in this report.
1 Excluding mortgage interest payments, council tax and Northern Ireland rates. Mortgage interest payments can be found in category 13.

Source: Office for National Statistics

Table A9

Household expenditure by age of household reference person

UK, financial year ending 2022

	Less than 30	30 to 49	50 to 64	65 to 74	75 or over	All house-holds
Weighted number of households (thousands)	2,610	9,410	7,890	4,490	4,100	28,500
Total number of households in sample	360	1,820	1,640	1,140	670	5,630
Total number of persons in sample	760	5,410	3,660	1,970	1,050	12,850
Total number of adults in sample	630	3,380	3,270	1,950	1,040	10,260
Weighted average number of persons per household	2.2	3.1	2.3	1.7	1.5	2.3
Commodity or service	Average weekly household expenditure (£)					
1 Food & non-alcoholic drinks	44.50	69.80	68.00	56.90	50.20	62.20
2 Alcoholic drinks, tobacco & narcotics	5.80	10.90	16.00	14.80	8.70	12.20
3 Clothing & footwear	12.40	22.50	19.90	14.60	8.50	17.60
4 Housing(net)[1], fuel & power	138.10	106.50	81.50	59.50	54.90	87.70
5 Household goods & services	26.40	35.30	39.50	38.60	25.10	34.70
6 Health	3.40	7.60	10.30	12.40	10.20	9.10
7 Transport	61.60	84.90	94.60	61.70	33.50	74.40
8 Communication	19.00	23.70	23.80	18.40	15.20	21.20
9 Recreation & culture	38.30	60.80	67.20	53.90	37.50	56.10
10 Education	[7.10]	8.50	5.20	[1.50]	..	5.20
11 Restaurants & hotels	32.00	39.20	40.70	32.00	18.20	34.80
12 Miscellaneous goods & services	31.00	47.80	41.60	34.30	35.40	40.60
1-12 All expenditure groups	419.70	517.70	508.20	398.70	297.70	455.70
13 Other expenditure items	56.90	90.70	74.50	56.60	58.60	73.10
Total expenditure	**476.60**	**608.40**	**582.70**	**455.30**	**356.30**	**528.80**
Average weekly expenditure per person (£) **Total expenditure**	**219.40**	**198.70**	**253.30**	**265.80**	**237.20**	**226.70**

Note: The commodity and service categories are not comparable to those in publications before 2001-02.
Please see background notes for symbols and conventions used in this report.
1 Excluding mortgage interest payments, council tax and Northern Ireland rates. Mortgage interest payments can be found in category 13.

Source: Office for National Statistics

Table A10

Household expenditure as a percentage of total expenditure by age of household reference person

UK, financial year ending 2022

	Less than 30	30 to 49	50 to 64	65 to 74	75 or over	All house-holds
Weighted number of households (thousands)	2,610	9,410	7,890	4,490	4,100	28,500
Total number of households in sample	360	1,820	1,640	1,140	670	5,630
Total number of persons in sample	760	5,410	3,660	1,970	1,050	12,850
Total number of adults in sample	630	3,380	3,270	1,950	1,040	10,260
Weighted average number of persons per household	2.2	3.1	2.3	1.7	1.5	2.3
Commodity or service	Percentage of total expenditure					
1 Food & non-alcoholic drinks	9	11	12	13	14	12
2 Alcoholic drinks, tobacco & narcotics	1	2	3	3	2	2
3 Clothing & footwear	3	4	3	3	2	3
4 Housing(net)[1], fuel & power	29	18	14	13	15	17
5 Household goods & services	6	6	7	8	7	7
6 Health	1	1	2	3	3	2
7 Transport	13	14	16	14	9	14
8 Communication	4	4	4	4	4	4
9 Recreation & culture	8	10	12	12	11	11
10 Education	[1]	1	1	[0]	..	1
11 Restaurants & hotels	7	6	7	7	5	7
12 Miscellaneous goods & services	7	8	7	8	10	8
1-12 All expenditure groups	88	85	87	88	84	86
13 Other expenditure items	12	15	13	12	16	14
Total expenditure	**100**	**100**	**100**	**100**	**100**	**100**

Note: The commodity and service categories are not comparable to those in publications before 2001-02.

Please see background notes for symbols and conventions used in this report.

1 Excluding mortgage interest payments, council tax and Northern Ireland rates. Mortgage interest payments can be found in category 13.

Source: Office for National Statistics

Table A12

Household expenditure by gross income quintile group where the household reference person is aged under 30

UK, financial year ending 2020 to financial year ending 2022

This table is under review to be removed from future publications.
If you use this table for your analysis, please get in contact here.

	Lowest twenty per cent	Second quintile group	Third quintile group	Fourth quintile group	Highest twenty per cent	All house-holds
Lower boundary of group (£ per week)[1]		369	612	918	1,366	
Average weighted number of households (thousands)	360	490	650	650	390	2,530
Total number of households in sample (over 3 years)	170	220	280	280	150	1,100
Total number of persons in sample (over 3 years)	350	450	630	630	400	2,460
Total number of adults in sample (over 3 years)	220	310	510	560	370	1,970
Weighted average number of persons per household	2.1	2.1	2.3	2.3	2.7	2.3

Commodity or service	Average weekly household expenditure (£)					
1 Food & non-alcoholic drinks	35.80	38.30	51.80	54.20	64.80	49.70
2 Alcoholic drinks, tobacco & narcotics	6.70	5.70	7.00	9.90	11.60	8.10
3 Clothing & footwear	7.50	11.80	15.00	19.40	21.80	15.40
4 Housing(net)[2], fuel & power	100.50	123.60	139.20	144.00	249.50	148.40
5 Household goods & services	17.60	16.60	27.10	33.10	43.50	27.80
6 Health	1.50	1.70	3.10	3.90	6.10	3.30
7 Transport	21.70	37.90	62.90	83.80	99.80	63.20
8 Communication	14.10	15.90	21.70	23.20	21.20	19.80
9 Recreation & culture	17.00	23.20	43.70	45.90	64.50	39.80
10 Education	..	[10.00]	[9.70]	[15.40]	[30.10]	13.10
11 Restaurants & hotels	15.10	19.80	32.60	40.10	64.70	34.50
12 Miscellaneous goods & services	17.20	25.60	36.70	45.70	49.20	36.00
1-12 All expenditure groups	255.90	330.10	450.60	518.60	726.80	459.20
13 Other expenditure items	20.70	32.40	55.70	85.30	106.80	61.80
Total expenditure	**276.60**	**362.50**	**506.30**	**603.90**	**833.70**	**521.00**
Average weekly expenditure per person (£) **Total expenditure**	**131.40**	**175.60**	**221.10**	**264.50**	**309.30**	**228.40**

Note: The commodity and service categories are not comparable to those in publications before 2001-02.

Please see background notes for symbols and conventions used in this report.

This table is based on a three year average.

1 Lower boundary of 2021-22 gross income quintile groups (£ per week).

2 Excluding mortgage interest payments, council tax and Northern Ireland rates. Mortgage interest payments can be found in category 13.

Source: Office for National Statistics

Table A12Eq

Household expenditure by equivalised disposable income quintile group (OECD-modified scale) where the household reference person is aged under 30

UK, financial year ending 2020 to financial year ending 2022

This table is under review to be removed from future publications. If you use this table for your analysis, please get in contact here.

	Lowest twenty per cent	Second quintile group	Third quintile group	Fourth quintile group	Highest twenty per cent	All house-holds
Lower boundary of group (£ per week)[1]		263	369	494	663	
Average weighted number of households (thousands)	420	410	540	690	480	2,530
Total number of households in sample (over 3 years)	190	180	240	300	190	1,100
Total number of persons in sample (over 3 years)	520	410	510	630	390	2,460
Total number of adults in sample (over 3 years)	300	290	420	590	380	1,970
Weighted average number of persons per household	2.7	2.4	2.2	2.1	2.2	2.3

Commodity or service	Average weekly household expenditure (£)					
1 Food & non-alcoholic drinks	45.10	50.10	47.10	50.10	55.10	49.70
2 Alcoholic drinks, tobacco & narcotics	7.20	6.90	6.90	9.10	10.00	8.10
3 Clothing & footwear	10.80	12.10	14.90	17.10	20.70	15.40
4 Housing(net)[2], fuel & power	104.80	152.10	137.80	137.80	213.50	148.40
5 Household goods & services	18.60	16.80	23.80	31.40	45.20	27.80
6 Health	1.30	1.60	3.80	3.90	5.00	3.30
7 Transport	27.60	41.20	60.10	80.80	91.30	63.20
8 Communication	15.80	17.70	20.90	22.40	19.80	19.80
9 Recreation & culture	23.10	26.40	41.90	43.10	58.60	39.80
10 Education	..	..	[14.40]	[16.50]	..	13.10
11 Restaurants & hotels	17.10	22.80	27.40	42.50	57.30	34.50
12 Miscellaneous goods & services	20.40	30.40	34.80	44.20	45.50	36.00
1-12 All expenditure groups	296.00	393.50	433.80	499.00	634.80	459.20
13 Other expenditure items	24.30	33.90	58.30	72.60	110.20	61.80
Total expenditure	**320.30**	**427.40**	**492.10**	**571.50**	**745.00**	**521.00**
Average weekly expenditure per person (£) **Total expenditure**	**117.60**	**175.60**	**228.30**	**273.40**	**342.00**	**228.40**

Note: The commodity and service categories are not comparable to those in publications before 2001-02.

Please see background notes for symbols and conventions used in this report.

This table is based on a three year average.

1 Lower boundary of 2021-22 gross income quintile groups (£ per week).

2 Excluding mortgage interest payments, council tax and Northern Ireland rates. Mortgage interest payments can be found in category 13.

Source: Office for National Statistics

Table A13

Household expenditure by gross income quintile group where the household reference person is aged 30 to 49

UK, financial year ending 2020 to financial year ending 2022

This table is under review to be removed from future publications. If you use this table for your analysis, please get in contact here.

	Lowest twenty per cent	Second quintile group	Third quintile group	Fourth quintile group	Highest twenty per cent	All house-holds
Lower boundary of group (£ per week)[1]		369	612	918	1,366	
Average weighted number of households (thousands)	980	1,430	1,900	2,420	2,710	9,430
Total number of households in sample (over 3 years)	530	810	1,070	1,400	1,500	5,320
Total number of persons in sample (over 3 years)	1,070	2,060	3,250	4,430	4,990	15,790
Total number of adults in sample (over 3 years)	660	1,210	1,940	2,820	3,180	9,810
Weighted average number of persons per household	2.1	2.7	3.1	3.2	3.3	3.0
Commodity or service	Average weekly household expenditure (£)					
1 Food & non-alcoholic drinks	45.50	55.10	66.60	78.10	91.30	72.70
2 Alcoholic drinks, tobacco & narcotics	8.90	8.00	10.90	12.80	14.80	11.80
3 Clothing & footwear	9.80	14.70	19.40	25.60	34.50	23.60
4 Housing(net)[2], fuel & power	83.70	109.30	109.10	94.50	105.50	101.60
5 Household goods & services	16.70	21.60	31.90	38.50	60.30	38.60
6 Health	3.20	4.30	5.30	6.30	10.00	6.50
7 Transport	26.20	45.10	63.80	89.40	129.10	82.40
8 Communication	13.70	18.90	23.70	24.60	28.70	23.60
9 Recreation & culture	24.90	33.10	44.50	61.80	107.00	63.10
10 Education	[2.80]	3.90	3.30	4.80	19.40	8.30
11 Restaurants & hotels	14.00	18.20	32.50	41.90	68.80	41.20
12 Miscellaneous goods & services	17.10	27.30	38.30	48.00	71.20	46.40
1-12 All expenditure groups	266.60	359.40	449.30	526.30	740.60	519.90
13 Other expenditure items	27.40	44.10	68.00	94.60	156.90	92.50
Total expenditure	**294.00**	**403.50**	**517.40**	**620.80**	**897.50**	**612.40**
Average weekly expenditure per person (£) **Total expenditure**	**142.70**	**150.30**	**166.00**	**193.70**	**268.70**	**202.30**

Note: The commodity and service categories are not comparable to those in publications before 2001-02.

Please see background notes for symbols and conventions used in this report.

This table is based on a three year average.

1 Lower boundary of 2021-22 gross income quintile groups (£ per week).

2 Excluding mortgage interest payments, council tax and Northern Ireland rates. Mortgage interest payments can be found in category 13.

Source: Office for National Statistics

Table A13Eq

Household expenditure by equivalised disposable income quintile group (OECD-modified scale) where the household reference person is aged 30 to 49

UK, financial year ending 2020 to financial year ending 2022

> **This table is under review to be removed from future publications.**
> **If you use this table for your analysis, please get in contact here.**

		Lowest twenty per cent	Second quintile group	Third quintile group	Fourth quintile group	Highest twenty per cent	All house-holds
Lower boundary of group (£ per week)[1]			263	369	494	663	
Average weighted number of households (thousands)		1,640	1,660	1,870	1,950	2,320	9,430
Total number of households in sample (over 3 years)		860	910	1,100	1,150	1,290	5,320
Total number of persons in sample (over 3 years)		2,730	2,990	3,430	3,280	3,360	15,790
Total number of adults in sample (over 3 years)		1,440	1,650	2,070	2,210	2,440	9,810
Weighted average number of persons per household		3.3	3.4	3.1	2.9	2.6	3.0
Commodity or service		Average weekly household expenditure (£)					
1	Food & non-alcoholic drinks	62.80	71.10	72.40	74.90	79.40	72.70
2	Alcoholic drinks, tobacco & narcotics	8.20	10.00	12.40	13.90	13.40	11.80
3	Clothing & footwear	17.10	18.80	21.60	27.20	30.20	23.60
4	Housing(net)[2], fuel & power	103.60	107.10	97.40	92.30	107.90	101.60
5	Household goods & services	22.40	29.60	35.20	39.30	58.50	38.60
6	Health	3.60	5.30	5.40	7.30	9.70	6.50
7	Transport	42.90	59.60	72.60	95.50	123.20	82.40
8	Communication	18.90	23.50	23.90	25.60	25.10	23.60
9	Recreation & culture	31.80	43.80	54.30	72.20	98.30	63.10
10	Education	3.80	2.50	4.40	6.90	20.20	8.30
11	Restaurants & hotels	19.20	26.30	35.90	48.90	65.20	41.20
12	Miscellaneous goods & services	25.70	35.10	43.70	50.80	67.40	46.40
1-12	All expenditure groups	360.00	432.80	479.40	554.90	698.40	519.90
13	Other expenditure items	38.20	57.00	83.20	103.10	154.70	92.50
Total expenditure		**398.20**	**489.80**	**562.60**	**657.90**	**853.10**	**612.40**
Average weekly expenditure per person (£) **Total expenditure**		**119.70**	**145.80**	**178.90**	**227.10**	**329.10**	**202.30**

Note: The commodity and service categories are not comparable to those in publications before 2001-02.

Please see background notes for symbols and conventions used in this report.

This table is based on a three year average.

1 Lower boundary of 2021-22 gross income quintile groups (£ per week).

2 Excluding mortgage interest payments, council tax and Northern Ireland rates. Mortgage interest payments can be found in category 13.

Source: Office for National Statistics

Table A14

Household expenditure by gross income quintile group where the household reference person is aged 50 to 64

UK, financial year ending 2020 to financial year ending 2022

This table is under review to be removed from future publications. If you use this table for your analysis, please get in contact here.

	Lowest twenty per cent	Second quintile group	Third quintile group	Fourth quintile group	Highest twenty per cent	All house-holds
Lower boundary of group (£ per week)[1]		369	612	918	1,366	
Average weighted number of households (thousands)	1,500	1,300	1,450	1,600	2,020	7,880
Total number of households in sample (over 3 years)	930	810	890	990	1,150	4,770
Total number of persons in sample (over 3 years)	1,270	1,520	1,920	2,520	3,490	10,720
Total number of adults in sample (over 3 years)	1,200	1,350	1,730	2,240	3,030	9,550
Weighted average number of persons per household	1.4	1.9	2.2	2.6	3.2	2.3
Commodity or service	Average weekly household expenditure (£)					
1 Food & non-alcoholic drinks	39.10	56.40	66.30	78.40	102.10	71.10
2 Alcoholic drinks, tobacco & narcotics	11.00	12.80	15.50	18.90	24.80	17.30
3 Clothing & footwear	7.20	13.60	15.20	25.10	36.30	20.90
4 Housing(net)[2], fuel & power	62.30	74.40	78.10	77.00	87.30	76.60
5 Household goods & services	16.00	29.30	34.80	44.40	65.10	40.00
6 Health	3.50	6.00	5.60	11.90	16.20	9.20
7 Transport	29.70	53.30	81.90	104.60	162.80	92.60
8 Communication	13.20	17.80	21.70	26.60	33.50	23.50
9 Recreation & culture	30.10	40.10	60.90	81.40	116.90	70.20
10 Education	[2.40]	3.40	[1.40]	4.20	16.50	6.40
11 Restaurants & hotels	13.70	22.10	33.40	45.20	75.00	40.90
12 Miscellaneous goods & services	20.00	30.40	34.40	52.20	71.60	44.20
1-12 All expenditure groups	248.20	359.40	449.40	570.00	808.10	512.90
13 Other expenditure items	26.80	42.40	67.50	79.10	137.00	75.80
Total expenditure	**275.00**	**401.90**	**516.80**	**649.10**	**945.10**	**588.70**
Average weekly expenditure per person (£) **Total expenditure**	**203.60**	**206.70**	**235.80**	**249.60**	**296.90**	**252.90**

Note: The commodity and service categories are not comparable to those in publications before 2001-02.

Please see background notes for symbols and conventions used in this report.

This table is based on a three year average.

1 Lower boundary of 2021-22 gross income quintile groups (£ per week).

2 Excluding mortgage interest payments, council tax and Northern Ireland rates. Mortgage interest payments can be found in category 13.

Source: Office for National Statistics

Table A14Eq

Household expenditure by equivalised disposable income quintile group (OECD-modified scale) where the household reference person is aged 50 to 64

UK, financial year ending 2020 to financial year ending 2022

> **This table is under review to be removed from future publications.**
> **If you use this table for your analysis, please get in contact here.**

	Lowest twenty per cent	Second quintile group	Third quintile group	Fourth quintile group	Highest twenty per cent	All house-holds
Lower boundary of group (£ per week)[1]		263	369	494	663	
Average weighted number of households (thousands)	1,570	1,300	1,460	1,670	1,870	7,880
Total number of households in sample (over 3 years)	950	800	910	1,000	1,110	4,770
Total number of persons in sample (over 3 years)	1,760	1,720	2,120	2,500	2,620	10,720
Total number of adults in sample (over 3 years)	1,520	1,490	1,880	2,260	2,390	9,550
Weighted average number of persons per household	1.9	2.2	2.4	2.6	2.4	2.3
Commodity or service	Average weekly household expenditure (£)					
1 Food & non-alcoholic drinks	50.90	62.30	70.80	78.60	87.60	71.10
2 Alcoholic drinks, tobacco & narcotics	11.20	14.00	16.80	18.60	23.70	17.30
3 Clothing & footwear	9.60	13.70	21.50	23.40	32.50	20.90
4 Housing(net)[2], fuel & power	69.40	71.60	77.60	77.00	85.00	76.60
5 Household goods & services	20.20	31.30	35.10	44.90	62.60	40.00
6 Health	4.30	6.00	8.60	8.30	16.90	9.20
7 Transport	38.30	65.90	83.30	109.00	149.50	92.60
8 Communication	15.40	20.90	23.60	26.30	29.30	23.50
9 Recreation & culture	34.50	45.20	61.60	82.30	113.40	70.20
10 Education	3.40	3.40	5.10	5.70	12.60	6.40
11 Restaurants & hotels	17.60	26.30	32.70	49.80	68.70	40.90
12 Miscellaneous goods & services	24.50	30.70	41.00	49.40	67.70	44.20
1-12 All expenditure groups	299.20	391.20	477.80	573.30	749.40	512.90
13 Other expenditure items	34.10	46.20	61.20	86.50	133.20	75.80
Total expenditure	**333.40**	**437.50**	**539.00**	**659.80**	**882.60**	**588.70**
Average weekly expenditure per person (£)						
Total expenditure	**171.50**	**197.10**	**223.40**	**257.40**	**360.50**	**252.90**

Note: The commodity and service categories are not comparable to those in publications before 2001-02.

Please see background notes for symbols and conventions used in this report.

This table is based on a three year average.

1 Lower boundary of 2021-22 gross income quintile groups (£ per week).

2 Excluding mortgage interest payments, council tax and Northern Ireland rates. Mortgage interest payments can be found in category 13.

Source: Office for National Statistics

Table A15

Household expenditure by gross income quintile group where the household reference person is aged 65 to 74

UK, financial year ending 2020 to financial year ending 2022

This table is under review to be removed from future publications. If you use this table for your analysis, please get in contact here.

		Lowest twenty per cent	Second quintile group	Third quintile group	Fourth quintile group	Highest twenty per cent	All house-holds
Lower boundary of group (£ per week)[1]			369	612	918	1,366	
Average weighted number of households (thousands)		1,270	1,160	920	620	350	4,330
Total number of households in sample (over 3 years)		860	890	720	480	260	3,200
Total number of persons in sample (over 3 years)		1,020	1,490	1,400	1,040	600	5,540
Total number of adults in sample (over 3 years)		1,020	1,480	1,390	1,010	580	5,480
Weighted average number of persons per household		1.2	1.6	2.0	2.2	2.4	1.7
Commodity or service		Average weekly household expenditure (£)					
1	Food & non-alcoholic drinks	38.70	55.00	69.20	80.20	92.70	60.00
2	Alcoholic drinks, tobacco & narcotics	9.40	13.20	17.90	17.80	29.10	15.00
3	Clothing & footwear	6.80	10.80	16.50	20.70	28.30	13.70
4	Housing(net)[2], fuel & power	51.00	56.30	58.00	69.80	77.30	58.90
5	Household goods & services	16.00	28.00	37.20	45.20	83.30	33.30
6	Health	4.00	8.80	11.10	15.00	15.30	9.40
7	Transport	23.90	45.40	69.10	93.50	120.80	57.40
8	Communication	12.20	16.60	20.40	24.00	27.00	18.00
9	Recreation & culture	27.30	48.80	75.20	91.50	99.90	58.80
10	Education	..	..	[0.30]	..	[10.70]	1.30
11	Restaurants & hotels	11.40	22.50	35.90	47.30	66.70	29.50
12	Miscellaneous goods & services	17.00	31.60	39.70	48.70	73.30	34.90
1-12	All expenditure groups	217.80	337.90	450.60	554.70	724.30	390.10
13	Other expenditure items	26.00	44.50	60.00	83.30	120.00	54.50
Total expenditure		**243.80**	**382.40**	**510.60**	**638.10**	**844.30**	**444.60**
Average weekly expenditure per person (£) **Total expenditure**		**206.30**	**232.00**	**260.70**	**285.50**	**348.70**	**257.70**

Note: The commodity and service categories are not comparable to those in publications before 2001-02.

Please see background notes for symbols and conventions used in this report.

This table is based on a three year average.

1 Lower boundary of 2021-22 gross income quintile groups (£ per week).

2 Excluding mortgage interest payments, council tax and Northern Ireland rates. Mortgage interest payments can be found in category 13.

Source: Office for National Statistics

Table A15Eq

Household expenditure by equivalised disposable income quintile group (OECD-modified scale) where the household reference person is aged 65 to 74

UK, financial year ending 2020 to financial year ending 2022

This table is under review to be removed from future publications.
If you use this table for your analysis, please get in contact here.

	Lowest twenty per cent	Second quintile group	Third quintile group	Fourth quintile group	Highest twenty per cent	All house-holds
Lower boundary of group (£ per week)[1]		263	369	494	663	
Average weighted number of households (thousands)	980	1,100	940	700	600	4,330
Total number of households in sample (over 3 years)	670	810	730	540	460	3,200
Total number of persons in sample (over 3 years)	930	1,380	1,330	1,030	880	5,540
Total number of adults in sample (over 3 years)	920	1,360	1,310	1,030	870	5,480
Weighted average number of persons per household	1.4	1.7	1.8	2.0	1.9	1.7
Commodity or service	Average weekly household expenditure (£)					
1 Food & non-alcoholic drinks	42.20	55.20	63.40	71.10	79.10	60.00
2 Alcoholic drinks, tobacco & narcotics	10.20	13.70	15.80	15.30	23.70	15.00
3 Clothing & footwear	6.30	11.90	15.50	16.90	22.20	13.70
4 Housing(net)[2], fuel & power	51.60	55.80	61.80	60.60	69.80	58.90
5 Household goods & services	15.70	28.20	29.40	44.50	64.90	33.30
6 Health	4.50	6.50	11.20	12.40	16.10	9.40
7 Transport	27.00	38.50	63.90	81.80	101.90	57.40
8 Communication	12.50	16.40	18.80	22.90	23.00	18.00
9 Recreation & culture	31.50	42.60	62.60	88.00	92.40	58.80
10 Education	..	..	..	..	[6.40]	1.30
11 Restaurants & hotels	12.40	20.60	29.30	42.40	57.70	29.50
12 Miscellaneous goods & services	17.00	26.50	39.10	43.80	61.60	34.90
1-12 All expenditure groups	231.10	316.90	411.40	499.80	618.90	390.10
13 Other expenditure items	25.20	39.40	56.00	68.30	109.90	54.50
Total expenditure	**256.30**	**356.30**	**467.40**	**568.10**	**728.80**	**444.60**
Average weekly expenditure per person (£) **Total expenditure**	**186.50**	**209.50**	**255.50**	**290.10**	**381.70**	**257.70**

Note: The commodity and service categories are not comparable to those in publications before 2001-02.

Please see background notes for symbols and conventions used in this report.

This table is based on a three year average.

1 Lower boundary of 2021-22 gross income quintile groups (£ per week).

2 Excluding mortgage interest payments, council tax and Northern Ireland rates. Mortgage interest payments can be found in category 13.

Source: Office for National Statistics

Table A16

Household expenditure by gross income quintile group where the household reference person is aged 75 or over

UK, financial year ending 2020 to financial year ending 2022

This table is under review to be removed from future publications. If you use this table for your analysis, please get in contact here.

		Lowest twenty per cent	Second quintile group	Third quintile group	Fourth quintile group	Highest twenty per cent	All house-holds
Lower boundary of group (£ per week)[1]			369	612	918	1,366	
Average weighted number of households (thousands)		1,530	1,250	720	340	160	4,010
Total number of households in sample (over 3 years)		720	660	420	200	90	2,080
Total number of persons in sample (over 3 years)		830	1,030	780	410	190	3,250
Total number of adults in sample (over 3 years)		830	1,030	780	410	180	3,230
Weighted average number of persons per household		1.1	1.5	1.9	2.1	2.1	1.5
Commodity or service		Average weekly household expenditure (£)					
1	Food & non-alcoholic drinks	35.00	49.50	62.00	78.90	80.40	50.10
2	Alcoholic drinks, tobacco & narcotics	5.50	7.40	11.30	15.80	23.10	8.70
3	Clothing & footwear	5.20	8.50	12.10	17.00	16.60	8.90
4	Housing(net)[2], fuel & power	46.00	49.40	55.90	65.20	64.80	51.20
5	Household goods & services	16.30	25.20	27.40	41.90	48.60	24.50
6	Health	5.30	10.90	13.30	21.40	20.00	10.50
7	Transport	12.30	29.30	47.10	54.30	90.20	30.60
8	Communication	11.00	15.00	18.90	21.30	24.70	15.20
9	Recreation & culture	20.10	32.40	55.30	84.60	88.70	38.20
10	Education	..	..	..	..	..	[0.40]
11	Restaurants & hotels	7.50	13.40	26.00	40.30	63.10	17.30
12	Miscellaneous goods & services	19.70	30.50	44.10	57.40	80.10	33.00
1-12	All expenditure groups	184.00	271.40	373.70	499.90	606.00	288.60
13	Other expenditure items	24.60	43.80	58.00	106.90	158.90	49.40
Total expenditure		**208.60**	**315.20**	**431.70**	**606.80**	**764.90**	**338.00**
Average weekly expenditure per person (£) **Total expenditure**		**184.80**	**211.50**	**233.00**	**290.40**	**357.20**	**226.00**

Note: The commodity and service categories are not comparable to those in publications before 2001-02.

Please see background notes for symbols and conventions used in this report.

This table is based on a three year average.

1 Lower boundary of 2021-22 gross income quintile groups (£ per week).

2 Excluding mortgage interest payments, council tax and Northern Ireland rates. Mortgage interest payments can be found in category 13.

Source: Office for National Statistics

Table A16Eq

Household expenditure by equivalised disposable income quintile group
(OECD-modified scale) where the household reference person is aged 75 or over
UK, financial year ending 2020 to financial year ending 2022

**This table is under review to be removed from future publications.
If you use this table for your analysis, please get in contact here.**

	Lowest twenty per cent	Second quintile group	Third quintile group	Fourth quintile group	Highest twenty per cent	All house-holds
Lower boundary of group (£ per week)[1]		263	369	494	663	
Average weighted number of households (thousands)	1,020	1,160	840	620	360	4,010
Total number of households in sample (over 3 years)	490	600	450	340	200	2,080
Total number of persons in sample (over 3 years)	680	930	730	580	340	3,250
Total number of adults in sample (over 3 years)	680	920	730	570	340	3,230
Weighted average number of persons per household	1.3	1.5	1.5	1.6	1.7	1.5
Commodity or service	Average weekly household expenditure (£)					
1 Food & non-alcoholic drinks	39.10	46.40	52.60	60.10	69.10	50.10
2 Alcoholic drinks, tobacco & narcotics	5.50	7.40	8.60	12.50	16.20	8.70
3 Clothing & footwear	6.80	6.60	9.80	11.70	15.20	8.90
4 Housing(net)[2], fuel & power	49.20	48.20	52.50	52.00	63.20	51.20
5 Household goods & services	15.90	22.80	23.90	34.30	40.10	24.50
6 Health	5.90	8.30	14.10	14.10	15.40	10.50
7 Transport	14.00	25.30	33.50	44.60	63.40	30.60
8 Communication	11.40	13.80	16.70	18.20	21.20	15.20
9 Recreation & culture	20.40	29.20	41.20	56.60	84.20	38.20
10 Education	:	..	..	..	..	[0.40]
11 Restaurants & hotels	8.20	11.30	20.00	25.90	44.90	17.30
12 Miscellaneous goods & services	22.10	23.80	38.20	44.30	63.70	33.00
1-12 All expenditure groups	198.60	243.20	311.40	374.80	499.90	288.60
13 Other expenditure items	23.90	35.50	46.30	63.30	147.60	49.40
Total expenditure	**222.50**	**278.70**	**357.80**	**438.10**	**647.50**	**338.00**
Average weekly expenditure per person (£) **Total expenditure**	166.60	190.00	232.70	265.70	385.00	226.00

Note: The commodity and service categories are not comparable to those in publications before 2001-02.

Please see background notes for symbols and conventions used in this report.

This table is based on a three year average.

1 Lower boundary of 2021-22 gross income quintile groups (£ per week).

2 Excluding mortgage interest payments, council tax and Northern Ireland rates. Mortgage interest payments can be found in category 13.

Source: Office for National Statistics

Table A23

Expenditure by household composition

UK, financial year ending 2022

| | Retired households | | | | Non-retired | | Retired and non-retired households | | | | | | |
| | State pension[1] | | Other retired | | | | One adult | | Two adults | | | Three or more adults | |
	One person	Two adults	One person	Two adults	One person	Two adults	with one child	with two or more children	with one child	with two children	with three or more children	without children	with children
Weighted number of households (thousands)	760	450	2,920	2,960	4,640	6,340	650	590	2,140	2,710	890	2,330	1,130
Total number of households in sample	130	100	530	690	920	1,340	120	100	410	520	150	420	180
Total number of persons in sample	130	210	530	1,380	920	2,670	240	330	1,240	2,090	810	1,390	890
Total number of adults in sample	130	210	530	1,380	920	2,670	120	100	830	1,050	310	1,390	620
Weighted average number of persons per household	1.0	2.0	1.0	2.0	1.0	2.0	2.0	3.3	3.0	4.0	5.3	3.4	5.0

Commodity or service	Average weekly household expenditure (£)												
1 Food & non-alcoholic drinks	34.50	60.80	35.00	69.00	33.50	63.70	42.70	52.30	74.70	86.30	85.50	87.90	106.10
2 Alcoholic drinks, tobacco & narcotics	5.40	10.50	7.70	15.60	10.00	14.50	4.40	4.50	11.70	12.00	9.90	17.90	15.10
3 Clothing & footwear	5.60	10.50	6.40	14.90	9.80	17.60	13.00	14.20	26.20	22.90	28.70	30.40	36.10
4 Housing(net)[2], fuel & power	53.20	56.80	47.30	60.80	85.30	95.70	115.80	121.20	89.40	103.40	119.00	105.00	127.10
5 Household goods & services	13.40	37.80	22.70	37.40	24.30	40.60	24.40	14.70	39.80	40.30	33.20	50.80	42.40
6 Health	6.60	10.50	7.20	17.00	4.40	9.00	4.50	4.20	8.00	7.30	7.90	16.90	10.20
7 Transport	11.90	41.70	24.90	62.00	42.80	89.30	32.20	47.70	109.00	107.30	88.20	125.70	113.10
8 Communication	10.90	14.00	12.60	20.40	14.70	22.40	16.20	18.70	25.60	26.30	31.60	30.80	31.50
9 Recreation & culture	17.70	42.80	26.60	64.90	35.20	64.50	37.20	36.30	67.00	81.10	83.80	70.00	68.60
10 Education	:	:	..	..	3.90	1.50	[28.60]	..	10.70	8.80	[14.20]	[9.00]	[15.20]
11 Restaurants & hotels	7.80	24.90	13.70	34.00	20.30	43.50	18.40	25.60	41.40	48.40	33.30	56.70	49.20
12 Miscellaneous goods & services	24.10	28.00	24.70	44.50	22.90	44.30	29.20	26.50	54.30	56.70	46.10	55.10	55.90
1-12 All expenditure groups	191.30	338.20	229.00	441.40	307.10	506.60	366.70	366.60	557.90	600.80	581.30	656.20	670.60
13 Other expenditure items	25.00	37.70	51.50	68.80	54.00	82.20	49.60	35.60	104.80	112.40	81.70	79.30	73.40
Total expenditure	**216.30**	**376.00**	**280.50**	**510.20**	**361.10**	**588.80**	**416.30**	**402.20**	**662.70**	**713.20**	**663.10**	**735.50**	**744.00**
Average weekly expenditure per person (£)													
Total expenditure	**216.30**	**188.00**	**280.50**	**255.10**	**361.10**	**294.40**	**208.10**	**120.30**	**220.90**	**178.30**	**125.30**	**219.10**	**149.40**

Note: The commodity and service categories are not comparable to those in publications before 2001-02.

Please see background notes for symbols and conventions used in this report.

1 Mainly dependent on state pensions and not economically active - see Methodology - Economically Inactive.

2 Excluding mortgage interest payments, council tax and Northern Ireland rates Mortgage interest payments can be found in category 13.

Source: Office for National Statistics

Table A26

Expenditure of one adult non-retired households by gross income quintile group[1]

UK, financial year ending 2020 to financial year ending 2022

> **This table is under review to be removed from future publications and replaced with disposable equivalised income tables.**
> **If you use this table for your analysis, please get in contact here.**

	Lowest twenty per cent	Second quintile group	Third quintile group	Fourth quintile group	Highest twenty per cent	All house-holds
Lower boundary of group (gross income: £ per week)[2]		369	612	918	1,366	
Average weighted number of households (thousands)	1,820	1,220	880	430	240	4,590
Total number of households in sample (over 3 years)	1,070	740	500	250	120	2,670
Total number of persons in sample (over 3 years)	1,070	740	500	250	120	2,670
Total number of adults in sample (over 3 years)	1,070	740	500	250	120	2,670
Weighted average number of persons per household	1.0	1.0	1.0	1.0	1.0	1.0
Commodity or service	Average weekly household expenditure (£)					
1 Food & non-alcoholic drinks	31.00	32.50	36.00	39.30	49.00	34.10
2 Alcoholic drinks, tobacco & narcotics	10.10	8.40	8.80	12.10	13.80	9.70
3 Clothing & footwear	5.40	9.20	10.20	15.00	16.00	8.80
4 Housing(net)[3], fuel & power	66.00	85.20	76.80	86.70	111.10	77.40
5 Household goods & services	13.30	16.60	26.80	33.50	59.00	21.00
6 Health	2.90	4.50	4.80	9.30	6.90	4.50
7 Transport	21.00	39.10	51.10	76.10	87.50	40.20
8 Communication	11.00	14.30	16.50	17.10	17.50	13.80
9 Recreation & culture	21.10	27.20	44.20	44.60	43.70	30.70
10 Education	[2.60]	[3.10]	..	[4.60]	..	2.60
11 Restaurants & hotels	10.50	15.80	26.00	30.50	46.90	18.80
12 Miscellaneous goods & services	15.10	23.40	30.80	37.70	45.30	23.90
1-12 All expenditure groups	210.00	279.20	332.80	406.60	499.20	285.50
13 Other expenditure items	23.70	42.30	75.00	82.50	177.90	52.10
Total expenditure	**233.70**	**321.50**	**407.80**	**489.10**	**677.10**	**337.60**
Average weekly expenditure per person (£)						
Total expenditure	**233.70**	**321.50**	**407.80**	**489.10**	**677.10**	**337.60**

Note: The commodity and service categories are not comparable to those in publications before 2001-02.

Please see background notes for symbols and conventions used in this report.

This table is based on a three year average.

1 Mainly dependent on state pensions and not economically active - see Methodology - Economically Inactive.

2 Lower boundary of 2021-22 gross income quintile groups (£ per week).

3 Excluding mortgage interest payments, council tax and Northern Ireland rates. Mortgage interest payments can be found in category 13.

Source: Office for National Statistics

Table A29

Expenditure of two adult non-retired households by gross income quintile group[1]

UK, financial year ending 2020 to financial year ending 2022

> **This table is under review to be removed from future publications and replaced with disposable equivalised income tables.**
>
> **If you use this table for your analysis, please get in contact here.**

	Lowest twenty per cent	Second quintile group	Third quintile group	Fourth quintile group	Highest twenty per cent	All house-holds
Lower boundary of group (gross income: £ per week)[2]		369	612	918	1,366	
Average weighted number of households (thousands)	510	880	1,430	1,860	1,620	6,300
Total number of households in sample (over 3 years)	310	570	870	1,120	960	3,820
Total number of persons in sample (over 3 years)	620	1,140	1,740	2,230	1,920	7,650
Total number of adults in sample (over 3 years)	620	1,140	1,740	2,230	1,920	7,650
Weighted average number of persons per household	2.0	2.0	2.0	2.0	2.0	2.0
Commodity or service	Average weekly household expenditure (£)					
1 Food & non-alcoholic drinks	54.20	60.40	61.90	65.10	74.30	65.20
2 Alcoholic drinks, tobacco & narcotics	10.50	15.00	16.50	15.60	17.90	15.90
3 Clothing & footwear	10.70	12.60	13.30	21.40	26.20	18.70
4 Housing(net)[3], fuel & power	76.70	79.20	94.70	96.20	109.40	95.40
5 Household goods & services	24.50	35.80	33.90	37.50	64.70	42.40
6 Health	3.80	6.90	5.90	9.00	11.70	8.20
7 Transport	46.70	55.70	76.20	90.60	120.50	86.60
8 Communication	18.20	18.70	21.80	23.50	25.60	22.50
9 Recreation & culture	41.70	44.60	55.30	68.90	98.20	67.70
10 Education	..	[2.20]	1.80	1.90	2.50	2.00
11 Restaurants & hotels	25.40	26.90	36.60	43.70	61.90	42.90
12 Miscellaneous goods & services	29.60	32.90	34.80	45.30	60.30	43.70
1-12 All expenditure groups	342.70	390.80	452.80	518.70	673.20	511.30
13 Other expenditure items	36.60	44.90	58.70	85.40	135.20	82.50
Total expenditure	**379.30**	**435.60**	**511.40**	**604.20**	**808.40**	**593.80**
Average weekly expenditure per person (£) **Total expenditure**	**189.70**	**217.80**	**255.70**	**302.10**	**404.20**	**296.90**

Note: The commodity and service categories are not comparable to those in publications before 2001-02.

Please see background notes for symbols and conventions used in this report.

This table is based on a three year average.

1 Mainly dependent on state pensions and not economically active - see Methodology - Economically Inactive.

2 Lower boundary of 2021-22 gross income quintile groups (£ per week).

3 Excluding mortgage interest payments, council tax and Northern Ireland rates. Mortgage interest payments can be found in category 13.

Source: Office for National Statistics

Table A32

Household expenditure by tenure

UK, financial year ending 2022

	Owners			Social rented from			Private rented[4]				All tenures
	Owned outright	Buying with a mortgage[1]	All	Council[2]	Registered Social Landlord[3]	All	Rent free	Rent paid, unfurnished[5]	Rent paid, furnished	All	
Weighted number of households (thousands)	10,140	9,010	19,150	2,130	1,930	4,060	260	4,280	750	5,290	28,500
Total number of households in sample	2,300	1,830	4,130	360	320	680	40	680	110	830	5,630
Total number of persons in sample	4,430	5,040	9,470	830	670	1,500	110	1,560	220	1,890	12,850
Total number of adults in sample	4,150	3,590	7,730	590	510	1,100	80	1,150	200	1,430	10,260
Weighted average number of persons per household	1.9	2.8	2.3	2.5	2.3	2.4	2.7	2.5	2.1	2.4	2.3
Commodity or service	Average weekly household expenditure (£)										
1 Food & non-alcoholic drinks	61.00	72.60	66.50	54.70	48.60	51.80	56.00	55.60	48.20	54.50	62.20
2 Alcoholic drinks, tobacco & narcotics	12.90	13.50	13.20	10.90	8.20	9.60	8.90	10.90	8.30	10.40	12.20
3 Clothing & footwear	14.90	24.60	19.50	11.60	13.90	12.70	30.70	14.10	10.40	14.40	17.60
4 Housing(net)[6], fuel & power	51.30	55.20	53.10	93.40	117.00	104.60	39.10	203.30	236.10	199.90	87.70
5 Household goods & services	35.80	47.10	41.10	22.00	21.30	21.70	13.80	23.60	12.70	21.60	34.70
6 Health	12.40	9.50	11.00	3.10	4.00	3.50	12.40	6.60	2.20	6.30	9.10
7 Transport	73.80	103.50	87.80	29.00	39.00	33.70	52.40	61.00	37.70	57.30	74.40
8 Communication	19.70	25.60	22.50	18.30	16.80	17.60	20.00	20.30	14.40	19.50	21.20
9 Recreation & culture	59.80	74.60	66.80	27.30	34.90	30.90	28.90	39.90	20.90	36.70	56.10
10 Education	2.70	7.80	5.10	..	..	[2.20]	..	4.30	..	7.70	5.20
11 Restaurants & hotels	33.90	48.00	40.50	12.60	15.80	14.10	43.50	29.20	30.00	30.00	34.80
12 Miscellaneous goods & services	41.40	52.90	46.90	20.00	19.30	19.70	47.80	31.50	45.50	34.30	40.60
1-12 All expenditure groups	419.60	535.00	473.90	304.30	341.70	322.10	370.50	500.60	489.50	492.60	455.70
13 Other expenditure items	63.00	128.20	93.70	20.50	23.10	21.70	56.10	38.60	30.20	38.30	73.10
Total expenditure	**482.60**	**663.20**	**567.50**	**324.80**	**364.80**	**343.80**	**426.60**	**539.20**	**519.70**	**530.90**	**528.80**
Average weekly expenditure per person (£) **Total expenditure**	**256.60**	**240.10**	**247.30**	**130.30**	**160.10**	**143.80**	**160.70**	**218.60**	**246.40**	**218.90**	**226.70**

Note: The commodity and service categories are not comparable to those in publications before 2001-02.

Please see background notes for symbols and conventions used in this report.

1 Including shared owners (who own part of the equity and pay mortgage, part rent).

2 "Council" includes local authorities, New Towns and Scottish Homes, but see note 3 below.

3 Formerly Housing Associations.

4 All tenants whose accommodation goes with the job of someone in the household are allocated to "rented privately",
  even if the landlord is a local authority or housing association or Housing Action Trust, or if the accommodation is
  rent free. Squatters are also included in this category

5 "Unfurnished" includes the answers: "partly furnished".

6 Excluding mortgage interest payments, council tax and Northern Ireland rates. Mortgage interest payments can be found in category 13.

Source: Office for National Statistics

Table 3.3

Expenditure of one adult non-retired households by disposable income quintile group

UK, financial year ending 2022

> This table is under review to be removed from future publications and replaced with disposable equivalised income tables.
>
> If you use this table for your analysis, please get in contact here.

Commodity or service	Lowest twenty per cent	Second quintile group	Third quintile group	Fourth quintile group	Highest twenty per cent	All house-holds
Lower boundary of group (£ per week)[1]		411	652	887	1230	
Weighted number of households (thousands)	2,420	1,290	540	220	190	4,640
Total number of households in sample	480	260	100	40	30	920
Total number of persons in sample	480	260	100	40	30	920
Total number of adults in sample	480	260	100	40	30	920
Weighted average number of persons per household	1.0	1.0	1.0	1.0	1.0	1.0
Commodity or service	Average weekly household expenditure (£)					
1 Food & non-alcoholic drinks	30.00	34.70	36.10	39.30	54.90	33.50
2 Alcoholic drinks, tobacco & narcotics	10.20	7.70	10.10	17.50	13.30	10.00
3 Clothing & footwear	7.10	10.70	10.30	12.00	35.50	9.80
4 Housing (net)[2], fuel & power	80.00	78.20	99.10	96.80	150.50	85.30
5 Household goods & services	15.50	22.70	37.80	58.90	69.70	24.30
6 Health	3.40	5.20	5.20	7.10	[6.10]	4.40
7 Transport	27.80	52.00	65.50	64.80	83.60	42.80
8 Communication	12.30	17.40	15.20	18.80	19.90	14.70
9 Recreation & culture	22.80	49.70	43.90	27.90	81.10	35.20
10 Education	[4.60]	..	..	..	..	3.90
11 Restaurants & hotels	11.30	24.80	29.80	41.70	52.80	20.30
12 Miscellaneous goods & services	17.40	23.00	33.00	42.10	40.50	22.90
1-12 All expenditure groups	242.40	329.00	390.20	428.10	613.00	307.10
13 Other expenditure items	29.20	78.00	62.80	75.90	160.60	54.00
Total expenditure	**271.60**	**406.90**	**453.00**	**504.00**	**773.60**	**361.10**
Average weekly expenditure per person (£)						
Total expenditure	**271.60**	**406.90**	**453.00**	**504.00**	**773.60**	**361.10**

Note: The commodity and service categories are not comparable to those in publications before 2001-02.

Please see background notes for symbols and conventions used in this report.

1 Quintile groups have been calculated separately for retired and non-retired households.

2 Excluding mortgage interest payments, council tax and Northern Ireland rates. Mortgage interest payments can be found in category 13.

Source: Office for National Statistics

Table 3.3E
Expenditure of one adult non-retired households by disposable equivalised income quintile group (OECD-modified scale)
UK, financial year ending 2022

	Lowest twenty per cent	Second quintile group	Third quintile group	Fourth quintile group	Highest twenty per cent	All house-holds
Lower boundary of group (£ per week)[1]		277	399	530	705	
Weighted number of households (thousands)	1,260	1,080	750	790	770	4,640
Total number of households in sample	260	210	160	150	150	920
Total number of persons in sample	260	210	160	150	150	920
Total number of adults in sample	260	210	160	150	150	920
Weighted average number of persons per household	1.0	1.0	1.0	1.0	1.0	1.0

Commodity or service	Average weekly household expenditure (£)					
1 Food & non-alcoholic drinks	28.40	31.10	35.10	35.20	41.70	33.50
2 Alcoholic drinks, tobacco & narcotics	10.60	9.40	7.20	9.80	12.50	10.00
3 Clothing & footwear	5.70	8.70	12.70	8.10	17.00	9.80
4 Housing (net)[2], fuel & power	71.80	90.60	77.90	81.70	111.10	85.30
5 Household goods & services	15.30	15.70	20.50	26.30	52.80	24.30
6 Health	3.20	3.40	6.80	3.50	6.40	4.40
7 Transport	22.90	32.40	56.90	46.00	73.10	42.80
8 Communication	10.70	14.10	16.40	17.60	17.30	14.70
9 Recreation & culture	25.40	19.10	33.60	57.40	52.70	35.20
10 Education	..	..	..	..	..	3.90
11 Restaurants & hotels	9.30	13.30	18.70	30.40	39.10	20.30
12 Miscellaneous goods & services	15.20	19.50	24.00	25.60	36.20	22.90
1-12 All expenditure groups	219.50	266.20	310.50	345.60	464.50	307.10
13 Other expenditure items	23.30	34.50	56.60	91.00	91.20	54.00
Total expenditure	**242.80**	**300.70**	**367.20**	**436.60**	**555.80**	**361.10**
Average weekly expenditure per person (£) **Total expenditure**	**242.80**	**300.70**	**367.20**	**436.60**	**555.80**	**361.10**

Note: The commodity and service categories are not comparable to those in publications before 2001-02.
Please see background notes for symbols and conventions used in this report.
1 Quintile groups have been calculated separately for retired and non-retired households.
2 Excluding mortgage interest payments, council tax and Northern Ireland rates. Mortgage interest payments can be found in category 13.

Source: Office for National Statistics

Table 3.7

Expenditure of two adult non-retired households by disposable income quintile group

UK, financial year ending 2022

This table is under review to be removed from future publications and replaced with disposable equivalised income tables. If you use this table for your analysis, please get in contact here.

	Lowest twenty per cent	Second quintile group	Third quintile group	Fourth quintile group	Highest twenty per cent	All house-holds
Lower boundary of group (£ per week)[1]		411	652	887	1230	
Weighted number of households (thousands)	800	1,140	1,530	1,670	1,200	6,340
Total number of households in sample	170	260	320	330	260	1,340
Total number of persons in sample	340	510	640	670	510	2,670
Total number of adults in sample	340	510	640	670	510	2,670
Weighted average number of persons per household	2.0	2.0	2.0	2.0	2.0	2.0

Commodity or service	Average weekly household expenditure (£)					
1 Food & non-alcoholic drinks	54.50	58.10	62.20	66.80	72.80	63.70
2 Alcoholic drinks, tobacco & narcotics	12.80	13.70	13.50	13.90	18.60	14.50
3 Clothing & footwear	9.80	13.00	13.00	24.30	23.60	17.60
4 Housing (net)[2], fuel & power	83.50	80.50	91.50	99.50	118.50	95.70
5 Household goods & services	24.70	35.30	36.60	35.00	69.30	40.60
6 Health	7.80	8.70	8.20	8.30	12.20	9.00
7 Transport	54.20	66.90	78.80	103.10	128.20	89.30
8 Communication	19.90	20.50	22.90	22.70	24.70	22.40
9 Recreation & culture	34.90	40.90	66.30	68.40	98.90	64.50
10 Education	..	..	..	..	[4.20]	1.50
11 Restaurants & hotels	25.00	32.20	36.50	47.30	70.50	43.50
12 Miscellaneous goods & services	23.10	32.50	34.20	47.90	77.60	44.30
1-12 All expenditure groups	350.90	402.40	465.20	538.00	719.00	506.60
13 Other expenditure items	38.00	53.30	66.00	95.60	141.30	82.20
Total expenditure	**388.90**	**455.70**	**531.20**	**633.60**	**860.30**	**588.80**
Average weekly expenditure per person (£) **Total expenditure**	**194.40**	**227.80**	**265.60**	**316.80**	**430.20**	**294.40**

Note: The commodity and service categories are not comparable to those in publications before 2001-02.
Please see background notes for symbols and conventions used in this report.
1 Quintile groups have been calculated separately for retired and non-retired households.
2 Excluding mortgage interest payments, council tax and Northern Ireland rates. Mortgage interest payments can be found in category 13.

Source: Office for National Statistics

Table 3.7E
Expenditure of two adult non-retired households by disposable equivalised income
quintile group (OECD-modified scale)
UK, financial year ending 2022

	Lowest twenty per cent	Second quintile group	Third quintile group	Fourth quintile group	Highest twenty per cent	All house-holds
Lower boundary of group (£ per week)[1]		277	399	530	705	
Weighted number of households (thousands)	820	810	1,230	1,620	1,860	6,340
Total number of households in sample	180	180	260	330	390	1,340
Total number of persons in sample	350	370	530	660	770	2,670
Total number of adults in sample	350	370	530	660	770	2,670
Weighted average number of persons per household	2.0	2.0	2.0	2.0	2.0	2.0
Commodity or service	Average weekly household expenditure (£)					
1 Food & non-alcoholic drinks	54.90	57.90	61.50	62.30	72.70	63.70
2 Alcoholic drinks, tobacco & narcotics	12.60	13.90	16.30	12.00	16.60	14.50
3 Clothing & footwear	9.80	11.20	13.20	20.40	24.20	17.60
4 Housing (net)[2], fuel & power	82.50	75.80	91.80	92.00	116.00	95.70
5 Household goods & services	24.70	35.40	42.70	31.40	56.60	40.60
6 Health	7.70	7.50	9.10	6.90	12.10	9.00
7 Transport	54.10	67.30	71.30	92.70	123.20	89.30
8 Communication	20.00	21.50	22.10	22.30	24.10	22.40
9 Recreation & culture	34.70	43.20	51.40	76.30	85.20	64.50
10 Education	..	:	..	..	[2.90]	1.50
11 Restaurants & hotels	24.80	33.90	31.90	44.10	63.20	43.50
12 Miscellaneous goods & services	24.00	31.30	32.80	42.40	68.10	44.30
1-12 All expenditure groups	350.50	399.00	444.30	504.80	664.80	506.60
13 Other expenditure items	38.10	50.10	61.40	83.50	128.20	82.20
Total expenditure	**388.60**	**449.10**	**505.70**	**588.30**	**793.00**	**588.80**
Average weekly expenditure per person (£) **Total expenditure**	**194.30**	**224.60**	**252.90**	**294.10**	**396.50**	**294.40**

Note: The commodity and service categories are not comparable to those in publications before 2001-02.
Please see background notes for symbols and conventions used in this report.
1 Quintile groups have been calculated separately for retired and non-retired households.
2 Excluding mortgage interest payments, council tax and Northern Ireland rates. Mortgage interest payments can be found in category 13.

Source: Office for National Statistics

Table 3.12
Percentage of households by composition in each disposable and equivalised income decile group (OECD-modified scale)
UK, financial year ending 2022

This table is under review to be removed from future publications and replaced with disposable equivalised income tables.
If you use this table for your analysis, please get in contact here.

	Income decile group									
	Lowest ten per cent		Second		Third		Fourth		Fifth	
	Disposable	Equivalised	Disposable	Equivalised	Disposable	Equivalised	Disposable	Equivalised	Disposable	Equivalised
Lower boundary of group (£ per week)			247	196	349	263	443	315	555	369
Average size of household	1.4	2.1	1.5	2.3	1.7	2.3	2.1	2.3	2.4	2.3
One adult retired mainly dependent on state pensions[1]	17.0	9.0	8.0	11.0	..	[2.00]	:	[3.00]	:	..
One adult, other retired	22.0	12.0	30.0	14.0	21.0	17.0	15.0	16.0	6.0	13.0
One adult, non-retired	37.0	27.0	30.0	14.0	27.0	15.0	20.0	17.0	18.0	16.0
One adult, one child	4.0	4.0	[3.00]	[3.00]	5.0	4.0	4.0	3.0	[2.00]	..
One adult, two or more children	[3.00]	6.0	4.0	6.0	[4.00]	[3.00]	[4.00]	..	[2.00]	..
Two adults, retired mainly dependent on state pensions[1]	..	[2.00]	3.0	6.0	8.0	5.0	3.0	[1.00]	..	..
Two adults, other retired	..	3.0	6.0	8.0	10.0	11.0	20.0	15.0	18.0	14.0
Two adults, non-retired	10.0	14.0	10.0	12.0	14.0	12.0	14.0	9.0	24.0	19.0
Two adults, one child	..	5.0	[3.00]	[3.00]	[2.00]	6.0	6.0	7.0	7.0	8.0
Two adults, two children	..	[4.00]	..	9.0	[2.00]	9.0	7.0	9.0	9.0	11.0
Two adults, three children	..	[4.00]	..	[4.00]	..	[4.00]	..	[3.00]	[3.00]	[2.00]
Two adults, four or more children	..	..	..	..	:	..	..	..	..	..
Three adults	..	[1.00]	..	[2.00]	..	4.0	..	5.0	5.0	6.0
Three adults, one or more children	..	..	..	4.0	..	[2.00]	..	[3.00]	[3.00]	[3.00]
All other households without children	:	..	:	..	..	..	..	[4.00]	..	..
All other households with children	:	..	:	..	:	..	..	..	..	..

	Income decile group									
	Sixth		Seventh		Eighth		Ninth		Highest ten per cent	
	Disposable	Equivalised	Disposable	Equivalised	Disposable	Equivalised	Disposable	Equivalised	Disposable	Equivalised
Lower boundary of group (£ per week)	668	429	795	494	928	569	1,127	663	1,438	829
Average size of household	2.5	2.4	2.7	2.4	2.9	2.4	3.0	2.4	3.2	2.3
One adult retired mainly dependent on state pensions[1]	:	:								
One adult, other retired	4.0	9.0	[2.00]	9.0	..	5.0	..	5.0	..	3.0
One adult, non-retired	11.0	13.0	8.0	14.0	5.0	16.0	[4.00]	15.0	[4.00]	17.0
One adult, one child	[3.00]	[3.00]	..	..	..	..	..	..	..	..
One adult, two or more children	..	..	..	..	..	..	:	..	..	:
Two adults, retired mainly dependent on state pensions[1]	:	..	..	..	:					
Two adults, other retired	16.0	14.0	13.0	13.0	8.0	10.0	8.0	10.0	3.0	7.0
Two adults, non-retired	29.0	22.0	32.0	26.0	36.0	33.0	30.0	35.0	25.0	41.0
Two adults, one child	9.0	11.0	12.0	8.0	12.0	8.0	10.0	7.0	11.0	10.0
Two adults, two children	13.0	13.0	11.0	10.0	15.0	11.0	20.0	10.0	17.0	7.0
Two adults, three children	[3.00]	..	[3.00]	[2.00]	[3.00]	..	[3.00]	..	[3.00]	..
Two adults, four or more children	..	..	..	..	..	..	..	..	..	..
Three adults	5.0	6.0	7.0	8.0	10.0	8.0	12.0	8.0	14.0	9.0
Three adults, one or more children	[2.00]	[3.00]	[4.00]	[3.00]	4.0	[3.00]	6.0	..	5.0	..
All other households without children	..	[3.00]	[3.00]	[3.00]	[2.00]	[3.00]	4.0	6.0	12.0	[2.00]
All other households with children	..	..	..	..	[3.00]	..	[2.00]	..	[4.00]	..

Please see background notes for symbols and conventions used in this report.

1 Mainly dependent on state pensions and not economically active - see Methodology - Economically Inactive.

Source: Office for National Statistics

Background notes

Symbols and conventions used in Family Spending tables

[ ] Figures should be used with extra caution because they are based on fewer than 20 reporting households.

.. The data is suppressed if the unweighted sample counts are less than 10 reporting households.

. No figures are available because there are no reporting households.

~ The figure is greater than 0 but rounds to 0.

Rounding: Individual figures have been rounded independently. The sum of component items does not therefore necessarily add to the totals shown.

Averages: These are averages (means) for all households included in the column or row, and unless specified, are not restricted to those households reporting expenditure on a particular item or income of a particular type.

Impact of the coronavirus (COVID-19) pandemic on the Living Costs and Food Survey (LCF) for the financial year ending 2020

Following Government guidance in relation to the coronavirus (COVID-19) pandemic, a pause in data collection led to interviews being conducted for 13 fewer days in March 2020 than planned. Final March interviews took place on Monday March 16th. All households that were not interviewed as a result were treated as non-responders and data were weighted to account for reduced data collection in March 2020 compared to previous years.

Data collected in March 2020 may have covered changes to spending habits around the start of the first UK lockdown on March 23rd, for example panic buying beforehand and reduced spending during lockdown when people were advised to stay at home and many businesses were closed. However, due to reduced data collection in the latter half of March data may not accurately reflect the impact of lockdown on spending and the annual estimates reported in this release will not be significantly impacted.

Office for
National Statistics

Family Spending

Workbook 3 - Expenditure by Region

Contents:

ONS Social Surveys

Office for National Statistics

March 2023

A number of tables within the family spending workbooks have been placed under review to be removed from future publications. Tables under review are specified within the workbooks. If you use these for your analysis, please contact us via family.spending@ons.gov.uk**.**

Table A33

Household expenditure by countries and regions

UK, financial year ending 2020 to financial year ending 2022

	United Kingdom	England	North East	North West	Yorkshire and The Humber	East Midlands	West Midlands	East	London	South East	South West	Wales	Scotland	Northern Ireland
	K02000001	E92000001	E12000001	E12000002	E12000003	E12000004	E12000005	E12000006	E12000007	E12000008	E12000009	W92000004	S92000003	N92000002
Average weighted number of households (thousands)	28,170	23,540	1,210	3,110	2,450	2,080	2,450	2,620	3,380	3,790	2,450	1,370	2,500	760
Total number of households in sample (over 3 years)	16,470	12,480	720	1,670	1,370	1,260	1,330	1,400	1,220	1,910	1,610	710	2,360	920
Total number of persons in sample (over 3 years)	37,760	28,930	1,580	3,830	3,060	2,910	3,110	3,260	3,040	4,420	3,730	1,600	5,000	2,230
Total number of adults in sample (over 3 years)	30,030	22,910	1,280	3,030	2,420	2,330	2,490	2,570	2,350	3,490	2,970	1,290	4,110	1,720
Weighted average number of persons per household	2.3	2.4	2.2	2.3	2.2	2.3	2.4	2.4	2.7	2.4	2.3	2.3	2.1	2.5
Commodity or service						Average weekly household expenditure (£)								
1 Food & non-alcoholic drinks	65.00	65.50	56.30	62.90	58.20	63.90	64.20	66.40	71.50	71.60	65.20	61.00	60.10	73.70
2 Alcoholic drinks, tobacco & narcotics	13.10	12.90	11.60	13.70	13.50	12.80	12.50	13.40	10.10	14.00	14.00	12.90	14.30	14.40
3 Clothing & footwear	18.50	18.40	15.30	19.20	15.70	18.30	19.00	17.40	21.40	18.70	17.90	16.50	18.30	23.90
4 Housing(net)[1], fuel & power	85.10	88.40	64.50	77.10	65.70	70.50	79.10	86.30	141.80	92.00	84.90	68.30	71.80	57.70
5 Household goods & services	35.20	35.60	33.80	33.50	35.90	35.40	35.20	37.30	30.40	41.20	36.10	33.30	32.70	35.40
6 Health	8.00	8.30	5.30	6.80	7.90	8.30	9.60	7.40	8.30	10.90	8.30	6.00	5.50	9.20
7 Transport	72.30	73.30	58.80	68.90	64.50	80.00	72.60	82.40	64.80	83.80	76.20	62.30	69.20	68.50
8 Communication	21.20	21.30	19.00	21.40	18.80	21.60	21.60	22.40	21.30	22.60	21.50	19.90	20.30	21.30
9 Recreation & culture	58.80	60.30	45.90	61.80	53.30	60.20	56.30	60.40	52.30	73.90	66.70	54.10	51.80	45.20
10 Education	6.00	6.60	[0.40]	2.50	3.00	5.50	3.80	5.80	11.70	13.00	6.30	4.30	2.40	3.00
11 Restaurants & hotels	35.30	36.30	27.90	34.10	31.80	35.70	32.80	35.70	43.20	39.90	37.10	27.40	31.00	35.10
12 Miscellaneous goods & services	41.20	42.10	29.00	40.60	38.00	43.40	41.20	41.80	44.90	47.70	42.00	34.90	36.00	40.60
1-12 All expenditure groups	459.60	469.00	367.70	442.50	406.40	455.60	448.00	476.70	521.70	529.20	476.30	400.80	413.40	428.20
13 Other expenditure items	73.10	75.70	53.10	66.10	59.80	69.00	67.50	75.30	93.00	95.10	75.80	61.80	62.50	48.80
Total expenditure	**532.70**	**544.70**	**420.80**	**508.60**	**466.20**	**524.60**	**515.50**	**552.00**	**614.70**	**624.20**	**552.10**	**462.60**	**475.90**	**476.90**
Average weekly expenditure per person (£) **Total expenditure**	**227.00**	**229.90**	**194.80**	**218.60**	**210.60**	**228.60**	**214.30**	**232.90**	**231.50**	**260.50**	**242.80**	**204.50**	**221.80**	**193.00**

Note: The commodity and service categories are not comparable to those in publications before 2001-02.
Please see background notes for symbols and conventions used in this report.
This table is based on a three year average.

1 Excluding mortgage interest payments, council tax and Northern Ireland rates. Mortgage interest payments can be found in category 13.

Source: Office for National Statistics

Table A34

Household expenditure as a percentage of total expenditure by countries and regions
UK, financial year ending 2020 to financial year ending 2022

	United Kingdom	England	North East	North West	Yorkshire and The Humber	East Midlands	West Midlands	East	London	South East	South West	Wales	Scotland	Northern Ireland
	K02000001	E92000001	E12000001	E12000002	E12000003	E12000004	E12000005	E12000006	E12000007	E12000008	E12000009	W92000004	S92000003	N92000002
Average weighted number of households (thousands)	28,170	23,540	1,210	3,110	2,450	2,080	2,450	2,620	3,380	3,790	2,450	1,370	2,500	760
Total number of households in sample (over 3 years)	16,470	12,480	720	1,670	1,370	1,260	1,330	1,400	1,220	1,910	1,610	710	2,360	920
Total number of persons in sample (over 3 years)	37,760	28,930	1,580	3,830	3,060	2,910	3,110	3,260	3,040	4,420	3,730	1,600	5,000	2,230
Total number of adults in sample (over 3 years)	30,030	22,910	1,280	3,030	2,420	2,330	2,490	2,570	2,350	3,490	2,970	1,290	4,110	1,720
Weighted average number of persons per household	2.3	2.4	2.2	2.3	2.2	2.3	2.4	2.4	2.7	2.4	2.3	2.3	2.1	2.5
Commodity or service	Percentage of total expenditure													
1 Food & non-alcoholic drinks	12	12	13	12	12	12	12	12	12	11	12	13	13	15
2 Alcoholic drinks, tobacco & narcotics	2	2	3	3	3	2	2	2	2	2	3	3	3	3
3 Clothing & footwear	3	3	4	4	3	3	4	3	3	3	3	4	4	5
4 Housing(net)[1], fuel & power	16	16	15	15	14	13	15	16	23	15	15	15	15	12
5 Household goods & services	7	7	8	7	8	7	7	7	5	7	7	7	7	7
6 Health	1	2	1	1	2	2	2	1	1	2	2	1	1	2
7 Transport	14	13	14	14	14	15	14	15	11	13	14	13	15	14
8 Communication	4	4	5	4	4	4	4	4	3	4	4	4	4	4
9 Recreation & culture	11	11	11	12	11	11	11	11	9	12	12	12	11	9
10 Education	1	1	[0]	0	1	1	1	1	2	2	1	1	1	1
11 Restaurants & hotels	7	7	7	7	7	7	6	6	7	6	7	6	7	7
12 Miscellaneous goods & services	8	8	7	8	8	8	8	8	7	8	8	8	8	9
1-12 All expenditure groups	86	86	87	87	87	87	87	86	85	85	86	87	87	90
13 Other expenditure items	14	14	13	13	13	13	13	14	15	15	14	13	13	10
Total expenditure	100	100	100	100	100	100	100	100	100	100	100	100	100	100

Note: The commodity and service categories are not comparable to those in publications before 2001-02.
Please see background notes for symbols and conventions used in this report.
This table is based on a three year average.
1 Excluding mortgage interest payments, council tax and Northern Ireland rates. Mortgage interest payments can be found in category 13.

Source: Office for National Statistics

Table A35
Detailed household expenditure by countries and regions
UK, financial year ending 2020 to financial year ending 2022

	United Kingdom	England	North East	North West	Yorkshire and the Humber	East Midlands	West Midlands	East	London	South East	South West	Wales	Scotland	Northern Ireland
	K02000001	E92000001	E12000001	E12000002	E12000003	E12000004	E12000005	E12000006	E12000007	E12000008	E12000009	W92000004	S92000003	N92000002
Average weighted number of households (thousands)	28,170	23,540	1,210	3,110	2,450	2,080	2,450	2,620	3,380	3,790	2,450	1,370	2,500	760
Total number of households in sample (over 3 years)	16,470	12,480	720	1,670	1,370	1,260	1,330	1,400	1,220	1,910	1,610	710	2,360	920
Total number of persons in sample (over 3 years)	37,760	28,930	1,580	3,830	3,060	2,910	3,110	3,260	3,040	4,420	3,730	1,600	5,000	2,230
Total number of adults in sample (over 3 years)	30,030	22,910	1,280	3,030	2,420	2,330	2,490	2,570	2,350	3,490	2,970	1,290	4,110	1,720
Weighted average number of persons per household	2.3	2.4	2.2	2.3	2.2	2.3	2.4	2.4	2.7	2.4	2.3	2.3	2.1	2.5
Commodity or service						Average weekly household expenditure (£)								
1 Food & non-alcoholic drinks	**65.00**	**65.50**	**56.30**	**62.90**	**58.20**	**63.90**	**64.20**	**66.40**	**71.50**	**71.60**	**65.20**	**61.00**	**60.10**	**73.70**
1.1 Food	59.40	60.00	51.20	57.10	53.30	58.40	58.30	60.60	66.00	65.70	60.20	55.30	54.30	66.60
1.1.1 Bread, rice and cereals	5.70	5.70	4.80	5.50	5.20	5.70	5.60	5.80	6.50	6.10	5.50	5.20	5.40	6.70
1.1.2 Pasta products	0.50	0.50	0.40	0.40	0.40	0.40	0.40	0.50	0.60	0.50	0.40	0.40	0.40	0.50
1.1.3 Buns, cakes, biscuits etc.	4.10	4.10	3.80	4.00	3.60	4.40	4.20	4.20	4.20	4.30	4.10	3.90	4.00	5.50
1.1.4 Pastry (savoury)	1.00	1.00	1.00	1.00	0.90	1.10	1.00	1.00	0.90	1.10	1.00	0.90	1.00	0.90
1.1.5 Beef (fresh, chilled or frozen)	2.00	1.90	1.90	2.20	1.80	2.00	1.80	2.00	1.80	2.00	1.90	2.00	1.90	3.50
1.1.6 Pork (fresh, chilled or frozen)	0.60	0.60	0.60	0.50	0.50	0.60	0.60	0.60	0.60	0.60	0.60	0.60	0.40	0.70
1.1.7 Lamb (fresh, chilled or frozen)	0.60	0.70	0.30	0.60	0.60	0.60	0.80	0.60	1.10	0.80	0.60	0.60	0.20	0.60
1.1.8 Poultry (fresh, chilled or frozen)	2.40	2.40	2.00	2.40	2.00	2.20	2.70	2.30	2.80	2.40	2.50	2.20	2.00	2.70
1.1.9 Bacon and ham	0.80	0.80	0.80	0.80	0.80	0.90	0.90	0.80	0.50	0.90	0.90	1.00	0.80	1.30
1.1.10 Other meat and meat preparations	6.80	6.70	6.70	7.40	6.30	7.00	6.60	6.90	5.90	7.10	6.80	6.80	7.20	9.00
1.1.11 Fish and fish products	3.20	3.30	2.50	3.10	3.00	2.90	2.90	3.40	4.30	3.70	2.90	2.70	2.70	2.30
1.1.12 Milk	2.10	2.10	1.90	2.20	2.00	2.10	2.20	2.00	2.00	2.10	2.30	1.90	1.80	2.30
1.1.13 Cheese and curd	2.30	2.30	1.90	2.10	2.10	2.30	2.10	2.40	2.40	2.70	2.60	2.10	2.00	2.00
1.1.14 Eggs	0.80	0.80	0.60	0.70	0.70	0.70	0.70	0.70	1.00	0.90	0.80	0.70	0.70	0.80
1.1.15 Other milk products	2.50	2.50	2.10	2.30	2.20	2.40	2.30	2.60	2.70	2.80	2.60	2.30	2.20	2.60
1.1.16 Butter	0.50	0.50	0.40	0.50	0.40	0.40	0.50	0.40	0.50	0.60	0.60	0.60	0.40	0.70
1.1.17 Margarine, other vegetable fats and peanut butter	0.60	0.60	0.60	0.60	0.70	0.70	0.60	0.70	0.50	0.70	0.60	0.60	0.70	0.50
1.1.18 Cooking oils and fats	0.40	0.40	0.30	0.30	0.40	0.30	0.30	0.40	0.60	0.40	0.30	0.30	0.30	0.30
1.1.19 Fresh fruit	4.10	4.20	3.00	3.60	3.50	3.80	4.00	4.10	5.30	4.80	4.20	3.50	3.50	4.00
1.1.20 Other fresh, chilled or frozen fruits	0.50	0.50	0.30	0.40	0.40	0.40	0.50	0.50	0.70	0.50	0.50	0.40	0.50	0.50
1.1.21 Dried fruit and nuts	0.90	1.00	0.50	0.80	0.80	0.80	0.90	1.00	1.50	1.10	1.00	0.80	0.70	0.60
1.1.22 Preserved fruit and fruit based products	0.20	0.20	0.20	0.10	0.20	0.10	0.10	0.20	0.20	0.20	0.20	0.10	0.10	0.20
1.1.23 Fresh vegetables	4.60	4.80	3.30	3.90	3.90	4.30	4.40	4.60	6.40	5.50	5.00	3.80	3.50	3.60
1.1.24 Dried vegetables	0.10	0.10	0.00	0.10	0.10	0.00	0.10	0.10	0.10	0.10	0.10	0.00	0.10	0.00
1.1.25 Other preserved or processed vegetables	2.00	2.10	1.70	1.80	1.80	1.90	2.00	2.00	2.50	2.40	2.00	1.70	1.70	1.90
1.1.26 Potatoes	0.70	0.70	0.60	0.60	0.60	0.60	0.70	0.70	0.60	0.70	0.70	0.70	0.60	1.10
1.1.27 Other tubers and products of tuber vegetables	1.90	1.80	2.00	1.90	1.70	2.00	1.90	1.90	1.60	1.90	1.90	2.00	2.10	2.70
1.1.28 Sugar and sugar products	0.40	0.40	0.30	0.40	0.40	0.40	0.40	0.40	0.50	0.50	0.50	0.40	0.40	0.40
1.1.29 Jams, marmalades	0.30	0.30	0.20	0.30	0.30	0.30	0.30	0.40	0.50	0.40	0.40	0.30	0.30	0.40
1.1.30 Chocolate	2.40	2.40	2.20	2.20	2.20	2.50	2.20	2.50	2.20	2.60	2.50	2.50	2.40	3.10
1.1.31 Confectionery products	0.90	0.80	0.90	0.80	0.70	0.90	0.90	0.80	0.70	1.00	0.80	0.80	1.00	1.20
1.1.32 Edible ices and ice cream	0.80	0.80	0.80	0.70	0.70	0.80	0.80	0.80	1.00	1.00	0.80	0.80	0.80	0.90
1.1.33 Other food products	2.90	3.00	2.50	2.70	2.50	2.90	2.90	3.10	3.30	3.40	2.80	2.90	2.70	3.00
1.2 Non-alcoholic drinks	5.60	5.50	5.00	5.80	4.90	5.50	5.80	5.80	5.50	5.90	5.00	5.70	5.80	7.10

Table A35

Detailed household expenditure by countries and regions

UK, financial year ending 2020 to financial year ending 2022

	United Kingdom	England	North East	North West	Yorkshire and the Humber	East Midlands	West Midlands	East	London	South East	South West	Wales	Scotland	Northern Ireland
	K02000001	E92000001	E12000001	E12000002	E12000003	E12000004	E12000005	E12000006	E12000007	E12000008	E12000009	W92000004	S92000003	N92000002
1.2.1 Coffee	1.10	1.10	0.90	1.10	1.00	1.20	1.10	1.20	1.00	1.30	1.10	1.30	1.00	1.00
1.2.2 Tea	0.50	0.50	0.50	0.40	0.40	0.50	0.50	0.50	0.50	0.50	0.50	0.50	0.40	0.50
1.2.3 Cocoa and powdered chocolate	0.10	0.10	0.10	0.10	0.10	0.10	0.20	0.20	0.10	0.10	0.10	0.10	0.10	0.10
1.2.4 Fruit and vegetable juices (inc. fruit squash)	1.10	1.10	0.90	1.20	1.00	1.10	1.20	1.20	1.20	1.30	1.00	1.00	1.00	1.20
1.2.5 Mineral or spring waters	0.40	0.40	0.30	0.40	0.20	0.30	0.40	0.30	0.60	0.30	0.30	0.20	0.30	0.50
1.2.6 Soft drinks (inc. fizzy and ready to drink fruit drinks)	2.40	2.30	2.40	2.50	2.00	2.30	2.40	2.40	2.10	2.40	2.00	2.60	2.90	3.70

Note: The commodity and service categories are not comparable to those in publications before 2001-02.

The numbering system is sequential, it does not use actual COICOP codes.

Please see background notes for symbols and conventions used in this report.

This table is based on a three year average.

Table A35

Detailed household expenditure by countries and regions (cont.)

UK, financial year ending 2020 to financial year ending 2022

Commodity or service	United Kingdom	England	North East	North West	Yorkshire and The Humber	East Midlands	West Midlands	East	London	South East	South West	Wales	Scotland	Northern Ireland
	Average weekly household expenditure (£)													
2 Alcoholic drink, tobacco & narcotics	**13.10**	**12.90**	**11.60**	**13.70**	**13.50**	**12.80**	**12.50**	**13.40**	**10.10**	**14.00**	**14.00**	**12.90**	**14.30**	**14.40**
2.1 Alcoholic drinks	10.00	9.90	8.70	10.90	10.30	9.80	9.30	10.50	7.40	11.10	10.70	10.20	10.20	9.80
2.1.1 Spirits and liqueurs (brought home)	2.30	2.20	2.10	2.70	2.20	2.30	2.20	2.40	1.40	2.30	2.50	2.30	2.80	2.60
2.1.2 Wines, fortified wines (brought home)	4.90	4.90	3.70	4.90	4.70	4.70	4.30	5.30	3.90	6.10	5.40	4.40	4.80	4.60
2.1.3 Beer, lager, ciders and perry (brought home)	2.80	2.80	2.80	3.20	3.40	2.80	2.80	2.80	2.10	2.60	2.80	3.50	2.60	2.40
2.1.4 Alcopops (brought home)	0.00	0.00	[0.00]	[0.00]	[0.00]	[0.00]	[0.00]	[0.00]	..	[0.00]	[0.00]	..	0.00	[0.10]
2.2 Tobacco and narcotics	3.10	3.00	2.80	2.80	3.20	2.90	3.20	2.90	2.70	2.90	3.40	2.70	4.00	4.70
2.2.1 Cigarettes	2.10	2.00	2.00	1.90	2.20	2.20	2.20	2.00	1.90	1.90	1.80	1.30	2.90	3.60
2.2.2 Cigars, other tobacco products and narcotics	1.00	1.00	0.80	0.90	1.00	0.80	1.00	0.90	0.80	1.00	1.60	1.40	1.10	1.10
3 Clothing & footwear	**18.50**	**18.40**	**15.30**	**19.20**	**15.70**	**18.30**	**19.00**	**17.40**	**21.40**	**18.70**	**17.90**	**16.50**	**18.30**	**23.90**
3.1 Clothing	14.90	14.90	12.30	15.60	12.80	15.00	15.00	13.80	17.50	15.10	14.50	13.60	14.70	18.60
3.1.1 Men's outer garments	3.60	3.60	2.80	3.80	2.70	3.60	3.30	3.00	4.60	3.70	3.60	3.60	3.50	4.50
3.1.2 Men's under garments	0.40	0.40	0.40	0.40	0.40	0.50	0.50	0.50	0.60	0.40	0.40	0.40	0.40	0.50
3.1.3 Women's outer garments	6.40	6.40	5.30	6.90	5.20	6.30	6.60	5.80	7.50	6.20	6.30	5.60	6.30	8.10
3.1.4 Women's under garments	1.00	1.00	0.90	1.00	1.00	1.10	1.00	0.90	1.20	1.10	1.00	0.80	1.00	1.30
3.1.5 Boys' outer garments (5-15)	0.60	0.60	0.70	0.70	0.60	0.50	0.50	0.90	0.60	0.70	0.40	0.60	0.70	1.00
3.1.6 Girls' outer garments (5-15)	0.80	0.80	0.90	1.00	0.80	0.80	0.90	0.90	0.60	0.80	0.80	0.70	0.90	1.00
3.1.7 Infants' outer garments (under 5)	0.50	0.50	0.30	0.60	0.40	0.60	0.70	0.50	0.60	0.50	0.40	0.50	0.60	0.50
3.1.8 Children's under garments (under 16)	0.40	0.40	0.30	0.40	0.40	0.40	0.40	0.20	0.40	0.40	0.30	0.40	0.40	0.60
3.1.9 Accessories	0.70	0.80	0.50	0.60	0.90	1.00	0.90	0.60	0.70	0.90	0.70	0.50	0.60	0.80
3.1.10 Haberdashery, clothing materials and clothing hire	0.30	0.30	0.30	0.20	0.30	0.20	0.20	0.30	0.30	0.30	0.40	0.60	0.30	0.10
3.1.11 Dry cleaners, laundry and dyeing	0.20	0.20	..	0.10	[0.10]	[0.10]	[0.10]	0.20	0.40	0.20	0.10	[0.10]	0.20	0.20
3.2 Footwear	3.50	3.50	3.00	3.60	2.90	3.20	4.00	3.50	3.90	3.50	3.50	2.90	3.60	5.30

Commodity or service	United Kingdom	England	North East	North West	Yorkshire and The Humber	East Midlands	West Midlands	East	London	South East	South West	Wales	Scotland	Northern Ireland
4 Housing (net)[1], fuel & power	**85.10**	**88.40**	**64.50**	**77.10**	**65.70**	**70.50**	**79.10**	**86.30**	**141.80**	**92.00**	**84.90**	**68.30**	**71.80**	**57.70**
4.1 Actual rentals for housing	51.80	54.60	41.00	41.50	35.10	37.20	43.50	49.70	117.30	51.70	46.70	37.10	40.10	30.60
4.1.1 Gross rent	51.70	54.50	41.00	41.40	35.10	37.20	43.50	49.70	117.10	51.50	46.60	37.10	39.90	30.60
4.1.2 *less housing benefit, rebates & allowances rec'd*	10.60	10.50	13.10	8.70	9.30	7.20	7.60	8.70	21.10	8.60	8.20	11.70	10.80	11.40
4.1.3 Net rent[2]	41.10	44.00	27.90	32.70	25.80	30.00	35.90	40.90	96.00	42.90	38.40	25.40	29.20	19.20
4.1.4 Second dwelling rent	[0.10]	[0.10]	..	..	..	..	..	..	..	..	..	..	..	..
4.2 Maintenance and repair of dwelling	9.20	9.40	5.90	9.70	7.60	8.00	9.00	10.80	7.20	12.10	11.00	8.50	9.20	6.70
4.3 Water supply and miscellaneous services relating to the dwelling	10.20	10.80	8.40	10.00	9.30	8.50	10.10	10.10	14.40	11.90	11.00	9.30	8.40	0.80
4.4 Electricity, gas and other fuels	24.40	24.10	22.40	24.60	23.10	23.90	24.20	24.40	23.90	25.00	24.50	25.00	25.00	31.00
4.4.1 Electricity	12.90	12.80	11.10	12.50	11.60	12.40	12.50	13.30	12.80	13.50	13.70	12.80	13.40	14.70
4.4.2 Gas	10.20	10.40	10.50	11.30	10.60	10.60	10.80	9.40	11.00	10.30	9.10	9.60	10.00	5.10
4.4.3 Other fuels	1.40	1.00	0.70	0.70	0.80	0.90	0.80	1.70	0.10	1.20	1.70	2.60	1.50	11.20

Note: The commodity and service categories are not comparable to those in publications before 2001-02.

The numbering system is sequential, it does not use actual COICOP codes.

Please see background notes for symbols and conventions used in this report.

This table is based on a three year average.

1 Excluding mortgage interest payments, council tax and Northern Ireland rates. Mortgage interest payments can be found in category 13.

2 The figure included in total expenditure is net rent as opposed to gross rent.

Table A35
Detailed household expenditure by countries and regions (cont.)
UK, financial year ending 2020 to financial year ending 2022

Commodity or service	United Kingdom	England	North East	North West	Yorkshire and The Humber	East Midlands	West Midlands	East	London	South East	South West	Wales	Scotland	Northern Ireland
	Average weekly household expenditure (£)													
5 Household goods & services	**35.20**	**35.60**	**33.80**	**33.50**	**35.90**	**35.40**	**35.20**	**37.30**	**30.40**	**41.20**	**36.10**	**33.30**	**32.70**	**35.40**
5.1 Furniture and furnishings, carpets and other floor coverings	17.70	17.80	20.20	17.00	18.10	16.10	17.40	19.10	14.70	20.80	17.30	16.70	16.80	18.10
5.1.1 Furniture and furnishings	14.30	14.40	16.00	13.90	14.10	11.90	14.20	14.80	12.60	17.20	14.50	13.90	13.20	14.30
5.1.2 Floor coverings	3.40	3.40	4.20	3.10	3.90	4.20	3.30	4.20	2.10	3.50	2.90	2.80	3.60	3.80
5.2 Household textiles	2.00	2.00	2.00	2.10	2.10	2.00	2.70	1.90	2.00	1.60	2.30	1.60	2.10	2.10
5.3 Household appliances	3.50	3.50	1.90	2.80	4.50	6.10	3.50	3.00	3.10	3.60	3.40	2.90	3.50	3.00
5.4 Glassware, tableware and household utensils	2.00	2.00	1.70	1.90	1.90	1.80	2.00	2.00	2.00	2.50	2.10	2.10	1.80	2.00
5.5 Tools and equipment for house and garden	3.20	3.20	2.30	3.10	3.30	3.30	3.40	3.50	2.20	3.90	3.30	3.50	3.00	3.10
5.6 Goods and services for routine household maintenance	6.80	7.00	5.80	6.60	6.00	6.20	6.30	7.70	6.50	8.80	7.70	6.50	5.40	7.20
5.6.1 Cleaning materials	2.70	2.70	2.30	2.60	2.70	2.70	2.70	2.90	2.70	3.10	2.70	2.40	2.40	3.20
5.6.2 Household goods and hardware	2.00	2.00	1.60	1.90	1.80	2.00	1.90	2.00	2.00	2.30	2.20	1.90	1.70	2.20
5.6.3 Domestic services, carpet cleaning and hire/repair of furniture/furnishings	2.20	2.30	1.90	2.00	1.40	1.50	1.70	2.80	1.90	3.40	2.90	2.20	1.30	1.80
6 Health	**8.00**	**8.30**	**5.30**	**6.80**	**7.90**	**8.30**	**9.60**	**7.40**	**8.30**	**10.90**	**8.30**	**6.00**	**5.50**	**9.20**
6.1 Medical products, appliances and equipment	4.40	4.60	3.20	3.30	4.80	5.60	4.70	4.80	4.50	5.40	4.50	3.90	3.30	3.80

	United Kingdom	England	North East	North West	Yorkshire and The Humber	East Midlands	West Midlands	East	London	South East	South West	Wales	Scotland	Northern Ireland
6.1.1 Medicines, prescriptions, healthcare products and equipment	2.70	2.90	2.20	2.30	2.60	3.80	2.60	3.30	3.20	3.10	2.50	1.90	1.90	2.10
6.1.2 Spectacles, lenses, accessories and repairs	1.70	1.70	1.00	1.00	2.20	1.80	2.10	1.50	1.30	2.30	2.10	2.10	1.40	1.70
6.2 Hospital services	3.60	3.70	2.10	3.50	3.10	2.70	4.90	2.60	3.80	5.50	3.80	2.10	2.20	5.40
7 Transport	**72.30**	**73.30**	**58.80**	**68.90**	**64.50**	**80.00**	**72.60**	**82.40**	**64.80**	**83.80**	**76.20**	**62.30**	**69.20**	**68.50**
7.1 Purchase of vehicles	29.00	29.40	21.90	27.10	25.10	36.90	32.20	33.80	25.40	29.30	32.50	25.90	28.50	21.10
7.1.1 Purchase of new cars and vans	8.90	8.90	7.20	6.60	6.40	13.00	9.30	10.90	9.80	8.40	8.40	7.90	11.10	4.50
7.1.2 Purchase of second hand cars or vans	18.90	19.40	14.50	19.80	18.20	21.80	22.30	22.10	14.40	19.70	20.90	16.70	16.80	16.30
7.1.3 Purchase of motorcycles and other vehicles	1.10	1.20	[0.30]	[0.70]	[0.50]	2.10	0.60	[0.80]	[1.20]	1.20	3.30	[1.40]	0.60	
7.2 Operation of personal transport	28.60	28.70	23.80	26.90	26.90	32.10	28.30	32.20	19.40	34.20	33.80	27.20	25.80	37.00
7.2.1 Spares and accessories	2.50	2.60	1.70	2.00	2.50	2.90	2.00	2.90	2.10	3.20	3.80	1.80	1.90	2.70
7.2.2 Petrol, diesel and other motor oils	17.50	17.30	16.80	17.50	16.30	19.30	18.00	19.70	10.30	19.40	19.50	17.00	16.60	27.50
7.2.3 Repairs and servicing	6.50	6.60	3.70	5.10	6.10	8.00	6.30	7.40	4.70	8.70	8.10	6.40	5.70	5.70
7.2.4 Other motoring costs	2.20	2.20	1.60	2.20	2.00	2.00	2.00	2.20	2.20	2.90	2.40	2.00	1.70	1.10
7.3 Transport services	14.70	15.20	13.00	15.00	12.60	11.00	12.20	16.40	20.00	20.30	9.90	9.10	14.80	10.40
7.3.1 Rail and tube fares	2.40	2.60	1.30	1.40	1.20	1.40	1.70	3.80	5.10	4.20	1.30	1.20	1.20	0.50
7.3.2 Bus and coach fares	0.90	0.90	0.90	1.10	1.10	1.10	0.90	0.80	0.80	0.80	0.80	0.70	1.20	0.90
7.3.3 Combined fares	0.20	0.30						[0.20]	1.50					
7.3.4 Other travel and transport	11.20	11.30	10.80	12.40	10.30	8.50	9.50	11.60	12.60	15.20	7.70	7.30	12.40	9.00
8 Communication	**21.20**	**21.30**	**19.00**	**21.40**	**18.80**	**21.60**	**21.60**	**22.40**	**21.30**	**22.60**	**21.50**	**19.90**	**20.30**	**21.30**
8.1 Postal services	0.80	0.80	0.50	0.60	0.50	0.90	0.80	0.80	0.60	1.10	1.00	0.90	0.80	0.50
8.2 Telephone and telefax equipment	1.10	1.20	0.90	1.00	0.90	1.00	1.60	1.50	0.80	1.30	1.70	0.60	0.70	1.80
8.3 Telephone and telefax services[3]	8.60	8.70	7.40	8.60	7.60	8.80	8.80	9.00	9.70	8.90	8.30	7.70	7.70	9.20
8.4 Internet subscription fees (ex. combined packages)	0.70	0.70	0.90	0.70	0.80	0.60	0.80	0.60	1.10	0.70	0.60	0.60	0.80	0.70
8.5 Combined telecom services[4]	10.00	9.90	9.30	10.50	9.10	10.20	9.60	10.60	9.20	10.70	10.00	10.10	10.30	9.00

Note: The commodity and service categories are not comparable to those in publications before 2001-02.

The numbering system is sequential, it does not use actual COICOP codes.

Please see background notes for symbols and conventions used in this report.

This table is based on a three year average.

3 For FYE 2019 onwards, excludes payments made as part of a combined bill.

4 For FYE 2019 onwards, all telecoms bills that include more than one service. Due to the nature of combined packages, this also includes packages that includes television services.

Table A35
Detailed household expenditure by countries and regions (cont.)
UK, financial year ending 2020 to financial year ending 2022

	United Kingdom	England	North East	North West	Yorkshire and The Humber	East Midlands	West Midlands	East	London	South East	South West	Wales	Scotland	Northern Ireland
Commodity or service						Average weekly household expenditure (£)								
9 Recreation & culture	**58.80**	**60.30**	**45.90**	**61.80**	**53.30**	**60.20**	**56.30**	**60.40**	**52.30**	**73.90**	**66.70**	**54.10**	**51.80**	**45.20**
9.1 Audio-visual, photographic and information processing equipment	4.60	4.50	2.90	4.70	3.80	4.60	4.40	6.00	3.80	5.40	3.90	4.60	5.20	4.10
9.1.1 Audio equipment and accessories, CD players	0.90	1.00	0.70	0.70	0.80	1.20	0.90	1.00	0.90	1.30	1.10	0.60	1.00	0.40
9.1.2 TV, video and computers	3.30	3.20	1.90	3.60	2.60	3.10	3.50	4.60	2.90	3.30	2.60	3.70	4.10	3.60
9.1.3 Photographic, cine and optical equipment	0.30	0.30		[0.40]	[0.30]			[0.40]		0.80	[0.20]	[0.30]	[0.10]	
9.2 Other major durables for recreation and														

culture	2.80	3.10	[1.10]	5.90	1.70	2.10	3.40	2.40	[0.40]	3.10	6.80	[1.20]	1.50	[0.90]
9.3 Other recreational items and equipment, gardens and pets	16.20	16.40	11.70	16.70	16.20	18.70	15.40	18.00	12.10	19.00	18.70	18.70	13.40	14.20
9.3.1 Games, toys and hobbies	3.00	3.00	2.40	3.50	2.90	3.00	3.20	3.70	2.30	3.10	2.70	4.00	3.00	2.50
9.3.2 Computer software and games	1.00	1.00	1.00	1.30	0.60	0.70	1.10	0.90	1.10	1.40	1.00	1.00	0.90	1.10
9.3.3 Equipment for sport, camping and open-air recreation	1.80	1.80	1.20	2.90	0.80	2.90	1.90	1.60	1.20	1.90	2.20	2.60	1.30	0.60
9.3.4 Horticultural goods, garden equipment and plants	3.60	3.70	2.80	3.20	4.60	3.40	3.40	4.00	3.00	3.90	4.40	3.30	3.10	3.30
9.3.5 Pets and pet food	6.80	6.90	4.20	5.80	7.30	8.60	5.80	7.70	4.60	8.70	8.30	7.90	5.10	6.70
9.4 Recreational and cultural services	15.70	16.20	11.50	15.10	13.40	15.20	14.00	16.30	19.70	19.50	16.30	11.70	13.70	11.50
9.4.1 Sports admissions, subscriptions, leisure class fees and equipment hire	5.70	6.10	2.50	5.90	3.90	4.80	4.60	5.40	9.40	8.10	6.00	3.40	4.00	2.70
9.4.2 Cinema, theatre and museums etc.	2.00	2.10	1.30	1.40	2.00	1.90	1.80	2.30	3.00	2.30	2.10	0.90	1.60	1.90
9.4.3 TV, video, satellite rental, cable subscriptions and TV licences [5]	5.20	5.20	4.90	5.00	5.10	5.10	5.00	5.30	4.90	5.90	5.10	5.30	5.20	4.50
9.4.4 Miscellaneous entertainments	1.10	1.20	0.70	1.10	0.90	1.40	0.90	1.40	1.10	1.50	1.60	1.00	0.70	0.50
9.4.5 Development of film, deposit for film development, passport photos, holiday and school photos	0.20	0.20	[0.00]	0.20	0.10	0.20	0.20	0.20	0.20	0.10	0.10	[0.10]	0.40	0.20
9.4.6 Gambling payments	1.50	1.50	2.10	1.60	1.40	1.80	1.50	1.80	1.10	1.50	1.30	1.20	1.80	1.70
9.5 Newspapers, books and stationery	4.90	5.00	3.80	4.30	4.00	4.90	4.70	5.20	5.10	5.90	5.80	4.20	4.70	4.70
9.5.1 Books	1.20	1.20	0.80	1.10	0.80	1.10	1.20	1.10	1.60	1.40	1.60	0.90	1.20	1.00
9.5.2 Diaries, address books, cards etc.	2.10	2.20	1.50	1.80	1.80	2.20	2.10	2.40	2.20	2.60	2.40	1.80	1.70	1.70
9.5.3 Newspapers	1.00	1.00	1.00	0.90	0.90	1.00	0.90	1.10	0.80	1.20	1.20	0.90	1.30	1.50
9.5.4 Magazines and periodicals	0.60	0.60	0.50	0.60	0.50	0.50	0.60	0.60	0.50	0.70	0.60	0.60	0.50	0.60
9.6 Package holidays	14.60	15.00	14.90	15.10	14.20	14.70	14.20	12.50	11.10	20.90	15.30	13.70	13.40	9.70
9.6.1 Package holidays - UK	1.50	1.60	1.60	1.70	1.30	1.40	1.80	1.90	1.00	1.70	1.80	1.70	0.90	:
9.6.2 Package holidays - abroad	13.10	13.40	13.30	13.40	12.90	13.20	12.40	10.60	10.20	19.20	13.50	12.00	12.50	9.40
10 Education	6.00	6.60	[0.40]	2.50	3.00	5.50	3.80	5.80	11.70	13.00	6.30	4.30	2.40	3.00
10.1 Education fees	5.70	6.30	:	2.30	2.90	5.40	3.60	5.40	11.10	12.40	6.00	4.10	2.20	2.80
10.2 Payments for school trips, other ad-hoc expenditure	0.30	0.30	:	[0.20]	:	[0.10]	[0.20]	[0.30]	[0.60]	0.60	[0.30]	:	[0.20]	[0.30]
11 Restaurants & hotels	35.30	36.30	27.90	34.10	31.80	35.70	32.80	35.70	43.20	39.90	37.10	27.40	31.00	35.10
11.1 Catering services	26.80	27.30	22.50	27.00	23.80	26.60	24.80	27.20	32.60	28.90	26.80	21.60	23.80	30.80
11.1.1 Restaurant and café meals	12.30	12.60	9.80	11.70	10.30	13.00	11.10	13.70	14.00	14.30	13.10	10.40	10.70	13.00
11.1.2 Alcoholic drinks (away from home)	5.00	5.10	4.10	6.10	4.60	4.80	4.50	4.60	5.70	5.30	5.10	4.00	4.40	3.90
11.1.3 Take away meals eaten at home	5.00	5.00	4.60	4.70	4.50	4.40	4.80	4.70	7.00	5.00	4.30	4.00	4.80	7.90
11.1.4 Other take-away and snack food	3.40	3.40	2.80	3.40	3.30	3.30	3.10	3.30	4.60	3.30	3.20	2.40	3.20	4.60
11.1.5 Contract catering (food) and canteens	1.10	1.10	1.20	1.10	1.10	1.00	1.20	0.90	1.30	1.10	1.10	0.80	0.80	1.40
11.2 Accommodation services	8.60	9.00	5.40	7.10	8.10	9.10	8.00	8.50	10.60	11.00	10.30	5.70	7.20	4.30
11.2.1 Holiday in the UK	6.00	6.30	4.40	4.70	6.40	6.80	6.50	6.90	5.20	7.30	7.60	4.50	5.30	2.40
11.2.2 Holiday abroad	2.50	2.60	[0.90]	2.40	1.60	2.20	1.50	1.50	5.40	3.60	2.50	1.20	1.90	1.90
11.2.3 Room hire	0.10	0.10	:	:	:	:	:	:	:	[0.10]	:	:	:	:

Note: The commodity and service categories are not comparable to those in publications before 2001-02.

The numbering system is sequential, it does not use actual COICOP codes.

Please see background notes for symbols and conventions used in this report.

This table is based on a three year average.

5 For FYE 2019 onwards, excludes payments made as part of a combined bill.

Table A35

Detailed household expenditure by countries and regions (cont.)

UK, financial year ending 2020 to financial year ending 2022

Commodity or service	United Kingdom	England	North East	North West	Yorkshire and The Humber	East Midlands	West Midlands	East	London	South East	South West	Wales	Scotland	Northern Ireland
	Average weekly household expenditure (£)													
12 Miscellaneous goods & services	**41.20**	**42.10**	**29.00**	**40.60**	**38.00**	**43.40**	**41.20**	**41.80**	**44.90**	**47.70**	**42.00**	**34.90**	**36.00**	**40.60**
12.1 Personal care	11.50	11.70	8.90	10.90	10.90	12.00	12.00	12.00	12.40	12.70	11.20	8.90	11.20	12.10
12.1.1 Hairdressing, beauty treatment	3.20	3.20	2.70	3.00	3.10	3.50	3.00	3.20	2.80	3.70	3.10	2.40	3.60	3.20
12.1.2 Toilet paper	0.90	0.90	0.80	0.90	0.90	0.90	1.00	1.00	0.90	1.00	0.90	0.90	0.80	1.10
12.1.3 Toiletries and soap	2.50	2.60	2.00	2.50	2.00	2.60	2.40	2.60	2.80	3.10	2.40	2.10	2.30	2.90
12.1.4 Baby toiletries and accessories (disposable)	0.50	0.50	0.30	0.50	0.40	0.60	0.50	0.70	0.60	0.50	0.50	0.60	0.40	0.60
12.1.5 Hair products, cosmetics and electrical personal appliances	4.40	4.50	3.10	3.90	4.50	4.30	5.10	4.60	5.30	4.60	4.30	3.00	4.10	4.30
12.2 Personal effects	3.20	3.30	2.40	3.00	2.40	2.80	4.50	2.20	4.00	4.20	3.00	2.00	3.50	2.30
12.3 Social protection	2.50	2.50	1.10	3.00	2.10	1.70	2.20	1.70	4.60	2.40	2.50	[1.70]	2.80	2.20
12.4 Insurance	18.80	19.20	14.90	19.00	17.40	18.80	18.80	20.50	19.70	22.00	18.30	17.40	15.00	18.30
12.4.1 Household insurances - structural, contents and appliances	5.00	5.10	4.00	4.90	4.60	4.70	4.50	5.60	5.40	5.80	4.90	5.20	4.80	4.60
12.4.2 Medical insurance premiums[6]	2.40	2.50	1.20	2.00	1.70	2.00	1.90	2.40	3.20	4.20	2.40	1.80	1.20	1.90
12.4.3 Vehicle insurance including boat insurance	10.80	11.10	9.30	11.70	10.70	11.60	11.80	11.90	10.40	11.20	10.40	10.00	8.40	11.40
12.4.4 Non-package holiday, other travel insurance[7]	0.60	0.60	0.40	0.40	0.40	0.60	0.50	0.50	0.70	0.70	0.70	0.40	0.50	0.40
12.5 Other services	5.20	5.30	1.80	4.70	5.20	8.10	3.70	5.50	4.30	6.40	6.90	4.80	3.60	5.70
12.5.1 Moving house	2.40	2.50	0.90	2.30	1.80	2.80	1.80	2.30	2.10	3.60	3.90	2.80	1.40	1.10
12.5.2 Bank, building society, post office, credit card charges	0.60	0.60	0.20	0.60	0.50	0.50	0.50	0.50	0.50	0.70	0.70	0.50	0.60	0.20
12.5.3 Other services and professional fees	2.20	2.20	0.70	1.80	2.80	4.80	1.40	2.70	1.60	2.10	2.30	1.60	1.60	4.40
1-12 All expenditure groups	**459.60**	**469.00**	**367.70**	**442.50**	**406.40**	**455.60**	**448.00**	**476.70**	**521.70**	**529.20**	**476.30**	**400.80**	**413.40**	**428.20**
13 Other expenditure items	**73.10**	**75.70**	**53.10**	**66.10**	**59.80**	**69.00**	**67.50**	**75.30**	**93.00**	**95.10**	**75.80**	**61.80**	**62.50**	**48.80**
13.1 Housing: mortgage interest payments council tax etc.	51.60	53.40	38.00	46.70	42.50	48.60	47.70	57.20	62.80	66.50	53.30	47.70	43.70	29.10
13.2 Licences, fines and transfers	3.80	3.90	3.10	3.40	3.40	3.90	3.70	4.10	3.60	4.80	4.00	4.00	3.00	3.80
13.3 Holiday spending	4.80	4.80	[4.30]	4.10	[2.60]	3.10	2.40	3.80	11.80	4.70	4.20	[2.60]	6.20	4.90
13.4 Money transfers and credit	12.90	13.60	7.80	11.80	11.30	13.40	13.80	10.30	14.70	19.00	14.30	7.50	9.60	10.90
13.4.1 Money, cash gifts given to children	0.30	0.30	..	[0.10]	..	..	[0.40]	[0.70]	[0.40]	[0.30]	0.60	..	[0.10]	..
13.4.2 Cash gifts and donations	11.60	12.20	7.10	10.80	10.50	12.30	12.40	8.80	13.10	17.40	12.30	6.60	8.60	9.90
13.4.3 Club instalment payments (child) and interest on credit cards	1.00	1.00	0.60	1.00	0.70	0.90	0.90	0.80	1.30	1.20	1.50	0.80	0.90	0.90
Total expenditure	**532.70**	**544.70**	**420.80**	**508.60**	**466.20**	**524.60**	**515.50**	**552.00**	**614.70**	**624.20**	**552.10**	**462.60**	**475.90**	**476.90**
14 Other items recorded														
14.1 Life assurance, contributions to pension funds	35.10	36.00	24.80	30.90	28.80	30.50	32.20	38.60	49.50	43.50	30.90	28.20	31.70	30.80
14.2 Other insurance inc. friendly societies	2.20	2.30	1.70	2.20	2.00	2.50	2.40	2.40	1.60	3.00	2.80	1.80	2.10	0.60
14.3 Income tax, payments less refunds	109.30	115.00	59.30	87.30	79.70	94.70	96.30	125.50	173.80	152.80	98.80	77.70	83.40	74.90
14.4 National insurance contributions	41.30	42.60	29.90	37.90	33.40	38.20	39.50	44.50	59.80	48.40	36.50	33.10	35.70	34.20
14.5 Purchase or alteration of dwellings, mortgages	66.30	70.20	38.40	54.40	46.00	56.20	55.30	79.40	81.40	114.50	62.30	48.70	48.00	39.60
14.6 Savings and investments	5.90	6.40	3.80	4.70	4.90	6.30	5.20	3.70	7.80	11.80	5.40	2.80	4.10	2.40
14.7 Pay off loan to clear other debt	2.10	2.10	1.40	2.30	1.70	1.70	1.70	1.60	3.00	2.20	2.90	1.60	1.90	[0.80]
14.8 Windfall receipts from gambling etc[8]	0.60	0.60	0.70	1.40	0.40	0.40	0.40	0.50	0.40	0.60	0.30	0.30	0.60	0.70

Note: The commodity and service categories are not comparable to those in publications before 2001-02.

The numbering system is sequential, it does not use actual COICOP codes.

Please see background notes for symbols and conventions used in this report.

This table is based on a three year average.

6 For FYE 2019 onwards, critical illness cover, personal accident insurance and other medical insurance are included here. They were not included in previous years.

7 For FYE 2019 onwards, information about insurance for non-package holiday and other travel insurance was collected in the questionnaire in addition to the diary. In previous years, this was based on diary data only.

8 Expressed as an income figure as opposed to an expenditure figure.

Source: Office for National Statistics

Table A36
Household expenditure by urban/rural areas
Great Britain[1], financial year ending 2020 to financial year ending 2022

	Urban	Rural
Average number of weighted households (thousands)	21,570	5,840
Total number of households in sample (over 3 years)	11,780	3,770
Total number of persons in sample (over 3 years)	26,990	8,540
Total number of adults in sample (over 3 years)	21,380	6,930
Weighted average number of persons per household	2.4	2.3

Commodity or service	Average weekly household expenditure (£)	
1 Food & non-alcoholic drinks	64.00	67.70
2 Alcoholic drinks, tobacco & narcotics	12.40	15.20
3 Clothing & footwear	18.40	18.00
4 Housing (net)[2], fuel & power	88.90	74.60
5 Household goods & services	33.70	40.90
6 Health	7.60	9.10
7 Transport	67.10	91.70
8 Communication	21.10	21.30
9 Recreation & culture	55.60	71.90
10 Education	6.20	5.80
11 Restaurants & hotels	35.10	35.60
12 Miscellaneous goods & services	40.30	44.20
1-12 All expenditure groups	450.50	496.10
13 Other expenditure items	71.80	80.90
Total expenditure	**522.30**	**577.10**
Average weekly expenditure per person (£)		
Total expenditure	**221.30**	**253.00**

Note: The commodity and service categories are not comparable to those in publications before 2001-02.

Please see background notes for symbols and conventions used in this report.

This table is based on a three year average.

1 Combined urban/rural classification for England & Wales and Scotland - see Methodology - Urban and rural areas.

2 Excludes mortgage interest payments, council tax. Mortgage interest payments can be found in category 13.

Source: Office for National Statistics

Background notes

Symbols and conventions used in Family Spending tables

[ ]   Figures should be used with extra caution because they are based on fewer than 20 reporting households.

:   The data is suppressed if the unweighted sample counts are less than 10 reporting households.

.   No figures are available because there are no reporting households.

~   The figure is greater than 0 but rounds to 0.

Rounding: Individual figures have been rounded independently. The sum of component items does not therefore necessarily add to the totals shown.

Averages: These are averages (means) for all households included in the column or row, and unless specified, are not restricted to those households reporting expenditure on a particular item or income of a particular type.

Impact of the coronavirus (COVID-19) pandemic on the Living Costs and Food Survey (LCF) for the financial year ending 2020

Following Government guidance in relation to the coronavirus (COVID-19) pandemic, a pause in data collection led to interviews being conducted for 13 fewer days in March 2020 than planned. Final March interviews took place on Monday March 16th. All households that were not interviewed as a result were treated as non-responders and data were weighted to account for reduced data collection in March 2020 compared to previous years.

Data collected in March 2020 may have covered changes to spending habits around the start of the first UK lockdown on March 23rd, for example panic buying beforehand and reduced spending during lockdown when people were advised to stay at home and many businesses were closed. However, due to reduced data collection in the latter half of March data may not accurately reflect the impact of lockdown on spending and the annual estimates reported in this release will not be significantly impacted.

161

Family Spending

Workbook 4 - Expenditure by Household Characteristics

Contents:

ONS Social Surveys

Office for National Statistics

March 2023

A number of tables within the family spending workbooks have been placed under review to be removed from future publications. Tables under review are specified within the workbooks. If you use these for your analysis, please contact us via family.spending@ons.gov.uk**.**

Correction

04 August 2022

A correction has been made to Family spending workbook 4: expenditure by household characteristic (table A48 only) affecting the periods FYE 2021 and FYE 2020. This minor error has been caused by processing/code errors introduced in the creation of table A48 and affects the percentage of households with durable goods, (fridge-freezer or deep freezer, tumble dryer, dishwasher, telephone, home computer and internet connection). You can see the original content in the superseded version. We apologise for any inconvenience

Table A17

Household expenditure by economic activity status of the household reference person

UK, financial year ending 2022

	Employees			Self-employed	All in employ-ment[1]	Unem-ployed	All economi-cally active[1]	Economically inactive			All house-holds
	Full-time	Part-time	All					Retired	Other	All	
Weighted number of households (thousands)	12,330	2,960	15,290	1,900	17,220	370	17,590	7,440	3,470	10,910	28,500
Total number of households in sample	2,390	580	2,970	390	3,370	70	3,430	1,530	670	2,200	5,630
Total number of persons in sample	6,270	1,470	7,740	1,070	8,820	140	8,960	2,500	1,390	3,890	12,850
Total number of adults in sample	4,670	1,060	5,730	810	6,540	100	6,650	2,490	1,130	3,620	10,260
Weighted average number of persons per household	2.7	2.7	2.7	2.8	2.7	2.1	2.7	1.6	2.3	1.8	2.3
Commodity or service					Average weekly household expenditure (£)						
1 Food & non-alcoholic drinks	68.40	65.10	67.70	74.30	68.40	42.60	67.90	52.40	54.30	53.00	62.20
2 Alcoholic drinks, tobacco & narcotics	12.70	11.40	12.50	14.50	12.70	6.40	12.60	11.00	12.50	11.50	12.20
3 Clothing & footwear	21.90	17.60	21.10	23.10	21.30	8.00	21.00	10.80	14.80	12.10	17.60
4 Housing (net)[2], fuel & power	99.90	96.30	99.20	107.50	100.50	134.80	101.20	55.20	88.90	65.90	87.70
5 Household goods & services	39.60	27.70	37.30	51.40	38.80	23.30	38.50	29.70	26.40	28.60	34.70
6 Health	8.90	6.50	8.40	8.80	8.50	4.80	8.40	11.80	6.80	10.20	9.10
7 Transport	96.90	72.40	92.20	98.00	92.70	43.00	91.60	42.70	54.90	46.60	74.40
8 Communication	24.70	21.20	24.10	23.50	24.00	14.10	23.80	16.40	18.70	17.10	21.20
9 Recreation & culture	66.20	50.20	63.10	71.00	63.90	34.30	63.20	44.20	45.30	44.50	56.10
10 Education	6.70	7.10	6.70	8.00	6.90	:	6.90	[0.40]	6.30	2.30	5.20
11 Restaurants & hotels	44.90	33.30	42.70	41.40	42.50	16.50	41.90	23.00	24.10	23.30	34.80
12 Miscellaneous goods & services	46.90	42.80	46.10	51.20	46.60	25.30	46.20	33.90	27.00	31.70	40.60
1-12 All expenditure groups	537.80	451.70	521.10	572.50	526.60	363.40	523.20	331.40	380.00	346.80	455.70
13 Other expenditure items	94.60	66.90	89.30	80.30	88.20	35.80	87.10	55.50	40.10	50.60	73.10
Total expenditure	632.40	518.50	610.40	652.80	614.80	399.20	610.30	386.90	420.10	397.50	528.80
Average weekly expenditure per person (£) Total expenditure	238.20	191.00	228.90	232.10	229.30	189.10	228.70	245.60	186.60	222.00	226.70

Note: The commodity and service categories are not comparable to those in publications before 2001-02.
Please see background notes for symbols and conventions used in this report.

1 Includes households where household reference person was on a Government supported training scheme.
2 Excluding mortgage interest payments, council tax and Northern Ireland rates. Mortgage interest payments can be found in category 13.

Source: Office for National Statistics

Table A18

Household expenditure by gross income: the household reference person is a full-time employee

UK, financial year ending 2022

> This table is under review to be removed from future publications and replaced with disposable equivalised income tables.
> If you use this table for your analysis, please get in contact here.

	Lowest twenty per cent	Second quintile group	Third quintile group	Fourth quintile group	Highest twenty per cent	All house-holds
Lower boundary of group (£ per week)[1]		369	612	918	1,366	
Weighted number of households (thousands)	230	1,390	2,610	3,690	4,410	12,330
Total number of households in sample	40	280	500	710	860	2,390
Total number of persons in sample	60	460	1,170	1,930	2,640	6,270
Total number of adults in sample	50	370	880	1,440	1,930	4,670
Weighted average number of persons per household	1.4	1.7	2.4	2.7	3.1	2.7

Commodity or service	Average weekly household expenditure (£)					
1 Food & non-alcoholic drinks	35.20	39.20	57.80	67.20	86.50	68.40
2 Alcoholic drinks, tobacco & narcotics	10.00	6.60	10.70	11.90	16.70	12.70
3 Clothing & footwear	[4.90]	11.60	14.20	22.30	30.30	21.90
4 Housing (net)[2], fuel & power	97.60	99.10	98.10	95.00	105.50	99.90
5 Household goods & services	9.20	19.70	29.90	37.60	54.90	39.60
6 Health	[1.40]	4.70	4.00	6.20	15.70	8.90
7 Transport	28.50	40.30	64.60	90.10	143.20	96.90
8 Communication	13.40	16.70	22.50	25.10	28.80	24.70
9 Recreation & culture	18.20	22.60	48.00	58.40	99.70	66.20
10 Education	..	[1.90]	..	[4.90]	13.70	6.70
11 Restaurants & hotels	18.30	16.50	28.70	39.10	69.70	44.90
12 Miscellaneous goods & services	15.20	24.80	29.80	46.10	66.30	46.90
1-12 All expenditure groups	252.30	303.80	408.80	504.00	731.00	537.80
13 Other expenditure items	41.30	44.10	63.60	83.50	141.10	94.60
Total expenditure	**293.60**	**347.90**	**472.40**	**587.50**	**872.10**	**632.40**
Average weekly expenditure per person (£) **Total expenditure**	**207.40**	**201.60**	**199.80**	**214.40**	**280.30**	**238.20**

Note: The commodity and service categories are not comparable to those in publications before 2001-02.

Please see background notes for symbols and conventions used in this report.

1 Lower boundary of 2021-22 gross income quintile groups (£ per week).

2 Excluding mortgage interest payments, council tax and Northern Ireland rates. Mortgage interest payments can be found in category 13.

Source: Office for National Statistics

Table A18Eq

Household expenditure by equivalised disposable income (OECD-modified scale): the household reference person is a full-time employee
UK, financial year ending 2022

	Lowest twenty per cent	Second quintile group	Third quintile group	Fourth quintile group	Highest twenty per cent	All house-holds
Lower boundary of group (£ per week)[1]		263	369	494	663	
Weighted number of households (thousands)	470	1,590	2,780	3,400	4,090	12,330
Total number of households in sample	90	290	560	670	790	2,390
Total number of persons in sample	300	860	1,480	1,690	1,930	6,270
Total number of adults in sample	170	550	1,060	1,310	1,580	4,670
Weighted average number of persons per household	3.6	3.1	2.7	2.5	2.4	2.7
Commodity or service	Average weekly household expenditure (£)					
1 Food & non-alcoholic drinks	66.10	64.00	64.10	66.10	75.10	68.40
2 Alcoholic drinks, tobacco & narcotics	10.10	8.70	11.80	12.10	15.70	12.70
3 Clothing & footwear	18.70	16.00	16.40	22.30	28.00	21.90
4 Housing (net)[2], fuel & power	125.50	102.40	93.90	89.00	109.20	99.90
5 Household goods & services	29.20	24.80	32.10	40.70	50.70	39.60
6 Health	5.80	4.20	5.70	7.40	14.50	8.90
7 Transport	53.90	56.20	71.60	97.60	134.40	96.90
8 Communication	21.50	26.00	23.10	24.90	25.60	24.70
9 Recreation & culture	30.50	37.00	48.00	68.20	92.30	66.20
10 Education	..	..	4.80	4.60	12.40	6.70
11 Restaurants & hotels	22.60	23.50	30.10	44.30	66.40	44.90
12 Miscellaneous goods & services	34.10	30.30	40.20	46.70	59.60	46.90
1-12 All expenditure groups	418.90	394.40	441.70	524.10	683.80	537.80
13 Other expenditure items	53.30	54.50	72.20	94.30	130.60	94.60
Total expenditure	**472.20**	**448.80**	**513.90**	**618.40**	**814.40**	**632.40**
Average weekly expenditure per person (£) **Total expenditure**	**131.90**	**145.40**	**189.00**	**243.90**	**334.40**	**238.20**

Note: The commodity and service categories are not comparable to those in publications before 2001-02.

Please see background notes for symbols and conventions used in this report.

1 Lower boundary of 2021-22 equivalised disposable income quintile groups (£ per week).

2 Excluding mortgage interest payments, council tax and Northern Ireland rates. Mortgage interest payments can be found in category 13.

Source: Office for National Statistics

Table A19

Household expenditure by gross income: the household reference person is self-employed

UK, financial year ending 2020 to financial year ending 2022

This table is under review to be removed from future publications and replaced with disposable equivalised income tables. If you use this table for your analysis, please get in contact here.

	Lowest twenty per cent	Second quintile group	Third quintile group	Fourth quintile group	Highest twenty per cent	All house-holds
Lower boundary of group (£ per week)[1]		369	612	918	1,366	
Average weighted number of households (thousands)	280	450	440	450	420	2,040
Total number of households in sample (over 3 years)	160	260	270	260	240	1,180
Total number of persons in sample (over 3 years)	250	640	730	730	760	3,110
Total number of adults in sample (over 3 years)	210	450	520	570	600	2,340
Weighted average number of persons per household	1.6	2.5	2.8	3.0	3.3	2.7
Commodity or service	Average weekly household expenditure (£)					
1 Food & non-alcoholic drinks	44.00	64.30	76.90	81.00	98.80	75.10
2 Alcoholic drinks, tobacco & narcotics	8.30	11.70	15.10	19.10	21.70	15.70
3 Clothing & footwear	9.50	14.10	23.50	22.70	35.00	21.80
4 Housing(net)[2], fuel & power	99.30	97.30	97.60	105.30	106.50	101.20
5 Household goods & services	18.20	35.60	35.50	49.10	90.60	47.50
6 Health	7.10	4.00	7.10	8.90	10.30	7.50
7 Transport	54.60	60.80	78.50	112.50	127.40	89.10
8 Communication	13.30	19.00	22.50	25.80	32.90	23.40
9 Recreation & culture	32.10	40.20	63.70	80.30	115.10	68.50
10 Education	..	[3.10]	[4.40]	[3.00]	19.60	6.40
11 Restaurants & hotels	20.30	26.50	38.50	48.30	61.60	40.50
12 Miscellaneous goods & services	30.20	40.40	40.40	51.20	76.80	49.00
1-12 All expenditure groups	338.10	416.90	503.70	607.40	796.20	545.80
13 Other expenditure items	43.10	54.10	72.40	94.70	148.80	85.30
Total expenditure	**381.20**	**471.00**	**576.10**	**702.10**	**945.00**	**631.10**
Average weekly expenditure per person (£) **Total expenditure**	**232.30**	**185.00**	**204.40**	**234.50**	**289.00**	**231.00**

Note: The commodity and service categories are not comparable to those in publications before 2001-02.

Please see background notes for symbols and conventions used in this report.

This table is based on a three year average.

1 Lower boundary of 2021-22 gross income quintile groups (£ per week).

2 Excluding mortgage interest payments, council tax and Northern Ireland rates. Mortgage interest payments can be found in category 13.

Source: Office for National Statistics

Table A19Eq

Household expenditure by equivalised disposable income (OECD-modified scale): the household reference person is self-employed

UK, financial year ending 2020 to financial year ending 2022

		Lowest twenty per cent	Second quintile group	Third quintile group	Fourth quintile group	Highest twenty per cent	All house-holds
Lower boundary of group (£ per week)[1]			263	369	494	663	
Average weighted number of households (thousands)		410	390	400	370	460	2,040
Total number of households in sample (over 3 years)		230	230	230	210	280	1,180
Total number of persons in sample (over 3 years)		610	670	630	550	650	3,110
Total number of adults in sample (over 3 years)		400	450	470	460	560	2,340
Weighted average number of persons per household		2.8	3.0	2.8	2.7	2.4	2.7
Commodity or service		Average weekly household expenditure (£)					
1	Food & non-alcoholic drinks	64.10	77.00	75.20	78.00	80.90	75.10
2	Alcoholic drinks, tobacco & narcotics	7.90	14.70	15.40	16.80	22.30	15.70
3	Clothing & footwear	14.60	20.00	21.30	30.00	23.10	21.80
4	Housing(net)[2], fuel & power	99.20	105.50	98.10	96.00	105.00	101.20
5	Household goods & services	25.20	47.70	35.90	57.20	71.20	47.50
6	Health	7.00	5.60	7.50	6.00	10.60	7.50
7	Transport	65.80	86.00	80.70	94.80	114.20	89.10
8	Communication	18.00	24.10	24.80	24.70	25.30	23.40
9	Recreation & culture	39.00	48.50	64.30	82.20	102.00	68.50
10	Education	[1.80]	[4.90]	[2.70]	9.10	13.80	6.40
11	Restaurants & hotels	25.20	33.30	38.60	43.50	58.30	40.50
12	Miscellaneous goods & services	39.30	40.90	45.20	47.20	69.70	49.00
1-12	All expenditure groups	407.20	508.30	509.70	585.60	696.30	545.80
13	Other expenditure items	49.60	63.20	82.40	93.30	132.40	85.30
Total expenditure		**456.80**	**571.50**	**592.10**	**678.90**	**828.80**	**631.10**
Average weekly expenditure per person (£) **Total expenditure**		**161.50**	**188.20**	**212.60**	**249.70**	**352.50**	**231.00**

Note: The commodity and service categories are not comparable to those in publications before 2001-02.

Please see background notes for symbols and conventions used in this report.

This table is based on a three year average.

1 Lower boundary of 2021-22 gross income quintile groups (£ per week).

2 Excluding mortgage interest payments, council tax and Northern Ireland rates. Mortgage interest payments can be found in category 13.

Source: Office for National Statistics

Table A20
Household expenditure by number of persons working
UK, financial year ending 2022

	Number of persons working					All house-holds
	None	One	Two	Three	Four or more	
Weighted number of households (thousands)	9,850	7,740	9,160	1,480	280	28,500
Total number of households in sample	1,980	1,550	1,810	250	40	5,630
Total number of persons in sample	3,220	3,120	5,370	940	200	12,850
Total number of adults in sample	3,000	2,450	3,850	790	180	10,260
Weighted average number of persons per household	1.6	2.1	3.0	3.8	4.7	2.3
Weighted average age of head of household	68	49	43	51	54	54
Employment status of the household reference person[1]:						
- % working full-time or self-employed	0	64	86	85	83	49
- % working part-time	0	20	12	13	14	10
- % not working	100	16	2	2	2	40

Commodity or service	Average weekly household expenditure (£)					
1 Food & non-alcoholic drinks	49.30	55.40	75.50	91.50	113.90	62.20
2 Alcoholic drinks, tobacco & narcotics	10.50	11.80	13.00	19.00	17.20	12.20
3 Clothing & footwear	10.00	16.30	23.60	31.70	52.90	17.60
4 Housing(net)[2], fuel & power	64.60	99.50	97.80	111.00	117.90	87.70
5 Household goods & services	27.00	32.90	41.20	52.40	50.60	34.70
6 Health	9.40	7.80	8.40	15.50	26.40	9.10
7 Transport	40.30	66.10	105.70	135.00	160.80	74.40
8 Communication	15.70	19.40	25.90	34.30	41.10	21.20
9 Recreation & culture	39.60	53.00	73.80	65.80	87.40	56.10
10 Education	1.90	8.90	5.30	[4.50]	..	5.20
11 Restaurants & hotels	20.50	31.20	48.50	57.40	69.50	34.80
12 Miscellaneous goods & services	29.80	34.50	53.40	59.60	77.20	40.60
1-12 All expenditure groups	318.50	436.80	572.10	677.70	829.90	455.70
13 Other expenditure items	48.70	63.40	104.60	88.00	91.20	73.10
Total expenditure	**367.30**	**500.20**	**676.70**	**765.70**	**921.20**	**528.80**
Average weekly expenditure per person (£) **Total expenditure**	**225.00**	**239.60**	**226.40**	**203.20**	**194.00**	**226.70**

Note: The commodity and service categories are not comparable to those in publications before 2001-02.

Please see background notes for symbols and conventions used in this report.

1 Excludes households where the household reference person was on a Government-supported training scheme.

2 Excluding mortgage interest payments, council tax and Northern Ireland rates. Mortgage interest payments can be found in category 13.

Source: Office for National Statistics

Table A21

Household expenditure by age at which the household reference person completed continuous full-time education

UK, financial year ending 2022

	Aged 14 and under	Aged 15	Aged 16	Aged 17 and under 19	Aged 19 and under 22	Aged 22 or over
Weighted number of households (thousands)	130	1,220	5,790	5,480	4,450	4,590
Total number of households in sample	20	280	1,160	1,100	870	900
Total number of persons in sample	50	570	2,840	2,740	2,200	2,270
Total number of adults in sample	30	490	2,230	2,090	1,610	1,680
Weighted average number of persons per household	2.8	2.1	2.6	2.6	2.6	2.5
Weighted average age of head of household	49	58	52	46	44	44
Commodity or service	Average weekly household expenditure (£)					
1 Food & non-alcoholic drinks	38.10	57.00	63.90	65.80	67.30	68.20
2 Alcoholic drinks, tobacco & narcotics	[9.20]	15.40	15.20	11.70	12.60	10.70
3 Clothing & footwear	[11.40]	13.20	18.60	19.10	20.60	24.10
4 Housing(net)[1], fuel & power	85.50	68.60	85.60	96.60	98.30	110.90
5 Household goods & services	[11.90]	30.70	34.40	34.70	44.90	35.80
6 Health	[1.70]	4.90	8.50	8.60	8.50	9.30
7 Transport	[32.30]	62.50	82.90	84.00	92.30	90.10
8 Communication	36.40	20.20	23.30	23.10	23.10	21.60
9 Recreation & culture	10.90	44.20	58.60	57.60	65.60	67.20
10 Education	..	..	2.80	2.00	3.50	15.70
11 Restaurants & hotels	..	22.60	33.20	36.70	44.20	48.40
12 Miscellaneous goods & services	[23.10]	30.30	36.00	40.80	48.40	52.00
1-12 All expenditure groups	280.40	369.80	463.00	480.70	529.20	554.10
13 Other expenditure items	[22.70]	43.30	60.10	69.80	96.60	105.20
Total expenditure	**303.10**	**413.10**	**523.10**	**550.60**	**625.80**	**659.30**
Average weekly expenditure per person (£)						
Total expenditure	**108.60**	**194.50**	**203.20**	**211.90**	**243.10**	**258.90**

Note: The commodity and service categories are not comparable to those in publications before 2001-02.

Please see background notes for symbols and conventions used in this report.

1 Excluding mortgage interest payments, council tax and Northern Ireland rates. Mortgage interest payments can be found in category 13.

Source: Office for National Statistics

Table A22

Household expenditure by socio-economic classification of household reference person

UK, financial year ending 2022

	Large employers and higher managerial	Higher profess- ional	Lower manag- erial and profess- ional	Inter- mediate	Small employ- ers	Lower super- visory	Semi- routine	Routine	Long- term unem- ployed[1]	Students	Occupation not stated[2]	All house- holds
Weighted number of households (thousands)	1,090	3,580	5,720	2,390	1,550	1,200	1,520	1,950	60	500	8,940	28,500
Total number of households in sample	220	700	1,140	470	320	230	290	370	10	90	1,810	5,630
Total number of persons in sample	610	1,840	2,860	1,080	890	600	670	950	30	210	3,110	12,850
Total number of adults in sample	450	1,370	2,150	820	660	460	500	720	20	160	2,960	10,260
Weighted average number of persons per household	2.9	2.6	2.6	2.4	2.9	2.8	2.6	2.7	3.3	2.6	1.7	2.3
Commodity or service	Average weekly household expenditure (£)											
1 Food & non-alcoholic drinks	87.30	73.60	67.00	59.40	72.30	63.10	57.40	56.60	..	49.50	53.10	62.20
2 Alcoholic drinks, tobacco & narcotics	19.80	13.10	12.50	10.50	12.80	13.30	11.10	13.70	..	6.50	11.00	12.20
3 Clothing & footwear	31.10	23.30	21.60	17.50	22.00	15.80	14.80	16.70	..	13.70	11.50	17.60
4 Housing (net)[3], fuel & power	98.80	98.10	98.70	93.00	99.10	96.00	98.10	108.00	..	159.30	60.50	87.70
5 Household goods & services	43.00	48.80	40.70	34.90	43.80	29.30	27.00	24.20	..	15.70	28.10	34.70
6 Health	11.80	12.10	9.80	7.80	6.90	6.30	4.10	3.00	..	6.50	10.60	9.10
7 Transport	151.40	104.30	95.70	75.60	95.50	80.20	58.70	58.60	..	70.80	41.40	74.40
8 Communication	28.60	22.30	24.40	21.90	24.40	25.20	22.40	22.00	..	18.30	16.40	21.20
9 Recreation & culture	86.30	75.80	73.80	53.90	63.70	48.00	33.80	33.30	..	41.50	43.30	56.10
10 Education	[17.50]	8.10	8.80	[1.80]	[2.20]	..	..	[1.60]	..	[51.20]	[1.00]	5.20
11 Restaurants & hotels	66.40	56.70	44.30	31.50	34.00	37.30	21.00	25.10	..	21.00	22.20	34.80
12 Miscellaneous goods & services	62.40	54.50	50.60	39.30	44.60	36.90	30.40	29.20	..	27.60	31.40	40.60
1-12 All expenditure groups	704.40	590.80	547.80	447.10	521.20	453.70	379.10	392.00	..	481.80	330.50	455.70
13 Other expenditure items	132.10	122.00	87.30	72.70	68.80	71.70	49.00	46.90	..	34.70	50.80	73.10
Total expenditure	**836.50**	**712.90**	**635.10**	**519.80**	**590.00**	**525.50**	**428.10**	**438.90**	**..**	**516.50**	**381.20**	**528.80**
Average weekly expenditure per person (£) Total expenditure	**292.40**	**274.00**	**248.70**	**217.60**	**203.20**	**186.10**	**167.30**	**165.20**	**..**	**199.60**	**223.20**	**226.70**

Note: Changes to categories of socio-economic classification were made in 2011. See Appendix B for details.

The commodity and service categories are not comparable to those in publications before 2001-02.

Please see background notes for symbols and conventions used in this report.

1 Includes those who have never worked - see Methodology - National Statistics Socio-economic Classification (NS-SEC)

2 Includes those who are economically inactive - see Methodology - Economically inactive

3 Excludes mortgage interest payments, council tax and Northern Ireland rates. Mortgage interest payments can be found in category 13.

Source: Office for National Statistics

Table A45 Percentage of households with durable goods[1,2]
UK, 1970 to financial year ending 2022

> **This table is under review to be removed from future publications.**
> **If you use this table for your analysis, please get in contact here.**

	Car/ van	Central heating[3]	Tele- phone	Mobile phone[4]	Home computer	Internet connec- tion
1970	52	30	35	--	--	--
1975	57	47	52	--	--	--
1980	60	59	72	--	--	--
1985	63	69	81	--	13	--
1990	67	79	87	--	17	--
1994-95	69	84	91	--	--	--
1995-96	70	85	92	--	--	--
1996-97	69	87	93	16	27	--
1997-98	70	89	94	20	29	--
1998-99	72	89	95	26	32	9
1998-99[5]	72	89	95	27	33	10
1999-2000	71	90	95	44	38	19
2000-01	72	91	93	47	44	32
2001-02[6]	74	92	94	64	49	39
2002-03	74	93	94	70	55	45
2003-04	75	94	92	76	58	49
2004-05	75	95	93	78	62	53
2005-06	74	94	92	79	65	55
2006[7]	76	95	91	80	67	59
2006[8]	74	95	91	79	67	58
2007	75	95	89	78	70	61
2008	74	95	90	79	72	66
2009	76	95	88	81	75	71
2010	75	96	87	80	77	73
2011	75	96	88	87	79	77
2012	75	96	88	87	81	79
2013	76	96	89	92	83	82
2014	76	96	88	94	85	84
2014-15	76	96	88	94	85	84
2015-16	78	95	88	95	88	88
2016-17	79	95	89	95	88	89
2017-18	78	95	85	95	88	89
2018-19	79	97	83	96	89	91
2019-20	80	96	82	90	89	94
2020-21	81	96	81	93	90	96
Latest year	81	97	79	93	91	96

Please see background notes for symbols and conventions used in this report.

-- Data not available.

1 The questions asking about owership of washing machines, microwaves and DVD players were removed from the FYE 2020 questionnaire.

2 The questions asking about owership of dishwashers and tumble driers were removed from the FYE 2021 questionnaire.

3 Full or partial.

4 From FYE 2020 onwards, the calculation of whether a household owns a landline/mobile/internet connection is based on whether they report any spending on these services in the questionnaire. Prior to FYE 2020, households were explicity asked whether they owned these goods.

5 From this version of 1998-99, figures shown are based on weighted data and including children's expenditure.

6 From 2001-02 onwards, weighting is based on the population figures from the 2001 census.

7 From 1998-99 to this version of 2006, figures shown are based on weighted data using non-response weights based on the 1991 Census and population figures from the 1991 and 2001 Census.

8 From this version of 2006, figures shown are based on weighted data using updated weights, with non-response weights and population figures based on the 2001 Census.

Source: Office for National Statistics

Table A46

Percentage[1] of households with durable goods[2,3] by income group and household composition
UK, financial year ending 2022

> This table is under review to be removed from future publications.
> If you use this table for your analysis, please get in contact here.

	Central heating[4]	Home computer	Internet connection	Tele-phone	Mobile phone[5]
All households	**97**	**91**	**96**	**79**	**93**
Gross income decile group					
Lowest ten per cent	92	65	83	67	86
Second decile group	97	77	89	79	89
Third decile group	98	85	94	82	90
Fourth decile group	96	92	97	80	92
Fifth decile group	96	95	100	80	96
Sixth decile group	98	97	99	78	95
Seventh decile group	97	99	100	79	95
Eighth decile group	97	98	99	79	97
Ninth decile group	97	99	100	81	96
Highest ten per cent	97	99	99	80	97
Household composition					
One adult, retired mainly dependent on state pensions [6]	95	52	67	81	67
One adult, other retired	97	73	81	89	82
One adult, non-retired	94	86	97	68	94
One adult, one child	97	88	99	66	97
One adult, two or more children	98	92	100	65	100
Two adults, retired mainly dependent on state pensions [6]	96	83	93	92	87
Two adults, other retired	97	94	98	96	92
Two adults, non-retired	97	96	99	75	96
Two adults, one child	97	94	100	72	95
Two adults, two children	97	98	100	79	97
Two adults, three children	97	96	100	80	100
Two adults, four or more children	100	91	100	79	100
Three adults	98	98	99	83	98
Three adults, one or more children	100	98	99	84	96
All other households without children	95	100	100	81	97
All other households with children	94	97	98	83	98

Please see background notes for symbols and conventions used in this report.

1 See table A47 for number of recording households.
2 The questions asking about owership of washing machines, microwaves and DVD players were removed from the FYE 2020 questionnaire.
3 The questions asking about owership of dishwashers and tumble driers were removed from the FYE 2021 questionnaire.
4 Full or partial.
5 From FYE 2020 onwards, the calculation of whether a household owns a landline/mobile/internet connection is based on whether they report any spending on these services in the questionnaire. Prior to FYE 2020, households were explicity asked whether they owned these goods.
6 Mainly dependent on state pensions and not economically active - see Methodology - Economically Inactive.

Source: Office for National Statistics

Table A47

Percentage of households with cars by income group, tenure and household composition

UK, financial year ending 2022

This table is under review to be removed from future publications.
If you use this table for your analysis, please get in contact here.

	One car/van	Two cars/vans	Three or more cars/vans	All with cars/vans	Weighted number of house-holds (000s)	House-holds in the sample (number)
All households	*45*	*28*	*7*	*81*	*28,500*	*5,630*
Gross income decile group						
Lowest ten per cent	44	5	..	49	2,860	530
Second decile group	49	8	..	58	2,850	540
Third decile group	59	11	..	71	2,850	560
Fourth decile group	63	15	[3]	81	2,850	580
Fifth decile group	55	28	4	87	2,850	580
Sixth decile group	45	35	7	87	2,850	570
Seventh decile group	44	42	8	94	2,850	570
Eighth decile group	34	47	12	94	2,850	580
Ninth decile group	27	49	16	92	2,850	560
Highest ten per cent	32	44	19	95	2,850	560
Tenure of dwelling						
Owners						
Owned outright	50	27	8	85	10,140	2,300
Buying with a mortgage [1]	39	45	10	93	9,010	1,830
All	45	35	9	89	19,150	4,130
Social rented from						
Council [2]	43	9	..	54	2,130	360
Registered social landlord [3]	46	9	..	57	1,930	320
All	44	9	[2]	55	4,060	680
Private rented [4]						
Rent free	[41]	[28]	..	72	260	40
Rent paid, unfurnished [5]	51	20	3	74	4,280	680
Rent paid, furnished	38	[9]	..	48	750	110
All	49	19	3	70	5,290	830
Household composition						
One adult, retired mainly dependent on state pensions [6]	43	..	:	44	760	130
One adult, other retired	58	[2]	..	61	2,920	530
One adult, non-retired	61	5	..	66	4,640	920
One adult, one child	67	..	:	69	650	120
One adult, two or more children	58	..	:	65	590	100
Two adults, retired mainly dependent on state pensions [6]	57	24	:	80	450	100
Two adults, other retired	53	34	4	91	2,960	690
Two adults, non-retired	39	42	6	86	6,340	1,340
Two adults, one child	39	45	6	91	2,140	410
Two adults, two children	34	53	5	92	2,710	520
Two adults, three children	43	43	[9]	95	670	120
Two adults, four or more children	[44]	[25]	..	86	220	30
Three adults	22	41	30	93	1,630	310
Three adults, one or more children	33	35	25	94	760	130
All other households without children	21	22	47	91	700	110
All other households with children	[33]	[33]	[27]	94	370	50

Please see background notes for symbols and conventions used in this report.

1 Including shared owners (who own part of the equity and pay mortgage, part rent).

2 "Council" includes local authorities, New Towns and Scottish Homes, but see note 3 below.

3 Formerly housing association.

4 All tenants whose accommodation goes with the job of someone in the household are allocated to "rented privately",
 even if the landlord is a local authority or housing association or Housing Action Trust, or if the accommodation is
 rent free. Squatters are also included in this category.

5 "Unfurnished" includes the answers: "partly furnished".

6 Mainly dependent on state pensions and not economically active - see Methodology - Economically Inactive.

Source: Office for National Statistics

Table A48

Percentage of households with durable goods[1,2] by countries and regions

UK, financial year ending 2020 to financial year ending 2022

> **This table is under review to be removed from future publications.**
> **If you use this table for your analysis, please get in contact here.**

	United Kingdom	England	North East	North West	Yorkshire and the Humber	East Midlands	West Midlands	East	London	South East	South West	Wales	Scotland	Northern Ireland
	K02000001	E92000001	E12000001	E12000002	E12000003	E12000004	E12000005	E12000006	E12000007	E12000008	E12000009	W92000004	S92000003	N92000002
Average weighted number of households (thousands)	28,170	23,540	1,210	3,110	2,450	2,080	2,450	2,620	3,380	3,790	2,450	1,370	2,500	760
Total number of households in sample (over 3 years)	16,470	12,480	720	1,670	1,370	1,260	1,330	1,400	1,220	1,910	1,610	710	2,360	920
Percentage of households														
by region and Country														
Car/van	80	80	74	79	79	85	83	88	64	86	85	83	77	84
One	46	46	46	45	46	44	44	49	47	42	47	47	48	44
Two	28	28	23	28	27	32	31	30	13	35	29	29	25	30
Three or more	7	7	5	6	6	9	8	8	4	9	9	8	4	10
Central heating full or partial	96	96	97	96	97	98	97	97	92	95	97	97	97	99
Tumble dryer[1,2]	57	57	62	58	54	62	62	59	42	60	62	63	54	64
Dishwasher[1,2]	50	50	41	42	39	47	46	55	52	63	58	50	46	54
Telephone	81	81	75	81	79	84	81	85	73	84	85	83	81	76
Mobile phone[3]	92	93	89	92	92	93	92	92	93	94	92	85	90	92
Home computer	90	90	84	89	86	90	87	92	93	94	91	90	88	85
Internet connection	95	95	94	95	93	95	94	96	96	97	96	94	95	94

Please see background notes for symbols and conventions used in this report.

This table is based on a three year average.

1 The questions asking about ownership of dishwashers and tumble dryers were removed from the FYE 2021 questionnaire.

2 For FYE 2020, the placement of the dishwashers and tumble driers ownership questions were moved to the household improvements section of the questionnaire.

3 From FYE 2020 onwards, the calculation of whether a household owns a landline/mobile/internet connection is based on whether they report any spending on these services in the questionnaire. Prior to FYE 2020, households were explicitly asked whether they owned these goods.

Source: Office for National Statistics

Table A49

Percentage of households by size, composition and age in each gross income decile group

UK, financial year ending 2022

	Lowest ten per cent	Second decile group	Third decile group	Fourth decile group	Fifth decile group	Sixth decile group	Seventh decile group	Eighth decile group	Ninth decile group	Highest ten per cent	All house-holds
Lower boundary of group (£ per week)		253	369	479	612	761	918	1,102	1,366	1,808	
Weighted number of households (thousands)	2,860	2,850	2,850	2,850	2,850	2,850	2,850	2,850	2,850	2,850	28,500
Number of households in the sample	530	540	560	580	580	570	570	580	560	560	5,630
Size of household											
One person	76	64	44	38	25	17	13	6	5	5	29
Two persons	16	25	42	37	45	44	46	44	37	30	36
Three persons	5	7	8	11	12	16	20	24	21	24	15
Four persons	..	[2]	5	8	11	17	14	19	26	32	14
Five persons	..	..	[3]	[4]	5	[3]	5	5	8	7	4
Six or more persons	..	..	..	..	[3]	[2]	[3]	..	[3]	[3]	2
All sizes	100	100	100	100	100	100	100	100	100	100	100
Household composition											
One adult, retired mainly dependent on state pensions[1]	18	7	..	:	:	:	:	:	:	:	3
One adult, other retired	22	30	21	16	6	[3]	[2]	..	..	:	10
One adult, non-retired	35	27	22	22	18	14	11	6	5	5	16
One adult, one child	4	[4]	5	[3]	[2]	[3]	..	..	..	..	2
One adult, two or more children	[3]	4	6	[2]	[2]	..	..	..	..	..	2
Two adults, retired mainly dependent on state pensions[1]	..	4	8	[2]	..	:	:	:	:	:	2
Two adults, other retired	..	6	13	19	18	16	12	9	5	3	10
Two adults, non-retired	9	11	15	13	24	25	32	35	31	27	22
Two adults, one child	..	[3]	[2]	7	6	10	10	12	10	12	7
Two adults, two children	..	..	[2]	8	7	12	11	14	19	19	9
Two adults, three children	..	..	..	[3]	[3]	[2]	[2]	[3]	[4]	[3]	2
Two adults, four or more children	..	..	:	..	..	..	..	:	..	..	1
Three adults	..	..	..	[3]	5	5	8	12	11	11	6
Three adults, one or more children	..	..	..	..	[4]	[2]	[4]	[4]	6	5	3
All other households without children	:	:	..	..	..	[4]	..	[3]	[5]	10	2
All other households with children	:	:	:	..	..	..	..	..	[3]	[4]	1
All compositions	100	100	100	100	100	100	100	100	100	100	100
Age of household reference person											
15 and under 20 years	:	..	:	:	:	:	:	:	:	:	..
20 and under 25 years	[3]	..	[3]	[3]	[3]	[5]	[3]	..	..	:	3
25 and under 30 years	[4]	[4]	5	5	8	7	11	10	8	[4]	6
30 and under 35 years	[2]	[3]	5	7	8	13	11	11	8	8	8
35 and under 40 years	4	[3]	6	9	8	9	9	14	12	10	9
40 and under 45 years	5	5	7	6	8	8	8	10	15	16	9
45 and under 50 years	5	[4]	5	4	7	9	9	10	12	16	8
50 and under 55 years	8	10	7	6	7	7	10	10	15	18	10
55 and under 60 years	9	7	7	8	8	9	10	11	9	12	9
60 and under 65 years	11	9	8	8	9	9	9	9	8	9	9
65 and under 70 years	12	10	11	11	9	8	7	5	4	3	8
70 and under 75 years	13	12	11	10	10	7	6	4	3	[2]	8
75 and under 80 years	8	10	11	8	7	5	5	[2]	[2]	..	6
80 and under 85 years	7	8	9	7	6	[4]	[2]	..	..	..	5
85 and under 90 years	7	8	[5]	..	..	..	..	..	..	..	3
90 years or more	..	[3]	..	..	..	..	..	..	:	..	1
All ages	100	100	100	100	100	100	100	100	100	100	100

Please see background notes for symbols and conventions used in this report.

1 Mainly dependent on state pensions and not economically active - see Methodology - Economically Inactive.

Source: Office for National Statistics

Table A50

Percentage of households by economic activity, tenure and socio-economic classification in each gross income decile group

UK, financial year ending 2022

	Lowest ten per cent	Second decile group	Third decile group	Fourth decile group	Fifth decile group	Sixth decile group	Seventh decile group	Eighth decile group	Ninth decile group	Highest ten per cent	All house-holds
Lower boundary of group (£ per week)		253	369	479	612	761	918	1,102	1,366	1,808	
Weighted number of households (thousands)	2,860	2,850	2,850	2,850	2,850	2,850	2,850	2,850	2,850	2,850	28,500
Number of households in the sample	530	540	560	580	580	570	570	580	560	560	5,630
Number of economically active persons in household											
No person	78	71	54	44	29	20	15	8	5	[3]	33
One person	19	24	39	41	41	35	24	18	15	14	27
Two persons	[3]	5	7	14	27	40	53	61	62	62	33
Three persons	:	:	..	..	[3]	5	6	11	15	16	6
Four or more persons	:	:	..	..	..	..	..	..	[3]	6	1
All economically active persons	100	100	100	100	100	100	100	100	100	100	100
Tenure of dwelling											
Owners											
Owned outright	37	46	46	48	40	36	31	26	23	22	36
Buying with a mortgage [1]	6	7	12	18	27	33	41	52	56	63	32
All	43	54	58	66	66	69	73	79	79	86	67
Social rented from											
Council [2]	21	16	11	6	8	5	[4]	..	..	..	7
Registered social landlord [3]	17	13	9	8	7	6	[4]	..	..	..	7
All	38	28	21	13	14	11	7	[4]	[3]	..	14
Private rented [4]											
Rent free	..	..	..	..	..	..	..	..	..	..	1
Rent paid, unfurnished [5]	15	16	19	18	15	16	16	14	12	9	15
Rent paid, furnished	[2]	..	[2]	[2]	[3]	[3]	[2]	[3]	[4]	..	3
All	19	18	22	21	19	20	20	17	18	12	19
All tenures	100	100	100	100	100	100	100	100	100	100	100
Socio-economic classification											
Higher managerial and professional											
Large employers/higher managerial	..	..	..	..	[2]	[2]	[3]	4	9	15	4
Higher professional	[2]	..	[2]	4	8	10	15	19	27	37	13
Lower managerial and professional	7	7	12	17	21	22	26	31	29	30	20
Intermediate	3	7	10	9	10	13	12	9	7	[4]	8
Small employers	5	4	5	7	7	8	4	6	5	[2]	5
Lower supervisory	[3]	[2]	[3]	[2]	4	6	7	7	5	[3]	4
Semi-routine	4	8	10	8	6	6	4	4	[2]	..	5
Routine	9	9	6	9	9	7	8	6	4	[2]	7
Long-term unemployed [6]	..	..	..	..	:	:	:	:	:	:	..
Students	[3]	[2]	[2]	[3]	..	..	[2]	..	..	..	2
Occupation not stated [7]	62	60	50	40	31	24	18	13	9	5	31
All occupational groups	100	100	100	100	100	100	100	100	100	100	100

Note: Changes to categories of socio-economic classification were made in 2011. Please see Appendix B for details.

Please see background notes for symbols and conventions used in this report.

1 Including shared owners (who own part of the equity and pay mortgage, part rent).

2 "Council" includes local authorities, New Towns and Scottish Homes, but see note 3 below.

3 Formerly housing association.

4 All tenants whose accommodation goes with the job of someone in the household are allocated to "rented privately", even if the landlord is a local authority or housing association or Housing Action Trust, or if the accommodation is rent free. Squatters are also included in this category.

5 "Unfurnished" includes the answers: "partly furnished".

6 Includes those who have never worked.

7 Includes those who are economically inactive - see Methodology - Economically Inactive.

Source: Office for National Statistics

Table A56

Expenditure of households with children by gross income quintile group
UK, financial year ending 2020 to financial year ending 2022

	Lowest twenty per cent	Second quintile group	Third quintile group	Fourth quintile group	Highest twenty per cent	All house-holds
Lower boundary of group (gross income: £ per week)[1]		369	612	918	1,366	
Average weighted number of households (thousands)	680	1,260	1,620	2,030	2,370	7,960
Total number of households in sample (over 3 years)	370	660	890	1,160	1,340	4,420
Total number of persons in sample (over 3 years)	1,100	2,270	3,390	4,470	5,350	16,570
Total number of adults in sample (over 3 years)	500	1,100	1,760	2,470	3,020	8,850
Weighted average number of persons per household	3.1	3.5	3.9	3.9	4.0	3.8
Commodity or service	Average weekly household expenditure (£)					
1 Food & non-alcoholic drinks	55.90	66.00	78.50	88.10	105.20	85.10
2 Alcoholic drinks, tobacco & narcotics	7.80	7.40	10.20	12.70	16.00	11.90
3 Clothing & footwear	13.70	18.40	23.00	27.30	38.40	27.20
4 Housing(net)[2], fuel & power	94.10	118.50	114.30	91.80	97.30	102.40
5 Household goods & services	20.10	23.60	34.60	40.90	61.40	41.20
6 Health	3.40	3.40	4.70	6.60	11.40	6.90
7 Transport	32.30	50.60	68.10	95.90	146.00	92.50
8 Communication	16.20	20.40	25.60	27.10	31.70	26.20
9 Recreation & culture	31.20	36.10	49.90	67.70	119.10	71.20
10 Education	[2.30]	6.70	3.70	6.00	31.20	12.80
11 Restaurants & hotels	14.70	19.90	32.90	42.10	73.60	43.70
12 Miscellaneous goods & services	20.50	30.40	40.40	53.70	77.60	51.60
1-12 All expenditure groups	312.20	401.50	485.90	559.90	808.90	572.70
13 Other expenditure items	28.70	40.60	66.70	95.10	160.00	94.30
Total expenditure	**340.90**	**442.10**	**552.60**	**655.00**	**968.80**	**667.10**
Average weekly expenditure per person (£) **Total expenditure**	**109.70**	**125.10**	**142.30**	**167.40**	**239.50**	**174.70**

Note: The commodity and service categories are not comparable to those in publications before 2001-02.

Please see background notes for symbols and conventions used in this report.

This table is based on a three year average.

1 Lower boundary of 2021-22 gross income quintile groups (£ per week).

2 Excluding mortgage interest payments, council tax and Northern Ireland rates. Mortgage interest payments can be found in category 13.

Source: Office for National Statistics

Table A57

Expenditure of households without children by gross income quintile group

UK, financial year ending 2020 to financial year ending 2022

	Lowest twenty per cent	Second quintile group	Third quintile group	Fourth quintile group	Highest twenty per cent	All house-holds
Lower boundary of group (gross income: £ per week)[1]		369	612	918	1,366	
Average weighted number of households (thousands)	4,960	4,370	4,020	3,600	3,260	20,210
Total number of households in sample (over 3 years)	2,840	2,730	2,490	2,190	1,800	12,050
Total number of persons in sample (over 3 years)	3,440	4,270	4,590	4,560	4,320	21,180
Total number of adults in sample (over 3 years)	3,440	4,270	4,590	4,560	4,320	21,180
Weighted average number of persons per household	1.2	1.5	1.8	2.1	2.5	1.8
Commodity or service	Average weekly household expenditure (£)					
1 Food & non-alcoholic drinks	36.40	48.90	59.10	68.70	84.40	57.10
2 Alcoholic drinks, tobacco & narcotics	8.60	10.60	13.90	16.20	21.60	13.50
3 Clothing & footwear	6.10	10.10	13.70	21.60	29.70	15.10
4 Housing(net)[2], fuel & power	56.90	66.70	79.30	89.90	112.20	78.30
5 Household goods & services	15.70	25.60	31.60	40.20	62.30	32.90
6 Health	4.00	7.90	8.10	11.20	13.40	8.40
7 Transport	21.30	40.80	66.80	88.70	131.30	64.30
8 Communication	12.00	16.00	20.30	23.40	28.30	19.20
9 Recreation & culture	24.30	37.30	57.10	71.50	97.70	53.90
10 Education	1.10	1.80	2.20	4.90	8.40	3.30
11 Restaurants & hotels	11.20	18.80	32.30	43.70	68.00	32.00
12 Miscellaneous goods & services	18.30	29.20	37.10	47.30	64.70	37.00
1-12 All expenditure groups	216.00	313.50	421.40	527.30	722.00	415.10
13 Other expenditure items	25.50	43.30	62.70	85.20	133.00	64.70
Total expenditure	**241.50**	**356.80**	**484.20**	**612.50**	**855.00**	**479.80**
Average weekly expenditure per person (£) **Total expenditure**	**202.40**	**232.40**	**262.10**	**292.50**	**342.90**	**271.50**

Note: The commodity and service categories are not comparable to those in publications before 2001-02.

Please see background notes for symbols and conventions used in this report.

This table is based on a three year average.

1 Lower boundary of 2021-22 gross income quintile groups (£ per week).

2 Excluding mortgage interest payments, council tax and Northern Ireland rates. Mortgage interest payments can be found in category 13.

Source: Office for National Statistics

Background notes

Symbols and conventions used in Family Spending tables

[ ] Figures should be used with extra caution because they are based on fewer than 20 reporting households.

.. The data is suppressed if the unweighted sample counts are less than 10 reporting households.

. No figures are available because there are no reporting households.

~ The figure is greater than 0 but rounds to 0.

Rounding: Individual figures have been rounded independently. The sum of component items does not therefore necessarily add to the totals shown.

Averages: These are averages (means) for all households included in the column or row, and unless specified, are not restricted to those households reporting expenditure on a particular item or income of a particular type.

Impact of the coronavirus (COVID-19) pandemic on the Living Costs and Food Survey (LCF) for the financial year ending 2020

Following Government guidance in relation to the coronavirus (COVID-19) pandemic, a pause in data collection led to interviews being conducted for 13 fewer days in March 2020 than planned. Final March interviews took place on Monday March 16th. All households that were not interviewed as a result were treated as non-responders and data were weighted to account for reduced data collection in March 2020 compared to previous years.

Data collected in March 2020 may have covered changes to spending habits around the start of the first UK lockdown on March 23rd, for example panic buying beforehand and reduced spending during lockdown when people were advised to stay at home and many businesses were closed. However, due to reduced data collection in the latter half of March data may not accurately reflect the impact of lockdown on spending and the annual estimates reported in this release will not be significantly impacted.

Office for
National Statistics

Family Spending

Workbook 5 - Housing

Contents:

ONS Social Surveys

Office for National Statistics

March 2023

A number of tables within the family spending workbooks have been placed under review to be removed from future publications. Tables under review are specified within the workbooks. If you use these for your analysis, please contact us via family.spending@ons.gov.uk**.**

Table 2.2

Housing expenditure

UK, financial year ending 2019 to financial year ending 2022

	2018-19			2019-20			2020-21			2021-22		
	£ per week	% of total expend-iture	% of housing expend-iture	£ per week	% of total expend-iture	% of housing expend-iture	£ per week	% of total expend-iture	% of housing expend-iture	£ per week	% of total expend-iture	% of housing expend-iture
Weighted number of households (thousands)	27,480			27,820			28,200			28,500		
Total number of households in sample	5,480			5,440			5,400			5,630		
Total number of persons in sample	12,790			12,670			12,240			12,850		
Total number of adults in sample	9,980			9,880			9,880			10,260		
Weighted average number of persons per household	2.4			2.4			2.3			2.3		
Commodity or service												
Primary dwelling												
Rent	**50.20**	**6**	**28**	**52.50**	**6**	**30**	**51.00**	**7**	**28**	**51.50**	**6**	**26**
Gross rent	50.20	6	28	52.50	6	30	51.00	7	28	51.50	6	26
less *housing benefit, rebates and*												
allowances received	12.90	2	7	12.40	1	7	9.70	1	5	9.70	1	5
Net rent[1]	37.30	4	21	40.10	5	23	41.30	6	22	41.90	5	21
Mortgage	**49.40**	**6**	**27**	**51.50**	**6**	**29**	**52.90**	**7**	**29**	**52.50**	**7**	**27**
Mortgage interest payments	20.80	2	12	22.30	3	13	22.20	3	12	22.20	3	11
Mortgage protection premiums	1.10	0~	1	1.00	0~	1	0.90	0~	1	0.70	0~	0~
Capital repayment of mortgage	27.60	3	15	28.20	3	16	29.80	4	16	29.50	4	15
Outright purchase, including deposits	**[0.10]**	**0~**	**0~**	**[0.80]**	**0~**	**0~**	**[2.30]**	**0~**	**1**	**[6.10]**	**1**	**3**
Secondary dwelling	**17.40**	**2**	**10**	**4.50**	**1**	**3**	**10.10**	**1**	**5**	**8.50**	**1**	**4**
Rent	..	0~	0~	..	0~	0~	[0.10]	0~	0~	..	0~	0~
Council tax, mortgage, insurance												
(secondary dwelling)	0.80	0~	0~	1.10	0~	1	1.20	0~	1	**1.40**	**0~**	**1**
Purchase of second dwelling	16.50	2	9	3.40	0~	2	8.80	1	5	7.10	1	4
Charges	**34.30**	**4**	**19**	**36.40**	**4**	**21**	**37.60**	**5**	**20**	**38.60**	**5**	**20**
Council tax, domestic rates	24.50	3	14	26.00	3	15	27.60	4	15	28.20	4	14
Water charges	8.10	1	5	8.20	1	5	7.80	1	4	8.20	1	4
Other regular housing payments including												
service charge for rent	**1.50**	**0~**	**1**	**2.10**	**0~**	**1**	**1.90**	**0~**	**1**	**2.00**	**0~**	**1**
Refuse collection, including skip hire	0.10	0~	0~	0.10	0~	0~	0.30	0~	0~	0.20	0~	0~
Moving house	**2.40**	**0~**	**1**	**2.00**	**0~**	**1**	**1.50**	**0~**	**1**	**2.30**	**0~**	**1**
Property transaction - purchase and sale	1.20	0~	1	0.90	0~	1	0.90	0~	0~	1.20	0~	1
Property transaction - sale only	0.50	0~	0~	0.40	0~	0~	0.30	0~	0~	0.50	0~	0~
Property transaction - purchase only	0.50	0~	0~	0.40	0~	0~	0.30	0~	0~	0.50	0~	0~
Property transaction - other payments	0.20	0~	0~	0.20	0~	0~	0.10	0~	0~	0.20	0~	0~
Maintenance and repair of dwelling	**7.50**	**1**	**4**	**8.00**	**1**	**5**	**10.00**	**1**	**5**	**9.70**	**1**	**5**
Central heating repairs	0.80	0~	0~	1.20	0~	1	1.20	0~	1	1.20	0~	1
House maintenance etc.	4.60	1	3	4.70	1	3	5.60	1	3	6.00	1	3
Paint, wallpaper, timber	1.20	0~	1	1.20	0~	1	1.90	0~	1	1.50	0~	1
Equipment hire, small materials	0.90	0~	0~	0.80	0~	0~	1.40	0~	1	1.00	0~	1
Alterations and improvements to dwelling	**26.40**	**3**	**15**	**28.10**	**3**	**16**	**24.10**	**3**	**13**	**30.80**	**4**	**16**
Central heating installation	1.60	0~	1	1.40	0~	1	1.10	0~	1	1.50	0~	1
DIY improvements: double glazing,												
kitchen units, sheds etc.	1.30	0~	1	1.40	0~	1	1.30	0~	1	**1.40**	**0~**	**1**
Home improvements - contracted out	22.50	3	13	24.50	3	14	19.80	3	11	26.70	3	14
Bathroom fittings	0.70	0~	0~	0.40	0~	0~	1.00	0~	1	0.50	0~	0~
Purchase of materials for Capital Improvements	0.30	0~	0~	0.40	0~	0~	0.80	0~	0~	0.80	0~	0~
Household insurances	**5.10**	**1**	**3**	**4.90**	**1**	**3**	**5.20**	**1**	**3**	**5.00**	**1**	**3**
Structure	2.40	0~	1	2.30	0~	1	2.50	0~	1	2.30	0~	1
Contents	2.30	0~	1	2.10	0~	1	2.30	0~	1	2.30	0~	1
Household appliances[2]	0.50	0~	0~	0.50	0~	0~	0.40	0~	0~	0.40	0~	0~
Housing expenditure	**180.00**	**21**	**100**	**176.40**	**21**	**100**	**185.00**	**25**	**100**	**195.40**	**24**	**100**
Total expenditure[3]	843.30			842.50			739.70			802.80		

Please see background notes for symbols and conventions used in this report.

1 The figure included in total expenditure is net rent as opposed to gross rent.

2 For FYE 2019 onwards, information about insurance for household appliances was collected in the questionnaire in addition to the diary. In previous years, this was based on diary data only.

3 This total includes all categories recorded in the LCF, including those outside the 'COICOP' total expenditure.

Source: Office for National Statistics

Table 2.3

Housing expenditure by gross income decile group

UK, financial year ending 2022

	Gross income decile group										
	1	2								10	All
Weighted number of households (thousands)	2,860	2,850	2,850	2,850	2,850	2,850	2,850	2,850	2,850	2,850	28,500
Total number of households in sample	530	540	560	580	580	570	570	580	560	560	5,630
Total number of persons in sample	710	830	990	1,170	1,310	1,400	1,460	1,590	1,650	1,750	12,850
Total number of adults in sample	630	720	850	950	1,060	1,110	1,160	1,250	1,240	1,310	10,260
Weighted average number of persons per household	1.4	1.5	1.8	2.1	2.4	2.6	2.6	2.8	3.0	3.2	2.3
Commodity or service	Average weekly household expenditure (£)										
Primary dwelling											
Rent	**68.40**	**65.50**	**57.00**	**49.90**	**52.50**	**49.70**	**46.40**	**40.90**	**46.30**	**38.80**	**51.50**
Gross rent	68.40	65.50	57.00	49.90	52.50	49.70	46.40	40.90	46.30	38.80	51.50
less housing benefit, rebates and allowances received	36.10	28.50	12.80	6.80	7.40	2.80	1.40	[0.30]	[0.50]	..	9.70
Net rent[1]	32.30	36.90	44.20	43.10	45.20	46.90	45.00	40.60	45.90	38.60	41.90
Mortgage	**7.40**	**6.60**	**10.70**	**19.10**	**29.10**	**40.90**	**54.80**	**84.10**	**110.30**	**161.70**	**52.50**
Mortgage interest payments	3.40	2.50	3.60	8.90	12.00	16.90	22.80	34.70	46.30	70.80	22.20
Mortgage protection premiums	..	[0.10]	0.30	0.20	0.40	0.70	0.90	1.50	1.40	1.50	0.70
Capital repayment of mortgage	4.00	4.00	6.80	10.00	16.70	23.30	31.00	47.90	62.60	89.40	29.50
Outright purchase, including deposits	..	:	..	..	:	..	:	..	..	..	[6.10]
Secondary dwelling	..	..	..	..	..	..	..	[1.80]	[4.10]	71.00	8.50
Rent	:	..	..	:	..	..	:	:	..	..	..
Council tax, mortgage, insurance (secondary dwelling)	..	..	:	..	..	:	..	..	..	[7.30]	1.40
Purchase of second dwelling	..	..	:	..	..	..	..	..	..	[63.40]	7.10
Charges	**22.50**	**27.10**	**31.90**	**35.40**	**38.60**	**40.20**	**42.10**	**44.60**	**48.20**	**55.20**	**38.60**
Council tax, domestic rates	13.60	17.90	23.20	26.60	28.50	30.00	32.00	33.50	35.30	41.70	28.20
Water charges	6.10	6.30	6.80	7.40	7.90	8.10	8.30	9.40	10.60	10.50	8.20
Other regular housing payments including service charge for rent	2.70	2.80	1.80	1.30	2.00	1.70	1.70	1.50	2.00	2.30	2.00
Refuse collection, including skip hire	..	..	..	..	..	..	[0.10]	..	..	..	0.20
Moving house	**[2.00]**	**[1.10]**	**[1.40]**	**1.30**	**[0.90]**	**[1.00]**	**2.10**	**3.60**	**4.60**	**5.20**	**2.30**
Property transaction - purchase and sale	[1.30]	..	..	..	..	..	..	[2.10]	[1.90]	2.70	1.20
Property transaction - sale only	..	..	..	..	..	:	..	..	[1.00]	..	0.50
Property transaction - purchase only	..	..	..	..	..	..	[0.70]	[0.80]	[0.90]	[0.80]	0.50
Property transaction - other payments	..	..	..	..	..	..	..	..	[0.80]	[0.40]	0.20
Maintenance and repair of dwelling	**3.40**	**5.50**	**4.70**	**8.50**	**9.30**	**7.70**	**10.20**	**13.90**	**13.70**	**20.00**	**9.70**
Central heating repairs	0.70	0.80	0.50	1.20	1.80	1.00	1.20	1.40	1.40	1.80	1.20
House maintenance etc.	1.30	3.30	3.10	5.40	4.40	4.50	6.60	9.10	7.70	14.40	6.00
Paint, wallpaper, timber	0.70	0.80	0.70	1.10	2.50	1.30	1.90	2.40	1.70	2.20	1.50
Equipment hire, small materials	[0.70]	0.50	0.40	0.90	0.60	0.80	0.60	1.10	2.80	1.50	1.00
Alterations and improvements to dwelling	**9.70**	**7.70**	**15.30**	**14.70**	**21.00**	**25.00**	**27.30**	**31.60**	**64.50**	**91.40**	**30.80**
Central heating installation	[0.80]	..	[0.80]	[1.40]	[0.70]	[1.80]	1.50	[1.50]	3.00	2.70	1.50
DIY improvements: double glazing, kitchen units, sheds etc.	..	..	..	..	..	[1.70]	..	[1.20]	[1.30]	[2.10]	1.40
Home improvements - contracted out	8.80	7.10	8.70	12.00	19.10	18.70	24.60	25.10	57.90	84.70	26.70
Bathroom fittings	..	:	..	[0.60]	[0.40]	[0.30]	..	[0.80]	[1.00]	..	0.50
Purchase of materials for capital improvements	..	..	..	..	..	..	..	..	[1.40]	..	0.80
Household insurances	**2.90**	**3.50**	**3.60**	**4.80**	**4.50**	**5.00**	**4.90**	**5.90**	**6.50**	**8.40**	**5.00**
Structure	1.40	1.50	1.60	2.10	2.10	2.40	2.20	2.90	3.10	4.30	2.30
Contents	1.40	1.70	1.60	2.40	2.00	2.10	2.40	2.60	3.00	3.70	2.30
Household appliances[2]	0.20	0.30	0.40	0.30	0.40	0.50	0.30	0.40	0.40	0.40	0.40
Housing expenditure	**94.30**	**89.90**	**139.90**	**127.40**	**149.60**	**170.60**	**188.20**	**226.20**	**298.00**	**469.80**	**195.40**
Total expenditure[3]	**286.10**	**311.90**	**437.90**	**499.10**	**625.80**	**703.30**	**829.00**	**1007.00**	**1260.80**	**2068.40**	**802.80**

Please see background notes for symbols and conventions used in this report.

1 The figure included in total expenditure is net rent as opposed to gross rent.

2 For FYE 2019 onwards, information about insurance for household appliances was collected in the questionnaire in addition to the diary. In previous years, this was based on diary data only.

3 This total includes all categories recorded in the LCF, including those outside the 'COICOP' total expenditure.

Source: Office for National Statistics

Table 2.4

Housing expenditure by age of household reference person

UK, financial year ending 2022

	Under 30	30 to 49	50 to 64	65 to 74	75 or over	All
Weighted number of households (thousands)	2,610	9,410	7,890	4,490	4,100	28,500
Total number of households in sample	360	1,820	1,640	1,140	670	5,630
Total number of persons in sample	760	5,410	3,660	1,970	1,050	12,850
Total number of adults in sample	630	3,380	3,270	1,950	1,040	10,260
Weighted average number of persons per household	2.2	3.1	2.3	1.7	1.5	2.3
Commodity or service	Average weekly household expenditure (£)					
Primary dwelling						
Rent	**111.10**	**70.50**	**39.80**	**27.80**	**18.50**	**51.50**
Gross rent	111.10	70.50	39.80	27.80	18.50	51.50
less housing benefit, rebates and allowances received	7.60	9.30	9.10	13.10	9.30	9.70
Net rent[1]	103.50	61.20	30.70	14.80	9.30	41.90
Mortgage	**49.00**	**96.70**	**54.30**	**6.20**	..	**52.50**
Mortgage interest payments	25.00	43.60	18.00	3.20	..	22.20
Mortgage protection premiums	0.80	1.20	0.80	[0.10]	:	0.70
Capital repayment of mortgage	23.20	51.90	35.50	2.80	..	29.50
Outright purchase, including deposits	..	..	..	:	:	**[6.10]**
Secondary dwelling	..	9.10	18.20	[2.20]	..	8.50
Rent	..	:	..	..	..	..
Council tax, mortgage, insurance (secondary dwelling)	..	[1.50]	[2.40]	..	..	1.40
Purchase of second dwelling	:	[7.70]	[15.60]	..	..	7.10
Charges	**32.50**	**39.00**	**39.70**	**38.20**	**39.70**	**38.60**
Council tax, domestic rates	22.40	28.30	29.60	28.60	28.60	28.20
Water charges	7.20	8.90	8.50	7.80	6.90	8.20
Other regular housing payments including service charge for rent	3.00	1.70	1.20	1.50	4.00	2.00
Refuse collection, including skip hire	:	[0.10]	[0.50]	[0.30]		0.20
Moving house	**2.30**	**3.20**	**1.90**	**1.60**	**[2.00]**	**2.30**
Property transaction - purchase and sale	..	1.60	1.00	[0.90]	[1.30]	1.20
Property transaction - sale only	:	0.70	[0.40]	..	..	0.50
Property transaction - purchase only	[1.60]	0.60	[0.30]	..	..	0.50
Property transaction - other payments	..	0.30	[0.20]	..	..	0.20
Maintenance and repair of dwelling	**5.00**	**8.40**	**12.60**	**10.00**	**9.60**	**9.70**
Central heating repairs	0.40	1.00	1.10	1.60	1.60	1.20
House maintenance etc.	2.80	5.20	7.70	5.70	6.90	6.00
Paint, wallpaper, timber	[1.60]	1.50	1.80	1.90	0.60	1.50
Equipment hire, small materials	[0.20]	0.70	1.90	0.80	0.50	1.00
Alterations and improvements to dwelling	**11.80**	**34.60**	**33.50**	**41.20**	**17.70**	**30.80**
Central heating installation	..	1.20	1.90	1.80	1.50	1.50
DIY improvements: double glazing, kitchen units, sheds etc.	..	1.40	0.70	[0.80]	..	1.40
Home improvements - contracted out	10.20	30.10	29.90	36.70	12.00	26.70
Bathroom fittings	..	0.80	0.50	[0.30]	..	0.50
Purchase of materials for capital improvements	..	[1.10]	[0.50]	[1.60]	..	0.80
Household insurances	**2.20**	**4.30**	**5.70**	**6.10**	**5.90**	**5.00**
Structure	0.90	2.00	2.70	2.90	2.60	2.30
Contents	1.10	2.00	2.60	2.60	2.70	2.30
Household appliances[2]	0.20	0.30	0.40	0.50	0.50	0.40
Housing expenditure	**208.70**	**273.90**	**197.50**	**120.20**	**84.70**	**195.40**
Total expenditure[3]	**696.50**	**1007.20**	**916.00**	**578.00**	**429.20**	**802.80**

Please see background notes for symbols and conventions used in this report.

1 The figure included in total expenditure is net rent as opposed to gross rent.

2 For FYE 2019 onwards, information about insurance for household appliances was collected in the questionnaire in addition to the diary.

In previous years, this was based on diary data only.

3 This total includes all categories recorded in the LCF, including those outside the 'COICOP' total expenditure.

Source: Office for National Statistics

Table 2.5

Housing expenditure by countries and regions

UK, financial year ending 2022

	United Kingdom K02000001	England E92000001	North East E12000001	North West E12000002	Yorkshire and the Humber E12000003	East Midlands E12000004	West Midlands E12000005	East E12000006	London E12000007	South East E12000008	South West E12000009	Wales W92000004	Scotland S92000003	Northern Ireland N92000002
Weighted number of households (thousands)	28,500	23,700	1,190	3,010	2,450	1,960	2,440	2,670	3,540	3,920	2,510	1,450	2,580	770
Total number of households in sample	5,630	4,260	210	520	460	380	450	510	480	670	580	230	820	330
Total number of persons in sample	12,850	9,830	440	1,210	1,010	910	1,060	1,180	1,170	1,510	1,340	480	1,710	830
Total number of adults in sample	10,260	7,790	350	940	810	730	840	930	920	1,210	1,070	410	1,410	650
Weighted average number of persons per household	2.3	2.4	2.2	2.4	2.2	2.5	2.4	2.3	2.5	2.3	2.2	2.1	2.1	2.5
Commodity or service	Average weekly household expenditure (£)													
Primary dwelling														
Rent	**51.50**	**54.90**	**38.60**	**41.50**	**37.60**	**40.20**	**43.10**	**49.10**	**116.20**	**50.70**	**45.20**	**29.20**	**39.10**	**30.70**
Gross rent	51.50	54.90	38.60	41.50	37.60	40.20	43.10	49.10	116.20	50.70	45.20	29.20	39.10	30.70
less housing benefit, rebates and allowances received	9.70	9.30	8.50	7.60	9.90	4.60	5.70	6.60	18.30	9.30	9.00	10.40	11.70	11.50
Net rent[1]	41.90	45.60	30.10	33.90	27.70	35.60	37.50	42.40	97.90	41.40	36.10	18.80	27.40	19.20
Mortgage	**52.50**	**53.80**	**37.50**	**46.00**	**43.40**	**49.40**	**51.10**	**55.10**	**62.90**	**65.40**	**54.50**	**55.10**	**43.50**	**36.80**
Mortgage interest payments	22.20	22.70	14.60	19.00	17.80	19.00	19.80	25.00	27.70	28.50	23.50	26.30	17.60	12.70
Mortgage protection premiums	0.70	0.70	0.90	0.70	0.80	1.00	0.70	0.70	0.50	0.70	0.60	0.80	0.80	1.70
Capital repayment of mortgage	29.50	30.40	22.10	26.30	24.80	29.40	30.70	29.50	34.70	36.30	30.40	27.90	25.20	22.40
Outright purchase, including deposits	**[6.10]**	..	..	..	..	..	..	..	..	..	..	..	..	..
Secondary dwelling	**8.50**	**9.80**	..	..	..	..	..	**[42.70]**	**[22.30]**	**[4.20]**	..	..	**[1.30]**	..
Rent	1.40	1.30	..	..	..	..	..	..	..	..	..	..	..	..
Council tax, mortgage, insurance (secondary dwelling)	7.10	8.40	..	..	..	..	..	..	..	[3.00]	..	..	[0.60]	..
Purchase of second dwelling														
Charges	**38.60**	**40.00**	**31.00**	**39.00**	**35.70**	**36.90**	**37.50**	**41.10**	**41.90**	**45.80**	**41.30**	**38.40**	**33.00**	**15.60**
Council tax, domestic rates	28.20	29.00	24.10	29.00	25.80	28.00	28.00	30.10	27.70	33.30	30.50	28.10	24.80	15.10
Water charges	8.20	8.50	6.50	9.00	8.40	7.90	8.00	8.40	8.80	8.70	9.10	8.80	7.30	
Other regular housing payments including service charge for rent	2.00	2.20		1.10	1.10	1.00	1.40	1.50	5.20	3.60	1.60	1.50	0.80	0.20
Refuse collection, including skip hire	0.20	0.20								[0.20]	[0.20]			
Moving house	**2.30**	**2.50**	..	**2.40**	**1.70**	**[2.50]**	**2.10**	**[2.20]**	**2.70**	**4.30**	**2.20**	..	**1.80**	..
Property transaction - purchase and sale	1.20	1.30		[1.00]	[1.00]					2.60	[0.70]		[1.10]	
Property transaction - sale only	0.50	0.60												
Property transaction - purchase only	0.50	0.50								[0.60]	[0.60]		[0.60]	
Property transaction - other payments	0.20	0.20												
Maintenance and repair of dwelling	**9.70**	**9.90**	**7.40**	**11.00**	**9.00**	**8.30**	**9.20**	**14.30**	**5.60**	**12.40**	**10.00**	**7.80**	**9.70**	**6.90**
Central heating repairs	1.20	1.30	1.50	0.60	1.90	1.00	0.90	1.90	1.30	1.50	0.90	0.80	0.60	0.60
House maintenance etc.	6.00	6.20	2.60	7.80	5.60	5.80	4.50	8.30	2.70	8.50	7.40	4.50	6.30	1.80
Paint, wallpaper, timber	1.50	1.50	1.60	1.60	1.00	1.20	1.60	2.50	1.30	1.70	0.90	[1.20]	2.20	1.70
Equipment hire, small materials	1.00	0.90	1.70	1.10	0.50	0.30	2.20	1.60	[0.30]	0.70	0.70	1.30	0.60	2.80
Alterations and improvements to dwelling	**30.80**	**31.80**	**17.20**	**28.10**	**30.50**	**19.60**	**26.80**	**24.30**	**21.90**	**63.30**	**32.00**	**26.10**	**28.20**	**16.20**
Central heating installation	1.50	1.50			[1.10]		[1.30]	[2.40]	[1.10]	2.60	1.70		1.40	[1.20]
DIY improvements: double glazing, kitchen units, sheds etc.	1.40	1.40								[1.40]		[1.20]	[0.40]	
Home improvements - contracted out	26.70	27.70	14.30	25.60	28.30	18.20	18.20	20.10	20.20	55.00	29.10	20.40	25.10	10.50
Bathroom fittings	0.50	0.50						[0.50]			[0.40]			
Purchase of materials for capital improvements	0.80	0.80												
Household insurances	**5.00**	**5.00**	**3.70**	**4.80**	**4.90**	**4.70**	**4.60**	**6.00**	**4.90**	**5.40**	**4.70**	**5.10**	**5.00**	**5.20**
Structure	2.30	2.30	1.70	2.30	2.40	2.30	2.10	2.90	2.20	2.50	2.20	2.60	2.40	2.70
Contents	2.30	2.30	1.70	2.20	2.30	2.00	2.10	2.80	2.40	2.50	2.20	2.20	2.30	2.50

Table 2.5

Housing expenditure by countries and regions

UK, financial year ending 2022

	United Kingdom	England	North East	North West	Yorkshire and the Humber	East Midlands	West Midlands	East	London	South East	South West	Wales	Scotland	Northern Ireland
	K02000001	E92000001	E12000001	E12000002	E12000003	E12000004	E12000005	E12000006	E12000007	E12000008	E12000009	W92000004	S92000003	N92000002
Household appliances[2]	0.40	0.40	0.30	0.30	0.30	0.40	0.50	0.40	0.40	0.40	0.30	0.30	0.40	[0.10]
Housing expenditure	195.40	205.60	127.40	166.10	157.00	159.90	171.80	242.10	260.00	273.80	183.80	157.60	150.90	101.00
Total expenditure[3]	802.80	823.80	580.10	750.20	717.20	771.10	796.70	852.40	919.10	973.00	802.00	676.00	718.60	674.80

Please see background notes for symbols and conventions used in this report.

1 The figure included in total expenditure is net rent as opposed to gross rent.

2 For FYE 2019, information about insurance for household appliances was collected in the questionnaire in addition to the diary. In previous years, this was based on diary data only.

3 This total includes all categories recorded in the LCF, including those outside the 'COICOP' total expenditure.

Source: Office for National Statistics

Table 2.6

Housing expenditure by socio-economic classification of household reference person

UK, financial year ending 2022

	Large employers and higher managerial	Higher professional	Lower managerial and professional	Intermediate	Small employers	Lower supervisory	Semi-routine	Routine	Long-term unemployed[1]	Students	Occupation not stated[2] and not classifiable	All groups
Weighted number of households (thousands)	1,090	3,580	5,720	2,390	1,550	1,200	1,520	1,950	60	500	8,940	28,500
Total number of households in sample	220	700	1,140	470	320	230	290	370	10	90	1,810	5,630
Total number of persons in sample	610	1,840	2,860	1,080	890	600	670	950	30	210	3,110	12,850
Total number of adults in sample	450	1,370	2,150	820	660	460	500	720	20	160	2,960	10,260
Weighted average number of persons per household	2.9	2.6	2.6	2.4	2.9	2.8	2.6	2.7	3.3	2.6	1.7	2.3

Commodity or service — Average weekly household expenditure (£)

Commodity or service	Large employers and higher managerial	Higher professional	Lower managerial and professional	Intermediate	Small employers	Lower supervisory	Semi-routine	Routine	Long-term unemployed[1]	Students	Occupation not stated[2] and not classifiable	All groups
Primary dwelling	**41.10**	**45.00**	**52.10**	**54.90**	**57.20**	**55.50**	**73.60**	**84.30**	..	**139.60**	**36.30**	**51.50**
Rent	41.10	45.00	52.10	54.90	57.20	55.50	73.60	84.30	..	139.60	36.30	51.50
Gross rent	..	..	..	..	..	..	..	..	..	..	..	..
less housing benefit, rebates and allowances received	..	0.50	2.80	3.70	5.10	5.30	12.80	14.90	..	15.00	19.30	9.70
Net rent[1]	40.50	44.50	49.30	51.20	52.10	50.10	60.80	69.30	..	124.60	17.00	41.90
Mortgage	**135.30**	**119.50**	**82.10**	**57.20**	**53.00**	**63.90**	**38.50**	**29.60**	..	**[18.20]**	**3.30**	**52.50**
Mortgage interest payments	57.60	52.80	34.80	24.50	20.70	24.50	14.40	10.80	..	[7.80]	1.60	22.20
Mortgage protection premiums	1.90	1.10	1.20	0.90	0.80	0.80	0.70	0.90	..	[0.00]	[0.00]	0.70
Capital repayment of mortgage	75.80	65.50	46.00	31.80	31.40	38.60	23.50	17.90	..	[10.20]	1.60	29.50
Outright purchase, including deposits	..	**[20.30]**	**4.50**	..	**[37.40]**	..	..	..	..	..	**[0.70]**	**[6.10]**
Secondary dwelling	..	..	..	..	..	..	..	..	..	..	..	**8.50**
Rent	..	..	..	..	..	..	..	..	..	..	..	..
Council tax, mortgage, insurance (secondary dwelling)	..	..	[2.50]	..	..	..	..	..	..	..	..	1.40
Purchase of second dwelling	..	..	[1.70]	..	..	..	..	..	..	..	..	7.10
Charges	**50.30**	**46.90**	**41.70**	**37.60**	**40.50**	**38.60**	**31.00**	**31.30**	..	**24.10**	**35.60**	**38.60**
Council tax, domestic rates	37.40	34.70	30.70	27.60	31.10	28.80	22.20	22.60	..	12.10	25.80	28.20
Water charges	10.10	9.50	8.60	8.20	8.60	8.60	7.90	7.80	..	7.00	7.20	8.20
Other regular housing payments including service charge for rent	2.50	1.90	2.20	1.80	0.80	1.00	0.90	0.90	..	[4.70]	2.50	2.00
Refuse collection, including skip hire	..	..	[0.20]	..	..	..	..	..	..	..	0.20	0.20
Moving house	**5.20**	**4.40**	**3.30**	**[1.60]**	**[2.50]**	..	..	..	..	..	**1.30**	**2.30**
Property transaction - purchase and sale	..	2.00	1.50	..	..	..	..	..	..	..	0.80	1.20
Property transaction - sale only	..	..	[0.70]	..	..	..	..	..	..	..	..	0.50
Property transaction - purchase only	1.30	1.30	0.70	..	..	..	..	..	..	..	..	0.50
Property transaction - other payments	[0.40]	[0.40]	[0.40]	..	..	..	..	..	..	..	..	0.20
Maintenance and repair of dwelling	**15.20**	**14.10**	**11.40**	**8.40**	**7.70**	**11.60**	**5.60**	**5.70**	..	**[2.10]**	**8.60**	**9.70**
Central heating repairs	1.50	1.50	1.30	1.10	1.40	0.40	1.00	0.30	..	..	1.30	1.20
House maintenance etc.	8.30	8.70	7.20	5.30	4.70	6.50	3.10	3.50	..	[2.00]	5.40	6.00
Paint, wallpaper, timber	3.70	1.70	1.70	1.30	1.00	[4.00]	1.00	1.40	..	..	1.20	1.50
Equipment hire, small materials	[1.70]	2.30	1.30	0.70	[0.50]	[0.70]	[0.50]	0.50	..	..	0.70	1.00
Alterations and improvements to dwelling	**59.00**	**50.30**	**37.60**	**28.90**	**24.30**	**29.70**	**15.60**	**9.50**	..	..	**26.10**	**30.80**
Central heating installation	..	2.80	1.40	[1.10]	[1.50]	..	..	..	..	..	1.50	1.50

187

Table 2.6

Housing expenditure by socio-economic classification of household reference person

UK, financial year ending 2022

	Large employers and higher managerial	Higher profess-ional	Lower manag-erial and profess-ional	Inter-mediate	Small employ-ers	Lower super-visory	Semi-routine	Routine	Long-term unem-ployed[1]	Students	Occupation not stated[2] and not classifiable	All groups
DIY improvements: double glazing, kitchen units, sheds etc.	..	[1.40]	[0.70]	..	..	..	..	..	..	..	2.20	1.40
Home improvements - contracted out	51.60	44.30	32.90	27.50	20.00	26.90	13.80	8.00	..	..	21.30	26.70
Bathroom fittings	..	[1.10]	1.00	..	..	..	..	..	..	..	0.30	0.50
Purchase of materials for capital improvements	..	..	..	..	..	..	..	..	..	..	[0.80]	0.80
Household insurances	**9.20**	**5.90**	**5.20**	**4.20**	**5.30**	**3.60**	**3.10**	**3.00**	**..**	**2.30**	**5.30**	**5.00**
Structure	4.70	3.10	2.50	1.90	2.50	1.80	1.20	1.10	..	0.80	2.40	2.30
Contents	4.20	2.60	2.50	2.00	2.30	1.70	1.60	1.40	..	1.30	2.40	2.30
Household appliances[2]	[0.40]	0.30	0.30	0.30	0.50	[0.20]	0.30	0.40	..	..	0.50	0.40
Housing expenditure	**327.80**	**336.30**	**244.60**	**190.90**	**225.50**	**246.30**	**162.40**	**150.50**	**..**	**173.50**	**97.80**	**195.40**
Total expenditure[3]	**1605.40**	**1313.60**	**1025.30**	**766.10**	**763.40**	**853.00**	**581.00**	**588.20**	**..**	**601.00**	**467.40**	**802.80**

Note: Changes to categories of socio-economic classification were made from 2011. Please see Appendix B for details.

Please see background notes for symbols and conventions used in this report.

1 The figure included in total expenditure is net rent as opposed to gross rent.

2 For FYE 2019 now, information about insurance for household appliances was collected in the questionnaire in addition to the diary. In previous years, this was based on diary data only.

3 This total includes all categories recorded in the LCF, including those outside the 'COICOP' total expenditure.

Source: Office for National Statistics

Table 2.7
Housing expenditure by household composition

UK, financial year ending 2022

| | Retired households | | Non-retired | | Retired and non-retired households | | | |
	One Person	Two adults	One Person	Two adults	One adult with children	Two adults with children	Three or more adults without children	Three or more adults with children
Weighted number of households (thousands)	3,670	3,410	4,640	6,340	1,240	5,730	2,330	1,130
Total number of households in sample	670	800	920	1,340	220	1,090	420	180
Total number of persons in sample	670	1,590	920	2,670	580	4,140	1,390	890
Total number of adults in sample	670	1,590	920	2,670	220	2,180	1,390	620
Weighted average number of persons per household	1.0	2.0	1.0	2.0	2.6	3.8	3.4	5.0

Commodity or service	Average weekly household expenditure (£)							
Primary dwelling								
Rent	**28.60**	**14.60**	**67.90**	**52.00**	**105.10**	**56.50**	**52.80**	**81.70**
Gross rent	28.60	14.60	67.90	52.00	105.10	56.50	52.80	81.70
less housing benefit, rebates & allowances received	17.30	5.60	16.00	3.90	23.60	5.70	6.30	15.00
Net rent[1]	11.30	8.90	51.90	48.10	81.40	50.70	46.50	66.80
Mortgage	**[1.80]**	**2.30**	**34.70**	**68.30**	**34.00**	**112.90**	**54.20**	**62.30**
Mortgage interest payments	[1.10]	1.40	14.80	29.40	14.20	49.60	17.20	23.10
Mortgage protection premiums	..	..	0.40	1.10	[0.40]	1.50	0.70	[0.70]
Capital repayment of mortgage	..	[0.90]	19.50	37.70	19.40	61.80	36.40	38.50
Outright purchase, including deposits	:	:	..	..	:	..	..	..
Secondary dwelling	..	..	**[3.00]**	**12.20**	..	**4.60**	..	..
Rent	..	:	:	..	:	..	..	..
Council tax, mortgage, insurance (secondary dwelling)	..	..	..	[1.80]	..	[2.60]	..	:
Purchase of second dwelling	..	..	[1.50]	[10.20]	:	[2.00]	..	..
Charges	**31.00**	**46.10**	**28.20**	**41.80**	**26.60**	**43.30**	**45.10**	**40.70**
Council tax, domestic rates	20.90	35.50	18.80	31.60	16.90	32.70	33.00	29.40
Water charges	5.90	8.40	5.90	8.40	8.00	9.70	10.20	10.70
Other regular housing payments including service charge for rent	4.10	1.80	3.40	1.70	[1.00]	0.80	1.10	[0.60]
Refuse collection, including skip hire	..	[0.40]	..	..	..	[0.10]	..	..
Moving house	**[1.10]**	**[2.00]**	**2.20**	**3.10**	..	**3.30**	**[0.80]**	..
Property transaction - purchase and sale	..	[1.10]	[1.10]	1.40	..	2.00	..	..
Property transaction - sale only	..	..	..	[0.60]	..	[0.80]	..	..
Property transaction - purchase only	..	..	0.80	0.60	..	[0.50]	..	..
Property transaction - other payments	..	..	..	[0.40]	..	..	..	..
Maintenance and repair of dwelling	**6.30**	**12.80**	**6.20**	**12.00**	**3.30**	**9.70**	**13.10**	**12.10**
Central heating repairs	1.40	1.80	0.80	1.20	0.90	1.20	1.20	0.60
House maintenance etc.	4.20	8.00	3.60	7.00	1.30	6.10	8.50	9.00
Paint, wallpaper, timber	0.30	2.20	1.10	2.20	[0.90]	1.60	1.90	1.50
Equipment hire, small materials	0.40	0.80	0.80	1.60	..	0.90	1.60	[1.10]
Alterations and improvements to dwelling	**12.60**	**48.10**	**13.10**	**32.30**	**5.50**	**47.90**	**34.80**	**35.10**
Central heating installation	1.30	2.30	1.60	1.30	..	1.50	[1.60]	..
DIY improvements: double glazing, kitchen units, sheds etc.	..	[4.10]	..	1.00	:	[1.80]	..	..
Home improvements - contracted out	10.00	39.20	10.90	29.00	5.00	41.80	30.90	33.10
Bathroom fittings	..	[0.50]	..	0.30	..	1.20	..	..
Purchase of materials for capital improvements	..	[2.00]	..	[0.60]	:	..	..	..
Household insurances	**5.00**	**6.70**	**3.50**	**5.20**	**2.30**	**5.30**	**5.80**	**4.90**
Structure	2.30	3.10	1.50	2.50	0.90	2.60	2.80	2.20
Contents	2.30	3.00	1.70	2.30	1.30	2.50	2.50	2.20
Household appliances[2]	0.40	0.60	0.20	0.40	0.20	0.30	0.60	[0.50]
Housing expenditure	**69.90**	**127.30**	**155.80**	**222.90**	**155.10**	**291.10**	**226.50**	**310.50**
Total expenditure[3]	**310.00**	**619.10**	**550.70**	**930.70**	**521.10**	**1138.40**	**1131.70**	**1203.00**

Please see background notes for symbols and conventions used in this report.

1 The figure included in total expenditure is net rent as opposed to gross rent.

2 For FYE 2019 onwards, information about insurance for household appliances was collected in the questionnaire in addition to the diary. In previous years, this was based on diary data only.

3 This total includes all categories recorded in the LCF, including those outside the 'COICOP' total expenditure.

Source: Office for National Statistics

Table 2.8

Expenditure on rent[1] by renters
UK, financial year ending 2020 to financial year ending 2022

	2019-20 £[2]	2019-20 % of total expenditure	2020-21 £[2]	2020-21 % of total expenditure	2021-22 £[2]	2021-22 % of total expenditure
Weighted number of households (thousands)	9,360		9,280		9,310	
Total number of households in sample	1,740		1,350		1,500	
Total number of persons in sample	4,030		2,940		3,350	
Total number of adults in sample	2,900		2,230		2,510	
Weighted average number of persons per household	2.4		2.4		2.4	
Total expenditure for renters	**610.10**		**560.20**		**614.10**	
Rent	**156.00**	**25.6**	**155.00**	**27.7**	**157.80**	**25.7**
Gross rent	156.00	25.6	155.00	27.7	157.80	25.7
less housing benefit, rebates and						
allowances received	36.80	6.0	29.60	5.3	29.60	4.8
Net rent[3]	119.20	19.5	125.50	22.4	128.20	20.9

Please see background notes for symbols and conventions used in this report.

1 Primary dwelling.

2 Average weekly household expenditure (£).

3 The figure included in total expenditure is net rent as opposed to gross rent.

Source: Office for National Statistics

Table 2.9

Expenditure on mortgages[1] by mortgage holders
UK, financial year ending 2020 to financial year ending 2022

	2019-20 £[2]	2019-20 % of total expenditure	2020-21 £[2]	2020-21 % of total expenditure	2021-22 £[2]	2021-22 % of total expenditure
Weighted number of households (thousands)	8,360		8,520		8,790	
Total number of households in sample	1,600		1,730		1,800	
Total number of persons in sample	4,620		4,820		4,970	
Total number of adults in sample	3,220		3,440		3,530	
Weighted average number of persons per household	2.9		2.8		2.8	
Total expenditure for mortgage payers	**1,271.40**		**1,117.10**		**1,164.70**	
Mortgage	**169.20**	**13.3**	**172.60**	**15.5**	**167.70**	**14.4**
Mortgage interest payments	73.10	5.8	72.40	6.5	70.80	6.1
Mortgage protection premiums	3.40	0.3	3.10	0.3	2.30	0.2
Capital repayment of mortgage	92.60	7.3	97.20	8.7	94.50	8.1

Please see background notes for symbols and conventions used in this report.

1 Primary dwelling.

2 Average weekly household expenditure (£).

Source: Office for National Statistics

Table 2.10

Expenditure on rent and mortgages[1] by renters and mortgage holders

by gross income decile group

UK, financial year ending 2022

	Gross income decile group										
	1	2	3	4	5	6	7	8	9	10	All
Weighted number of households (thousands)	1,590	1,320	1,210	990	940	900	790	590	570	410	9,310
Total number of households in sample	280	230	210	160	140	130	120	90	80	60	1,500
Total number of persons in sample	380	390	420	420	390	370	330	250	240	170	3,350
Total number of adults in sample	320	300	310	280	270	270	260	200	180	140	2,510
Weighted average number of persons per household	1.4	1.8	2.0	2.8	2.9	3.0	2.9	2.8	3.3	3.0	2.4

Commodity or service	Average weekly household expenditure (£)										
Rent for renters	**123.00**	**141.30**	**133.90**	**143.30**	**159.30**	**157.70**	**167.60**	**197.30**	**231.60**	**270.90**	**157.80**
Gross rent	123.00	141.30	133.90	143.30	159.30	157.70	167.60	197.30	231.60	270.90	157.80
less housing benefit, rebates and											
allowances received	64.90	61.60	30.10	19.50	22.40	8.90	4.90	[1.60]	[2.30]	..	29.60
Net rent[2]	58.10	79.70	103.90	123.90	136.90	148.80	162.60	195.70	229.30	269.70	128.20

	1	2	3	4	5	6	7	8	9	10	All
Weighted number of households (thousands)	160	200	310	470	750	920	1,140	1,490	1,570	1,770	8,790
Total number of households in sample	30	40	70	100	160	190	230	300	320	360	1,800
Total number of persons in sample	60	70	120	200	380	520	620	880	990	1,130	4,970
Total number of adults in sample	50	60	90	150	270	360	440	620	700	800	3,530
Weighted average number of persons per household	1.7	1.7	1.9	2.0	2.4	2.7	2.7	2.9	3.1	3.2	2.8

Commodity or service	Average weekly household expenditure (£)										
Mortgage for mortgage holders	**125.80**	**91.20**	**92.30**	**108.20**	**109.70**	**123.00**	**134.20**	**160.70**	**198.90**	**256.60**	**167.70**
Mortgage interest payments	57.00	34.30	30.40	50.40	45.30	50.40	55.90	66.30	83.60	112.30	70.80
Mortgage protection premiums	..	[2.10]	2.30	1.20	1.50	2.20	2.30	2.90	2.60	2.40	2.30
Capital repayment of mortgage	67.10	54.80	59.60	56.70	62.90	70.30	76.00	91.50	112.80	141.90	94.50

Please see background notes for symbols and conventions used in this report.

1 Primary dwelling.

2 The figure included in total expenditure is net rent as opposed to gross rent.

Source: Office for National Statistics

Table 2.11

Expenditure on rent and mortgages[1] by renters and mortgage holders, by countries and regions
UK, financial year ending 2022

	United Kingdom	England	North East	North West	Yorkshire & the Humber	East Midlands	West Midlands	East	London	South East	South West	Wales	Scotland	Northern Ireland
	K02000001	E92000001	E12000001	E12000002	E12000003	E12000004	E12000005	E12000006	E12000007	E12000008	E12000009	W92000004	S92000003	N92000002
Weighted number of households (thousands)	9,310	7,860	430	950	740	590	780	800	1,670	1,150	760	340	880	230
Total number of households in sample	1,500	1,150	60	130	120	90	120	120	200	170	140	40	230	80
Total number of persons in sample	3,350	2,640	120	290	230	220	280	310	510	370	310	80	440	180
Total number of adults in sample	2,510	1,950	90	210	170	170	210	200	380	280	240	60	350	140
Weighted average number of persons per household	2.4	2.5	2.1	2.4	2.1	2.6	2.6	2.6	2.8	2.4	2.3	1.9	2.0	2.3
Commodity or service						Average weekly household expenditure (£)								
Rent by renters														
Gross rent	157.80	165.70	108.10	131.80	124.80	133.00	135.30	163.90	246.70	172.10	150.30	124.00	115.10	103.00
less housing benefit, rebates and allowances received	29.60	28.20	23.90	24.10	32.80	15.10	17.70	22.10	38.80	31.60	30.00	44.20	34.50	38.60
Net rent[2]	128.20	137.50	84.20	107.70	92.00	117.90	117.60	141.80	207.80	140.60	120.30	79.80	80.60	64.40
Weighted number of households (thousands)	8,790	7,260	360	920	770	630	790	780	900	1,320	790	530	770	230
Total number of households in sample	1,800	1,360	60	160	150	130	150	150	130	230	200	80	250	100
Total number of persons in sample	4,970	3,800	170	490	390	380	410	420	350	640	560	200	660	310
Total number of adults in sample	3,530	2,690	120	320	280	270	290	300	260	460	400	150	490	210
Weighted average number of persons per household	2.8	2.8	2.8	3.0	2.7	3.1	2.8	2.7	2.7	2.8	2.7	2.6	2.6	2.9
Commodity or service						Average weekly household expenditure (£)								
Mortgage by mortgage holders	167.70	172.70	122.70	146.90	137.70	150.40	157.60	187.70	239.00	191.90	170.70	150.20	146.50	120.50
Mortgage interest payments	70.80	73.00	47.70	60.60	56.40	57.60	60.90	85.10	105.00	83.30	73.60	71.70	59.20	41.50
Mortgage protection premiums	2.30	2.20	2.90	2.20	2.40	3.10	2.00	2.20	1.80	2.00	1.90	2.30	2.60	5.60
Capital repayment of mortgage	94.50	97.60	72.20	84.10	78.80	89.70	94.60	100.40	132.20	106.60	95.20	76.20	84.70	73.40

Please see background notes for symbols and conventions used in this report.
1 Primary dwelling.
2 The figure included in total expenditure is net rent as opposed to gross rent.

Source: Office for National Statistics

Background notes

Symbols and conventions used in Family Spending tables

[]	Figures should be used with extra caution because they are based on fewer than 20 reporting households.
:	The data is suppressed if the unweighted sample counts are less than 10 reporting households.
..	No figures are available because there are no reporting households.
~	The figure is greater than 0 but rounds to 0.

Rounding: Individual figures have been rounded independently. The sum of component items does not therefore necessarily add to the totals shown.

Averages: These are averages (means) for all households included in the column or row, and unless specified, are not restricted to those households reporting expenditure on a particular item or income of a particular type.

Impact of the coronavirus (COVID-19) pandemic on the Living Costs and Food Survey (LCF) for the financial year ending 2020

Following Government guidance in relation to the coronavirus (COVID-19) pandemic, a pause in data collection led to interviews being conducted for 13 fewer days in March 2020 than planned. Final March interviews took place on Monday March 16th. All households that were not interviewed as a result were treated as non-responders and data were weighted to account for reduced data collection in March 2020 compared to previous years.

Data collected in March 2020 may have covered changes to spending habits around the start of the first UK lockdown on March 23rd, for example panic buying beforehand and reduced spending during lockdown when people were advised to stay at home and many businesses were closed. However, due to reduced data collection in the latter half of March data may not accurately reflect the impact of lockdown on spending and the annual estimates reported in this release will not be significantly impacted.